The Lost Decade

American University Studies

Series IX
History

Vol. 30

PETER LANG
New York · Bern · Frankfurt am Main · Paris

Gary H. Koerselman

The Lost Decade

A Story of America in the 1960's

PETER LANG
New York · Bern · Frankfurt am Main · Paris

Library of Congress Cataloging-in-Publication Data

Koerselman, Gary H.
The lost decade.

(American university studies. Series IX, History; Vol. 30)
Bibliography: p.
Includes index.
1. United States—Civilization—1945- .
2. United States—History—1961–1963. 3. United States—History—1963–1969. I. Title. II. Series.
E169.12.K58 1987 973.92 87-4237
ISBN 0-8204-0461-6
ISSN 0740-0462

CIP-Kurztitelaufnahme der Deutschen Bibliothek

Koerselman, Gary H.:
The lost decade : a story of America in the 1960's / Gary H. Koerselman. – New York; Bern; Frankfurt am Main; Paris: Lang, 1987.
(American University Studies: Ser. 9, History; Vol. 30)
ISBN 0-8204-0461-6

NE: American University Studies / 09

Printed by Weihert-Druck GmbH, Darmstadt, West Germany

TABLE OF CONTENTS

ACKNOWLEDGEMENTS

This is a special kind of history. It portrays the reactions of the American people to the dramatic events of the 1960's. By perusing several national magazines such as *Time* and *Newsweek*, quotations from representative Americans were sorted out and used liberally throughout the text in order to give the effect of an eye-witness account. I believe that contemporary perceptions must be a significant beginning in writing the history of any era.

The Age of Television also influenced the writing of this history. As a producer of numerous hours of television myself, I could not help but be influenced by the methods of video production. As much as possible, I attempt to make my points of historical interpretation through the words and thoughts of individuals on the scene. Thus, readers will notice that this book yields a certain aura of a television documentary minus the pictures.

This work was written in a style which encourages readers to reminisce and remember fondly times gone by. Some will say this is a book for "yuppies." I have discovered though, that young people are as interested in the Sixties as adults. The decade carries an intrigue all of its own.

This work would not have been possible without the generous support of others. It represents a community project similar to those of the Renaissance painter, Ghiberti, who developed and reworked his art in accordance with the advice and criticism offered by interested citizens who passed by to watch. Numerous students of all ages contributed unselfishly. As members of my Sixties classess, they diligently researched, gladly remembered, and offered helpful ideas, suggestions, and criticisms which sharpened my own ability to describe the mood and tone of the decade. Their interest and enthusiasm provided the inspiration and motivation necessary to bring this work to completion.

Some individuals contributed to the production of this work in a very special way. Meticulous editorial support was contributed by Dr. Albert Sellen and Marie Scheffer. The Lawrences -- Eric, Jennifer, and John; Greta Philips, Candace Davies, Agnus Donovan, Maxine Percell, and Brenda Oehlerking labored long hours diligently preparing the manuscript. Significant research was accomplished by Michael Fitzgibbons, Susan Greenly, and Marilyn Jensen.

My Morningside College colleagues graciously provided time and space to allow for the production of this work. Local Sioux City business people, especially Robert J. Hoefer and John W. Van Dyke, generously contributed funds to underwrite this project. Finally, I wish to express appreciation to my friends and family, especially daughters Amy and Ann, for their understanding, support, encouragement, and faith.

INTRODUCTION

The 1960's ranks as one of the most exciting and controversial decades in the annals of American history. It was a time when one momentous event after another seemed to explode upon the American scene with relentless frequency. It made Americans feel as if they had experienced the entire panorama of their history in just one short era. During the Sixties Americans experienced war and peace, prosperity and recession, radicalism and reaction, change and continuity, activism and complacency, and accomplishment and disaster, or near disaster, as in the Cuban missile crisis which placed the world on the edge of nuclear annihilation in 1962.

The decade of the Sixties witnessed tremendous cultural and social transformations. New ideas and trends struck with powerful consistency while older traditions and lifestyles persisted unremittingly. The American scene resembled that portrayed by British novelist Charles Dickens in _A Tale Of Two Cities._ "It was the best of times, it was the worst of times," wrote Dickens, "it was the age of wisdom, it was the age of foolishness, it was the epoch of incredulity, it was the season of light, it was the season of darkness, it was the spring of hope, it was the winter of despair." Indeed, as Dickens described it, "we had everything before us." These variegated patterns aptly described the kaleidoscope of American life in the Sixties.

The uncertain churning of events provided the decade with an aura of revolutionary striving. It was the kind of decade in which the great American poet Ralph Waldo Emerson would have wanted to be born. "If there is any period one would desire to be born in is it not the age of Revolution," Emerson queried, "when the old and the new stand side by side and admit of being compared; when the energies of all men are surrounded by fear and hope; when the historic glories of the old can be compensated by the rich possibilities of the new era?" The glamour of new beginnings and the luster of old endings certainly would have attracted the attention of Emerson to life in the Sixties.

Almost everything seemed possible in those fabulous, fateful, and frightening days of the Sixties. The decade featured a new generation born in this century and bent on surmounting every conceivable frontier. Science and technology glimmered more brightly than ever before, delivering moon landings and heart transplants. Colored television and cinema theater instilled a new glow of excitement in the lives of millions. The age of mass communications had dawned. The record books had literally to be rewritten in the field of sports. Even Babe Ruth's old record of 60 home runs in one season was topped in 1961, not by Mickey Mantle, but by Roger Maris of the venerable New York Yankees. The intensity of moral conscience and social organization resulted in civil rights legislation that brought new opportunities for countless Americans previously denied equal treatment in the marketplace. Meanwhile the U.S. Supreme Court methodically expanded and refined the meaning of democracy. Prosperity allowed for the accumulation of billions in new wealth as Americans sought to benefit from a relatively open and competitive free market political economy based on the profit motive.

The Sixties took on a tone of unbridled progress. The longest and most widespread period of prosperity ever experienced provided the impetus for reshaping the American landscape. Americans from suburban row to downtown began to believe that former President Herbert H. Hoover's promise of the Twenties had finally come true: a chicken in every pot and a car in every garage. The inner city skylines became transformed with the construction of a new generation of lofty skyscrapers. The throbbing heartbeat of life in the city placed history on notice that a new generation intended to excel beyond all times, even the 1920's. America hailed the glories of its new found urbanity with such songs as Petula Clark's 1964 Downtown , in which she sang that the lights are much brighter there and everything is waiting for you. Theologian Harvey Cox won widespread attention when he promoted a new perception of God in his 1964 book Secular City , in which he called for a God symbolizing the new urban reality rather than the outmoded rural imagery of the past. The celebration of sex took on bolder overtones. With the publication of Hugh Hefner's Playboy magazine, the production of the James Bond 007 cinema extravaganzas, and sensuous dress styles for women, sex became a centerpiece of American life, suggesting the liberality of the new era.

The sheer energy of the American people helped propel the nation to its summit of power and prestige. No nation dared to challenge the power and the glory of the United States directly, not even the Soviet Union. Along with the unprecedented prosperity, however, came fundamental changes in individual morals, which in turn began to reshape dramatically the nation's ideals and institutions. Alfred North Whitehead's famous observation that "the major advances in civilization are processes which all but wreck the societies in which they occur" applied well to America in the Sixties. The initial social challenge came mostly from youthful protesters who, more than anyone, felt themselves victims of the cutting edge of change. From the battlefields in Asia to the massive new university campuses back home youth felt uneasy and alienated by the prospects of modern life and began offering alternatives to the more established ways of the past.

The youthful cause was soon embraced by song poets such as Bob Dylan and the Beatles, reformers such as Ralph Nader, philosophers such as Herbert Marcuse, and politicians such as Senator Eugene McCarthy and Mayor John Lindsay. When established forces attempted to ignore and manipulate the zealous cries of youth, the movement spilled over into the streets. Advocacy turned to struggle. In 1968 the voices for change found themselves pitted in violent struggle against the recalcitrant establishment on the bloody streets of Mayor Daley's Chicago at the National Democratic Convention.

Youth lost the struggle to promote political and social change to the well-worn establishment forces of blue and gray, and sparked a vociferous political reaction from the right-wing elements of the middle class, calling itself the Silent Majority. The Silent Majority hailed such luminary leaders as Vice President Spiro T. Agnew, governors such as Ronald Reagan and George Wallace, evangelists such as Billy Graham, and songsters such as Johnny Cash and Merle Haggard, and bureaucrats such as the powerful F.B.I. Director J. Edgar Hoover, the master of subterfuge. The force of Silent Majority politics quelled the voices of rebellion as young people left politics and headed for the hills. Nevertheless, many of the youthful ideas and lifestyles penetrated the previously staid and boring veneer of American society. The American value system began to display a tolerance for social relationships and lifestyles previously unacceptable in a society of Victorian roots. One of the decade's preeminent young actors, Dustin Hoffman, called the social clashes and transformations "a great explosion! It hurt." Hoffman believed that the decade led to "the whole re-examination of what we are." They were "terrific times," remembered Hoffman, "a great opening."

Social turmoil diminished before the conservative reactionary forces of the Silent Majority. This provided balance in a decade turning disruptive. So the nation remained remarkably sturdy compared to what might have been. America remained a unique land of sprawling opportunity, energy, potential, immensity, and delightfully heterogeneous people. Plurality produced diversity and a special tolerance for things new and different. The nation continued to represent what novelist Thomas Wolfe described as "an incomparable experience." Wolfe marvelled at America's "sense of joy, its exultancy, its drunken and magnificent hope which, against reason knowledge, soars into a heaven of fabulous conviction." America "believes in the miracle and sees it invariably achieved," exulted Wolfe. With this same phenomenon in mind philosopher Eric Hoffer called America "the only new thing in history."

The new technology provided Americans with convenience and material comfort undreamed of by previous generations, but it also resulted in the creation of more diversity and contrast within the ranks of society. America had always been a land of contrast anyway. From the gently rolling plains of the Middle West to the rugged mountain tops of the far West, from the bitter cold bursts of the northern winters to the insufferable heat that marked the southern summers, from the bustle of city streets to the quietude of the countryside, from the urbane elitists educated in the Ivy Leagues to the semi-articulate drifters in Appalachia, America continued to present its interpreters with an almost impossible enigma. Wherever there was a rule, there would be an exception. An apparent characteristic produced a counter characteristic. Diversity seemed to breed more diversity. Yet contrasts existed which merit historical note.

One contrast that grew strikingly more apparent during the Sixties had to do with accumulation of wealth. The belief in the sanctity of private property continued almost unchallenged, but the development of new technology had a tendency to increase the gap between rich and poor. In spite of the Great Society Anti-Poverty programs, Americans continued to admire the rich and ignore the poor. Billionaire Howard Hughes, who multiplied his wealth by shrewd investments in the aerospace industry, lavished upon himself human pleasures unimaginable to previous generations. His every move drew widespread attention in the media and led to quizzical speculations in well-informed circles. "Wealth maketh many friends," stated Proverbs 19:4, "but the poor is separated from his neighbor."

But for every Howard Hughes there were thousands of losers who either ended in bankruptcy or never had the opportunity to succeed in the first place. Contrast the monuments erected by Hughes to the Potters Field monument for forgotten people on Hart Island in New York City. Potters Field was the final resting place for New York City's dead paupers. It cost the city about thirty dollars to seal them into cheap wooden boxes, haul them a dozen at a time on old trucks, and bury them in a mass grave ten boxes across, three boxes deep, and 148 bodies to a plot. Prosperity and opportunity were not a part of the America that these nameless victims of poverty knew. History had cruelly passed them by without even providing a mark for their grave.

So, the focus of attention in America continued to be

directed to the top echelons of society, heralding the winners and forgetting the losers. Americans continued to be intrigued with the exercise of power even while they were paranoid about the over-centralization of it. By the Sixties power was exercised most audaciously in the U.S. Presidency, an institution which had been expanding its influence since the days of the New Deal. The Presidency symbolized the nation's ideals, its vigor, and its might. No other office in the world held so much power, or drew so much attention. In the eyes of the world as well as many Americans the words and deeds of the President personified the United States.

Three presidents ascended to the helm of national leadership during the Sixties. Each struggled to manage the nation's destinies in an atmosphere known as the post-industrial age, an age fraught with unfamiliar mysteries. Each president made a significant impact on the American political scene and set the tones for the decade. Kennedy became known as a man of the sea, Johnson as a man of the range, and Nixon as a man of the closet.

Under John F. Kennedy the nation confidently grasped at the scepter of power, certain that the world, behind American leadership, could be made safe for peace and prosperity. Kennedy's tragic death came as a dreadful shock; but his New Frontier promises seemed secure in the steady hands of master politician and political manipulator Lyndon B. Johnson, protege of Franklin D. Roosevelt. Johnson's Great Society ambitions knew no limit. They were bigger than the Texas skies. Johnson believed that all Americans could be placed under the paternalistic umbrella of government programs.

Racial violence on the streets of the large cities, epitomized by the brutal assassination of civil rights leader Dr. Martin Luther King, frustration, destruction and death in Vietnam, and the intensity of the youth rebellion quickly stalled the liberal Johnsonian political momentum and finally drove Johnson unceremoniously from the Oval Office. By the time Richard M. Nixon reached the Presidency, the nation's confidence had been badly shaken and the optimism prevalent earlier in the decade had dissipated. The political atmosphere was pervaded by divisiveness and remorse over lost dreams. The nation could not find consensus under Nixon's leadership. Nixon lacked personality, and by now the great prosperity of the Sixties was grinding to an ominous halt. Divisions over law and order, controversial Supreme court appointments, defense spending, and the Vietnam War left the nation drifting in uncertainty about the future. The apparent contradictions in post-industrial society in America seemed too profound to be mitigated by the same old familiar political rhetoric.

By decade's end America languished in a time of introspection and self-criticism. Americans began singing the blues with B.B. King and sadly reminisced about the lost good times in such popular songs as "Those Were the Days My Friend" by Gene Raskin. Philosopher Max Lerner, aging commentator and resolute promoter of New Deal liberalism, now bemoaned national problems that he saw growing out of proportion. Disastrous events seemed to amplify Lerner's fears. Cultist leader Charlie Manson and his motley tribe of followers stormed the streets of Los Angeles leaving a bloody, murderous path. The Santa Barbara oil spill conjured up awesome images of a stinky and polluted future. The American way suddenly seemed threatened by incomprehensible and invincible new forces of rapid change. The American generation which had so confidently embraced Kennedy's promising mantle of hope now wished the decade away under Nixon.

The unpredictable whirlwind of happenings which marked the Sixties with great accomplishments as well as great disappointments renders the decade deserving of special historical attention. "This period was a watershed as important as the American Revolution or the Civil War in causing changes in the United States," contended Princeton historian Eric F. Goldman, who himself served as a special assistant to President Johnson during the high Sixties. The historical interpretation of the decade must begin. This work should be considered as an initial conceptualization of the era. It stands to be reshaped and remolded, and perhaps contradicted by those who follow.

CHAPTER I

AN AGE OF CONFRONTATION

The day was January 21, 1961. The eyes of the world were fixed upon events unfolding in the United States. The world's most powerful nation busily made final preparations for its premier occasion, the inauguration of a new president. Never had the American people seemed so self-assured about the glories of the past, so secure about the accomplishments of the present, and so confident about the limitless expectations of the future.

Inauguration day dawned uncommonly cold with brisk, chilly gusts of wind sweeping in from the north. Nevertheless, Washington, D. C., fairly glistened as sunbeams danced upon the freshly fallen snow. The White House and Capitol buildings sparkled majestically under a fresh coat of paint, symbolizing the excitement which comes when a new era marches boldly into the nation's governing city. The exuberant sounds of celebration swelled the air as Americans confidently marked their grand new beginning. The magic of television had come of age, allowing millions of Americans to share in the elaborate celebration. The glory of it all engendered an attentive trembling, a glad anticipation, and an exciting wonderment about the succession of a new, young president bearing good tidings of better tomorrows.

This was not an ordinary changing of the guard. The youngest president of the United States ever to be elected was about to replace the oldest. The nation watched intently. A young, vigorous John F. Kennedy, promising to "get the nation moving again," serenely accepted the mantle of the world's most powerful office from the amicable, aging Dwight D. Eisenhower, whose mild manner and reassuring smile had grown somewhat out of character in the highly charged atmosphere of hopeful expectations.

Suave and cosmopolitan, lean and vibrant, the new President--the first Roman Catholic ever elected to the office--quickly capitalized on the atmosphere of glad anticipation by giving the country renewed initiative. Kennedy stepped gracefully forward and literally transformed his Inaugural Address into a significant historical event. The substance, tone, and style captured the imagination of his compatriots and provided often repeated guideposts leading toward the future.

Standing abruptly upright, his narrow frame firmly fixed against the magnificent granite silhouettes of the Capitol buildings, Kennedy addressed the nation in an unforgettably crisp, elitist Boston accent. He confidently proclaimed the rise of a new generation, one that would command America on its final course to the pinnacle of power and potential. "Let the word go forth from this time and place, to friend and foe alike," intoned Kennedy, the upper frame of his body tilting now halfway forward toward the horizon where some enchanting destiny seemed to loom. "The torch has been passed to a new generation of Americans -- born in this century, tempered by war, disciplined by the hard and bitter peace, proud of our ancient heritage, and unwilling to witness or permit the slow undoing of those human rights to which this nation has always been committed."

Kennedy quickly asserted himself as the new standard-bearer of twentieth-century liberal American ideals. He promised to support the expansion of democratic institutions both at home and abroad. He presented a sagacious view of the future which would "not be finished in the first 100 days, nor will it be finished in the first 1000 days, nor in the life of this Administration, nor even perhaps in our lifetime on this planet," declared Kennedy, his right arm chopping sharply forward to accentuate the point, "but let us begin!" Kennedy resolved that "the energy, the faith and devotion which we bring to this endeavor will light our country and all who serve it, and the glow from that fire can truly light the world." He closed with a charge to the American people that would echo through the historical corridors of the decade. "And so my fellow Americans: ask not what your country can do for you -- ask what you can do for your country."

Kennedy's generation immediately became infatuated with the eloquent idealism of his message. Millions of Americans rallied to his cause. Exalted New Republic author Gerald Clarke: "The President was one of us, the government itself was ours, and the 'us' and the 'ours' were not the Democratic Party of the liberals, but the young and the vigorous." Young and old, rich and poor, all were attracted to the Kennedy style. They teemed into the capital from all corners of the nation. The celebrants made it almost impossible for the Democratic party faithful to control the occasion. The people came to see not only Kennedy but the many famous personalities from the entertainment world.

Celebrities Frank Sinatra, Leonard Bernstein, Nat King Cole, and Mahalia Jackson came to set forth praises in honor of the grandiose inaugural celebration.

Standing near the young President was America's most venerable aging poet, Robert Frost, who, at 86, was feeble but fiercely proud to be a part of the nation's reviving pioneer spirit. From the heartland he came to dedicate what he characterized as "the new Augustan Age." Gaunt and trembling from the infirmities that come with age, the sage poet held forth with all the intensity his frail body could muster. "Such as we were we gave ourselves outright/ To the land vaguely realizing westward/ But still unstoried, artless, unenhanced/ Such as she was, such as she will become." The brightness of the sun prevented Frost from reading his prepared poem which brilliantly captured the significance of the moment. "A golden age of poetry and power of which this noonday's the beginning hour." Frost saw in Kennedy a well-seasoned, resilient fabric molded by years of back pains and some near brushes with death. He saw in the new President a compassionate perspective that transcended the youthful years. Kennedy was "one acquainted with the night," asserted Frost.

The tone of the inauguration made it clear that President Kennedy intended to establish the greatness of his nation. One of his main campaign themes had read: "A Time for Greatness." Kennedy believed that his moral idealism could enhance America's opportunities to expand the frontiers of freedom. The promise of freedom seemed appropriate since it had provided the foundation for America's greatness in the first place. Freedom could provide the foundation for hope everywhere. "The hope of all mankind rests upon us," lectured Kennedy, "not simply upon those of us in this chamber, but upon the peasant in Laos, the fisherman in Nigeria, the exile from Cuba, the spirit that moves every man and nation who share our hopes for freedom and the future."

Kennedy raised the banners of freedom partly in an attempt to dwarf the feelings of fatalism and malaise which accompanied the dark side of progress. Without hope there would be no future. In spite of the regalia Kennedy knew that lurking just below the surface was a dreadful feeling that the world was drifting through one of the most dangerous times in human history. While the sparkling new technology had brought the United States to the summit of human achievement, it had also brought the human race to the brink of ultimate disaster, especially as it related to the development of nuclear weapons. Even as Kennedy delivered his Inaugural Address a huge Boeing 707 jet airliner hovered five miles in the sky just as it did 365 days a year. It contained the headquarters of the Airborne Emergency Command, prepared constantly to alert and protect the nation against a surprise nuclear attack.

Kennedy came to power in the 16th year of the nuclear age. As he gazed out of the windows in the Oval Office and reflected back over those years, the new President could take little comfort. Pictures of the bulging mushroom clouds ascending from Hiroshima and Nagasaki in 1945 flashed through his mind. The horrendous implications of that event would haunt Kennedy wherever he went. He remembered the lament of Albert Einstein, the scientist responsible for the nuclear formula: "The unleashed power of the atom has changed everything save our modes of thinking, and thus we drift toward unparalleled catastrophes." Kennedy wondered how his Administration could spare the world from the ultimate nuclear catastrophe.

In 16 years nuclear proliferation had made the world a far more dangerous place to live. After World War II President Truman had attempted to monopolize nuclear power through promotion of the Baruch Plan, aimed at strictly limiting nuclear weapons production. But the Soviet Union under Stalin's iron-fisted rule refused to be denied. By the middle Fifties Russia boasted of its own nuclear strike capability. Now a massive nuclear exchange could virtually destroy the industrialized world and threaten to annihilate the entire human race in only a matter of hours.

The bloody Hungarian crisis of 1954 clearly demonstrated to a nervous world how nuclear diplomacy on the part of both superpowers had become a stark reality in world affairs. Both sides vaguely understood that ways must be found to control the nuclear nemesis. President Eisenhower and Soviet leaders met at Geneva, Switzerland, in 1955 to establish some loose parameters of what would become known as "peaceful coexistence." The Geneva parley proved an important beginning, but the so-called "spirit of Geneva" had evaporated by the time the Soviets shot down an American U - 2 spy plane over Russian territory in 1960. Soviet Premier Nikita Khrushchev refused to have any further dealings with Eisenhower, and he travelled to the United Nations to pound his shoe on the podium while blatantly promising to bury capitalism.

During the 1960 election campaign Kennedy complained often about the Eisenhower-Khrushchev impasse. He charged that under Republican rule the United States had lost its strategic advantage and promised to close what he called the "missile gap." Kennedy's charge sounded all too plausible in the wake of the Soviet Union's successful launching of Sputnik into outer space in 1957. Kennedy's hawkishness represented in part his political strategy to avoid the unfortunate label of being "soft on communism," a label that had haunted liberal Democrats ever since the days of the ranting and raving Republican anti-communist Wisconsin Senator Joseph McCarthy.

In reality the Soviets never possessed a nuclear advantage. But Russia did represent a formidable ideological and military threat, even if it could not remotely match America's economic and industrial might. The apparent expansion of Soviet influence over Eastern Europe and China threatened America's hope to expand democratic and capitalistic institutions. The emergence of left-leaning movements in the Third World further threatened America's interests.

Soviet advances over 16 years had crystalized the feeling among the American people that they lived in a bipolar world which pitted Godless communism against freedom and democracy. The feeling spread fears that Armageddon might be at hand. Kennedy reflected those fears as he placed Soviet-American relations at the top of his Presidential agenda. "Domestic policy can only defeat us," he warned aides, "but foreign policy can kill us!"

Initially Kennedy assumed a hawkish stance toward the Russians. His policies followed along the traditional lines of Cold War containment principles first articulated by the intellectual diplomat George F. Kennan in his famous 1947 "Mr. X" article in Foreign Affairs, the journal most reflective of State Department thinking. According to Kennan's judgment Soviet aggression originated from a deeply rooted paranoia engendered by numerous invasions of the homelands and from a crusading mentality associated with communistic ideology. The Kennan doctrine held that the United States and its Free World allies must draw the line around the Soviet empire and confront Russian adventurism at any place with overwhelming military superiority. Economic sanctions and propaganda efforts were recommended to penetrate beyond the "Iron Curtain" so as to destabilize the Soviet empire from within. Meanwhile bold economic assistance policies and foreign aid should be applied in Western Europe and in the underdeveloped Third World in order to minimize communism's threat to the expansion of democratic capitalism.

Kennedy's initial proclamations concerning Soviet-American relations clearly cast him in the mold of a hawkish, perhaps even reckless, Cold Warrior. In his Inaugural Address Kennedy promised to "pay any price, bear any burden, meet any hardship, support any friend or oppose any foe in order to assure the survival and success of liberty." He spoke as if the Monroe Doctrine concerning the protection of Latin America now applied to the whole world. He insisted that "world peace and the security of the United States were one and the same thing." Kennedy frankly informed his advisors that "Khrushchev must *not* be certain that, where its vital interests are threatened, the United States will never strike first."

Under the assumption that overwhelming military superiority served as the best deterrent against Soviet aggression Kennedy instructed Secretary of Defense Robert S. McNamara -- known as one of the Harvard "Whiz Kids" and who helped enshrine computers in government -- to administer the largest military buildup in history. Under McNamara's direction the United States sought to establish both first- and second-strike capability. Hence, even if the Soviets struck first, the United States would still possess enough of a nuclear arsenal to inflict unacceptable damage on Russia. The threat of massive retaliation would hold the Russians in check and maintain the peace, so the theory went. A Kennedy military advisor reflected this thinking before a House Armed Services Committee hearing on the gigantic Titan missile: "The faster we can launch it, the more likely it is we'll never have to!"

The Kennedy-McNamara nuclear strategy was based upon a concept known as Triad, a triple complex of weapons systems--long-range bombers, submarines, and land-based intercontinental missiles. Any one of the systems alone possessed the capability of massive destruction; but, placed together, they offered the President deadly flexibility while keeping the Soviet defense planners off balance. The oldest of the three systems was the arsenal of 600 long-range B-52 bombers, called the "air-breathing leg" of the Triad. The bomber force was important for its flexibility. Bombers could carry warheads of various sizes depending on the amount of blast considered worthy to the particular crisis at hand. Once airborne the B-52s could be recalled in case last minute diplomacy averted the possibility of holocaust.

The Polaris submarine fleet, armed with Polaris and Poseidon missiles and independently targetable 40 to 200-kiloton H-bombs, could patrol the oceans unchallenged and essentially invulnerable to pre-emptive strikes. The third system, the ICBM leg, although most prominent in the imaginations of Americans, represented less than 30 percent of America's strategic capability. This system was deployed mainly in the wheat fields of the midwest. The most spectacular weapon in this arsenal was the giant Titan, known as the "blockbuster" or the "earth-splitter." It could forge a crater 1,000 feet deep and a mile across.

The Titan, used also to launch astronauts into outer space, was mounted with a single nine-megaton warhead. After mid-decade the Titan would be replaced with the Minuteman II, which carried less payload but had the advantage of accuracy. ICBMs could be launched to a height of 60 miles. At that point the H-bomb separated from the booster and under the force of gravity could coast up to 600 miles before descent. It could travel distances of 6,000 miles between launch and strike. The flight lasted about 30 minutes. The technology existed to mount many H-bombs on a single rocket and, through the use of sophisticated onboard computers, detonate the bombs toward a variety of targets. Unlike the B-52 bombers, ICBMs, once launched, could hardly be recalled; thus, this weapon represented the most terrifying and inflexible leg of the Triad.

The speculation about comparative destructive capabilities along with the intensification of Cold War feelings provided the impetus for a full-fledged national civil defense campaign. The President lent strong support to the movement. "To recognize the possibilities of nuclear war in the missile age without our citizens knowing what they should do and where they should go would be a failure of responsibility," declared Kennedy. At the forefront of the civil defense campaign stood liberal New York Governor Nelson A. Rockefeller, the Republican thought to have the best chance of defeating Kennedy for re-election in 1964. Rockefeller proposed a $4 million bomb shelter in the State Capitol complex at Albany, equipped with a "war room" and complete with bottled water, dog-biscuit survival rations and sanitary disposal bags. Communities around the nation soon followed suit. Most local governments established civil defense committees charged with developing survival plans in case of disaster. Such committees became responsible for building and stocking bomb shelters.

The matter of survival under atomic attack became a community dread not unlike the fear of smallpox epidemics in the old West. "At cocktail parties and P.T.A. meetings and family dinners, on busses and commuter trains and around office water coolers, talk turns to shelters," reported Time. Profit-minded private building contractors got into the act. They offered to construct a twelve by eighteen square foot underground bomb shelter for just $1,500. Manufacturers began selling prepackaged, high protein foods and "home survival kits" for families expecting a nuclear war. President Thomas J. Watson of International Business Machines went so far as to make available $1,000 loans to employees wishing to build bomb shelters. Before the bomb scare mania subsided, because of the hopeless realization that surviving a nuclear attack might be a fate worse than death, many local defense officials had put entire communities through the ordeal of bomb alert drills.

The nuclear bomb scare placed public opinion squarely behind President Kennedy's posture of toughness toward the Soviet Union. The massive military buildup of Kennedy's early years gave him powerful bargaining chips in his initial negotiating stance. But the fiesty Soviet Premier Khrushchev was not swayed from his own determination to challenge the limits of peaceful coexistence. Khrushchev was in a belligerent mood for several reasons. He was vexed by his government's inability to move the Soviet economy out of the doldrums of inefficiency and low productivity. His domestic agricultural and industrial policies seemed a failure. Khrushchev was deeply troubled by the Kennedy arms buildup and disturbed by the lack of settlement in West Berlin, but he was also flushed by the Sputnik success. Most of all the hard-bitten Soviet adversary was anxious to test the will of the new President who the Premier hoped would be naive and inexperienced enough to allow a major Soviet foreign policy victory.

Kennedy understood the dangers inherent in the Premier's growing attitude of belligerency. A way must be found to mollify him. Kennedy first resorted to Eisenhower's "sword and olive branch" approach. "Diplomacy and defense are not substitutes for one another," contended Kennedy. "We are neither warmongers nor appeasers, neither hard or soft, but determined to defend the frontiers of freedom." Peaceful coexistence to Kennedy meant "no action by either superpower to alter the existing balance of power and no attempt by either to interfere within the other's sphere of control."

Kennedy determined that personal diplomacy might best be employed to define the parameters controlling the delicate balance of power. He agreed to meet with the Premier in Vienna, Austria, during June of 1961. Kennedy prepared for the encounter meticulously. He studied Khrushchev's speeches so that he could contradict the Premier whenever there was duplicity. He watched film-strips to become familiar with the personality of this rambunctious and complicated man. Kennedy wanted to know about his pudgy hands, his abrupt movements, his moments of insecurity followed by explosive laughter, his bragging, and his mannerisms, anything that might be a clue to his personality. Kennedy even took to Vienna with him a model of the U.S.S. Constitution, an early American battleship, in order to demonstrate that warfare in previous times was innocuous compared to the horrendous stakes of modern conflagration.

The Vienna talks proved to be inordinately strained. It soon became apparent that Khrushchev came prepared to make a major issue out of the West Berlin situation. The German city existed as a flourishing island of democracy amidst a sea of communist totalitarianism. Every week hundreds of Eastern Europeans tried to escape through Berlin to freedom in the West. This embarrassed Khrushchev and his Politburo colleagues in the Kremlin. Khrushchev rudely called for the eradication of this "splinter from the heart of Europe," and demanded "an end to the occupation regime in West Berlin." He established December, 1961, as the final date for settlement and demanded that the "rotten tooth" of West Berlin be transformed "into a demilitarized free city." Kennedy was astonished and disappointed. On his way back to Washington the President predicted that "it will be a cold winter." A confrontation seemed sure to come.

As the crisis over Berlin mounted, Kennedy found his major foreign policy advisors divided over what should be the nature of the American response. Hard-bitten Cold Warriors such as former Secretary of State Dean Acheson, one of the original architects of the containment policy, urged strongly that the President proclaim a national emergency accompanied with an immediate reserve call up, a five billion dollar increase in military spending, broad new tax proposals, and standby wage and price controls. On the other side stood such original Cold Warriors as the sagacious W. Averell Harriman, former Ambassador to Russia with a life time of experience doing business there, who urged against over-reaction. Harriman knew the Russian mentality as well as anyone in America and argued that precipitous action would give the dangerous impression of hysteria, which could too easily set off the doomsday scenario. Harriman argued for a posture of patience and "unflinching resolve." President Kennedy pursued a middle course.

Kennedy's response to Berlin was carefully coupled with an appeal to worldwide public opinion, an act becoming more commonplace among world leaders in the age of television. In a nationwide television address on July 25 the President grimly informed Americans that the United States government would absolutely resist Soviet pressures against West Berlin. "I hear it said that West Berlin is militarily untenable," declared Kennedy, "and so was Bastogne. And, so, in fact, Stalingrad. Any dangerous spot is tenable if men -- brave men -- will make it so." Kennedy charged the Soviets with making the city "the greatest testing place of Western courage and will, a focal point where our solemn commitments. . . and Soviet ambitions now meet in basic confrontation." West Berlin would be protected "for the sake of the entire free world." The President then asked Congress for an additional $3.25 billion appropriation for strengthening America's military position in central Europe, tripled draft calls, ordered several National Guard units into active duty, and began reactivating dozens of older ships and planes.

At the end of his address Kennedy issued a somber warning along with a hint of conciliation. "In the days and months ahead, I shall not hesitate to ask the Congress for additional measures, or exercise any of the executive powers that I possess to meet this threat to peace," warned Kennedy sternly; but he added: "We recognize the Soviet Union's historical concern about their security in Central and Eastern Europe after a series of ravaging invasions, and we believe arrangements can be worked out which help to meet these concerns, and make it possible for both security and freedom to exist in this troubled area."

As the summer of 1961 wore on, Premier Khrushchev remained truculent. On August 7 at ceremonies honoring Soviet cosmonaut Titom he vehemently attacked what he labeled "Kennedy's military hysteria." He warned that Western intervention would result in "death to millions of people, and any state used as a springboard for an attack upon the Socialist camp will experience the full devastating power of our blow." During August Russian and East German troops began constructing the infamous Berlin Wall designed to squelch the refugee traffic. Kennedy ordered 1,500 American troops to travel the autobahn to West Berlin, where Vice President Johnson waited to greet them. Khrushchev charged Kennedy with using Berlin to ferry "revanchists, extremists and spies." Kennedy accused the Soviets of "deception, intimidation, provocation and irresponsibility." Refugees trying to escape across the wall were shot in cold blood.

Russian and American tanks pulled up to the wall as their nervous young crews stared suspiciously at each other. "The gap between war and peace had narrowed down to a few feet," reported _Newsweek._ When a West German teenager insulted an East German guard, a tank quickly responded with a high pressure stream of water that splashed two American soldiers guarding the Western side. The Americans quickly reached for their grenades. "For a moment of silence, the dreaded question of war and peace may have hovered in the balance between a youthful East German tank driver and the young American GI's," conjectured _Newsweek;_ "then, with agonizing slowness, the moment of crisis passed. The East German stopped squirting water; the GIs put back their grenades." The crisis point had passed.

Premier Khrushchev abruptly ended the three-year moratorium on nuclear testing in the atmosphere. Kennedy began underground nuclear testing in September. By October Khrushchev's blustering began to subside. The December deadline passed without incident. The young President's resolve had apparently helped dissipate the crisis. The President even had the last word when later he would stand at the Berlin Wall and tell thousands of cheering West Berliners: "Today, in the world of freedom, the proudest boast is _Ich bin ein Berliner."_ As the Kennedy Administration entered into the year 1962, however, the parameters of peaceful coexistence remained largely undefined. The coming confrontations over Cuba would change all of that.

The sugar-rich island of Cuba, just 90 miles from the Florida Keys, had always been of prime economic and strategic concern to the United States. Cuba belonged to the Spanish empire until 1898, when a threatening insurgency resulted in American support for Cuba's independence. Cuba's new democratic constitution contained provisions, however, which granted the United States broad powers of intervention. Throughout the 20th century Cuba suffered from political and economic instability while experiencing the overbearing burdens of autocratic rule, marked since World War II by the corrupt administration of Dictator Fulgencio Batista.

In 1959 Batista was abruptly deposed by a bearded teacher-patriot named Fidel Castro, who at first claimed to be a democrat and who obviously enjoyed widespread support among the Cuban people. In keeping with America's good neighbor pledges of nonintervention and self-determination, President Eisenhower granted Castro reluctant recognition. Soon thereafter Castro boldly announced his belief in socialistic principles and began expropriating American properties and investments. Eisenhower reversed his support and directed the Central Intelligence Agency (CIA), the covert arm of American diplomacy, to plan an invasion of the island led by disenchanted Cuban refugees opposed to the growing communist rule.

At first Kennedy paid little attention to events unraveling in Cuba. Berlin seemed much more serious. "If we solve the Berlin problem without war, Cuba will look pretty small," Kennedy told aide Ted Sorensen. "And if there is a war, Cuba won't matter much either." Thus Kennedy supported the CIA's clandestine invasion plan and went along with the public deception surrounding the ill-fated affair. While American Air Force officers in Guatemala and Nicaragua trained Cuban pilots to fly unmarked American jets, the President solemnly promised at a news conference that he would "make sure that there are no Americans involved in any actions inside Cuba." The invasion attempt began on April 15, 1961, when Cuban pilots, pretending to be defectors from Castro's regime, bombed airfields and other strategic targets inside Cuba. Two days later 1,500 hastily trained and tattered Cuban refugees, some of them very old men, invaded the island at a point known as the Bay of Pigs. The anticipated "general uprising" against Castro never materialized, and even while Kennedy characterized the invaders as the "most valiant men of the entire world," he quickly ordered a halt to the folly.

Public debate raged over the ill-conceived episode. Many Americans fervently called for a second invasion, but Kennedy, who felt betrayed by the CIA, firmly refused, saying that rather than make a martyr out of the embattled Castro, he would let the dictator "fashion his own noose." The newly instituted American boycott of Cuban sugar should help topple the determined dictator. Fearing American intentions, however, Castro turned to the waiting arms of the Russians for military and economic assistance. In March of 1962 Castro, garbed in old-fashioned military boots and wrinkled fatigues, journeyed to Moscow where the beaming and back-slapping Premier Khrushchev promised him solid support for the revolution.

To Kennedy's surprise Cuba, not Berlin, soon became the focal point of Soviet-American confrontation. By late summer Kennedy received some shocking intelligence reports of Russian SAM missile installations inside Cuba. In September the President warned Khrushchev against establishing "an offensive military base of significant capacity" in Cuba. By October American U-2 flights had discovered undisputable evidence of the construction of medium-range missile bases on the island. Completion of these bases could significantly alter the balance of power in the western hemisphere in a manner unfavorable to the United States. As soon as the dramatic implications of the latest Soviet adventurism became apparent, Kennedy resolved to take decisive action. He informed advisors at once that "the greatest danger of all would be to do nothing."

The President's advisors were again divided in their counsel concerning the most appropriate American response to this latest Russian intrigue. The military Joint Chiefs of Staff, supported by Acheson, strongly urged a swift series of preemptive air strikes. Under Secretary of State George C. Ball, a Harriman protege, strongly argued for restraint. Air strikes would amount to "a Pearl Harbor in reverse," contended Attorney General Robert F. Kennedy, the President's younger brother whose influence on the President was increasing significantly. The President opted for restraint. He believed that the most powerful defender of the status quo in this case could well afford to exercise moral restraint in the hope of promoting a safer world. He embarked upon the more moderate course of action, then, thinking that the full force of nuclear weaponry could always be resorted to later.

The crisis broke into the open on October 22, 1962, just a few weeks before mid-term Congressional elections. The day was filled with nervous reports that something was dreadfully wrong between the United States and Russia. From the nation's fields where farmers were busily completing harvest, from the workshops and factories, the office complexes, college classrooms, and kitchens attention was dramatically drawn to the ominous reports. It was announced that the President would address the nation on television that evening. The decade's most dangerous Soviet-American confrontation was about to begin. The entire world "paused at the nuclear precipice."

Kennedy began his address with a somber recitation of recent developments in Cuba and reaffirmed his fundamental determination to defend the western hemisphere. He announced a quarantine on Cuban ports in order to prevent further delivery of Soviet war materials and demanded that Russia dismantle the missile sites at once. Kennedy closed his address with a direct appeal to the Soviet Premier. "I call on Chairman Khrushchev to halt and eliminate this clandestine, reckless, and provocative threat to world peace and stable relations between our two nations," declared Kennedy. "I call upon him further to abandon this course of world domination and join in an historic effort to end the perilous arms race and to transform the history of man."

The world was thunderstruck and waited fearfully for events to unfold. The intense feelings of fear reminded one of an E. B. White statement: "For a few hours all life's dubious problems are dropped in favor of the clear task of keeping alive." Meanwhile the United States launched a blanket diplomatic offensive. At the United Nations the venerable UN Ambassador Adlai Stevenson led the attack against Soviet credibility. When Soviet Ambassador Dobrynin refused to clarify Russian intentions and actions leading up to the crisis Stevenson announced to the frustrated membership that he was prepared to wait until hell itself froze over for some credible answers. The United States also called the Organization of the American States into action. Diplomatic and military preparations for the worst possible case moved quickly forward.

The crisis of the Cuban confrontation was intensified by ominous military moves on the other side of the world. In eastern India Red China launched a major attack in the Himalayas. The invasion, which was aimed at control of Assam and Bengal, was timed to exploit the delicate political situation in Calcutta. India appealed desperately for American military assistance. Could it be that the two large communist superpowers had decided to commit serious aggression in concert? Some of Kennedy's more unnerved advisors now called for maximum response, but the President insisted upon restraint and watchful waiting for events around the world to sort themselves out.

As Premier Khrushchev and his Politburo colleagues scrambled nervously about inside the Kremlin walls contemplating their next move, a badly shaken world sullenly contemplated what the final holocaust might be like. The crisis mounted! On October 23 the Soviet flotilla of cargo ships and their submarine escorts continued to move unremittingly toward Cuban waters. American naval destroyers moved into their determined positions of opposition. Khrushchev placed Soviet armed forces on full alert and warned Kennedy that his aggressive action would ignite a thermonuclear war. Kennedy let it be known that he would not relax the blockade.

The weight of world history seemed to rest upon the shoulders of the young president as he listened to his advisors discuss the next move. Suddenly the future seemed so fragile. It rested completely upon the human factor involving the use of nuclear weapons. Kennedy shuddered at the thought. He clearly understood now how miscalculation, misjudgment, fear, mistrust, a lack of adequate procedure under great pressure, and a momentary breakdown in communications could almost by accident result in the final hurling of missiles that would mark the end of civilization.

Premier Khrushchev must have been thinking the same, gruesome thoughts. The reality of nuclear destruction had begun to chill the resolve on both sides. Finally Khrushchev presented Kennedy with two quite different messages. The first proposed an acceptable compromise -- Moscow would remove the missiles if Kennedy agreed not to invade Cuba. The second message asked for the withdrawal of American missiles from Turkey. The second message precipitated another stormy debate among the President's exhausted advisors. Kennedy settled the argument by responding to the first message and ignoring the second. A frank exchange of letters between the President and the Premier followed. Khrushchev ordered Soviet ships to turn back to their Russian ports. Kennedy relaxed the blockade. We were "eyeball to eyeball, and I think the other fellow just blinked," commented Secretary of State Dean Rusk.

So the crisis passed into history. A nuclear exchange was barely avoided. Careful and patient diplomacy prevailed. Steel nerves kept events from escalating out of hand. "The Administration set a new standard of prudence in dealing with the Soviet Union," wrote Harvard political scientist Richard Neustadt hopefully. "The standard of prudence, the hard thought given about the crisis as the Soviets would see it, thus giving our opponent as much room as possible--these were a model of Presidential conduct." The world received a respite. Life could go on, but with the horrible fear that perhaps in a future crisis an American president might not act so prudently. Life from now on would exist with the knowledge that death was as close as pushing the nuclear button.

The sobering effect of the Cuban missile crisis demonstrated the desperate need for the superpowers to define the parameters of peaceful coexistence in the dangerous atomic age. The crisis represented "two weeks when the history of the next twenty years was changed and rewritten because the world's two nuclear powers looked at each other and realized that neither of them wanted a nuclear war," wrote Kennedy aide Kenneth O'Donnell. The crisis led to "one of the turning points of history," declared British Prime Minister Harold Macmillan.

Leaders on both sides began making cautious statements reflecting a new more conciliatory mood. New initiatives were taken which might stabilize the international political situation.

In the United States Secretary of State Dean Rusk told a Senate committee that "we must keep everlastingly at this task of building a world community of order and law." Under questioning he argued that "the Soviets have a common interest with the West in attacking the dangerous anarchy of the armaments and nuclear weapons race, in maintaining order in outer space, and in other weapons to prevent our conflicting purposes from erupting into a mutually destructive war." He agreed that the Soviets had lied, tricked, cheated, and bullied; but he pointed out that they had also backed down under extreme pressure. The time had come to proceed carefully toward a new era of detente.

In Russia Premier Khrushchev told the Supreme Soviet in early 1963 that both sides must "exercise more sobermindedness and a greater desire to remove the roadblocks that cause friction and create tension among states." Russia might have survived a thermonuclear war, surmised the Premier, but "those who remained alive, and future generations too, would have suffered incredibly from the consequences of atomic radiation." A few months later Kennedy reciprocated by saying that "all we have built, all we have worked for, would be destroyed in the first 24 hours" of a nuclear exchange. As if to accentuate their good intentions, the two leaders established a "Hot Line" between the White House and the Kremlin for use during a crisis to prevent it from escalating out of control.

The dramatic turning point in Soviet-American relations became evident to the public on June 10, 1963, when President Kennedy delivered his famous American University address. The President was exhausted, having stopped at the White House only to shower and change clothes after flying all night back from Hawaii. But he was determined to make this his finest hour. He had spent too many long hours dreading the possibility of nuclear war. Now an attempt had to be made at limiting the dangers. He sensed a unique opportunity in the wake of the Cuban crisis to take advantage of events in order to positively change the course of history.

Kennedy's thinking about Soviet-American relations had been significantly tempered by the pressure of the recent crisis over Cuba. He felt that he could comprehend these relations with a wiser and perhaps more mellow perspective than in the earlier, more belligerent days of his Administration. He chose to deliver his remarks in an educational setting, where he hoped to summon all of the immense prestige afforded the Presidency. The strong determination in Kennedy's voice caused an immediate hush to fall over the audience which quickly sensed the historic significance of his message. "I speak of peace because of the new face of war," declared Kennedy. "We are not here distributing blame or pointing the finger of judgment," he continued, "but we must deal with the world as it is, and not as it might have been had the history of the last 18 years been different."

Kennedy now understood that only the President possessed a strong enough public forum to influence the citizens on such a fundamental issue as Soviet-American relations. Only the President stood in a position to mitigate feelings of bitterness and fear concerning Soviet intentions. For there to be peace the President must employ all of the prestige of his office to attract public acceptance of his efforts to chart an uneasy course toward creative and conciliatory diplomacy. "It is sad to read these Soviet statements. But it is also a warning to the American people," exhorted Kennedy, a warning "not to see conflict as inevitable, accommodation as impossible, and communication as nothing more that an exchange of threats." The American people "find communism profoundly repugnant as a negation of personal freedom and dignity," stated Kennedy, "but we can still hail the Russian people for their achievements in science and space, in culture and in acts of courage." Kennedy added that "among our common traits none is stronger than our abhorrence of war." He declared that the time had come for both sides to devote less money and energy for military armaments and more "to combating ignorance, poverty, and disease."

Kennedy pledged that as President he would devote his efforts to bringing Soviet-American relations back to paths leading to peace. "I realize that the pursuit of peace is not as dramatic as the pursuit of war--and frequently the words of the pursuer fall on deaf ears," admitted Kennedy, "but we have no more urgent task." According to Kennedy "peace and freedom walk together, and peace is a process - a way of solving problems." Kennedy let it be known that in his more conciliatory approach toward the Soviets he would be patient and pragmatic, not precipitous. "Let us focus not on a sudden revolution in human nature but on a gradual evolution in human institutions," he counseled. "No government or social system is so evil that its people must be considered as lacking in virtue. If we cannot end now our differences at least we can help make the world safe for diversity."

Kennedy even renounced the idea of "Pax-Americana enforced on the world by American weapons of war." He rejected "the peace of the grave or the security of the slave." He called for conciliation instead. He called for an end to the "vicious and dangerous cycle" in which "suspicion begets suspicion and new weapons beget counter-weapons." He announced to his appreciative audience that high-level discussions had already proceeded toward a comprehensive test ban treaty. Such a pact would "offer far more security and far fewer risks than an unabated, uncontrolled, unpredictable arms race," proclaimed the President. Kennedy's remarks drew resounding applause. Perhaps the spell of nuclear fear could be broken. A glimmer of hope once again appeared on the horizon of the future.

President Kennedy's thoughtful American University address hastened the momentum toward peaceful coexistence or detente. From the beginning Kennedy interpreted detente as a tough-minded process in which both the Soviets and Americans would seek to minimize their differences and maximize their similarities. Competition and conflict would continue to exist in many quarters, but mutuality of interests would lead to cooperation in some vital areas. Cooperation would be counted on to diminish the chances of a localized conflict leading to the nuclear threshold. Economic reality also dictated the need for cooperation. Neither side could afford the tremendous costs associated with the arms race. The Soviets needed American surplus grain to sustain their faltering agricultural system. The American farmers needed additional markets which the Soviets could provide in order to sustain family-sized farm capitalism.

Kennedy's appointment of Ambassador W. Averell Harriman as Chief Negotiator symbolized the great importance attached to detente. Harriman represented the most seasoned and experienced diplomat on the Democratic side of the foreign policy establishment. Harriman's many economic and political dealings with the Russians over four decades had earned their respect and trust. Harriman's main goal was to win Russian support for limiting the spread of nuclear weapons to other nations. Nuclear proliferation could greatly increase the danger of a massive exchange engendered by reckless diplomacy on the part of smaller nations. Harriman remembered well the President's words. "I am haunted by the feeling that by 1970, unless we are successful, there may be ten nuclear powers instead of four, and by 1975, fifteen or twenty." Nuclear weapons in the wrong hands would almost surely lead to disaster.

Harriman realized that halting the spread of nuclear technology worked in favor of both superpowers. It became a fundamental factor in their interest to continue domination in their respective spheres of influence. Red China and France realized this as well and refused to join in serious discussions surrounding the Test Ban Treaty. By July the details of a treaty were ready for presentation to the U.S. Senate, where a fierce debate raged for days. Several powerful Senators associated with the Armed Services Committee fought vigorously against passage. Democrats Richard Russell of Georgia and John Stennis of Mississippi joined with Republican Barry Goldwater of

Arizona to lead the battle against the treaty.

The credibility of the conservative opponents suffered somewhat because of their widely-known association with the influential military-industrial-complex. Yet their opposition carried with it legitimate foreign policy concerns. They feared that Russia would use the peace process to secretly build its own capacity to a point of superiority over American power. With that accomplished the Soviets could be in a position to employ nuclear blackmail in efforts to spread their doctrine and influence around the world at American expense. They believed that the Soviet impulse to dominate was unquenchable and that for the United States to lower its guard would only cause the Russians to use deception rather than confrontation to advance their arms and interests. They warned that the United States should not be lulled into discussions that would ultimately erode the American advantage.

The log jam in the Senate was broken when former President Eisenhower lent his critical support to the measure. No man in the United States other than Kennedy appreciated more the pressure of nuclear diplomacy than Ike, who himself had initiated a moratorium on atmospheric testing in 1958. He declared "this limited agreement may lead to other steps for lessening of tensions - and ultimately to genuine disarmament." The Senate passed the Test Ban Treaty in August, less than two months after Kennedy's American University address. Upon signing the treaty on August 5, 1963, Kennedy described it as "a shaft of light cut into the darkness, an important step towards reason - a step away from war." The foundation for a prolonged period of detente had been put into place.

Kennedy's detente would extend through the decade and beyond in spite of serious crises in Vietnam and the Middle East. It would lead to agreements expanding cultural exchange programs, a consular agreement providing legal protections for citizens traveling in the other country, and direct air service between New York and Moscow involving Pan American and the Soviet Aeroflot. Discussions concerning grain sales and other business relationships would begin in earnest. America's largest truck transport manufacturer, Mack Trucks Inc., entered into agreements that led to the sale of $700 million worth of equipment to the Soviets by 1970. This represented "a significant step in our continuing efforts to increase contacts and understanding between the American people and the peoples of the Soviet Union," stated then-President Lyndon B. Johnson, who capitalized upon the spirit of detente himself by conducting a summit conference with Premier Aleksei N. Kosygin at Glassboro, North Carolina, in June of 1967. The two leaders held amicable discussions on such wide-ranging issues as cooperation in space, trade relations, and arms control. The Glassboro talks led in turn to the Strategic Arms Limitations Talks (SALT) under President Richard M. Nixon and the signing of the Nuclear Non-Proliferation Treaty at the end of the decade.

With Soviet-American relations tilting toward detente, President Kennedy directed his attention toward bolstering the Atlantic Alliance. America's relationship with Western Europe represented Kennedy's second most vital diplomatic concern. In an age when the allies of both Russia and the United States demanded more independence from the superpowers, European diplomacy became complicated. Western Europe had made extraordinary political and economic gains since 1947 when President Truman established the Marshall Plan, which provided as much as $17 billion for the revitalization of economies left prostrate by war. In 1949 Truman engineered the establishment of the North Atlantic Treaty Organization (NATO), which provided military protection against the possibility of Russian aggression. Behind the nuclear shield Europe organized the Common Market, which helped to bring about unprecedented economic prosperity and political stability by the time Kennedy entered office.

Europe's recovery increased American dependency upon western European markets in order to sustain its own prosperity. American investments in western Europe would soon reach $50 billion annually. At the same time around half of American's exports went to Europe. Even though the growing interdependency became mutually beneficial, tensions began to surface which threatened the durability of the alliance.

Political and economic tensions stemmed from a growing wave of protectionism, balance of trade deficits, foreign currency exchanges, gold standard policies, and inflationary governmental spending policies. While American business interests feared a new round of competition from abroad, Europeans regretted the Americanization of their culture brought about by mass consumption of American goods. The growing friction was aptly reflected in the London Economist which asked "when will Ford close down Britain?" England's absence from membership in the Common Market only served to intensify the trade problem.

President Kennedy understood that America's economic prosperity and military security depended in large part upon maintaining a strong Atlantic Alliance. Thus he inaugurated the much heralded "Grand Design" for Europe. The policy called for tariff reductions, sharing of nuclear technology, and England's entry into the Common Market, a possibility previously limited by special economic advantages Great Britain enjoyed because of its relationship with the United Commonwealth and the European Free Trade Association.

Kennedy made his trade expansion proposal the top legislative priority of 1962 as he hastened to line up business and labor support for the measure. Top administration officials collaborated with the young free-lance journalist Joseph Kraft, who published a highly visible book on the subject entitled Grand Design. Kraft argued that Kennedy's trade expansion policy represented "the unifying intellectual principle of the New Frontier," and warned, "that in case of failure the United States will have to default on power, resign from history." Kennedy himself pressed Congress hard for resolution. "The two great Atlantic markets will either grow together or they will grow apart," warned the President. "That decision will either mark the beginning of a new chapter in the alliance of free nations - or a threat to the growth of Western unity."

Congress approved the Trade Expansion Act in September of 1962, granting the President broad authority to negotiate tariff reductions up to 50 percent with western European countries. An exhilarated President predicted confidently that "we can move forward to partnership with the nations of the Atlantic Community." The act set the stage for several rounds of talks called General Agreements on Tariff and Trade (GATT). The complicated and exhaustive bargaining sessions that followed managed to reduce tariffs on over 6,000 items by an average of 35 percent over the next five years. GATT policy enjoyed limited success, however; perhaps the most important success was that the talks kept things from getting worse. Europeans suspected from the beginning that Kennedy's main objective was to selfishly expand markets in order to stimulate America's own beleaguered economy. Ingrained protectionist instincts on both sides of the Atlantic seemed ineradicable.

A relatively small trade matter which became known as the "Chicken War of 1964," involving the United States and West Germany, best exemplified the nature of problems encountered over tariff adjustments. The clash of interests arose from a Common Market decision to raise tariffs on American poultry products, a decision which threatened to completely eliminate an annual $46 million poultry market for America in Europe. American negotiators at GATT threatened to retaliate by raising tariffs on selected products from West Germany, the nation which stood to gain the most from the protectionist policy concerning chickens. Both sides refused to budge. This proved once again that vested interests on both sides of the Atlantic preferred to follow traditional notions of "Free trade for everyone else, but not for me." As the decade wore on, GATT faded; and protectionism continued its relentless rise.

The military and political aspects of the Grand Design weighed more heavily on the mind of President Kennedy than did the economic aspects. Many European leaders demanded participation in nuclear decisions associated with NATO's strategic policy. President Eisenhower had raised expectation by discussing the possible creation of a Multilateral Force (MLF) which would involve joint operation of a Polaris submarine force. Ike had also entered into agreements with Great Britain to provide the Skybolt missile system to carry British nuclear warheads.

Thus Kennedy faced a crucial dilemma. It seemed reasonable that the partnership should involve Europeans in decisions fundamentally related to their destiny. But partnership involving the use of nuclear weapons also carried with it all of the dangerous implications associated with nuclear proliferation. Kennedy believed the nature of nuclear war demanded a unified deterrent. Secretary of Defense McNamara strongly and unequivocally agreed. The Defense Secretary ventured to the graduation ceremonies at the University of Michigan, Ann Arbor, during June of 1962 to state his strong beliefs. "There must not be competing and conflicting strategies to meet the contingency of nuclear war," insisted McNamara. "We are convinced that a general nuclear war target system is indivisible, and if, despite all our efforts, nuclear war should occur, our best hope lies in conducting a centrally controlled campaign against all of the enemy's vital nuclear capabilities." Independent nuclear forces according to McNamara would weaken rather than strengthen the hand of the West. "Limited nuclear capabilities, operating independently, are dangerous, expensive, prone to obsolescence, and lacking in credibility as a deterrent."

Both Kennedy and McNamara conceded that somehow Europeans should become involved in formulating nuclear policy. "We want and need a greater degree of Alliance participation in formulating nuclear weapons policy," admitted the President at one point. But as the Berlin crisis passed and the Cuban missile crisis mounted, Kennedy grew more adamant in his position that only an American president should make the fateful decisions concerning the use of nuclear weapons. So Kennedy instead offered Europeans a greater role in formulating policy for the strengthening of conventional weapons in Europe. Europeans demurred on this point, however, fearing that conventional arms build-ups would ultimately dissipate the impact of nuclear deterrents and serve only to increase the risk of Russian adventurism in the region.

In refusing to relinquish any control over the nuclear trigger, Kennedy assured monopolization of American participation in NATO nuclear stategy. Eventually this resulted in the cancellation of the Skybolt missile system for Britain, attempts by President De Gaulle to create an independent French nuclear force, and Kennedy's solemn promise to the Soviets that nuclear weapons would be kept out of the hands of the West Germans altogether. The Europeans were never satisified with this outcome, but the realities of nuclear war seemed to dictate it.

In spite of the difficulties inherent in bringing unity to western military and economic policy, Kennedy held out the hope that the Alliance would be all the better for the reasonable attempts to work out differences. Interwoven here were conflicting desires to achieve both more unity and more independence. Kennedy determined to work pragmatically within this framework. He chose this as the theme for his inspiring July 4, 1962, address at Independence Hall in Philadelphia. He equated the birth of the Atlantic partnership with the birth of the American union in 1776. He promised American support for a "more perfect union" in Europe, keeping in mind the principles of America's own "Declaration of Independence." Kennedy called for an alliance based on the fundamental principle of "indivisible liberty for all." Europe interpreted the Independence Hall address as an expression of Kennedy's sincerity concerning attempts to hold the Grand Alliance together.

After stabilizing Soviet-American relations and mending the cracks in the Atlantic Alliance, President Kennedy turned his attention to the underdeveloped Third World where industrialization was just beginning. Both Russia and the United States sought to assist development in the Third World, partly as another chapter in the contest between the two powers over which would rule the future. Thus Third World peoples seemed to have a choice between democratic capitalism or communistic socialism as they contemplated their industrial futures. "We can expect that it will be a decade of decision, and that the course of events during this period will determine whether most of the peoples in the emerging areas will live in open or closed societies," postulated Kennedy.

Kennedy surrounded himself with several so-called Charles River economists such as presidential advisor Walt Rostow, who pushed hard for a stronger American role in the Third World. "We cannot renounce our destiny. We are all over the globe," wrote Rostow in his book Our Global Strategy, and "given our history, this is a proud and natural responsibility." Kennedy realized that such global goals of Manifest Destiny would not come easily. In June of 1961 a special Task Force on Foreign Economic Assistance to the Third World reported that the decade "will be a period of continuing crisis, characterized by massive social and economic transformations and acute political instability in areas covering half the globe."

Kennedy also realized that the United States had become far more dependent upon good relations with the Third World in the Sixties than ever before. The growing dependency related to economic expansion as well as strategic military planning. The American economy could not flourish without trade expansion in the Third World. New markets were required for the disposition of American's growing agricultural and manufacturing surpluses. American bankers pressed for new investment opportunities in what could be called the new frontier areas of the world. Meanwhile American industry grew more dependent upon raw materials imported from abroad. During the Sixties approximately 30 percent of its iron ore, 90 percent of its bauxite, 35 percent of its lead, 45 percent of its copper, 60 percent of its zinc, and 60 percent of its oil had to be imported into the United States in order to keep the wheels of industry rolling. The expansion of democratic capitalism abroad was necessary to stimulate economic expansion, employment, and political stability at home.

These realities guided President Kennedy as he formulated his foreign policy toward the Third World. Alluding to the missile gap Kennedy declared the existence of an "economic gap, which constitutes an equally clear and present danger to our security." Kennedy called upon the United States to close the "gap in living standards and income and hope for the future." He called for a closing of the gap "between the stable, industrialized nations of the north and the overpopulated, underinvested nations of the south." Kennedy charged that the Eisenhower Administration had neglected Third World development, as witnessed by Vice President Richard M. Nixon's unfortunate Latin American tour of 1958. After facing serious and sometimes violent demonstrations, such as those in Caracas, Venezuela, Nixon returned to Washington complaining that "the threat of communism is greater than ever before." In the wake of Nixon's complications Kennedy called for a fresh policy toward the Third World. Eisenhower's disastrous reception in Japan in 1960 only served to increase the call for a new policy. "We take office in the wake of three and one-half years of slack, seven years of diminished economic growth, and nine years of falling farm income," admonished Kennedy, yet it represented an "economic challenge to which we have responded most sporadically, most timidly, and most inadequately."

The success of Kennedy's New Frontier policies depended to a large extent upon his ability to advance American ideals and interests abroad. Thus he called for the reorganization of foreign aid under a new office designated Aid for International Development (AID). By mid-decade AID employed almost 17,000 persons. Kennedy appointed Fowler Hamilton as coordinator of

AID. In exchange for American economic assistance Hamilton dutifully insisted on detailed plans for domestic democratic political reforms before any recipient nation could qualify for help from AID. In exchange for economic assistance recipient countries had to agree to monetary, trade, and taxation reforms usually more favorable to the interests of the United States than the recipient country itself. American assistance came for projects which would serve as a foundation for industrial development such as clearing new lands for agriculture, building market to market transportation facilities, bridges, and waterways, and organizing educational institutions.

South Korea became one of AID's success stories. To help organize the AID program Kennedy assigned the laconic career diplomat Samuel "Silent Sam" Berger as Ambassador to Korea. Berger patiently established the foundation for a spectacular industrial boom characteristic of American expanding frontiers, but he failed to persuade the new business establishment to expand the democratic institutions. America's other Pacific example of prosperity was the Philippines, where again the political establishment relied upon military avarice rather than yield very much to the democratization of its institutions.

What this meant, of course, was that Kennedy chose economic stability over human rights. He continued the policy of providing training and equipment for local military elites. Thousands of young men from the Third World came to the United States for military training under the auspices of AID. "Probably the greatest return on our military assistance investment comes from the training of selected officers and key specialists at our military schools and training centers in the United States and overseas," explained Defense Secretary McNamara. "These students are hand-picked by their countries to become instructors when they return home. They are the coming leaders, the men who will have the know-how and impart it to their own forces." These would be the forces to protect American interests. "I need not dwell upon the value of having in positions of leadership men who have first-hand knowledge of how Americans do things and how they think," asserted McNamara, "it is beyond price to us to make friends of such men." This represented the coldly calculated policy to expand American influence through subtle infiltration of Third World military and police elites.

Perhaps the most idealistic and distinctive feature of the AID program involved the Peace Corps, a program designed to send idealistic young Americans into Third World countries to provide educational and technical assistance. In order to make sure that the Peace Corps received his personal attention, Kennedy appointed his brother-in-law, Sargent Shriver, as director. Young people wishing to become involved with the program underwent several months of vigorous training at designated American universities in the history, language, and culture of the particular country they intended to serve. The actual field experience usually involved 18 months of services in the area of education, health, and agriculture. By 1963 over 7,000 enthusiastic young Americans served in 47 different countries, mostly in Latin America. In spite of widespread charges that these young American volunteers represented little more than advanced "agents of imperialism," most Third World people welcomed this laudatory example of American benevolence and good will. The Peace Corps became the bright side of America's attempt to integrate Third World peoples into a worldwide system of democratic capitalism. At least it presented the promise of rising standards of living.

President Kennedy's model for American relations with the Third World became the Alliance for Progress, a program designed to assist industrial and community development in Latin America. The Alliance for Progress represented "the most ambitious program ever directed toward Latin America," wrote historian William E. Leuchtenburg, and it "adopted a new goal for foreign aid: social change." The highly publicized program would provide $20 billion in United States assistance to be matched by an equal amount from Latin American countries for the purpose of economic development. "For too long my country, the wealthiest nation on a poor continent, has failed to carry out its full responsibilities to its sister Republics," announced Kennedy. "We have now accepted that responsibility."

Even though the basic principles of alliance strategy had already been developed under Eisenhower by such long-time Latin American specialists as Nelson Rockefeller, the Kennedy flair gave the program needed inspiration and momentum. "Our nations are the product of a common struggle--the revolt from colonial rule," declared Kennedy, "our unfulfilled task is to demonstrate to the entire world that man's unsatisfied aspiration for economic progress and social justice can best be achieved by free men working within a framework of democratic institutions."

Kennedy's Alliance for Progress combined idealism with concerns for hemispheric political stability and the economic expansion of the United States. In order to qualify for long-term, low-interest loans from the United States, Latin American governments had to adopt reforms in agriculture, banking practices, labor-management relations, housing, and education, all of these reforms commensurate with the development of democratic capitalism. True to the American work ethic, qualification for economic assistance depended on how well Latin American nations demonstrated a willingness to help themselves. Without a spirit of "self-help no amount of money in outside aid will do much good," warned U.N. Ambassador Adlai

Stevenson.

At Punta de Este, Uruguay, Treasury Secretary Douglas Dillon, who had also helped formulate the policy under Eisenhower, spelled out the terms of the Alliance for Progress policy. Taxes would have to be "assessed in accordance with ability to pay." Land reforms would be necessary "so that under-utilized soil is put to full use and so that farmers can own their land." This would "require lower interest rates on loans to small farmers and small businesses." The obvious ploy here was to create a system of small family-sized farm capitalism as the foundation for industrial progress, just as it had happened in the United States. In return for these reforms, Dillon announced, the United States would support a Latin American Free Trade Area (LAFTA), organized to reduce trade barriers among the nations of the western hemisphere.

Kennedy hoped that the Alliance for Progress would bring about inter-American economic prosperity and business expansion for the United States while preventing radical socialistic revolutions of the sort that had enveloped Cuba. "Unless necessary social reforms are freely made, unless we broaden the opportunity of all our people, unless the great mass of Americans share in increasing prosperity," admonished Kennedy, "our alliance, our revolution, our dream, and our freedoms will fail." Kennedy frankly told one group of Latin American diplomats that "those who make peaceful revolution impossible will make violent revolution inevitable."

President Kennedy's Alliance for Progress represented American big-brotherism at its best, but most Latin American leaders seemed to embrace it enthusiastically at first. The alliance, however, was doomed from the beginning. It faltered under the selfishness and conservative intransigence of the land-holding classes and military elites in Latin America, under the gross selfishness and narrow vision in public and private circles in the United States, and under the liberal naivete on both sides. Yet the legitimacy of the Kennedy approach stood as a constant reminder of what ought to be done.

President Kennedy thought of the world mostly in unilateral terms, yet he held to the hope that world conflicts could increasingly be settled under the auspices of the United Nations, established with so much expectation during the final days of President Franklin D. Roosevelt. The United Nations buildings, their abstract modern architecture rising boldly into the New York City skyline, served as a constant reminder that world order could be approached through sincere deliberation, persuasion, and peaceful compromise. Even though Roosevelt's original optimism about the effectiveness of the multilateral approach had evaporated in the face of unilateral actions,

Kennedy enthusiastically endorsed the organization as "the last best hope of mankind."

He demonstrated his enthusiasm by appointing Adlai Stevenson, the sagacious elder statesman and former Democratic presidential standard-bearer Ambassador to the United Nations. Stevenson's thoughtful and realistic appraisal of world affairs helped mollify those alienated by the Administration's earlier belligerency. "Power means the sum total of a nation's ability to influence the course of history," Stevenson reminded his colleagues at one point, but "peace cannot be won as war is won. Peace in the world, like good government at home, is a goal we approach but never finally or perfectly attain." Stevenson realized that world superpowers preferred unilateralism to multilateralism, but in his own pragmatic way reminded Kennedy that the United Nations could be "the effective second line of defense for peace." Stevenson proved that during the Cuban missile crisis.

The United Nations scored some notable successes during the Sixties. Under the astute leadership of Secretary General Dag Hammerskjold, author in the Fifties of the Uniting for Peace resolutions, the United Nations maintained a high profile. Under United Nations auspices special organizations contributed much to the age-old struggle against disease, hunger, and pestilence. The World Health Organization, for example, provided emergency aid for endless epidemics, issued birth control information, and conducted significant research toward the further eradication of disease. The United Nations Relief and Rehabilitation Administration distributed drugs, clothing, raw materials, seeds, and farm implements to disaster areas.

The United Nations Conference of Trade and Development, meeting in Geneva, Switzerland, developed important goals for the Third World nations receiving foreign aid. UNESCO (U.N. Education, Scientific, and Cultural Organization) promoted multifarious activities in child care and helped raise cultural standards by encouraging a healthy intellectual interchange between nations and peoples. As witnessed during the Cuban missile crisis, the United Nations provided a crucial avenue of communication and a worldwide forum where nations could at least talk about their differences. Such discussion, even when disjointed and bitter, could establish the basis for a future consensus on some matters. Finally, there was the powerful image of United Nations headquarters in New York City, where, daily, thousands of visitors from around the world traversed the chessboard floors, gazing up at the sea gulls gliding above as if to bless the proceedings. As these visitors watched and listened to the flap of more than 100 flags whipping back and forth in the cool oceanic breeze, the notion of peaceful and rational solutions to disputes became almost inescapable.

While President Kennedy was in office, the United Nations became deeply embroiled in a peacekeeping operation in the African Congo. The Congo had been granted independence from Belgium in 1960, and the new nation fell immediately into factionalism and civil war. The copper-rich land soon became an object of international intrigue by the United States and the Soviet Union. President Kasavubu's central government at Leopoldville requested United Nations intervention. When the pro-Soviet Premier Lumumba objected to such a predominate United Nations role, he was dismissed by Kasavubu. As he fled, Lumumba was captured and murdered. His followers established a pro-Soviet regime at Stanleyville. With the assistance of the American-supplied United nations peace keeping force, however, Kasavubu was able to contain the rebellion.

During the spring of 1961 events in the Congo took an ironic turn. The copper rich Katanga province, under the wily leadership of Moise Tshombe, declared its independence from the Congo. Now the central government faced two rebellions: one on the political left, the other on the right. Representatives of communist nations at the United Nations called for the quick annihilation of Tshombe's government, but the expeditious leader had strong support among conservative business forces around the world. With Kennedy's endorsement the United Nations swept into central Katanga and captured Jadetville, Tshombe's military stronghold. Tshombe was defeated, but a few months later he mysteriously became the new prime minister of the Congo.

The Congo intervention did much to erode the United Nations' prestige around the world. The Congo operation turned out to be offensive in nature, which conflicted with the peacekeeping intent of its original charter. Tshombe's ironic rise to power demonstrated the lack of impartiality in the Congo peacekeeping operation. It rendered the United Nations an instrument of American foreign policy, something bitterly resented by Russia and France. As a result both nations refused to pay their assessments in 1963 and 1964, obligating the United States to make a $200 million emergency loan to save the organization from bankruptcy.

When Dag Hammarskjold died in a mysterious plane crash over Africa, Russia pushed for a plan to replace him with a Troika representing both sides of the Iron Curtain and the neutral nations. After a series of explosive debates Hammarskjold was succeeded by Burma's U Thant who eventually became known as the "tower of jelly" for his lack of effectiveness with respect to such major issues as Red Chinese membership, Vietnam, the Middle East, and for the frivolous economic boycott of Rhodesia. During the decade the membership of the United Nations increased by 36, most of the new members coming from Africa. Although their gaudy robes, beaded headdresses, and Oxford and Sorbonne accents lent flavor and color to the proceedings, their anti-colonial vindictiveness, jealous determination to maintain a neutral stance, and lack of diplomatic sophistication greatly reduced the possibility of the General Assembly's achieving a working consensus. "The whole United Nations experiment has come close to collapse," lamented Time in 1965.

So in spite of Kennedy's early hopes about peaceful solutions to disputes through the United Nations, the actions of his own Administration and the realities of world politics greatly diminished the effectiveness of the organization. Later events would render the United Nations even more impotent. It would stand only as a forum for those wishing to make largely unheeded appeals to world public opinion. By then American's view of its own role in the world would also change under the pressure of new events and changing balances of power. Meanwhile, President Kennedy confidently turned the attention of his Administration toward domestic concerns.

CHAPTER II

NEW FRONTIERS: OLD SLOGANS

The domestic side of the Kennedy Administration earned the lofty designation of the New Frontier. Kennedy coined the term "New Frontier" during his acceptance speech at the Democratic National Convention in Los Angeles. It had become customary for Democratic administrations to enshrine their policies with such a designation ever since the days of Woodrow Wilson's New Freedom. Since Wilson, Franklin D. Roosevelt had had his New Deal and Harry S. Truman his Fair Deal. Kennedy choose the New Frontier designation in part to let it be known that his Administration would be philosophically consistent with the twentieth century liberal ideal of a chief executive who would exercise strong and aggressive leadership in domestic as well as foreign policy. "I believe the American people elect a President to act; if the President does not move, the nation does not move," asserted Kennedy. The President must be "the vital center of action."

In keeping with twentieth century liberal principles, Kennedy's New Frontier represented a mixture of reform, recovery, and relief; but for all its parading and high-sounding rhetoric, it did not contemplate any alteration in the basic foundations of the private enterprise system. "I regard the preservation and strengthening of the free market as the cardinal objective of this administration," declared Kennedy. The New Frontier sought to enrich and sustain the existing order by generating an ever higher level of prosperity. The patron saint of the Democratic Party, Thomas Jefferson, would have called it "enlarging the empire of liberty." Kennedy's philosophical framework was wholly consistent with the observation once made by Alexis de Tocqueville. "Two things are astonishing about America; the great changeableness of most human behavior and the singular fixity of certain principles," wrote the French philosopher. Americans "are forever varying, altering, and restoring secondary matters, but they are very careful not to touch fundamentals. They like change but they dread revolution."

Kennedy's New Frontier appealed to the liberal and centerist elements of the democratic capitalistic establishment who by the Sixties welcomed governmental assistance but abhorred socialistic tinkering with the basics. Such economic principles as free enterprise, risk for profit, right of contract, and the sanctity of private property continued to serve as givens in New Frontier policy. Kennedy was anxious to improve upon government's role in creating new economic frontiers for fueling the engines of capitalism, and he determined to employ the presidency vigorously to that end.

President Kennedy primarily concerned himself with arresting the economic lag inherited from the Eisenhower years. Activity in the market place must be restored. "Business, after all, is really the backbone of our whole way of life," counselled Kennedy. "We must move along the path to a higher rate of growth and full employment for this will mean tens of billions of dollars more in production, profits, wages and public revenue." If we can get the "tide to rise all the boats will rise," proffered Kennedy. In his efforts to restore business activity, Kennedy relied for advice on economists such as Paul Samuelson and Walter Heller, Chief of the President's Council of Economic Advisors. They provided the President with a series of neo-Keynesian tricks for fine-tuning the economy. Armed with computer analysis, advances in economic fact gathering, and better business forecasting techniques, the economists were confident that the federal government could stimulate the economy with much greater sophistication than before.

The influence of the "new economics" soon revealed itself in Kennedy's policy initiatives. Kennedy encouraged the Federal Reserve Board to ease credit and lower discount rates. He directed federal agencies to release additional funds for construction in depressed areas, ordered accelerated federal spending for post office and highway construction, increased farm supports, reduced interest rates on Federal Housing Administration and Small Business Administration loans, and made more credit available through the Federal Home Loan Banks.

On February 2, 1961, the President presented Congress with a seven-point economic recovery plan, billed in the press as the most far-reaching economic package since the early days of the New Deal. The plan would bring about "full recovery and sustained growth," predicted Kennedy confidently. By June Congress had obliged the President by approving all seven parts of the plan: (1) an increase in minimum wage and broadened coverage; (2) an increase in Social Security payments; (3) an expansion of federal relief to feed grain farmers; (4) aid for children of unemployed workers; (5) an expansion of assistance for federal home building and slum clearance; (6) a special thirteen-week supplement for unemployment benefits; and, (7) special funds for the redevelopment of economically depressed areas.

In early 1962 Kennedy prodded Congress into providing a seven percent tax credit for business investment on new machinery and equipment, as well as a liberalization of timetables and guidelines for equipment depreciation. This sweeping tax credit policy reduced all business taxes by an estimated $2.5 billion and corporation taxes by almost 11 percent. In 1963 Treasury Secretary Douglas Dillon, a liberal Republican holdover from the Eisenhower Administration, persuaded the President to ask Congress for an income tax cut amounting to almost $10 billion. This eventually passed Congress and generated more consumer spending in the private sector. Undaunted by conservative warnings that deficit spending would fuel the fires of inflation, Kennedy also systematically increased spending for military, space, health care, education, urban renewal, and welfare assistance programs.

Secretary of the Treasury Douglas Dillon became the most important influence on New Frontier economic policy. Unlike some of the professorial, idealistic economists surrounding the President, Dillon had a practical business background and enjoyed several important connections with the immensely influencial corporate boardroom elites who dominated the American political economy. According to Dillon's analysis economic lag had resulted from sluggish growth and a lack of investment incentives. The expansionary forces generated by World War II had dissipated. Increasing tax rates captured so much income as to prevent the private sector from reaching full employment. Without some new stimulus the national economy would be locked into permanent stagnation characterized by inadequate demand, increasing unemployment, and frequent recessions.

Hence Dillon strongly recommended the use of national fiscal policy as "a dynamic and affirmative agent in fostering economic growth." Expenditure, tax, debt management, and monetary policies were heartily endorsed by Dillon, but in time he came to the conclusion that only a dramatic tax cut could get the American economy moving again. The "Big Question" was "whether to increase government expenditures or to reduce taxes," argued Dillon, "or to come to the heart of the matter: whether to rely upon the latent energies of the private sector or to expand government activity." In convincing Kennedy to pursue the tax cut Dillon had persuaded the President to place the Administration's confidence in the "latent energies" of the private sector. The decision proved an expeditious one for the American economy.

As a result of Kennedy's New Frontier economic initiatives unemployment decreased from eight to five percent, manufacturing capacity increased from 72 to 87 percent, and spending for capital improvement increased by 20 percent. Meanwhile inflation held steady at only 1.2 percent. Dillon could rightfully be proud. "American economic policy and practice have taken new and dramatic turns for the better," he reported in an address to the Harvard Business School. "Our economy is no longer on the wane but surely and strongly on the rise," he confidently predicted and added that "we can now look forward, in all sober confidence, to the continuation of a peacetime economic recovery of greater durability and strength than in any comparable period in this century." Kennedy's $5 billion of additional spending for space programs also helped stimulate economic recovery.

The space spectaculars of the early Sixties highlighted Kennedy's New Frontier initiatives. Not only did the space extravaganza provide economic stimulation, but its exotic successes greatly enhanced national pride and increased America's international rapport. Ever since the Soviets launched Sputnik in 1957, the United States and Russia had been locked in a space race reminiscent of the days when British and Spanish explorers vied for position in the New World. "We had no choice in this," explained NASA's Dr. Francis Johnson. "If we hadn't at least done something to roughly compete with what the Russians were doing, we'd look much less prestigious on the world scene." Prior to Sputnik the American space effort had been little more than a "paper clip operation" headed by pioneer rocket expert Wernher Von Braun, one of the scientists inherited by the United States from defeated Germany after World War II. In the wake of Sputnik President Eisenhower, in 1958, created the National Aeronautics and Space Administration (NASA), a civilian agency granted a billion dollars to reverse America's fortunes in the space race.

Acting upon Eisenhower's sense of urgency, Von Braun developed the Jupiter C rocket which successfully launched the Explorer I satellite into space in 1958. Then, the ingenious Von Braun, who had been experimenting with rocketry since age 12, pioneered the Redstone rocket, destined to propel America's first astronaut aloft. He had already in mind the development of the huge Saturn V rocket which one day would carry astronauts to the moon.

As Director of NASA's Marshall Space Flight Center Von Braun visualized his historic task with brilliant enthusiasm and with abundant idealism. "I look forward to the time when mankind will join hands to apply the combined technological ingenuity of all nations to the exploration and utilization of outer space for peaceful uses," announced Von Braun, who had once developed Hitler's dreaded V-2 Rocket during World War II. When asked what would be involved in building a rocket for travel to the moon, Von Braun abruptly replied: "The will to do it."

It was this romantic, forthright dedication of spirit that especially attracted President Kennedy as he pondered the outermost frontiers of space. In April of 1961 as Kennedy thought about the decision to go to the moon, he had just suffered the humiliation of the Bay of Pigs, and the Russians had recently placed their first man in space. His science and budget advisors counseled caution. It would cost $40 billion, and the Russians might get to the moon first anyway. But for Kennedy the challenge was worth embracing. "We are going to the moon," he directed, determination in his voice.

The space program also attracted the President for practical, scientific reasons. A wide array of spinoff benefits would occur in communications, weather reporting, navigation, astronomy, medicine, agriculture, geology, oceanography, and industry. The cost of basic research in all of these areas was so high that only the federal government could afford it. Kennedy strongly endorsed NASA's Technology Utilization Program which was designed to disseminate advice to the non-aerospace technical community. Declaring it a "new age of exploration...and our great new frontier," Kennedy described the space program as "a great new American enterprise...which in many ways may hold the key to our future on earth."

Sensing these great possibilities, then, and with a careful eye on the development of space weaponry, Kennedy committed the American people to the goal of placing a man on the moon before the end of the decade. "No single project in this period will be more impressive to mankind, or more important for the long-range exploration of space," contended Kennedy, "and none will be more difficult or expensive to accomplish." The project leading to the moon landing alone would cost nearly $25 billion. Soon after the space decision the news was filled with stories about space feats involving weather satellites, Telstar communications satellites, and unmanned lunar and interplanetary probes. The real laurels of space, however, were reserved for the Manned Space Exploration Program, a series of three projects "designed immediately to achieve manned space flight in the vicinity of the earth, and ultimately to send manned spacecraft to the moon and the nearby planets."

The pioneer series, know as Project Mercury, placed astronaut Alan B. Shepard, decked in an elaborate space suit and laden with sophisticated instruments, into space for a 15 minute suborbital 300 mile flight on May 5, 1961. This was followed a few months later by a flight manned by Virgil (Gus) Grissom, who was destined to perish tragically a few years later in a space capsule fire during flight tests. The earlier flights were completely overshadowed, however, on February 20, 1962, when the amicable John H. Glenn boarded his Friendship 7 space craft. When the countdown reached zero, the thunder from Friendship's rockets echoed from horizon to horizon. The flash of fire from the gigantic engines fairly lit the atmosphere and the long trail of smoke in the distance excited America's enduring penchant for far-away places and exotic adventure. Glenn travelled three orbits around the earth. His flight signaled that America could take the lead in the space race. It put the nation "back in the space race with a vengeance, and gave the United States and the entire Free World a huge and badly needed boost," reported Time.

Not since Charles Lindbergh flew his "Spirit of St. Louis" across the Atlantic in 1927 had Americans possessed such an opportunity to admire a superhero. Clergymen pointed to his devotion, bureaucrats to his dedication, businessmen to his resourcefulness, professional men to his perseverance, and adventurers to his courage. In classrooms teachers heralded his moral qualities before enthusiastic young students who imagined themselves someday on an extravagantly organized mission into the outer limits of space.

"Glenn's an astronaut and a baseball player ain't nothing," exclaimed a 15-year-old admirer. Through Glenn's spectacular accomplishment Americans could celebrate their individualism, organizational genius, scientific and technological superiority, pioneering spirit, and above all, the pre-eminence of democratic capitalism and a free society. President Kennedy called the flight a "victory of technology and the human spirit." Glenn's flight represented the American impulse of exploration and adventure, pressing ever forward toward limitless new frontiers. Glenn's apparent courage accentuated America's image of itself, inventive and vigorous. Glenn's flight "lifted the self-doubt that had plagued the United States since Sputnik," observed Newsweek. "Gone was the nagging suspicion that the American economic and political system was somehow inadequate sense that the nation was somehow losing its technological reliance, modesty, and courage had been corrupted by the soft, mechanized affluence of modern life."

Glenn's flight gave Americans confidence in their ability to manage technology for progressive purposes and gave them a feeling that all was well with the destinies of the nation. Their faith in science, education, and democracy as the formula for progress had been restored. The sky was no longer the limit. Pan American Airways accepted 90,000 reservations for a trip to the moon by the end of the decade. A confident Barron

Hilton, head of the Hilton Hotel chain, announced plans for a 100-room Lunar Hilton to be constructed just below the crust of the moon's surface.

Space and other New Frontier spending programs generated enough prosperity to renew business confidence. Business asked for no more, but Kennedy yearned to employ the office of Presidency in a way that would insure more equity in the market place; his concept of the modern Presidency went well beyond the rather mundane task of expanding economic opportunity for private interest groups. In a positive mercantile sense Kennedy believed that the Presidency must act responsibly to moderate the natural conflicts in the market place, as well as to ensure fairness and equity in the distribution of the gains. He understood that America's highly integrated political economy functioned through carefully organized interest groups in business, labor, agriculture, and the professions, rather than through millions of independent individuals making random decisions in their own best interest, as in the time of Adam Smith. In order to achieve their economic goals, individual producers and laborers relied on the advantages and strength of organizational activities. Rank and file loyalty, allegiance, and confidence in the integrity of powerful, private leaders, therefore, was imperative to the successful functioning of the modern political economic system. If private leadership failed to act in its own, best, enlightened self-interest, the system might collapse under the pressure of social and political conflict, leaving Kennedy's own upper class with the most to lose.

Kennedy was enlightened enough to know that the brazen misuse of power by vested interest groups in the market place could ultimately bring about social and political dislocations that would threaten the entire fabric of democratic capitalism. He believed that the Presidency should be used "as a pulpit for economic education" in order to convince self-interest groups to be cognizant of the public interest. Kennedy shared Roosevelt's belief that the Presidency was "above all, a place of moral leadership," and that nowhere was moral leadership as important as in the market place. In that sense Kennedy was a true, modern aristocrat.

When the private market place failed to provide for the mollification of natural conflicts between economic groups or prevent certain groups from taking undue advantage, Kennedy believed that the administration should intervene in the name of fairness and for the sake of posterity. The presidency, the only nationally elected office that represented all of the people, could fulfill this task. "This administration will not be a business administration, nor a labor administration, nor a farmers' administration," promised Kennedy, "but an administration representing and seeking to serve all Americans."

The principles of an idealistic and paternalistic president, on the one hand, and a cold, calculating, pragmatic business community, on the other, came to loggerheads during the infamous Steel Crisis of 1962. Excessive wage and price settlements in basic industries could threaten to instigate an inflationary spiral which would eliminate the economic gains of the New Frontier and further reduce America's ability to compete in world markets. In January, 1962, the Council of Economic Advisors convinced the President to institute wage and price guidelines which would not exceed the three per cent annual growth in productivity. This came at a time when the mammoth steel industry was negotiating a new three-year contract. The President mailed letters to the leaders of the twelve largest steel companies urging them to refrain from price increases, and concomitantly asked David J. McDonald, president of the powerful United States Steel Workers Union, to press for a settlement well within the limits of productivity and price stability.

Kennedy allowed his intervention to be widely publicized. Secretary of Labor Arthur Goldberg carefully explained the President's philosophy. "In the past when government officials were called upon to assist in collective bargaining, their only aim was to achieve a settlement," lectured Goldberg, "but today, in light of our government's commitments both home and abroad, government must increasingly provide guidelines that are not only in the interest of the parties themselves, but which also take into account the public interest." In a tactful attempt to allay possible business and labor suspicion, Goldberg quickly added that "no one wants government intervention, of course," but he also reminded them that "everyone expects the government to assert and define the national interest."

Throughout the month of March Secretary Goldberg carefully monitored the steel negotiations. After the companies promised not to raise prices, he convinced a cautious McDonald to settle for less than a one per cent wage cost increase per hour. President Kennedy was elated and heartily congratulated the leaders of both sides for their astute display of "industrial statesmanship."

Ten days later--April 10, 1962--the big steel companies surprised the President and the nation by announcing a huge price increase of $6 a ton or 3.5 per cent. Roger Blough, the strong-willed president of United States Steel, the acknowledged price leader, personally flew to Washington from New York to audaciously deliver the *fait accompli* at the very doorstep of the White House. He cited mounting labor costs and "competitive pressures" from domestic producers and foreign importers as the reasons for the price increase.

The capricious policy of the steel companies infuriated the President. "My father always told me that all businessmen were sons-of-bitches, but I never realized 'til now how right he was," the President was heard to rage. Not only was the price increase apparently against the public interest, but such a defiance of the principles involved in cooperation between public and private interests threatened the rapport of the President with business, organized labor, and foreign interests. If the action was allowed to stand unchallenged, it would jeopardize Kennedy's influence over the future course of the economy and place the credibility of his leadership at stake.

Kennedy took the offensive at his regularly scheduled press conference the next day, April 11. He denounced the price increase as "a wholly unjustifiable and irresponsible defiance of the public." "A tiny handful of steel executives, whose pursuit of private power and profit exceeds their sense of public responsibility, shows utter contempt for the interest of 185 million Americans," asserted Kennedy. "Price and wage decisions in this country are and ought to be freely and privately made," admitted the angry President, "but the American people have a right to expect in return for that freedom a higher sense of business responsibility for the welfare of their country than has been shown in the last two days." Kennedy charged the steel companies with being unattentive to the national interest and bluntly promised to fight the increases with every arsenal available to the Administration.

The President moved swiftly and decisively. As Secretary Goldberg winged his way to New York City for "eyeball-to-eyeball" negotiations with the guileful Blough, Kennedy hinted that tariffs on steel would be reduced in order to allow cheaper foreign material into the American market. Defense Secretary McNamara stated that Pentagon contracts would be shifted where possible "to the companies which have not increased prices." The Justice Department allowed rumors to circulate that a Federal Grand Jury in New York would begin investigating United States Steel and others for violation of the antitrust laws. FBI agents were ordered to begin examining evidence of price collusion.

Kennedy applied enormous pressure on the smaller, often more efficient, steel companies such as Inland, Armco, and Kaiser, entreating them not to follow the lead of the larger companies. On April 12 the President scored a decisive victory when the highly competitive Inland Steel Corporation announced it would not raise prices after all. It would not be "in the national interest to raise prices at this time," announced Inland's independent-minded and daring vice president Leigh B. Block. A few minutes later Kaiser Steel followed suit. These announcements set in motion a flurry of activity as steel executives scrambled uneasily back and forth to rescind their price increase. By that evening the stone-face Roger Blough reluctantly announced that even the gigantic United States Steel would rescind its price increase. Privately he commented that his "father had always told me that Presidents were S.O.B.'s, and now I believe it."

Kennedy had won the struggle but not without cost. The business community recoiled in anger when it learned of Kennedy's strong-arm tactics which bordered on ruthless governmental interference. George McManus of Iron Age went so far as to lament the end of the free enterprise system. "It's almost certain historians will regard 1962 as a year in which a decisive change took place in the American system of free, private enterprise," complained McManus remorsefully. "A new doctrine of economic management by government was asserted. This doctrine was applied. It was challenged." According to McManus, "the confrontation that followed produced an authentic change in the role of government in the rules for business operation." Actually, McManus overdrew the picture. The recalcitrant reaction to his steel policy caused Kennedy to relax his efforts to establish price and wage guidelines and freed both organized labor and management to command an ever-increasing share of America's expanding prosperity. Still, Kennedy, more than any modern President, obliged vested business groups to consider the national interest.

Organized labor also received a chastising from the President. Labor leaders at that time demonstrated even less social consciousness than business. By the Sixties organized labor had come of age. We "now belong to the establishment," boasted an AFL-CIO lobbyist in Washington, and "want to be invited to the White House." The large number of powerful labor leaders at the inaugural ball, the inordinate influence of Labor Secretary Goldberg at the White House, and Kennedy's offer to appoint United Auto Workers Leonard Woodcock as ambassador to Taiwan all attested to the President's recognition of labor's strength. The gruff George Meany, president of the AFL-CIO, who hailed from the New York City Italo-Irish Pelham Bay District of the Bronx, put the matter of labor's power more bluntly. "I don't buy the idea that labor needs the Democratic party," he once grumbled, but "I am sure it is the other way around."

From his perch at Lafayette Park, across from the White House, Meany exerted power that would have seemed awesome in the days of Sam Gompers, the founder of the AFL. When it came to philosophy, attitudes, and tactics, however, Meany fell completely into the tradition established by the astute Gompers at the turn of the century. Meany stuck close to the "bread and butter" issues. He supported the liberal idea of an expansionary democratic capitalism. Labor would fight for higher wages, shorter hours, and better working conditions but would leave social causes and reform crusades to others. "Ideology is baloney," growled Meany. He lived by the principle that "you do good work for your people."

Meany's hot rhetoric was meant as much for organizational consumption as it was based on principle. The appearance of too much compromise with management could be disastrous for the leadership. David McDonald, for example, lost his position to I.W. Abel on the charge of "tuxedo unionism," partly occasioned by his cooperation with management and the government during the steel crisis. Perhaps a better example of the typical union leader was Tommy Gleason, who stood prepared to take his heavily featherbedded Longshoremen out on strike every two years during contract negotiations, thus halting all port shipping activity. "The men in this union fight like hell and walk out at the drop of a hat," snorted Gleason.

The possible exception to labor's rather crass approach was Walter Reuther, President of the United Auto Workers, a union so rich it could afford to be a little liberal. "His whole life has been a gigantic crusade against society's ills--be they poverty, disease, ignorance, or alienation," commented a Reuther cohort. Reuther advocated civil rights, opposed the Vietnam War, and called for tax reform. Even as he stood near death, he could be found marching hand-in-hand with the persistent Cesar Chavez in an effort to organize the down-trodden Mexican-American farm workers in California.

President Kennedy, influenced strongly by brother Robert, made James Hoffa, president of the powerful Teamsters Union, the object of his concern for reform in the labor movement. Labor leaders also had an obligation to act in their best, enlightened self-interest, the President believed. Investigations during the late Fifties by the Permanent Investigations Subcommittee of the Senate Labor Committee, under the chairmanship of Arkansas' unbending John McClellan (Robert Kennedy was Chief Counsel), had marked Hoffa as the most flagrant violator of labor's public trust. Hoffa's outspoken support for Richard Nixon in 1960 made him even more vulnerable to prosecution under a Democratic administration. Upon entering the White House, Kennedy let it be known that he was "not satisfied to see men like Hoffa be free," and ordered Attorney General Robert Kennedy to cooperate with a host of local authorities in seeking indictments against the Teamsters. By June of 1963 Teamster Union officials faced over sixty indictments.

On May 18, 1962, a United States grand jury in Nashville, Tennessee indicted Hoffa for accepting illegal payments of over one million dollars from commercial carriers in absolute violation of the Taft-Hartley Act. In July the Administration got the Senate Permanent Investigations Subcommittee to release a report accusing Hoffa of "defiant indifference to the interest of rank and file members...whose Treasury was being exploited and misused by corrupt and dishonest officials." On October 22 Hoffa's trial began, but by December an exasperated District Judge William E. Miller declared a mistrial on the grounds that Hoffa's colleagues had tampered with the jury. A prospective juror had been offered a bribe of $10,000.

Hoffa escaped charges of misappropriation of union pension funds and mail fraud, but on March 4, 1963, he was convicted for jury tampering, fined $10,000, and sentenced to eight years in prison. "You stand here convicted of having tampered, really, with the very soul of this nation...of having struck at the very foundation upon which everything else in the nation depends, the very basis of civilization itself, and that is the administration of justice," stated an exasperated Judge Frank W. Wilson at the sentencing. Hoffa crisply maintained his innocence but went to prison as an example of Kennedy's concern that private leaders exercise enlightened self-interest.

During his one-thousand day tenure in the world's most powerful office, President Kennedy virtually captured the imagination of the American people and the world. Americans had always venerated their presidents, regarding them almost as kings, but never had any president--not even the Roosevelts--won so much enthusiastic acclaim and admiration for a vigorous and graceful style of leadership. Veteran commentator Walter Lippmann assessed Kennedy "as more serious than Franklin D. Roosevelt, more physically akin to robust Teddy, and more politically educated and disciplined than either."

A descendant of poor Irish immigrants who had reached the pinnacle of power through a fashionable display of gallantry, elan, appreciation for beauty, and boldness of approach, Kennedy represented at the time what most Americans wanted to be. "He represented an ideal part of ourselves," wrote Redbook. Adlai Stevenson called him "the Contemporary man." "Government requires pageantry, and rulers are required to put on a show," wrote historian William G. Carleton, and "the Kennedys put on a superb one." Kennedy's eloquent personal demeanor represented a refreshing contrast to the harsh and humorless politics of the Fifties.

In one respect Kennedy represented grandeur. He performed common tasks in uncommon ways. He could turn common occasions into special affairs. For this he earned the respect and allegiance of Americans of all classes. But in another respect Kennedy exhibited a genuine commonness and personableness that appealed to the basic egalitarianism underpinning the American character. "I have a nice home, the office is nearby and the pay is good," he replied when questioned about his feelings concerning the presidency." "He was just a darn good, everyday American," replied an American worker when asked what he remembered most about Kennedy.

The Kennedy style quickly came to dominate the American scene. "The country, reflecting its new leader, had a new look. This was the New Frontier and Jack Kennedy was its trail blazer," reported Newsweek. Millions of confident Americans soon began to emulate the youthful President. The slick two-button suit, the swirling splash of hair over the forehead, narrow ties, and pointed shoes--all became fashionable for an entire generation of young Kennedy admirers. "The President was a two-button suit man," reported Look, and shortly it was the favorite of all the men of the New Frontier.

When Kennedy vigorously endorsed the 50-mile hike, physical fitness became a national fad. Rocking chairs became popular again because the President used one. Jacqueline Kennedy's hairstyle and clothing were copied by millions of American women who yearned to be part of Camelot. "For the first time in my life, the President of the United States was not an Olympian or remote grandfather figure," remarked social commentator Laura Bergquist in Look, "but a contemporary--brighter, wittier, more sure of his destiny and more disciplined than any of us, but still a superior equal who talked your language, read the books you read, knew the inside jokes."

"The difficult we do immediately," admonished Kennedy in his distinguished Bostonian accent, "the impossible shall take us a little longer." Hence Kennedy achieved charisma and established loyalty among faithful young followers. He gave to the Presidency a refreshing new character of genteel refinement. Kennedy valued the combination of youth, talent, resourcefulness, and toughmindedness. He attracted to his service people of elegance, charm, and tact, the reputed jet setter elites and Ivy Leaguers from Cambridge and New York.

Kennedy packed Washington, D.C., with "ideological soul-mates and eager beavers," observed columnist Holmes Alexander. "Not since the New Deal has Washington seen such an influx of bright young men," commented Newsweek. The Cabinet and White House staff became known as the Ministry of Talent. It included such notables as Robert S. McNamara, the "whiz-kid" from Ford Motor Company; McGeorge Bundy, the glasses-laden National Security Advisor from Yale; the debonair Theodore Sorenson, articulate and responsive; the conscientious Kenneth O'Donnell, poetic and sensitive; the courtly and loquacious Arthur Schlesinger, Jr.; and the golden haired, solid Larry O'Brien, watchful political housekeeper who faithfully kept the party regulars in line.

All of these men exuded youth and intellect and brought the same, cool dispassion of their master to their White House business. When they failed to match the elan of the master, it did not go unnoticed. One young White House aide wore a bright red sports jacket to work. "Hang up the red coat for the duration," cautioned Kennedy, "we're trying to create a responsible image of the New Frontier as well as projecting Red Fay as a serious-minded administrator and not just Grand Old Lovable." According to veteran columnist Joseph Alsop, "This novel combination in Washington--youth at the prow and brilliance at the helm, so to say--at first dazzled the country. The country's dazzlement in turn tended to bedazzle the new President and many of those around him," continued Alsop. "Anything seemed possible. All seemed within reach."

Kennedy's idealism and respect for culture, rather his politics, became the final elements in his power to influence the American people. "I look forward to an America which commands respect throughout the world not only for its strength but for its civilization as well," intoned Kennedy. Not since the days of Woodrow Wilson had the White House been so receptive to the arts and intellectuals. State dinners came adorned with an extra service of culture--a Shakespeare performance, Igor Stravinsky, Bach and Mozart, or a cello recital in the East Room. Pablo Casal's concert represented the first time since Theodore Roosevelt that a master cellist had appeared at the White House.

Never before has the White House been such a show place for the nation's art and artists," reported Newsweek, "the sense--and the semblance--of culture was everywhere." According to Look, the spotlight had "shifted from the Hill to the Mansion, not simply because a young President struggles there with bloodcurdling crises or because of the slow historical trickle of power from Congress to the Executive, or because Senators are suddenly avoiding publicity, but because the Mansion now jumps with interesting people and unlikely happenings." Like nineteenth-century nationalist Noah Webster, Kennedy wanted his nation to be first in letters as well as politics. "The life of the arts, far from being an interruption, a distraction in the life of a nation, is very close to the center of a nation's purpose and is a test of the quality of a nation's civilization," affirmed Kennedy. "If more politicians knew poetry, and more poets know politics, I am convinced the world would be a little better place in which to live," proffered Kennedy.

Even if Kennedy may have secretly abhorred intellectuals, as some suspected, his patronization of intellectualism gave the

Administration a fashionable political and social appeal. Intellectuals were welcomed at the White House. This careful attention deeply impressed the intellectual community, still smarting from the excruciating attacks of McCarthyism, and assured the young president sympathetic treatment in return from the intelligentsia.

Kennedy not only set himself forth as the nation's foremost politician but also as its foremost intellect. He prided himself in being a "writer of gifts" himself, and he went out of his way to include important intellectual appeals in speeches and public addresses. "The great enemy of truth is very often not the lie--deliberate, contrived, and dishonest--but myth, persistent, persuasive and unrealistic," admonished Kennedy at Yale University. "Too often we hold fast to the cliches of our forebears. We subject all facts to a prefabricated set of interpretations. We enjoy the comfort of opinion without the discomfort of thought." Hence, Kennedy brought intellectual courage, rationality, and spaciousness into American life.

Kennedy discreetly mixed his appeal to intellectualism with a goodly amount of sophisticated wit and humor. At an official luncheon observing the publication of some John Adams' presidential papers Kennedy jested with descendant Thomas Adams: "It is a pleasure to live in your family's old house, and we hope that you will come by and see us." On another occasion Kennedy sponsored a dinner for 29 Nobel Prize winners. "I believe this is the most extraordinary collection of talent, of human knowledge, that has ever been gathered together at the White House," beamed Kennedy, "with the possible exception of when Thomas Jefferson dined alone." When Kennedy telephoned Yale economics professor James Tobin asking him to become a member of the President's Council of Economic Advisors, Tobin hesitated initially. "I am an ivory tower economist," demurred Tobin. "That's fine. That's the best kind. I'm going to be an ivory tower President," retorted Kennedy goodnaturedly.

The zest for intellectualism demonstrated Kennedy's desire to leave for posterity a strong connection between culture and progress. In this sense the presidency became the major driving force behind the promotion of education. The President established the Hickory Hill School for young children of Administration members to gather for informal discussion of arts and politics. "When other children are still trying to master nursery rhymes," wrote _Life_, "the busy President of the United States was teaching his daughter short poems of Shakespeare and Edna St. Vincent Millay."

A major element in the Kennedy style involved the role of his vivacious young wife, Jacqueline. No First Lady since Dolly Madison received so much public attention. A beautiful, creative, versatile young woman of refinement and good taste,

"Jackie's" extravagant activities, whether skiing in the dangerous Alps or cruising the Mediterranean on Aristotle Onassis' luxurious Greek yacht, gave the administration a tantalizing dimension. The image of Jacqueline water skiing with Astronaut John Glenn on Lewis Bay, Massachusetts, presented an exciting new role for a First Lady. Millions of American women quickly copied her bouffant hairdo, and the fashion industry adopted her dress styles--the pillbox hat, box jacket, sleeveless dresses, uncluttered silhouettes, short skirts, and unusual colors. The American people "loved Mamie (Eisenhower), but left her in the peace she craved," reported Look. "They demanded to know what Jacqueline wore to the last gala."

The London Evening Standard, usually disdainful of American society and culture, contended that "Jacqueline Kennedy gave the American people one thing they have always lacked--majesty." The majesty was well reflected in her public appearances. "Her head was high and her eyes were bright, her smile was radiant. She swept regally past, her eyes looking far ahead, and the crowds loved it," commented Newsweek. Another observer described her as a "princess, the closest thing to royalty an American girl can be."

Jacqueline's popularity grew also from her willingness to defy White House conformity, her penchant for new design, while maintaining balance and good taste. She could "defy the system at times with considerable imagination and daring," wrote presidential photographer Cecil Stoughton, "but her eloquence and sense of history was so impressive the her 'differences' simply strengthened the public's fascination with her."

Even the unflappable, strictly composed, and unshakable French President Charles de Gaulle was enthralled with her touch of grandeur. In a rare moment of Gallic gallantry he observed that "the one thing I wish I could take back to France from America is Mrs. Kennedy." When the Kennedys visited Paris a few months later, the President good-naturedly observed that "I do not feel it inappropriate for me to introduce myself. I am the man who accompained Jacqueline Kennedy to Paris."

Hence, the Kennedy style--well-mannered, first class, and good humored--won and captured America's imagination. "Mr. and Mrs. Kennedy reached us, because they created a style that succeeded," wrote the editors of Smiling Through the Apocalypse. "He, because he was the pro, the operator, the man who made his score. She, because she played the pro's wife with an appreciation of the higher aspects of the situation, and because she looked like a movie star." The Kennedy style was best summed up by Time. He was a "vigorous, exciting man who loved the rough and tumble of political challenge, a vibrant man who loved he great thundering crowds of noisy cities, yet a thoughtful man who loved the solitude of the windswept coast of his native New England."

On the fateful afternoon of November 22, 1963, as President Kennedy and his entourage motored slowly down the winding streets of Dallas, Texas, as part of an attempt to mend Democratic Party differences there, the glamorous Augustan Age of Kennedy came to an abrupt and shocking end. The President was brutally assassinated by a restless malefactor named Lee Harvey Oswald. "Death, in full view, in the hands of obscure men, shocked everyone and shattered the pattern of history," reported Life. The nation was deeply grieved by this apparent aberration of the democratic process.

History will probably never declare John F. Kennedy a great president. His time in the presidency was too short, his accomplishments too mixed. His political skills with Congress and his ability to influence the establishment left much to be desired. New Deal Brains Truster Rexford Guy Tugwell believed that under Kennedy "in domestic affairs nothing of note was accomplished." Former Secretary of State Dean Acheson thought that in the presidency Kennedy was "really out of his depth." He charged that the Kennedy style amounted to a preoccupation of 'image.'" "It makes one look at oneself instead of at the problem," complained Acheson. "How will I look fielding this hot line drive to shortstop? This is a good way to miss the ball altogether." Acheson probably smarted a bit because of his lack of influence in the Kennedy Administration. In Tugwell had to admit that Kennedy's "sharp communication had been a striking change from Eisenhower's feisty blandness."

Although Kennedy's policies would have little effect on the course of American history, his political style would have a lasting influence. Form was sometimes as important as substance. What will endure was the great potential and style that marked President Kennedy when he tragically passed into the annals of history as a martyr.

Martyrdom itself became historically consequential since it prompted Americans to conjure up images of Kennedy's potential not possible had the young President lived to become tarnished by the political wars of later decades. Martyrdom also caused Americans to pause as they admired an invigorating style cut off in full bloom. The Kennedy legacy, then, would be an adorning image of a marriage between grace and power in American life, an image of leadership for the future. The Kennedys "presented us with a picture of a vigorous and graceful leadership moving the nation to a more imaginative, varied, rich life," asserted historian Eric F. Goldman. This image alone, even if unreal at times, became historically significant.

"Kennedy cracked the crust of the old politics wide open," recalled Suzannah Lessard in the Washington *Monthly*, "and if the crack was so fresh it closed up after his death, or whether his failings would have sabotaged the promise had he lived, does not invalidate the relevance of the experience to the present and the past." *Look* lamented that the "radiant Knight of Camelot" would not soon be forgotten. According to columnist Joseph Alsop, Kennedy's "time in office, for all its tragic shortness, was nonetheless a time of renovation and renewal, when our country found a new and better course after long years of search."

Not since Lincoln had the nation so profoundly mourned the loss of a President. Lincoln was remembered for what he finished, but as trusted Kennedy aide Ted Sorenson put it, John Kennedy "would be remembered for what he started." "Such was John F. Kennedy's contribution," wrote historian Peter Joseph, "a vast churning of energy, hope, action, an era of experimentation and new beginnings."

CHAPTER III

THE JOHNSON PRESIDENCY

Lyndon Baines Johnson rose unexpectedly to the pinnacle of power as a result of the Kennedy tragedy in Dallas, but it was not by accident that a man of Johnson's political savvy and experience should preside over the destinies of the nation during the middle Sixties. "No President in history reached office so well trained to govern the United States," observed Newsweek. "At the moment he took the oath of office, Mr. Johnson had thirty-one years of experience in manipulating the levers of the mammoth and intricate machinery of the Federal Government." Ever since 1938, when his great mentor, Franklin D. Roosevelt, had sponsored his election to Congress, the tall, slightly drooping Johnson had wanted to be President. In Congress he quickly established himself as a spokesman on national issues; and during the Fifties, when elected Senate Majority Leader, he became the most influential man in Washington outside of President Eisenhower. By 1960 Johnson was the only logical choice to become Kennedy's Vice-President in one of the most exceptional political marriages of convenience in history. Now, in the mournful atmosphere of November, 1963, the new President beckoned his fellow Americans, "let us continue."

In the first frustrating days after the assassination Johnson, a man susceptible to wolf-like habits but basically generous and committed to doing good, appeared somewhat flustered and constrained in the office of the Presidency. He sometimes stumbled when trying to read high-toned speeches authored by leftover Kennedy advisors. He demonstrated an obvious discomfort with the new, intimate, and scrutinizing interest of the press corps--an interest uncommon to the cloakroom politics and private arm-twisting associations which had catapulted him into power. In the "house of magnifying mirrors" called the modern presidency Johnson would never be able to develop a relaxed demeanor like that of FDR, and, thus, the people would never become comfortable with him either.

It soon became apparent, however, that LBJ was one of the most complex personalities ever to enter the White House. "Better to try and drain the Atlantic Ocean into a bathtub than to try and take one sentence to describe this President," observed LBJ's press secretary Bill D. Moyers. Nevertheless, LBJ, an abrasive, forceful Texan, whom Time called "the most boisterous, bumptious occupant of the White House in two decades," refused to be denied his place in history. Events were on the march, and Johnson determined to play a central role.

A fundamental believer in the American dream who was equipped with abundant optimism and a giant-sized Texas ego, Johnson had ambitions which ran without limit. "I want to be the president who educated young children to the wonders of the world. I want to be the president who helped feed the hungry. I want to be the president who helped the poor find their own way and who protected the right of every citizen to vote. I want to be the president who helped end hatred among his fellow men. I want to be the president who helped end war among the brothers of this earth," proclaimed Johnson. The President's appetite for accomplishment was unquenchable. "Nothing was beyond his desire. He wanted to be unifier and savior, uplifter of the poor at home and father of democracy in Asia," reported _Time._ "He yearned to be a latter-day Lincoln to the blacks, to outshine FDR's memory among reformers, to surpass Truman's humane but hardheaded foreign policy record, to evoke the affection accorded Eisenhower. Above all, Lyndon Johnson asked for the trust of today's voters and the respect of tomorrow's scholars."

Johnson's 42-button telephone in the Oval Office gave the unmistakable impression of a driving taskmaster in control and on top of every situation. Imposition of control came in both word and deed. When a young military officer offered to direct him to a waiting plane, LBJ retorted: "Son, let me tell you something. These over here are my planes. They're all my planes." The President demanded and received absolute loyalty from his staff and other associates. "They are afraid they'll be breathing out when he's breathing in," quipped Vermont Senator George Aiken.

Johnson insisted on involving every resource within the reach of the Presidency. "Lyndon had the ability to get you involved in whatever project was big on his mind," accorded Henry Ford II, President of Ford Motor Company. "He gave you a sense of urgency. He laid it right on the line when he got you on the phone. He was demanding, and he wanted the job done." Another Johnson associate reported that the President "could reach ten feet in either direction. Nothing could get by him." Political columnist Marianne Means described him as "a rare personal force with almost no outer limits." He would "leave his initials burned into the history of our land like a brand on a longhorn steer," wrote conservative columnist James J. Kilpatrick.

Johnson wished fervently to finish the work begun under Franklin D. Roosevelt's New Deal. He moved an old FDR desk into the Oval Office. "Now whenever I feel that I've done a good day's work, really accomplished something," pronounced LBJ with a windmill wave of his arm, "I look at the desk, and then I go back to work, because I know I've only begun."

A Johnsonian style soon began to emerge. It was a New Deal activist style with a Texas twist. As an activist president in the tradition of Roosevelt, LBJ sought to establish himself in the role of the great leader--always instructing, sometimes cajoling, inspiring the people onward and upward along the road of progress. "If you wish a sheltered and uneventful life, you are living in the wrong generation," proclaimed the President. "No one can promise you calm, or ease, or undisturbed comfort. But we can promise you this--we can promise enormous challenge and arduous struggle, hard labor, and great danger. And with them we can promise you triumph over all the enemies of man," continued LBJ as he prepared to overcome the threats of apocalypse. Thus, the President, who was fond of reminding his audiences that he was once just "a boy under the scattered Texas sky," greatly impressed his fellow Americans with his determination. "I like his direction in general. He is no McKinley," observed the aging poet Carl Sandburg.

Consensus and reconciliation were uppermost in the President's mind. "Come now, and let us reason together," LBJ would say in reference to his favorite Old Testament prophet Isaiah. "The President all but acknowledges that consensus is more important to him than the system of constitutional checks and balances," commented Newsweek. Johnson went to great lengths in his efforts to achieve consensus. "I dream that the least among us will find contentment, and the best among us will find greatness, and all will respect the dignity of the one and admire the achievements of the other," announced the President in one of his perorations. "This is my dream. It concerns the simple wants of people. But this is what America is really all about." At Detroit's fabulous Cadillac Square LBJ pronounced, "I have come here today to pledge that if all Americans will stand united, we will keep moving. This country is not going to turn from unity to hostility, from understanding to hate. Today I have come to call for national unity."

When the First Family attended church services at Christ Episcopal Church in Alexandria, Virginia, where George Washington had once served as vestryman, the Reverend William Sydnor sermonized that "perhaps the greatest single need of our world is reconciliation--reconciliation between husband and wife, labor and management, race and race, nation and nation." After the service the President leaned thoughtfully forward over his coffee in the parish hall and told Mrs. Sydnor that "the rector must have written that sermon for me. That's the business I'm in, you know, the business of reconciliation."

President Johnson's talk about consensus and reconciliation was quite in keeping with the current mood of the nation. Americans had come to believe that severe economic and social conflicts had been put behind them during the earlier decades when populists, socialists, and progressives found themselves locked in conflict over the nature of the modern American political economy. The arguments had finally been settled in the Thirties and Forties by the U.S. Supreme Court in favor of the New Deal Progressives from which LBJ hailed. "Out of the years of fire and faith in the 20th century," stated Johnson, "our diverse peoples have forged together a consensus such as we have not known before--a consensus on our national purposes, our national policies and the principles to guide them both."

According to LBJ's way of thinking, the vociferous ideological confrontations of the past had fallen before the pragmatic forces of progressive and administrative efficiency and consensus among intellectuals on political issues: "the acceptance of the welfare State; the desirability of decentralized power; a system of fixed economy and political pluralism," wrote Daniel Bell in a 1964 book appropriately called The End of Ideology. Meanwhile, a vigorous new school of "consensus" historians sought to rewrite American history to remove the emphasis on conflict which had been the preoccupation of the earlier "progressive" historians led by Frederick Jackson Turner and Charles Beard.

In his attempts to maintain consensus and at the same time be a folksy President, Johnson often acted impulsively, sometimes in a refreshing manner but often in a peculiar and homely way. Back in Texas it had been that way. His old neighbors had come to appreciate his homespun strain of humanity. "He was vitally interested in the people, their children, their churches, their schools and whatever went on," reported one who had sipped beer and chatted with him in the Stonewall Cafe near the LBJ Ranch. Now LBJ began practicing his folkloric political art in the nation's capital. At the Christ Episcopal Church's coffee hour he noticed a two-month old baby girl who had been baptized during the service; he promptly stalked over and proudly pinned his "LBJ '64'" tie clasp on the baby's dress. On another occasion at the Detroit airport, just before boarding his plane for Washington, the President abruptly broke away from the official party and strolled gingerly over to where the Redford High School band was waiting to give him a musical sendoff; he grabbed the baton from the leader and led the band in "Happy Days Are Here Again." Activities such as these not only helped LBJ achieve consensus but also demonstrated his deep yearning to be loved and cherished as a "people's President" in the tradition of FDR.

A Texas-like, homespun, spontaneous, down-on-the ranch, free-wheeling image of Johnson, replacing the more sophisticated and cosmopolitan image of John F. Kennedy. The LBJ Ranch, white Continental, and barbecue replaced Hyannisport, Honey Fitz, and golf as the major focus of leisure activity. When LBJ wished to entertain, he invited his guests down to the ranch for an elaborate cook-out with all of the western trimmings. "I've got to see the stars again," LBJ would say as he flew off for Texas. On the gently rolling hills of western Texas the real Johnson came to life. He enjoyed driving his guests around in his big white Lincoln Continental, beer in hand, showing them the landmarks and recollecting stories of the ranch's short tradition.

In this broad expanse far from the sophisticated and snobbish atmosphere of Washington where "running water," according to LBJ, was "the prettiest sound God ever made," the President could be a humorous and fun-loving man. Nancy Dickerson, CBS's vivacious, young news commentator, remembered one Presidential party arrived at the ranch to find a bright red fire engine sitting in the front yard, bequeathed to LBJ by a small Missouri town. LBJ was ecstatic. He bounded into the driver's seat and began driving it around in circles, laughing and shouting farcically, "This is why Barry Goldwater wants to be President." LBJ loved practical jokes. He once had an automobile equipped so that it could float in water and then, while showing guests around, he would suddenly veer off into LBJ Lake in order to alarm them.

Johnson hated solitude and craved attention. "His mood is not for solitary contemplation," wrote Theodore White. Like Teddy Roosevelt, LBJ wanted to be the bride at every wedding and the corpse at every funeral. He was unrivaled as a story-teller, imposing an anecdote on every occasion complete with illustrative gestures and mimicry. He was "in endless pursuit of public attention and affection and acclaim and still more recognition of his success," wrote Wall Street Journal correspondent Philip Geyelin. Johnson proved that in 1966 when, after returning from a hospital stay occasioned by the so-called "Executive Virus," he held a press conference in bed, his head propped on pillows. Often he surprised his guests by inviting them for a dip in the White House pool. Foreign visitors often wondered at the peculiar ways in which LBJ extended hospitality. He once loaded the Latin American Ambassadors on Air Force One for a weekend at the Lyndon B. Johnson Ranch, where they were adorned with red bandannas and Texas-shaped clasps, a tour of the ranch, and a historical pageant featuring a frenetic Mexican dance. The all too obvious motive behind the affair soon became clear when Johnson delivered a hard sell on the "Hemis-Fair" to be held in his beloved San Antonio in 1968.

Maurice Yameogo, President of Africa's Upper Volta, was one official foreign visitor to be favored with the southwestern style of hospitality dealt out by the profligate Texan in the White House. The little five-foot-six Yameogo received the red-carpet treatment, including a 21-gun salute welcome on the White House lawn. In a gala ceremony Johnson fervently praised him as a leader who had "steadfastly and wisely denied comfort to those who would subvert the hard-won freedom" of Africa. Before Yameogo could catch his breath, he was hustled into a glittering state dinner where he sat as the exalted guest of honor. After dinner LBJ jovially invited all guests to come to the lavish East Room where American Indian entertainment was provided. The room was elegantly decorated with richly adorned buffalo hides and gorgeous loin-clothes representing the heritage and culture of Johnson's own southwest. While Yameogo delightfully admired his surroundings, several dozen Indians from various American tribes "whooped, chanted, and clanged their way through five primitive dances."

As the final dance ended, the President steered Yameogo into an official limousine and whisked him off through the deserted streets of Washington for a visit to the Lincoln Memorial. Johnson ordered his astonished secret service attendants to illuminate the contemplative image of Lincoln, who he understood was Yameogo's favorite American historical figure. As the two men stood silently gazing at the awesome figure of Lincoln, they began quoting passages from the Gettysburg address. So effective was Johnson's ostentatiousness, reported one amazed journalist, that "Yameogo came to Washington a fan of Abraham Lincoln; he left a fan of Lyndon Baines Johnson."

Any consideration of the emerging Johnsonian style would be incomplete without pondering the role of Mrs. Johnson, whom the President fondly called "my Lady Bird." Lady Bird was a gracious and tactful woman, immensely sensitive and thoughtful. Her business and political acumen matched that of the President. She was proud to be known as a "hard-bargaining business woman." In many ways Lady Bird emulated Eleanor Roosevelt, wife of Franklin D. Roosevelt and matron figure of the Democratic Party. One White House aide described her as "remarkable...She always made you feel that you mattered."

Lady Bird became directly and intimately involved with issues that otherwise would have received little public attention. While the Johnsons occupied the White House, Lady Bird conducted forty "Discover America" trips, acting "as the eyes and ears of LBJ." She almost single-handedly alerted the nation to the dangers of pollution with her strong support of beautification programs. She combined her concern for blight in the countryside with that of the inner cities. She declared before the American Forestry Association at Grand Teton National Park: "Ugliness--the gray, dreary, unchanging world of deprived neighborhoods--has contributed to riots, mental ill health and to crime." Pushing her campaign against inequality, Lady Bird once joined over 6,000 Washington area children at a performance of the Ringling Brothers and Barnum and Bailey Circus. As the television cameras beamed in her direction, she sat down conspicuously between a black girl and a white girl and chatted with the children and the clowns.

On another occasion Lady Bird flew to St. Petersburg, Florida, in order to address the first VISTA graduating class and characteristically took advantage of the occasion to comment on the nation's responsibility to eradicate poverty through the operation of such agencies as VISTA. "America is many things," Lady Bird stoically reminded her audience, "but above all, more than any nation in the history of man, ever since the first frontiersman picked up his musket to help protect a neighbor, we have been a nation of volunteers. We have been a land in which the individual says, 'My neighbor needs me. I will do something.'" In such statements Lady Bird captured the idealism that the Johnsons hoped would serve as an underpinning to the Great Society.

For all of his sincere efforts to portray himself as the people's President, however, LBJ failed to win the general respect and approval of his fellow Americans. Somehow he could never shed the old clodhopper image of master politician, inside operator, and conscienceless cloakroom manipulator. Americans continued to view him skeptically as the broker in power, the political middleman who would probably sacrifice his birthright in trade for a strategic political victory. From the critical press corps to the average individual on the street, the people never quite accepted LBJ as their President--one, incidentally, who probably could not have reached the office except for the tragedy in Dallas.

Too often the President's actions bordered on the bombastic. He could not resist hyperbole. Creating the elaborate Oval Office network of television sets, lifting his pet beagles by the ears, showing off his gall bladder operation scar for reporters, hailing Diem as the Winston Churchill of South Asia, taking appointments while sitting on the bathroom stool, conspicuously consuming low calorie root beer and Texas steak while streaking above the clouds in Air Force One, playing with his automatic chair which raised and lowered at a touch, exercising on the ever-present bicycle bolted to the door of Air Force One for use above the clouds, making Vice-Presidential candidate Hubert Humphrey wait in the White House drive for thirty minutes before telling him of his selection, rejecting the Hurd portrait of himself, delivering a bust of himself to a surprised Pope Paul VI in the Vatican on Christmas Eve, leaning forward and locking eyes with Aleksei Kosygin at Glassboro and not blinking until the Soviet leader looked away--all of these idiosyncratic episodes curiously marked the man and left his followers amazed and puzzled.

Johnson failed to achieve a comfortable relationship with the press because of his insecurity, secretiveness, and mistrustful attitude toward those who were in a position to interpret his stewardship. He complained suspiciously that the Eastern seaboard metropolitan press purposefully interfered with his efforts toward national unity because of his Southern origins. He charged the press with possessing a short-sighted "disdain for the South that seems to be woven into the fabric of Northern experience." LBJ was not beyond lashing out at those in the press critical of him. Once he invited Washington Post publisher Katharine Graham into his bedroom after a dinner party to complain bitterly about a recent headline while he proceeded to undress for bed. He raised "unshirted hell with me," remembered the incensed publisher.

Television further disparaged LBJ's image. After Kennedy's vigorous dynamism Johnson came across as a disappointing, stern, colorless, and sometimes pathetic figure. The President's delivery could be "solemn, slow, almost doggedly prayerful and paternal," observed Time. All of this might have been overlooked, but LBJ's insistence on manipulating the press caused much resentment and bitterness, as did his exaggerations and lies. He applied the carrot-and-stick technique, rewarding those reporters who would write friendly stories about him, and punishing those critical of his actions and this in turn encouraged the punished to "dig up nasty stories," recalled LBJ's second press secretary, George E. Reedy.

Thoughtful critics became concerned about Johnson's ability to inspire the nation. His "Alamo psychology" was alien to what historian Eric Goldman called the "Metro-Americans--the educated, affluent, growing middle class." When Johnson would thunder, "Why, goddammit, can't these economists talk straight like Sylvia?" referring to the popularly serialized economist Sylvia Porter, he probably made populist anti-intellectual points in Texas but not in Metro-America, where citizens longed for the refinement of Kennedy. "Somehow Johnson has been cast--perhaps has cast himself--in the role of the Great Prestidigitator, the Miracle Worker," wrote Max Lerner, one of the nation's most astute political observers: "Step up and watch him, Ladies and Gentlemen. See how nimble, see how quick. Watch the incredible performance of this master." Lerner searched in vain for a sign of charisma. "It is a performance we watch with fascination, with admiration, in the end perhaps with acceptance tinged with boredom," complained Lerner. "Such a man can carry votes with him; he cannot lift our hearts nor stir our brains. Before you can get a society, great or small, you need more than a consensus," concluded Lerner. "You need a nexus: something to tie the parts into a whole, something to cement the individual wills, something to stir the nation's pulse, not continually feel it." "The nation needed to be engaged. It needed a personality that it could warm to and trust," wrote Time. "Instead, it got a preacher and teacher who ensured accomplishment in statistics that were irrelevant to the haves and incomprehensible to the have-nots."

This criticism of Johnson represented in part the disillusionment felt by the liberal-leaning northeastern Democrats who had been so infatuated with Kennedy. The Kennedy liberals never completely recovered from the shock of Dallas and soon became disenchanted with LBJ's overly sentimental, homely style, closet maneuvers, and earthy language; they detested his "stumping style of politics." Whenever the President "flailed his arms, pounded the lectern, shouted so hard his voice broke, leaned so far forward he was practically nose to nose with front-row listeners," the liberals flinched and turned away in disgust. The liberals resented LBJ's propensity to overdo things. "Kennedy could make a decision, or an appointment, or a speech and be convinced about it; it was enough for him that he was Kennedy and he was President," said one liberal critic. "With Johnson, he seems to feel a necessity for circuses, sideshows, Roman candles, klieg lights, to get his point across."

The liberals resented LBJ's rigid desire to follow strict protocol and his regal insistence upon establishing traditional lines of administrative organization. As exiles in watchful waiting, then, the Kennedy liberals granted Johnson only halfhearted support as they longed for the time when another Kennedy would rise to the White House and restore the spirit of the New Frontier.

This attitude of remorsefulness effectively removed many liberals from the counsels of the President and caused him to sway more toward the conservative wing of the party, which had become more concerned with building new frontiers in Vietnam than at home. Unfortunately, the liberals grossly underestimated Johnson's ability and resolve, and, as the ship of state moved sharply forward, many liberals found themselves excluded from the inner circles of power. "It was Johnson rather than Kennedy who moved the system," wrote historian William A. Williams. "The Kennedy machine was like a freeway cruiser: beautiful on the way to the White House or the moon, but of little help in getting coal to Grandma in the snow."

Johnson's inordinate ability to move the system resulted from his intimate relationship with Congress and his profound understanding of political matters. "The President possesses 'a safecracker's touch' for the sensibilities of congressmen," reported Newsweek. "The genius of Lyndon Johnson is that he not only calls you when he wants something, but he remembers to call you back and thank you for what you've done," commented

Connecticut's Senator Abraham Ribicoff. "The President never forgets a birthday," confided another Congressman. These were the marks of a patient and meticulous President seeking to establish a relationship of cooperation and mutual trust with Congress.

LBJ carefully tried to set this tone in his first address before Congress. "As one who has long served in both houses of Congress, I firmly believe in the independence and the integrity of the legislative branch. I promise you that I shall always respect this," declared Johnson firmly as he hesitated and cast a torridly anxious glance over his ornamental wirerimmed glasses as if to check on the attentiveness of his audience. Then in his famous half-grin, half-glare, he boomed, "it is deep in the marrow of my bones." Johnson paused a moment longer, still glaring over his glasses and cocking his head a little to one side now as if listening to his point sink in. "With equal firmness," he continued, "I believe in the capacity and I believe in the ability of Congress, despite the divisions of opinion which characterize our nation, to act--to act wisely, to act vigorously, to act speedily when the need arises." With that Johnson shot another determined glare over his glasses, braced himself, raised his fist, cocked his head in the air and declared unequivocally, "The need is here. The need is now."

In his first State of the Union message--delivered at 9:00 p.m. rather than the customary high noon for television purposes--Johnson clarified his intentions to Congress and the nation. "Our basic task is threefold," declared the President, "to keep our economy growing, to open for all Americans the opportunity that is now enjoyed by most Americans and to improve the quality of life for all." Following the address LBJ bombarded Congress with a myriad of legislative proposals. Telephone lines between the White House and Capitol Hill began to purr. Surprised Congressmen found themselves at the White House for some "face-to-face discussions" about the President's high priority bills. They soon discovered that Johnson was "thoroughly familiar with every weapon in the White House arsenal, from the invitation to ride in the Presidential plane to the authorization of a campaign contribution from Democratic funds, and from patronage to White House parties." Capitol Hill had not experienced so much action since the first one hundred days of the New Deal.

Johnson's legislative programs became know collectively as the Great Society. The term "great society," like Franklin D. Roosevelt's "new deal," originated almost accidentally, certainly without much forethought. The term itself was first employed in 1914 in a book written by the socialist Graham Wallas of the London School of Economics. The book analyzed the general social organization of a large, modern industrial state. President Johnson himself first acknowledged the term in his famous Great Society address during the 1964 commencement ceremonies at the University of Michigan. "It is not something brand new," conceded the President, "it is a dream as old as our civilization." According to Johnson, "a President did not shape a new and personal vision of America, he collected it from the scattered hopes of the American past."

President Johnson placed his Great Society vision squarely in the tradition of the "city on a hill" concept first enunciated by John Winthrop when the Puritans arrived on American shores in 1630. "We shall be as a city upon a Hill, the eyes of all are upon us," exhorted Winthrop in the belief that God had called his people out of decadent England to establish a "new Israel" in America. The new Israel would serve as an example to all the world. The concept had been secularized and updated through the years by great presidents such as Jefferson, Jackson, and Roosevelt; and now it was LBJ's turn to build upon that tradition. Rather than being just another nation in history, America embodies a special providence, contended the President. America's founders had "made a covenant with this land. Conceived in justice, written in liberty, bound in union, it was meant one day to inspire the hopes of all mankind." Johnson viewed the Great Society as a struggle for betterment. "I do not believe that the Great Society is the ordered, changeless and sterile battalion of the ants," LBJ told Washington Post reporter Dorothy McCardle after the Inaugural Ball in 1965. "It is the excitement of becoming--always becoming, trying, probing, falling, resting and trying again--but always trying and always gaining." Hence, the Great Society became a convenient, all-encompassing, even somewhat inspiring term employed to describe the Johnson years in the White House.

Actually the Great Society differed little from the New Frontier in operation and intent, except that it was much more ambitious. Johnson employed the memory of the fallen Kennedy in order to get his way with Congress and the American people. Unlike Kennedy, Johnson showed much more concern for expansion than for reform. "Most of the Great Society programs were directed toward putting people in a position where they could stand on their own two feet and pull off their own piece of the economic pie," admitted Johnson aide Joseph A. Califano bluntly. "During the New Deal right up until the Kennedy Administration, the great concern of politics was redistribution," commented Harvard political scientist Samuel Beer, but "Johnson is less concerned with the distribution of material things than he is with raising the general level." Business took kindly to LBJ's emphasis on expansion rather than reform. He wanted no part of the old antitrust wars that had raged during previous periods of Democratic rule. He sought, instead, expansion for all, large and small. This emphasis was reflected in his rhetoric. "Let us bring the capitalist and the manager and the worker and the

Government to one table to share in the fruits of all our dreams and all of our work," urged the President.

Before Johnson could fully assert himself, however, he faced a sensational political challenge from the Republicans in the election of 1964. The challenge came under the banner of conservative Arizona Senator Barry Goldwater. The outspoken Arizona Senator represented the New Conservatives, much more uncompromising, recalcitrant, militant, and less dedicated to fundamental nineteenth century ideals of free expression and reason than to the brand of twentieth-century Conservatism propounded by former President Hoover and the late Ohio Senator Robert Taft. Goldwaterism amounted to a blanket indictment of the twentieth century liberal New Deal-Great Society policies; it offered the American people "a choice, not an echo."

Conservative Republicans had been brooding over the course of the Grand Old Party ever since the fiesty old Progressive Alf Landon had become the standard-bearer in 1936. Wendell Wilkie's internationalism, Thomas D. Dewey's northeastern liberalism, and even Eisenhower's middle-of-the-roadism had enraged them. They branded it a mirage which in the final analysis only served to cater to the "creeping socialism" of the New Deal. Even Vice President Nixon's reactionary wrangling of the Fifties had not placated them. The infamous Nixon-Rockefeller Fifth Avenue Compact of 1960--in which in return for "Rocky's" support Nixon pledged to adopt a more moderate position on defense and civil rights--completely disillusioned the conservatives; after Nixon's defeat, they launched a concerted drive to capture control of the party. Leadership in the conservative crusade fell upon the shoulders of the impelling Goldwater.

Goldwater became to the new conservatism what Kennedy had been to the new liberalism of the Sixties. His honorific disposition and bold rhetorical style enabled him to command extraordinary devotion and loyalty from his followers. His crisp manner, western background, puritanical moral integrity, and simple straight forward answers ("telling it like it is") endeared him with those who wished to return to the homespun virtues of individualism, localisms, and Sunday piety. For younger conservatives, who viewed society as radically corrupt, Goldwater's flair for the military, his ability to fly his own plane, the <u>Yia Bi Kin</u> (Navajo for House in the Sky), gave them the image of a gallant leader, ready and willing to reverse the forces of decay and re-establish orderly processes.

In domestic policy the Goldwaterites made the growing power of the federal government the central issue. "Leaders of the present administration conceive of government as master, not servant," charged Goldwater. "Responsibility has shifted from the family to the bureaucrat, from the neighborhood to the arbitrary and distant agencies." The Goldwaterites opposed organized labor as an aberration of capitalism, warned that big government amounted to a dangerous interference with individual incentive and autonomy, accused the Supreme Court of permissiveness and un-Americanism, equated federal aid to education to steps toward totalitarianism, and saw Keynesian economics as deviously undermining the American system of morals and values. In his concern for the possibility that federal aid to education would interfere with states' rights, for example, Goldwater charged that it "would inevitably invite bureaucratic Federal control of school curricula, add wasteful freight charges on money collected by the Federal Government, and squeeze out the private school and the small college in favor of large public institutions." Goldwater demanded a return to the concept of the neighborhood school. "I do not want the federal government counseling my children," complained Goldwater.

In foreign policy the Goldwaterites claimed to be blatantly anti-communist, critical of the United States membership in the United Nations, opposed to accommodation with communistic or even neutralistic nations. Goldwater demonstrated this point by voting against the Test Ban Treaty and by strongly advocating more spending for defense programs. On the United Nations Goldwater charged that "we must never attempt to use the United Nations as a substitute for clear and resolute United States policy." It has never been more than a "useful forum...for valuable conciliation among nations," he contended. He frankly insisted that the "Red Chinese should never be allowed to shoot their way" into the organization. On foreign aid Goldwater contended that "we should adopt a discriminating foreign aid policy; aid should be furnished only to friendly, anti-communist nations that are willing to join with us in the struggle for freedom." He warned that "government-to-government aid" encouraged socialism and inefficiency in the recipient countries. "We are making it more difficult for free enterprise to take hold," he complained. "We should eliminate all government-to-government capital assistance and encourage substitution of American private investment." "Foreign aid is becoming a form of international charity," he lamented, and "we cannot, in the last analysis, be friends."

Goldwater charged that the liberal establishment had allowed America's defense posture to deteriorate ominously. "Since 1961 the United States has introduced no new weapons systems, thus leaving us defenseless against any advances the Communists may make," he complained. "This amounts to a one-sided disarmament. We need manned bombers, nuclear power for some of the big ships in our navy, and conventional armaments as well as a missile system which has been proven reliable." Goldwater called for a strengthening of the Atlantic Alliance. "The greatest force for freedom in the world today is the powerful Atlantic Alliance, the NATO Community," he declared. "It is the first line of defense of the entire free world. But the present administration has allowed NATO to drift into disarray."

Between 1961 and 1964, while the Republican moderates sat complacently aside attending to the more mundane aspects of politics, the Goldwater enthusiasts organized a political momentum that extended all the way down to the precinct grassroots level. After Nixon lost the race for governor of California, the only real opposition was Governor Nelson A. Rockefeller, whose energy, wealth, and jaunty political style made him a serious contender even though he announced his candidacy late in the campaign. For all of his waving, winking, and blowing kisses, however, the masterful Rockefeller was doomed from the start. His liberal gubernatorial policies made him an easy target of conservatives. His controversial divorce from his wife of twenty-six years in 1963, and then remarriage, did not go over well in the more conservative areas of the country. When Goldwater won the crucial California primary in June, the conservative steamroller was on. The last minute entry of Pennsylvania Governor William Scranton amounted to only a token move.

The jubilant Goldwaterites converged on the 1964 National Republican Convention at San Francisco's Cow Palace to the tune of "When The Saints Come Marching In," and nominated their hero on the first ballot. But the victory would be a hollow one since Goldwater haughtily refused to dilute his idealogical views in order to compromise with the party moderates. Goldwater directed the creation of a party platform upon which twelve of the fourteen Governors found it impossible to campaign. All hope of party compromise was eliminated when, in his acceptance address, Goldwater contended that "extremism in the defense of liberty is no vice. And let me remind you also that moderation in the pursuit of justice is no virtue." "Good God! He's going to run as Barry Goldwater," declared one commentator. The Goldwater statement sent the moderates scurrying for political shelter and even left many thoughtful conservatives pondering nervously. The statement brought doubts which could best be summarized by the haunting words of former Justice Louis Brandeis, who once observed that "the greatest dangers to liberty lurk in the insidious encroachment of men of zeal, well-meaning but without understanding."

During the campaign Goldwater made statements which alienated him even further from the party and left voters apoplectic. His frank criticism of social security, an American sacred cow, and his idea about making the system voluntary caused a defection among the elderly. His contention that civil rights should be left to the states alienated millions familiar with the traditions in the South. His reckless talk about employing low-yield nuclear warheads in Vietnam and granting NATO commanders more control of the decision to employ nuclear weaponry in Europe made him susceptible to charges of impulsiveness and warmongering. His thoughtless promise to appoint "a real dirt farmer" as Secretary of Agriculture, on top of his call to eliminate the farm program, seriously hampered his support in the agri-business community. "Goldwater's positions on national issues proved to be an insurmountable obstacle to his campaign ever getting off the ground," complained Ripon, a liberal Republican society which had been hurriedly organized in 1962 in order to stem the tide of conservatism in the party ranks.

Goldwater soon found himself linked with such radical rightist groups as the John Birch Society, headed by red-baiting Robert Welch, who, in his infamous Blue Book, had intimated that even General Eisenhower acted as an instrument of communistic infraction. These extremist groups included the Minutemen, who stored up weapons and strained secretly to stave off a communist invasion either from within or outside the country; the Ku Klux Klan, as anti-semitic and anti-black as ever; John Schwartz's Christian Anti-Communist Crusade; the Conservative Society of America; The National Indignation Convention; and the All American Society. Many of these groups advocated violence and circumvention of law as instruments in their crusade to restore America to their view of its first principles.

Finally, Goldwater's choice for Vice Presidential running mate of a parochial-minded New York Congressman named William E. Miller-a man of unyielding stance, abrupt mannerisms, and constricting vision of the future--proved stupefying. Goldwater's conservative and sometimes colorless political antics were simply out of step with the buoyant Great Society mood which pervaded the political atmosphere of 1964. Goldwaterism could have provided the American people with a serious and necessary critique of the contradictions inherent in Johnson's Great Society; but, unfortunately, the movement's conspiracy-mindedness, impulsiveness, extremism, and uncompromising political posture prompted the voters to merely dismiss the Goldwater candidacy as an irresponsible last gasp of the old Republican order.

If there was a genuinely responsible and respected conservative influence on the Great Society, it came not from Goldwater, the "grandson of a peddler," but from the aging grandson of a middlewestern prairie farmer, Senate Republican Minority Leader Everett McKinley Dirksen of Illinois, whose conservative credentials dated back to the 1952 Republican National Convention which found him berating the modern Republicanism of Thomas Dewey. Dirksen's infernal logic, his flow of white hair and voluptuous voice, combined with his quick wit gave him the beloved image of an old-fashioned Senator.

Not only did the Senator play a key role in the halls of Congress, but he also stirred the admiration of the nation by recording a popular hit called "Gallant Men" in 1967. He gained sentimental favor for his campaign to make the marigold the national flower. "There's something in you that craves expression, and it must come out," Dirksen once intoned. This was a fitting self-characterization of a leader of exceptional prowess. Dirksen employed sarcasm with telling brevity. "A billion here, and a billion there, and pretty soon you are talking about a lot of money," snapped the Senator.

Dirksen's steady rise to power in the Senate was predicated largely upon his shrewdness in parliamentary maneuver. Never zealous but a believer in the practical art of the possible, Dirksen laboriously placed his stamp of conservatism on Great Society legislation as it flowed through the Congressional process. "Progress was made not by what goes on the statute books, but by what comes off," he once stormed. "I am a legislator, not a moralist and my job is to make sure any bill we pass does not do more harm than good." Dirksen understood power and played his political chips with the skill of a pawn broker. In September, 1964, for example, when many of his colleagues felt desperately the need to start campaigning, Dirksen cleverly tendered a rider to a foreign aid bill which would have allowed states to delay compliance with the Supreme Court's reapportionment edict. "I can stay here until Christmas," insisted Dirksen, who was not up for re-election. "This issue will have to be solved." In order to appease the persistent Senator, the Democratic leadership promised him consideration of a Constitutional amendment after the election. The Senate recess became know as the "Dirksen Breather."

On another occasion Dirksen hobbled on to the Senate floor with crutches, the result of a minor bone injury. At a critical juncture in the debate he rose majestically to his feet, his tangled white mane of hair floundering in every direction. "If I have to, I can use these weapons," bellowed the crusty old Senator. "The Bible says Samson slew the Philistine with the jawbone of an ass; I may have to slay an ass with the jawbones of a crutch." The only Senator who came the least bit close to rivaling Dirksen's antics was Massachusetts' salty Leverett Saltonstall, ranking Republican on the powerful Senate Appropriations and Armed Services Committees. "Old Lew" was known for his reticence and crusty behavior. "No comment and that's off the record," he once told a reporter. Known for his ability to reconcile House and Senate differences, Saltonstall retired in 1967 to become "just a plain country fellow" on his Dover farm, thus leaving Dirksen as the last of the "old time" Senators.

From his perch in the Senate Dirksen applied pressure on the liberal bend of the Sixties. He often criticized the Supreme Court. Not only did he seek to amend its reapportionment decisions, but he also introduced a school prayer amendment (The Dirksen Rider) designed to reverse Engle vs. Vital. "I do not intend to let nine men tell 190 million Americans including children where and when they can say their prayers," protested the embattled old sage.

When Johnson offered a National Service Corps, which provided tutoring and counseling clinics for urban youth, Dirksen offered his own brazen formula for juvenile misbehavior. "When I played hooky, I could think up the fanciest excuses which ever came into a juvenile mind, but they did not score with my saintly mother," raged Dirksen, his face flushed with anger. "She had the remedy. She did not say, 'My son, come into the parlor, I'm going to counsel with you now.' No, that was not the way. Behind the kitchen door was a strap, and it was administered, and the people did not go in for some of the nonsense we have today."

Even President Johnson was careful not to cross the wise old Magus of the great plains and often sought to placate him. Once Dirksen complained that LBJ tried to drive Senators like cattle when instead he should be stirring them up like hogs one by one. When Dirksen complained about the "remarkable collection of hummingbird economists who can reverse themselves without first stopping," Johnson moved swiftly to pare down the Administration's public chatter about deficit spending.

Ironically, Dirksen's superlative and dramatic opposition to the Great Society programs eventually played a key role in their passage. He proved to be an "intermittent ally and legislative king maker" as far as the Democrats were concerned. Kennedy once conceded that "most of the time old Ev is a good man when the chips are down." Dirksen's belated support made passage of the Test Ban Treaty possible. The Civil Rights Act probably would have never passed without Dirksen's timely announcement that he would support cloture, thus choking off southern opposition. "I regret that I must cut off the voices of my distinguished colleagues," he pronounced solemnly in the best tradition of Senate decorum, "but with some measure of assurance that in the long veil of history, over the transient concerns of this fleeting day, they will find me not too far wrong." A few days later at a White House reception Eric Goldman, Johnson's noted intellectual-in-residence, congratulated Dirksen on his ingenuous role. "Nothing, nothing at all to my credit," Dirksen thundered, "I simply glimpsed duty and followed its inexorable path."

Despite all of the combined efforts of conservatism, President Johnson was not about to be denied his moment in the pages of history. Rejoicing to the popular tune of "Hello Dolly," the exuberant LBJ won easy renomination at the Democratic National Convention held in Atlanta, Georgia, in late August, 1964. While Goldwater and other conservatives stumbled and droned through the almost meaningless campaign, Johnson maintained a healthy Presidential aloofness, concentrating on the affairs of state. After the election dust of the Goldwater "debacle" settled, Republican strength in the Senate had been reduced to a mere 32, compared to 68 Democrats; in the House only 140 Republicans remained, compared to 295 Democrats.

The fabulous 89th Congress, laden with 90 freshmen Democratic Congressmen who had reached office because of Johnson's political coattails, posed itself to approve a record 323 of the 469--(69%)--proposals submitted by LBJ in 1965, earning him the nickname of "the Box Score President." Johnson's remarkable legislative successes prompted New York *Times* columnist James Reston to chide: "He's getting everything through Congress but the abolition of the Republican Party, and he hasn't tried that yet."

CHAPTER IV

THE GREAT SOCIETY

Bolstered by the power of electoral mandate, President Johnson moved quickly to expand further his Great Society program. He first turned his attention toward education, which, since the Sputnik scare of 1957, had enjoyed increasing support from the federal government. LBJ, who had once taught public speaking in a Texas high school, wanted to be known as a friend of education. Just call me "the teacher in the White House," he would fondly tell his visitors whenever he explained his goals of providing a maximum education for all Americans. "Every child must be encouraged to get as much education as he has the ability to take," asserted the President. Education was a popular cause, as American as apple pie. "The popular passion of Americans isn't politics, baseball, money or material things. It is education," concluded CBS commentator Eric Sevareid, as he lent strong media support for LBJ's educational goals.

Embracing traditional values, President Johnson associated education with the idea of progress. "As a son of a poor farmer, I know that education is the only valid passport from poverty," argued Johnson. "Health is important. So is beautification, civil rights, agriculture, defense posture, but all of these are nothing if we do not have education."

During his Presidency LBJ signed sixty laws pertaining to federal aid for education. These laws included funds for classroom and library construction, guaranteed loans for the purchase of instructional equipment, opportunity grants for needy students, and expanded funds for college and graduate training. Johnson's famous Education Act of 1965 passed Congress with little more than a whimper of opposition. America's great faith in education reflected what Alexis de Tocqueville had observed about the nation much earlier in its history. "They (Americans) have all a lively faith in the perfectibility of man," wrote the French philosopher. "They judge that the diffusion of knowledge must necessarily be advantageous, and the consequence of ignorance fatal."

Medicare joined education as a high priority concern of Great Society. Pointing to the "deafening applause" every time

Medicare was mentioned during the campaign, Johnson said , "Make no mistake about it, the people are ahead of us in this. They want this program. They will support this program. They are going to have this program." He told Senators that he wanted the bill passed before returning home in the fall so "that we can have, as we say in my country, the coonskins on the wall instead of just a lot of conversations about them."

In 1900 only 3.1 million or one of every twenty-five Americans was over 65 years old, by the Sixties the elderly numbered 21.8 million or one out of ten. Many of them suffered the ravages of cancer, heart disease, and stroke. One-fourth of the nation's elderly existed below the poverty level.

Johnson ceremoniously appointed a blue-ribbon panel of medical experts led by Houston's famous heart surgeon, Michael E. DeBakey, to study the health problems of aging and make recommendations. Such expert involvement would serve to strengthen the President's rationale. The DeBakey group reported that the country "suffered from too many premature deaths." "Every hour families are being plunged into tragedy that need not happen," concluded the report. "Medical miracles are in many instances available only to the fortunate few who can get to the unique medical institution or specialist who can perform that miracle."

Armed with the DeBakey report, Johnson told Congress, "Unless we do better, two-thirds of all Americans now living will suffer or die from cancer, heart disease, or stroke; I expect you to do something about it." Only the powerful American Medical Association offered significant opposition, arguing that Medicare would increase health costs by as much as 20 per cent, impair the fine quality of private medicine in the United States, and pave the way to a system of socialized medicine. "The elderly are not primarily interested in more money, more benefits, more handouts," asserted the AMA before a Congressional Committee. "Today's older Americans want involvement....They worry less about health and finances than they do about rejection." Moreover, argued the AMA, "there are no diseases of the aged; there are simply diseases among the aged." Such arguments did not impress Congress, and it promptly passed the Medicare Act in 1965.

The Medicare Act provided persons over 65 years of age with federal assistance for hospitalization, nursing home care, and such home health needs as "meals on wheels." It would be basically financed through a substantial increase in the social security tax. Health, Education, and Welfare (HEW) Secretary John W. Gardner, responsible for administering the program, glibly explained the functioning of Medicare by comparing it to a three-layer cake. First, came the basic hospital insurance benefits for the aged. This included 90 days of hospital care, up to 100 days of nursing home care, and 100 home health care visits and outpatient services. Secondly, the Supplementary Plan provided 80 per cent of additional medical services, including doctor bills, post-hospital extended care, and therapeutic services. Thirdly, Medicare extended the earlier Kerr-Mills Medical Assistance program of 1958 to include indigent and needy persons. About 20 million Americans became eligible for such assistance. In order to bolster the Medicare program, Congress authorized the creation of complicated associations of private insurance companies to sell--on a non-profit basis--federally approved insurance policies covering health costs not authorized under the new program. Soon millions of elderly flocked into the Medicare program with praises of Johnson's Great Society on their lips.

The next priority item on Lyndon B. Johnson's ambitious Great Society agenda was urban renewal. By the Sixties 74 per cent of the American people lived on only one per cent of the land. By the end of the century America's urban population would double, and the total amount and area needed would double as over one million acres annually fell to suburban sprawl. In the inner cities over five million dilapidated homes would require refurbishing each year. In order to avoid social chaos, "we will have to build in our cities as much as all that we have built since the first colonist arrived on these shores," explained Johnson. "It is as if we had 40 years to rebuild the entire United States." "It is harder and harder to live the good life in American cities today," warned the President in his Great Society Address. "Our society will never be great until our cities are great." According to Johnson the problems of the cities essentially represented "the problems of American society itself."

Congress had grown accustomed to considering federal housing proposals, having considered such stratagems since World War I when Woodrow Wilson asked for a United States Housing Corporation as a part of the mobilization effort. Herbert Hoover's Emergency and Relief Construction proposal of 1932 first authorized federal loans to states for municipal housing. After Franklin D. Roosevelt declared in his 1938 Inaugural Address, "I see one-third of the nation ill-housed, ill-clad, and ill-nourished," Congress authorized the first national low-rent housing and slum clearance program. In 1950, under Truman, Congress appropriated $101.4 million for the task. In an effort to stimulate the badly sagging post-Korean War economy during the Fifties, Dwight D. Eisenhower got Congress to expand the appropriation to $350 million annually.

President Kennedy raised the amount to almost a billion dollars a year and instituted much stricter regulations in the urban renewal project areas. Congress required local urban renewal agencies, upon the advice and consent of a committee of local citizens groups, to designate certain downtown sections as "project boundary areas." These were placed under federal control with the full powers of "eminent domain." The government purchased the land and resold it, usually at a substantial loss, to private developers who agreed to contract and build appropriate new structures in accordance with certain national specifications.

On March 2, 1965, an unsuspecting Congress assembled in methodical fashion to hear yet another Presidential urban renewal proposal. This time, however, its members were in for some surprises. Johnson presented a gigantic six-billion-dollar proposal and asked for some innovative new housing programs. He called for a cabinet-level Department of Housing and Urban Development (HUD) to serve as "a focal point for thought and innovation and imagination about the problems of our cities." He requested a commission of experts to unravel the complex conglomeration of state and local building codes and zoning restrictions in order to bring national uniformity to the housing industry. He also requested matching federal funds for cities to purchase and preserve land for future development, federal grants to assist cities to improve water and sewage systems, and special funds for cities to pursue beautification programs. That would "bring the beauty of nature to the city dweller" promised the President.

In addition, LBJ asked for a continuation of the public-housing program at a rate of 35,000 additional units yearly. He asked for funds to help low-income families rehabilitate existing housing. The real bombshell, however, was Johnson's request for a rent subsidy program which would provide 500,000 urban families with incomes under $8,000 a year with direct supplements for rent and mortgage payments. Such families, ghetto people who previously got along by the grace of God and the help of a neighbor, would receive assistance amounting to the difference between their actual housing cost and 20 per cent of their income. "The Rent Subsidy will prove to be the most effective instrument of our new housing policy," predicted Johnson as he laid the urban renewal challenge before the Congress and the nation.

Serious opposition confronted LBJ's proposals as weary Congressmen began debating the advantages and disadvantages of federally funded urban redevelopment. The opposition had been brewing for years, mostly among southern and middlewestern conservative but among some liberals, too. Opponents argued with some merit that such programs caused an overcentralization of planning in Washington which would ultimately lead to the "nationalization of American cities." Nationally defined priorities were not necessarily those best suited for local communities. Nebraska Congressman David Martin complained that "to qualify, a city must be prepared to surrender much of its independence." The U.S. Chamber of Commerce compared the federally-designated "local coordinator" to a "sort of commissar or czar who would possess vaguely defined powers."

Urban renewal policy contravened the traditional concerns about individual rights, private ownership of property, and the autonomy and independence of small business. Renewal projects abruptly uprooted poor families from familiar neighborhoods where they enjoyed warm personal ties and forced them to search for more expensive alternative housing elsewhere. It all "reminds me too much of the poor farm," remarked one elderly woman who intensely distrusted the high-minded bureaucrats from Washington who came in to administer the programs. In the old neighborhoods the poor could "work out for themselves a delicate balance in satisfying their emotional and material needs," argued The New Yorker; but under urban renewal they suffer from unfamiliarity and "regulated monotony." The upsetting experience of being rooted out of traditional and comfortable surroundings often caused increased crime, family breakdown, and a serious loss of identity. "Their right to their homes is just as precious to them as my right to my home," shouted one disconcerted congressman.

Private developers, dubbed as the "chosen instruments," came under severe criticism. Opponents believed that developers often waxed rich at the public expense by charging outlandish prices for cheaply erected buildings on the urban renewal sites. The program "has spawned corruption, produced gushers of profits for promoters and giant corporations, and pushed slum dwellers into worse pigsties," complained the Saturday Evening Post. "Urban renewal sounded splendid when first proposed, and all sorts of respectable people got behind what seemed a very good thing," complained LBJ's fellow Texan, Congressman John Dowdy; but "the lofty purpose of helping low-income families obtain decent housing has been deflected. Land grabbing and money grubbing have become the most important end." According to an editorial in Commentary the "basic error in the original design of urban renewal remains. It is still a method for eliminating slums in order to 'renew' the city, rather than a program for properly rehousing slum-dwellers."

Finally, opponents questioned the esthetic value of urban renewal, which too often was developed around an "exclusivist" theory in which structures were built as units largely independent of their surroundings and rendered unresponsive to the "life-giving needs and wants of users." Though LBJ harbored an exaggerated admiration for "modern architecture" and the "built in green spaces," opponents characterized the new high-rise buildings of glass skin construction as lifeless and expressionless "ice trays," "cigar boxes," and "cereal boxes" which mercilessly blotted out the sun and the stars as they protruded imposingly into the heavens. Green spaces, artificial by day and unsafe by night, would not convince the opponents, who saw these modern "towers of Babel" as threatening to the essential qualities of the American character. Urban renewal projects robbed cities of their character and diversity, replacing them with a "great blight of dullness," complained urbanologist Jane Jacobs.

In the liberal atmosphere of the Sixties, however, Johnson found it easy to dispense with conservative arguments against his housing policies. He argued that only the federal government possessed the necessary resources to save the cities from "blight and decay" and bring about responsible national planning. Besides, urban renewal increased the value of property, which resulted in an ever-expanding tax base for cities. To bolster his claims, Johnson sent Housing Director Robert C. Weaver to Congress to argue that "the program is generating private investment many times the amount of public funds expended. It has increased tax revenues and provided large desirable areas for good housing and neighborhoods." According to Weaver, "urban renewal had revitalized business and downtown areas, increased employment, provided land for public buildings and recreational use, and for cultural, medical and educational purposes." Commenting on the charge of neighborhood deterioration, Weaver pointed out that urban development "has given those who live in the central cities a new hope and a new dedication for their improvement," and he added confidently that the program would actually "preserve and protect from decay many historical older buildings and neighborhoods." A black himself who had grown up in an inner city, Weaver proved a difficult target for conservatives.

From around the country urban renewal sympathizers strongly spoke out in favor of Weaver's rationale. "Urban renewal generates new investments outside the project area," claimed William L. Slayton, United States Urban Renewal Administrator, and "this results in higher assessed valuations and tax levies." Slayton added that "urban renewal resulted also in an increase in the proportion of tax exempt land--parks, playgrounds, etc." Raymond R. Tucker, president of the United States Conference of Mayors, told the annual banquet of the National Housing Conference in Washington, D.C,. that "over the long term the program will do more good for more people and will have a greater effect on improving urban life than any other program I can think of." On this positive wave of public opinion Congress gave Lyndon B. Johnson his urban renewal program on July 7, 1965. Later Congress passed legislation guaranteeing up to $50 million plus interest payment on each approved developer's bonds in order to make them more acceptable to purchasers. Congress anticipated that the new city areas would become "giant mass-transit systems." America would become the best housed nation in history. Nothing less could be expected of a Great Society.

After focusing on education, Medicare, and urban renewal, Johnson turned his keen attention to the problems of poverty in the United States. Official records estimated that 13.3 per cent of the nation's population received income considered below the poverty level. One-third of all blacks and one-seventh of all children under age eighteen languished in poverty. "As your President, I hold a special responsibility to the distressed and disinherited, the hungry and the hopeless of this abundant nation," intoned Johnson. "This Administration here and now declares war on poverty in American." The effort would encompass "the field, every private home, every public office, from the courthouse to the White House."

In his 1965 State of the Union Address LBJ passionately asserted that "unfortunately many Americans live on the outskirts of hope--some because of their poverty, some because of their color, and all too many because of both." The President charged that "our task is to help replace their despair with opportunity." This represented the first Great Society legislation originating under Johnson rather than Kennedy, and the whole administration was expected to fall strongly into line. The President's genuine concern, as well as his attitude regarding poverty, was expressed lucidly by Attorney General Ramsey Clark: "The basic solution for most crime is economic--homes, health, education, employment, beauty. If the law is to be enforced--and rights fulfilled for the poor--we must end poverty."

Johnson's commitment to end poverty was demonstrated in his demeanor during the ceremony surrounding the signing of the Economic Opportunity Act. The President selected the placid setting of the White House Rose Garden for the ceremony. As he finished signing the bill, the President gazed emotionally across the east lawn toward the Lincoln memorial, his graying strands of hair blowing lazily in the late summer breeze. "On this occasion the American people and our American system are making history," the President spoke softly and swallowed hard. "For so long as man has lived on this earth, poverty has been his curse." Then, the President turned and squinted into the afternoon sunlight as though addressing the gods of posterity. "Today for the first time in all the history of the human race, a great nation is able to make and is willing to make a commitment to eradicate poverty among its people."

Congress proved exceptionally receptive to Johnson's initiatives on poverty. "The war on poverty is the finest human renewal program America has," affirmed the flamboyant and powerful New York Congressman Adam Clayton Powell, chairman of the House Education and Labor Committee and one of LBJ's most effective lieutenants in the poverty crusade. Congressman Philip M. Landrum of Virginia, floor leader for the poverty bill, agreed: "Doing something about poverty is economical in the long run," he claimed. We are going to "create taxpayers instead of tax eaters and end the ever-increasing cycle of a child of poverty becoming a parent of poverty." As space programs provided expanded economic opportunity for scientists, poverty programs would make the poor and previously unemployable productive members of society. It all sounded somewhat like the New Deal make-work projects of the Thirties.

In order to solidify the party behind his effort, Johnson appointed Kennedyite R. Sargent Shriver as Director of the Office of Economic Opportunity (OEO), the agency established to administer the ambitious new program. Shriver optimistically designated 1976, America's Bicentennial year, as "the target date for ending poverty in this land." Since the causes of poverty were so diverse, so were the diagnoses and cures. Nevertheless, Shriver promised that the ultimate goal of the program was to create employment. "Our aim is not only to relieve the symptoms of poverty but to cure it--and, above all, to prevent it," explained Shriver. "No single piece of legislation, however, will suffice."

The early successes of the anti-poverty initiative gave the impression that Johnson's Great Society was taking root. Examples of this success were the community action programs which encouraged the "maximum feasible participation of residents of the areas and members of the groups to be served." By 1966 the OEO had granted $653,500,000 to more than 5,000 local communities and agencies involved in such programs. In Mississippi STAR Inc. trained 3,400 functional illiterates by patiently providing the basic literacy, arithmetic, and social skills necessary to qualify them to enroll in manpower development and training programs. In California the Bay Area Neighborhood Development Foundation (BAND) helped the community establish a consumer action program which brought job training and other assistance to over 5,000 poor families. BAND founded four community credit unions to defend the interests of the poor from extortion on the part of corrupt creditors and private fixers, educated the poor on matters of money management and product selection, helped them develop healthy nutritional habits, and encouraged them to establish cooperative shopping strategies.

Operation CHAMP, with the enthusiastic backing of the President's Council on Physical Fitness, organized physical fitness and recreational programs for deprived youth in over a dozen cities. The Foster Grandparents program was established with the help of OEO to recruit and train low-income persons over sixty years of age to work with neglected and deprived children. Project Green Thumb trained the elderly for future employment in community betterment and beautification programs. All of these programs and many more gave local communities an opportunity to improve local conditions of life for more citizens.

Another important anti-poverty program was the Job Corps, a program reminiscent of the New Deal Civilian Conservation Corps, which provided useful skills for the unemployable. Under the program deprived youth between 16 and 22 years of age qualified for special job training. The Corps would not only make them into productive citizens but would also give them self-respect. Nearly 45 per cent of the youth enrolled came from broken homes, 40 per cent came from families on welfare, 75 per cent had never seen a medical doctor, 50 per cent were undernourished and underfed, and 10 per cent had never held full-time employment. Many of them could not read a newspaper. Many came from inner city and rural poverty areas. In order to improve the living standards of parents, each youth corpsman was asked to send home $25 of the $30 earned each month.

The Job Corps scored some early successes. By the end of 1966 it had created more than 70,000 new jobs. Although some communities proved unreceptive to the program and more than a few corpsmen could not overcome their apathy, many took advantage of this opportunity to establish an identity and a place in society. Government skills centers in Los Angeles provided training for 840 slum residents and found employment for 85 per cent of them in the two years after the 1965 Watts riots. In Boston the Action for Boston Community Development program trained 2,800 persons and placed most of them in productive employment. Some cases took on personal dimensions. A 17-year-old Kentuckian, for example, who could not read the first two lines of the beginning reader--"I am not an ant. I am a man"--arrived at his camp wearing a cocky Texas hat and boots, sporting a cigarette, and announcing that he would not cooperate. After several weeks of careful and patient attention, the same boy approached the instructor with prideful eyes and asked, "How soon will I be able to write my own letter home?" Examples such as this made the Job Corps seem worthwhile to millions of Americans.

Another unique anti-poverty offensive was the Legal Services Administration. No other agency held so much promise of serving the poor. It established a total of 500 offices throughout the country to provide legal services for poor and indigent persons who otherwise would have been unable to pay for the expense of defending themselves. According to the Johnson Administration, the poor were too often pathetic victims of unjust eviction, unfair garnishment of salaries, and even discriminatory treatment from government agencies.

A prime example of how the Legal Services Administration operated occurred in Washington, D.C., in 1966. An old washerwoman was evicted from her apartment after her landlord heard that she complained to the public housing authorities about her lurid living conditions. She sued for repossession, but the landlord was awarded a judgment by default. At this point a Washington Neighborhood Legal Services lawyer was contacted and intervened on the woman's behalf. He got the court to set the default judgment aside on the grounds that the eviction was retaliatory and wrongfully inhibited the tenant's constitutional right to inform the government of a violation of the law. When the landlord appealed the case, the lawyer obtained a ruling that the tenant need not post the usual expensive bond so long as she paid her regular rent on time. This was a significant maneuver on the part of the lawyer because the poor washerwoman would ordinarily have found the requirement to post bond so burdensome that it would have actually foreclosed her right to the appeal process. Thus, Legal Services brought justice to the washerwoman and many thousands of other indigent persons who otherwise would have had to bear the brunt of inequality.

The anti-poverty effort also comprised many other programs. Upward Bound provided job-training and counseling to secondary school students from impoverished areas who were adjudged to be potential dropouts. The Neighborhood Youth Corps provided community service employment after school and during summers for the sons and daughters of low-income families. VISTA, the domestic equal of Peace Corps, attracted volunteers from 18 to 80 years of age to work in city slums, migrant labor camps, and on Indian reservations for $50 per month and shelter.

Project Head Start provided preschool children in destitute areas with communicative skills and social training which would help them better adapt to the regular educational system. Head Start placed over two million students in the classroom by 1967. It "comes as close to having universal approval as any of the dozens of federal programs," wrote *Time.* It has "had a very major, very deep effect," commented Werner Hirsch, Director of the Institute of Government and Public Affairs at UCLA. Adult basic education courses provided several former dropouts with an opportunity to complete their high school education. It also provided technical training for adults whose previous skills had become obsolete. Adult education courses were taught in such offbeat places as farm houses, church basements, and abandoned stores. The rather quaint new learning atmospheres gave participants the grass-roots feeling that the Great Society was reaching the real needs of the American people.

OEO attempted to bring the opportunities of capitalism to the poor by making special loans to low-income persons for financing small businesses. One such loan opened the door of opportunity for David Flowers of Chicago's South Side. Flowers had been forced into early retirement from a back injury. His future looked hopeless until an OEO small business loan enabled him to purchase a franchise to open a 24-hour service station which he turned into a great success. In Missouri the OEO agreed to make a small business loan to a group of farmers in a six-county area to launch "Operation Porkchop," a project aimed at improving feeder pig production and marketing. OEO loans provided the beginning capital for the purchase of high-grade brood sows, modern farrowing pens, farm machinery, and the building improvements necessary to get the operation underway.

In addition, anti-poverty programs were supposed to assist American Indians and migrant workers, two minority groups which had largely been forgotten in the frantic scramble to take advantage of the benefits offered by the Great Society. Community services programs also disseminated information about birth control methods and health care to over twenty million American women of childbearing age. Federal work study programs were established to help needy students stay in college. By the end of the decade over $20 million helped nearly 400,000 students, including approximately 30 per cent of the blacks in school.

The Appalachian program, known as Johnson's "Little TVA," probably represented the greatest anti-poverty offensive of them all. The President's Appalachian plan called for Congress to appropriate over one billion dollars for highway and hospital construction, pollution control, soil improvement, vocational training, sewage treatment, and research for resource development. The Appalachian region, consisting of the Appalachian Mountain Range together with the Cumberland Plateau and the Allegheny Plateau to the west and the Blue Ridge Mountains to the east, had degenerated by the Sixties into America's most debilitated region. The once proud stretch of mighty highland, where some of America's strongest agrarian traditions had taken root and flourished, lay ravaged as a result of unwise agricultural practices and industrial shortsightedness. Its soil depleted and its coal and lumber resources used up, the cities of the region had been transformed from flourishing processing and trading centers into complacent way stations. Its population of 16 million had increased by merely one per cent during the Fifties compared to the national average of eighteen per cent. One out of every three Appalachian families lived on an annual income of less than $3,000. Only 32 per cent of its adults possessed a high school diploma; only five per cent had earned a college degree. Over one million were hopelessly unemployed.

Basing his rationale on these distressing statistics, LBJ enjoined Congress to take responsibility for rejuvenating the entire region. The President explained in true New Deal pump-priming fashion that his Appalachian bill would help the country as well as the region itself. "I can tell you that if Appalachia purchased retail goods at a rate proportionate to their population," predicted Johnson enthusiastically, "an additional $4 billion in goods" could be distributed in the area each year. Some Republicans criticized the excessively high $840 million included in the bill for highway and road construction, which left little for other facets of the program, but LBJ methodically defended the appropriation by explaining that new transportation facilities were necessary to make the region more accessible for tourism and industry. The skillful lobbyists who represented the entrenched highway construction industry heartily agreed with the President. LBJ argued so persuasively, and the tide of Johnsonianism ran so strong, that Congress passed the Appalachian bill without even changing a comma; and the Great Society kept marching on.

Between 1964 and 1969 the Great Society helped remove almost six million Americans from the Government's poverty rolls. But the cost of government began to grow, too. In 1961 there were 45 federal social programs with expenditures totaling $9.9 billion, compared to 435 programs costing $25.6 billion by 1969. Nevertheless, Johnson's anti-poverty initiative appeared so successful in the beginning that old-time liberal labor thinker Eric Hoffer predicted unequivocally that LBJ would "be the foremost President of the 20th Century."

Johnson agreed. Not only did his Great Society alleviate social ills, but it also helped unprecedented economic expansion. During Johnson's Presidency 8.5 million additional jobs were created, $460 billion was added to family net assets, and $535 billion was added to family income after taxes and inflation. Meanwhile, federal revenues increased by $70 billion. Business characteristically became the greatest benefactor of the Great Society programs. Many felt that not since the frugal Calvin Coolidge, who had patiently warned that "prosperity is only an instrument to be used, not a deity to be worshipped," had business found such a sympathetic ally in the White House.

Johnson's sympathy toward business expansion was reflected in his appointment of Harvard law professor Donald Turner to head the Antitrust Division of the Justice Department. Under Turner's benevolent tutelage the modern business conglomerate came into its own. During Turner's first year in office, 1965, there were 1,895 corporate mergers involving approximately $4 billion worth of assets; by 1968, his last year, 3,932 mergers involved $13 billion in assets. Modern day tycoons such as Felix Rohatyn of International Telephone and Telegraph put together complicated financial empires reminiscent of Charles Insull's gigantic utility holding companies of the Twenties, only much larger. Investment firms such as Lazard Freres earned millions of dollars in merger fees. By the end of the decade colossal conglomerates such as Long-Temco-Vought controlled billions in assets involving several smaller diversified industries. The Dallas-based LTV, under the leadership of James J. Long, grew from a $4 million contracting company in 1957 to the nation's 14th largest corporation in 1968 with sales of nearly $3 billion.

The merger movement coincided with the rise of the multinational corporation, a giant business organization with manufacturing or servicing facilities in several nations. Pepsi-Cola, for example, had expanded its markets to one hundred countries by the end of the Sixties. American goods produced abroad rose to $90 billion and investments abroad grew to $78 billion in 1970, while the total profits earned on business operations abroad rose to 40 per cent of the total profits at home. Whether mergers and multinational operations of this magnitude were in the national interest remained a debatable subject, but the billions in profits produced further enhanced prosperity and brought plaudits for the President from the upper echelons of the business community.

The Great Society prosperity, fueled by the ominous military buildup in Southeast Asia, proved to be the greatest since the Twenties. During 1965 alone the Dow Jones industrial averages, still the nation's most significant economic indicator, soared past the 900 mark. After a brief slump in 1966, caused by the Federal Reserve's tight money policy, the market climbed almost to the 1,000 mark in 1968. Around the country small investors, mostly professional people, scrambled into investment clubs where their money could be pooled for greater impact and profits.

All stocks seemed on the rise. George March, a civil engineer from Chicago, remembered how his investment club selected stocks by gingerly tossing darts at a list of possibilities pinned to the wall. "Performance became the watchword of the hour," according to <u>Time.</u> Small investors "sought aggressively to buy stocks that would rise faster than the market averages." Investors came to believe "that Keynesian economics had given governments the tools to control inflation and recession and keep business rising constantly," recalled Arnold Bernhard, president of Value Line Funds. "In the '60's stocks were bought on the assumption that growth would go on forever." LBJ's neo-Keynesian economic advisors, themselves filled with optimism, began to predict an era of permanent prosperity, claiming confidently that modern national planning and regulation of money supplies had eliminated the possibility of another great stock market crash like that of 1929.

Rising business activity seemed to bear them out. During the first quarter of 1965 alone the gross national product (GNP) increased by $14 billion, the largest single advance in American history. Consumer spending advanced by $11.7 billion. Profits climbed to all-time highs. Profits in the drugs and medicine industries rose by 18.8 per cent. Clary Corporation, maker of office machinery, reported an astonishing 28.7 per cent increase in profits, and the highly diversified Minnesota Mining and Manufacturing Corporation reported profit increases of 19.5 per cent. In 1966 corporation profits reached an all-time peak of $50.7 billion and remained at this high level through 1968. General Motors, America's largest corporation, enjoyed sales of over $20 billion annually by mid-decade; its wealth was greater than that of most nations in the world. Even the beleaguered railroad industry reported rising profits and operating revenues in 1965 and 1966. Meanwhile, unemployment dropped to 4.5 per cent, an eight-year low.

The economic future for business looked so bright that an exuberant Gardner Ackley, Chairman of the President's Council of Economic Advisors, could not locate "any dark spots" in the economy. "It's a good prosperity with good balance," exclaimed Ackley. "There has been no sign of excess in inventory stockpiling or in corporate investment." With an air of serene confidence Ackley boasted, "The economy does not seem to have any bottlenecks. Confidence is high in the consumer and the businessman."

This confidence was reflected in the attitudes of the business community. Business had not been so optimistic since the roaring prosperity of the Twenties. Henry Ford II, who described Johnson as a "terrific President," confidently predicted that the auto industry would have its biggest sales in history. "I've never seen people so optimistic," stated Robert H. Stewart, III, president of Dallas' First National Bank. "There's little doubt that our present economy is strong," declared John Brooks, colorful Board Chairman of Santa Monica's Lear Siegbe. "It's sure a different kind of country and economy than when I was a kid back in the '20's and '30's," mused Los Angeles sportswear tycoon Richard Woodwar. "With all these things going for us today, if we drop the ball we have nobody to blame but ourselves." According to Chicago banker Tilford C. Gaines, "the only words I can use are 'excellent', 'buoyant', and 'ebullient.'" If 18th century British author Dr. Samuel Johnson's comment that "a man is never so innocently occupied as when he is making money," ever held true for American business, it was during the high Sixties.

Organized labor benefited from the Great Society almost as much as business. Prosperity brought in its wake more employment, higher wages, and better working conditions. Real wages increased by 15 per cent during the Sixties, compared to no increase at all in the Seventies. In his 1965 State of the Union Address Johnson promised to support all of labor's priority demands. He promised to support legislation which would strike down state "right to work" laws. "This is the No. 1 goal of union leaders," contended Johnson. The President also promised to extend minimum wage coverage to more than two million additional workers. He promised to give unions more power to organize workers, more leeway to strike, and more freedom to picket. He promised to establish, by federal law, minimum payments to jobless workers under the unemployment insurance system. Organized labor leaders reveled at the President's sympathetic attitude.

Johnson's growing concern over inflation often interrupted his cordial relations with organized labor. In this concern LBJ proved especially attentive to liberal economist Arthur Okun, member and then Chairman of the President's Council of Economic Advisors. Okun's concern for productivity led him to the development of Okun's Law: for every three per cent increase in economic growth, unemployment would decrease by one per cent. Such theory matched well with the Great Society's goals of permanent peace and prosperity. However, Okun feared that if too much inflation were allowed, thus requiring recessionary policies, the poor and unorganized elements themselves would suffer most severely and negate the original aims of the Great Society. "Society can transport money from rich to poor only in a leaky bucket," warned Okun as he counseled the President to place economic efficiency as a priority over social equality. Therefore, government must place downward pressure on the price-wage spiral to prevent it from escalating out of hand. Traditionally, such pressures had favored business, and organized labor could be expected to demur.

LBJ decided to use the prestige of his office and his personal influence to keep wage and price increases below 3.2 per cent a year. The policy became known as "jawboning." "I shall not hesitate to draw public attention to major inflationary action," asserted the President in his annual economic message to the nation. Beginning with the preeminent George L. Meany, President of the AFL-CIO, labor leaders reacted adversely to Johnson's proposed guidelines of 3.2 per cent. "If we go down this road far enough, it leads to the end of free collective bargaining," complained Meany, the gruff old ex-plumber from the Bronx. "As far as I am concerned, I don't propose that labor at any time agree to go down this road." And he bluntly warned the President that organized labor did not need the Democratic Party as much as the Democrats needed labor.

The crucial test of LBJ's guidelines came in the summer of 1964 in the auto industry. The United Auto workers, under the masterful Walter Reuther, had long led the way in wage settlements. In 1964 he cleverly employed the threat of a strike in an election year and the old strategy of "divide and rule" among the major auto makers. In his marathon bargaining sessions with Chrysler, the weakest of the big three auto makers, Reuther demanded that the company pay all (rather than the customary half) of the employees' life and accident insurance, grant higher pensions, set aside extra annual vacation days, provide additional paid holidays (Good Friday and birthday), and extend by a dozen minutes the "john time" each day.

Reuther paid little heed to the President's protestations that an extreme settlement would induce an inflationary spiral. On September 9, 1964, after 23 hours of "nose to nose" haggling, Reuther wrangled a generous settlement from Chrysler. The adept bargainer immediately called the anxious LBJ at the White House, who said he was "delighted" about a settlement but wanted to know if the guidelines were intact." "Well," replied the sly Reuther, a little apologetically, "they're bent a little."

Indeed, the President's guideline had been bent badly, if not broken. By the time Reuther settled with all of the auto firms, he boasted an impressive 4.8 per cent increase in wage and benefits. "Reuther hit a home run," lamented John Linter of the Harvard Business School, "and we're going to see others swinging for triples and doubles when they might have gone only for singles." Linter's analysis proved essentially correct. In the next few years the United Steel Workers negotiated a four per cent increase package, followed by similar settlements for the Teamsters, Longshoremen, and the United Mine Workers, a union which had fallen under the dubious leadership of W. A. (Tony) Boyle, who had inherited the right to rule from the iron-fisted John L. Lewis in 1960. Teamsters Local 282 in New York City won a pension plan allowing its members to retire after twenty years at $300 a month, an agreement which made many shudder. Reuther himself, who by now had earned an almost statesmanlike reputation for his vigorous advocacy of national health insurance, tax reform, and civil rights, went so far as to advocate profit sharing, company paid auto insurance, and a guaranteed annual income. Clearly organized labor meant to possess as many of the Great Society's fruits as possible for itself.

The agricultural industry, although farmers were loath to admit it, also benefited immensely from Johnson's Great Society economic policies. During the Sixties mechanized agriculture became the most conspicuous example of modern American industrial efficency. "Across Iowa's corn country, huge machines with anteater snouts gulp the ears off eight-foot-high cornstalks, and an instant later spit golden kernels into selfcontained bins," boasted Time. "In California packing machines out in the fields seal freshly picked lettuce heads in plastic, drop them into cardboard boxes, then disgorge the boxes ready for market. On the farms of the Southwest, machines work the fields with surgical precision, injecting miniscule broccoli seeds one-by-one into the soil at measured intervals."

Since 1920 the actual farm population decreased from almost fifty per cent to seven per cent, while productivity increased by six percent a year compared to only three per cent for the rest of the economy. The average farmer produced enough to support thirty-nine other people, and one hour of farm labor produced seven and one-half times more than fifty years earlier. Consumers enjoyed the agricultural surge, for they only had to spend 16.6 per cent of their budget for food compared to twenty-three per cent 1951. Along with technical success American livestock breeding practices continued to improve resulting in faster-growing, more efficient animals. The better quality animals could be witnessed at the Chicago Annual International Live-Stock Exposition, "the Supreme Court of the livestock show world," where breeders and buyers from around the world came to purchase the best of 10,000 head of beef cattle, sheep and swine.

In spite of the great record of productive success agriculture generally languished in a state of hapless economic and social decline as the decade dawned. Agriculture suffered huge reversals as a result of the Eisenhower recession. The vicious cost-price squeeze that had always plagued farmers seemed to be growing worse. Between 1957 and 1962 the farmer's operating costs and living expenses rose by thirty-five per cent while his prices actually declined. Middlemen, such as processors, shippers, retailers, and wholesalers, continued to claim an ever-increasing share of the food dollar, as did organized labor in the processing and transportation industries. Out of the $100 billion Americans spent for food each year, the farmer received only about $25 billion or one out of every four dollars generated by agriculture. When Kennedy entered office, per capita farm income stood at only $903 compared to $2,181 non-farm income, or only 41.4 per cent. As many as one-half of America's farm families qualified for poverty relief.

The declining economic fortunes spawned a new, radical agricultural movement reminiscent of Milo Reno's cornbelt farm rebellion of the Thirties. A new, militant farm organization, the National Farmer's Organization--organized under the leadership of Oren E. Staley--rose to national prominence. The NFO advocated direct and vigorous "collective bargaining" between farm producers and the giant processors who purchased their products. Pointing to the continuing lag in parity and to the gross inconsistencies between supply and market prices, NFO leaders promised farmers that bargaining through collective action would significantly increase prices for the farmer without raising consumer prices. In other words the NFO would restore what it deemed to be the farmers' rightful share of the food dollar by taking it from the middlemen through collective bargaining, which involved holding products off the market.

According to the NFO, when the farmer gained control over his own product and hence his own destiny, collective bargaining would also bring to the smaller farmer a genuine autonomy in the complex modern marketing apparatus. The call for autonomy among smaller farmers who feared the corporate take-over struck a responsive cord as thousands joined the NFO. "In a way, this is an evangelical movement," boasted one NFO officer in the true populistic fashion, "a real belief that farmers can have a real say in the market instead of selling their products for whatever price they can get." According to the _New Republic's_ political observer Peter Barnes, NFO members represented modern-day populists, people who envisioned themselves as "little guys at the mercy of big financial institutions, transportation companies, and vertically integrated conglomerates."

The prestigious Committee for Economic Development provided a good example of NFO's wrath against big business. In 1962 the CED suggested that farm operators should be reduced because they misled investors and agri-business operators into retaining excessive resources in agriculture. The NFO understood the CED recommendation as a conspiracy against the family farm, hatched by the trusts themselves. Accordingly, NFO organized boycotts against firms whose executives belonged to the CED. Angry farmers gathered mail-order catalogs and dumped them in front of Sears Roebuck and Montgomery Ward stores and drove caravans of cars and tractors around Ford Motor and John Deere agencies. These protests obliged Sears and Ford to announce that their companies did not endorse the ill-fated CED report.

As the NFO movement spread, it largely became a farmer rebellion against the agricultural marketing establishment itself. Its foremost enemy was the American Farm Bureau Federation, which had dominated the agricultural scene since after World War I when it had been organized with generous support from big business and government. The Farm Bureau, which enjoyed a membership of almost two million, had lobbied successfully through the years for many key farm programs but, by the Sixties, had also earned a reputation for being one of the nation's most reactionary organizations; and many wondered whether it even represented its own members. In 1964, for example, Farm Bureau President Robert Shuman opposed LBJ's feed grain legislation, asking for a termination of all governmental protections of farm income. Yet most Farm Bureau members themselves participated in the lucrative federal program. The Farm Bureau opposed granting minimum wages and hours laws to farm workers as well as granting farm labor collective bargaining privileges. Yet it supported the importation of cheap foreign migratory labor. It opposed any welfare legislation from Medicare to the expansion of social security. Yet, it heartily supported subsidies through the granting of oil depletion allowances.

The NFO charged that the Farm Bureau had come to be dominated by big businessmen who showed little concern for the real needs of the small independent farmer. Even the cooperative marketing system, controlled mostly by Farm Bureau types, was criticized as operating outside of the farmer's control. Nonfarmers were not allowed to hold memberships in the NFO. During the early Sixties the NFO attracted increasing attention and membership. At times some predicted it would replace the Farmers' Union and the National Grange as the second most important organization representing farmers.

By the summer of 1962 the disgruntled NFO farmers had gained more national attention than any farm group had since the 1930's. On August 28 over 20,000 farmers jammed into the Veterans' Memorial Auditorium complex at Des Moines, Iowa, to grant their approval for a major national holding action. "American farmers are the most underpaid group in America," shouted President Staley. "They have retreated as far as they can go. We do not intend to retreat any further." Another NFO leader said, "Let the processors eat their damn money, we have food." This holding action like many others failed to diminish the central marketing position of processors, simply because, as President Kennedy put it at the time, "There are too many farmers, and they are so separated that it's not been possible to have them together to present a bargaining position."

That problem and others slowed the momentum of NFO. The

organization was too secretive for most farmers. The leadership steadfastly refused to disclose its membership lists, its full financial condition, or the contracts it purported to have forced upon unwilling processors. A majority of the hard-pressed farm producers did not possess the fortitude or the reserve of resources to stake their financial future on a holding action knowing that perishable goods could become almost worthless if the action failed. Also, the economic pressure and adverse publicity propagated in part by powerful middlemen, who themselves were not about to lose their favorable bargaining position, greatly discouraged many smaller farmers from joining the NFO.

The occasional violence which accompanied the NFO's demonstrations and holding actions greatly discouraged its growth. Its detractors, of course, anxiously tried to connect fist fights, tire slashings and roadside sniping to the NFO leadership. The violence reached a climax at Bonduel, Wisconsin, on September 15, 1964, where several local farmers, "unshaven and wearing sty-stained overalls," attempted to prevent trucks from making their deliveries to the Equity Cooperative Livestock Sales Association Yards. The confrontation was part of Staley's last ditch effort to call a nationwide holding action.

As the crowd of farmers grew larger and more ominous, most truckers simply turned back or waited along the road for the excitement to subside. Toward evening most of the 500 rambling farmers would have to return home to complete their chores and then the deliveries could be safely made. One driver, however, Ivan Mueller, was exasperated by the day's events; and in a fit of frustration and impatience he drove his truck through the long line of boycotting farmers. Armed with a pistol, Mueller moved his fancy Ford steadily forward as the frantic farmers shouted, "Take it back. Go home!" Suddenly two farmers slipped beneath the truck's huge rear wheels and were immediately crushed to death. The crowd went wild. Farmers surged toward Mueller's truck cab, throwing rocks and shattering his windshield with their bare fists. It took a contingent of sheriff's deputies several minutes to hustle Mueller away into custody. The unfortunate incident greatly disparaged the image of the NFO in the wary eyes of the public.

The most important factor behind the declining influence of the NFO, however, was the increasing prosperity visited upon the farm economy as a result of the Kennedy-Johnson farm policies. In 1961 Kennedy appointed former Minnesota Governor Orville Freeman as Secretary of Agriculture. Freeman, who once described himself as the man on the end of the pitchfork, proved sensitive to farm woes and promised "to end the drift in farm policy." He was retained by Johnson, which gave him an excellent opportunity to evolve a policy that had dated back to World War I; that is, a policy which combined the ambitious search for expanding foreign markets with domestic production and price controls.

In foreign markets Secretary Freeman doubled the efforts of the Food for Peace Program, a plan which had originated under Eisenhower's Agricultural Trade Development and Assistance Act of 1954. Under Food for Peace the Federal Government simply purchased farm surpluses in the domestic market and distributed them abroad under a variety of "give-away" programs. Food for Peace not only reduced domestic surpluses and increased prices but also served as a rather sophisticated diplomatic lever. "American agricultural abundance can be forged into both a significant instrument of foreign policy and a weapon against domestic hardship," explained Kennedy. "I don't regard agriculture surplus as a problem, I regard it as an opportunity." Kennedy continued, "I think the farmers can bring more credit, more lasting goodwill, more chance for peace, than almost any group of Americans in the next ten years, if we recognize that food is strength, and food is peace, and food is freedom, and food is a helping hand to people around the world whose goodwill and friendship we want."

By 1964 Food for Peace, under the leadership of South Dakota's George McGovern, was credited with bringing farm prices slowly upward as President Johnson increased the program by one-third. The program opened rich new markets in such far away places as Japan and Israel, contended Freeman. "Our chief objective in the department is to adjust American agriculture to the new dimensions of abundance with which this country is blessed."

As far as American farm production controls were concerned, Freeman relied upon a domestic allotment plan patterned after the New Deal's AAA and the old Brannan Plan forwarded during the Truman years. The Secretary prompted Congress to pass the Emergency Feed and Grain Act of 1961, which provided price supports and subsidy payments to farmers for keeping a percentage of their crop land out of production; this amounted to almost 60 million acres in 1966. The set aside program would achieve ninety per cent parity for farmers promised Freeman, while it would cost taxpayers almost $5 billion a years. It would save huge storage bills, however. "Instead of letting unwanted grain accumulate and run up immoderate storage bills for the government," commented _Fortune_, "Supply management has held down output." The passage of LBJ's Food and Agriculture Act of 1965 by the 89th Congress provided long-term cropland retirement provisions and price supports which would be readjusted annually by the Secretary of Agriculture. It was "a workable balance between supply and demand at lower costs to the government," claimed LBJ.

The relative success of the Kennedy-Johnson production price management policies would remain a hotly debated issue. Many argued that its success declined because farmers tended to retire their worst land and continued to apply more and better fertilizers and pesticides, which simply increased production on the non-government program lands. Others complained that federal subsidy payments favored the huge farm operators over small producers. In 1969, for example, 396 farm operators, of 2,517,304 receiving assistance, got government checks in excess of $100,000. J.G. Boswell Co., Corcoran, California, received total payments in that year of $4,370,657.

Another significant aspect of Freeman's agricultural initiative involved the Food Stamp program, billed by many as the domestic equivalent of Food for Peace. The program combined the need to reduce domestic food surpluses with the goal of alleviating poverty. Under the program "needy" people could obtain coupons for the portion of their income normally expended on food. For every six dollars paid for coupons, participants could purchase up to ten dollars of food from the local retail grocery store. Sometimes local agencies distributed additional stamps to indigent persons in order to enable them to expand their purchasing power. Retail stores redeemed the food coupons through the commercial banking system just as other cash receipts and commercial paper. Ultimately, the Federal Reserve banks redeemed them through a speical account maintained by the United States Treasury. The whole process significantly increased the domestic consumption of food and further bolstered farm prices.

When Johnson entered office, only 380,000 Americans benefited from the food stamp program. In hopes of further increasing farm prices, Johnson decided to greatly expand the program and sent Secretary Freeman to Congress in order to provide the rationale. "This program represents an expression of our belief that every American citizen should have an adequate, nutritious diet," argued Freeman; "To me this is both a spiritual and moral principle." Freeman solemnly explained to the wavering members of the House Committee on Agriculture that "some 13 per cent of the American people, because of unemployment, old age, physical disability, have serious nutritional shortages." As far as he was concerned, "the farmer, backed by the scientist and the engineer, had demonstrated that we have the resources to insure adequate diets." Now it was the time for Congress to "demonstrate the will to meet the moral responsibility" of guaranteeing that every American received enough food to live a happy life. "History will write of our generation as the age when man began to explore the universe," exhorted Freeman, "but I suspect that the brightest page of that book will be the one which describes not our scientific achievements but our achievements in simple humanity--of our efforts to abolish hunger."

Congress responded dutifully to LBJ's lanky Secretary of Agriculture. "You cannot teach a hungry child, and you cannot train a hungry man," lectured New York Congressman William Ryan. Congress was so eager to assent to Johnson's wishes that it failed to heed Iowa's canny Congressman Charles B. Hoeven's warnings that food stamps might too often go for caviar, steaks, drugs, automobile parts and "what not." By the end of the decade over ten million Americans were receiving food stamps monthly. The program eventually extended to over five million children through school lunch programs. All but twenty of the nation's 3,129 counties had a food stamp program. Meanwhile farmers enjoyed their highest prices ever, from $2,875 per farm family in 1960 to $5,769 in 1968, yet a Farm Journal poll found that 63 per cent of the farmers questioned favored an abrupt end to the food stamp program. Many argued that the increasing demand generated by the escalating Vietnam War had more to do with agricultural prosperity than any of the domestic programs.

The objections of many farmers to Freeman's farm policies grew out of their deep concern for the fate of the family farm, an institution which was virtually hallowed as one of America's primary moral and ethical foundations. The Freeman policies led to more consolidation and actually hastened the 20th century flight of people from the land into the already over-crowded cities, where farmers usually believed immoral influences ran rampant. Freeman and his Great Society planners understood that Johnson's farm policies would not protect the small farmer not efficient enough to compete in the market place. "You can't take care of low-income farmers with commodity programs," admitted Budget Chief Kermit Gordon in 1965. In one of his classic understatements the stern Freeman man conjectured that "no price-support program will do any good for a guy on forty acres with a mule."

Some argued that Freeman's programs further enhanced the rise of corporate farming, smothered the rich agrarian tradition, and snuffed out hundreds of thousands of small, happy communities where once the fullness of American life had flourished in undisturbed quietude. Indeed, the "giant checkerboard of green and yellow fields" was significantly enlarged under Freeman's tenure. The average size of the American farm increased from 288 acres in 1960 to nearly 400 acres by the end of the decade, and the number of farm families decreased from 3.8 to 2.6 million. Journalist John Bird of the Saturday Evening Post estimated that farms disappeared at a rate of 356 a day or 130,000 per year in 1965. Such ominous statistics caused the remaining 11 million rural Americans deep concern no matter what become of the prices. In traditional fashion, however, the farmers could boast of one thing: when agriculture flourished, the nation flourished.

And flourish the American political economic system did. "Our prosperity is broad and deep. It's brought record profits, the highest in our history, record wages," pronounced Johnson. "Our gross national product has grown more in the last five years than in any other period in our nation's history." From 1960 to 1970 individual income increased by 69 per cent, from $1,850 to $3,119. During the apex period, 1964-66, economic growth reached 5.7 per cent a year, prices increased by only two per cent, and unemployment averaged a low of 4.5 per cent. The United States had not been expected to reach a trillion-dollar economy until 1975, but now economists were predicting that for 1970. "My classic example of underestimation is the Trillion-Dollar economy," quipped Martin Gainsburgh, chief economist for the National Industrial Conference Board. In the past ten years the growth of the American economy had far outstripped the comprehension of most individuals; "Even the economists are at a loss for an abstract theory to explain it," wrote Time, "but beyond dispute is the fact that never before has man transmuted energy and raw materials into wealth at such a fantastic rate."

Never before had opportunity for the creation of new wealth seemed more abundant. The old Horatio Alger myth enjoyed a refreshing new lift as stories of individuals who rose from rags to riches began deluging the headlines; the number of millionaires increased during the decade from 40,000 to 100,000. One such person was Colonel Harlan Sanders, who in 1960 worked as a penniless filling station attendant but made his first million at age seventy-three by promoting his famous Kentucky Fried Chicken recipe. Another example young Max Palevsky, who amassed a fortune by concentrating on a previously neglected area in the burgeoning data processing industry. In 1961 he organized Scientific Data, which boasted profits of $4.3 million by 1967. Charles Percy of Illinois won a U.S. Senate seat in 1966 from veteran New Dealer Paul Douglas largely on the basis of his uncanny ability to become a millionaire as the daring young president of Bell and Howell Corporation.

Some of the fortunate benefactors of the new prosperity became downright haughty about their newly won success. Bart Lytton, for example, known to many as "Black Bart," was a man who arrived in California with $30 in his pocket at about the same time LBJ arrived in Washington and then went on to shepherd the phenomenal rise of Lytton Industries into a $685 million conglomerate, the fifth largest in the United States. Lytton boasted, "I am the most successful businessman in this decade in the United States." "The only ism for me is narcissism," snapped Lytton in traditional egotistical, hard-nosed business manner. "If I cared about my image, I'd never do the gutsy things I do. I say, the day I turn mellow, I hope they melt me."

Many of the new rich glaringly defied the Horatio Alger principles by pursuing lavish, exotic life styles, yet the old puritanical principle of frugality was not completely lost. Billionaire John D. MacArthur, for example, founder of Bankers Life and Casualty, made it a conspicuous practice to pocket desserts not finished on airplane flights and picked up discarded bottles for deposit refunds. And in Seattle Lloyd Hilman Fjestad occupied a simple $30-a-month room living on a hamburger a day and old bread. He used his meager savings to accumulate nearly $200,000 in U. S. Savings Bonds. "I live on as little as I can, I don't have any luxuries," he said. "I eat and sleep."

Of all the Horatio Alger types none raised more speculation and suspicion than the phantom billionaire recluse Howard Hughes, who had not been seen in the public since 1953. According to freelance writer William Bates, the Hughes empire represented "a junkyard: a scrapheap of commerce onto which the rusting fruits of enterprise have been tossed." Throughout most of the Sixties Hughes directed his empire from his secluded Desert Inn penthouse in Las Vegas, where his gambling holdings were extensive and where his control was secured through substantial contributions to Nevada's ruling politicians.

Hughes' eccentric business practices always remained a mystery, even to his closest advisors. His only official headquarters was an answering service in Los Angeles. Some of his closest associates waited months for a returned telephone call. Hughes made important business arrangements from pay telephone booths and in the front seat of old Chevies. He surrounded himself with Mormon bodyguards because they neither smoked nor drank. His secretaries were required to wear surgical gloves for typing. He once paid a barber $1,200 a month to remain on call in case he wanted a haircut, which he never got.

Most of Hughes' economic power resulted from the connections his Hughes Aircraft Corporation enjoyed in Washington, D.C., with representatives of almost every division of the federal government, especially the Defense Department. Hughes practiced the art of political influencing to the hilt. Bureaucrats who played a role in awarding lucrative government contracts to Hughes Aircraft could expect high-paying executive positions from Hughes after leaving government service. Politicians, and especially presidents, received favors whether they asked for them or not. Political party made no difference.

For John F. Kennedy it was an airplane of entertainers from Los Angeles to Washington for the inaugural festivities and the purchase of several $10,000 boxes for viewing the inaugural parade. For Lyndon Baines Johnson it was putting friend Abe Fortas' law firm on retainer in the legal battle with TWA, a firm once controlled by Hughes. For Richard M. Nixon it was a $100,000 campaign contribution made through Florida banker and real estate dealer Bebe Rebozo.

Hughes' attempts to influence the political establishment were usually subtle and difficult to document. His efforts paid handsome profits, however. Hughes Aircraft received government contracts of close to $6 billion during the decade. Hughes Aircraft was owned by the Howard Hughes Medical Institute, a charitable foundation which financed some important medical research but which also served as a comfortable tax shelter for Hughes' business operations. One critic estimated that Hughes collected over $1.5 million from the American taxpayers each day. Hughes' power was immense, as he told chief assistant Robert Maheu, "I can buy any man in the world, or I can destroy him."

Hughes' personal life was as intriguing and mystifying as his business and political life. Once an aggressive womanizer and dynamic social entertainer of well-placed people, Hughes, during the Sixties, became increasingly introverted and paranoid. He arranged to have the 1967 golf Tournament of Champions moved from the Desert Inn to the Stardust in order to avoid an influx of germs so close to his penthouse. In later years he owned only germ-proof automobiles. He paid $22.5 million for the adjoining Frontier Hotel out of fear that a 189-foot-high, $1 million sign in front of the hotel would fall on his Desert Inn, injuring him.

Fearful of race riots, Hughes offered $100,000 for the construction of a new community center in the city's black neighborhood. Hughes also feared the press might shed some "light of day" on his operations. He made a $4 million, thirty-five year, three per cent interest loan to Herman M. Greenspun, Editor of the Las Vegas _Sun_, with the expectation of favorable and sympathetic coverage. The _Sun_ published several editorials extolling the tycoon's virtues and accomplishments. Hence, Howard Hughes loomed as another peculiar figure who had gained an enormous fortune through his participation in America's modern, highly integrated political economy, made rich by the policies of Johnson's Great Society.

The exceptionally good fortune of the few multiplied the appetite of millions more for wealth. The scramble for wealth was reflected by the fact that Morton Shulman's _Anyone Can Make a Million_ (1966) became an all-time best seller. The thriving hustle and bustle of the market place recalled an observation once made by Alexis de Tocqueville, who surmised that "in America, everyone finds facilities unknown elsewhere for making or increasing his fortune. The spirit of gain is always on the stretch."

Exuberance and confidence in American capitalism reigned supreme. The amazing growth in material wealth prompted historian Daniel J. Boorstin to describe modern democracy in America as a system which gave "everything to everybody." And the great prosperity led journalist Henry Luce to exult that "the American economic system is one of the greatest achievements of all times. The present and foreseeable flood of abundance is not only producing the means for a great civilization, it is forcing us to think in these terms." After the accomplishment of abundant wealth Americans turned their attention to building a great civilization.

CHAPTER V

AMERICAN CIVILIZATION AT HIGH TIDE

Affluence marked the mid-Sixties as American civilization flourished at high tide; everywhere life seemed on the upbeat. Affluence magnified the traditional features of what historian Frederick Jackson Turner had once described loosely as the American character. "The coarseness and strength combined with acuteness and inquisitiveness; that practical, inventive turn of mind, quick to find expedients; that masterful grasp of material things, powerful to effect great ends; that restless, nervous energy; and with all that buoyance and exuberance which comes with freedom," wrote Turner; these were the elements of character which illuminated the American people in good times.

Some of Turner's followers later envisioned the city rather than the countryside as the ultimate American frontier, and by the Sixties the urban lifestyle had arrived in all its complexity and brilliance. An infatuation with urbanism swept through the nation. The new spirit of urbanity was probably best demonstrated in St. Louis, where a massive 630-foot Gateway Arch towered over the riverfront, symbolizing the city's role in pioneering the Old West, as well as its role in the pathway to the future. A promotional piece stated that the Arch represented a "new hustle, a new zest for living," an inscription which could have captured the mood of the American people during the High Sixties.

British songstress Petula Clark established the tone of the new urban mood with the popular song "Downtown": "When you're alone and life is making you lonely, you can always go Downtown/ When you've got worries, all the noise and the hurry seems to help/ I know, Downtown/ Just listen to the music of the traffic in the city/ Linger on the sidewalk where the neon signs are pretty/ How can you lose/ The lights are much brighter there/ You can forget all your troubles/ Forget all your cares/ So go Downtown/ Things will be great when you're Downtown/ No finer place for sure Downtown/ Everything's waiting for you."

The affable sound of "Downtown" fairly illuminated the clumps of mammoth new skyscrapers which were in the process of transforming the urban skylines and stood like monuments to a new age of progress. "All cultures that can be called cultures have built monuments--that is, buildings of unusual size and expenditure of effort, that have aroused pride and enjoyment as well as utility," wrote architect Philip Johnson. And so it was. New York's 1,300-foot-high Twin Towers, Chicago's John Hancock, and San Francisco's Transamerica placed history on notice that this generation had reached even greater heights of grandeur than its proud forebears of the 1920's, who had erected the Empire State Building.

The new skylines resulted in part from new technological improvements in building equipment; new construction techniques; stronger, more flexible steel; thicker, more durable glass; better grades of aluminum; and reinforced concrete. Not to be ignored was the resourcefulness and imagination demonstrated by such luminary architects as Chicago's Mies Von der Rohe, who firmly believed that "at its best, architecture touches and expresses the very innermost structure of the civilization from which it springs." He believed in the ultimate truth of architecture, that it could be adapted over the years until architecture became a great science. "I tried to make an architecture for a technological society," asserted Von der Rohe as he led his profession in the quest to fashion the modern temples of glass and steel.

Previously unthought of architectural feats complemented the atmosphere of the Sixties. In Manhattan Philip Johnson's Seagram Building, a virtual "Parthenon" of glass-grid architecture, marked the international style, restless and stylish like the urbanity it represented. An ingenious new staged elevator system made architect Emory Roth's World Trade Center Twin Towers possible. New York City's new 13-story Madison Square Garden Center--featuring a 48-lane bowling center, a 5,227 seat forum, a 501 seat cinema, the Hall of Fame, and the National Art Museum of Sport--was hung 45 feet above the Penn Central railroad station by steel girders, trusses, and cables, thus eliminating the need for the old standard columns. The fan-shaped amphitheater of the Saratoga Performing Arts Center, home of the New York Ballet, was supported by a slender steel framed acoustical canopy over the orchestra, giving patrons an exciting new blend of acoustical and visual perfection.

In Baltimore the enchanting Mechanic Theater, set like a "Blocky fortress" above a row of shops, provided the spark for a revitalized central-city area. In the burgeoning new western city of San Diego development centered around the downtown Concourse building, a convention, city administrative, cultural, and civic nerve center. The Concourse came equipped with an ambitious plan to install a massive computer system to make city administration quick, efficient, and unerring. The San Diego Municipal Command, it was said, could "do everything" from noting the failure to pay a light bill to informing firemen which way the wind was blowing.

The bustling new construction activity often threatened to blot out all traces of the city's dingy if colorful past, except in instances where momentary passions of nostalgia prevailed. In Denver, the "mile high city," the rustic old-fashioned block of Larimer Street was left unrenewed as a pensive gesture to "preserve its memory." In Boston an embattled group of civic-minded citizens staged an almost futile effort to save from the "bulldozing" redevelopers the historic area around Faneuil Hall marketplace, the once vibrant business center which had fostered such mercantile masters as Peter Faneuil and Josiah Quincy--the men who had proudly nicknamed the area the Hub (of the universe).

In places such as San Francisco's Noble Bay and Chicago's Lake Michigan spiraling self-contained apartment complexes, each housing hundreds of families, provided homes for those who wished to live among the bustling grandeur. Architect Bertrand Goldberg, who designed the nation's foremost vertical community, Chicago's Marina City Towers, accommodated its inhabitants with indoor shopping, parking, and almost every conceivable amenity of life so that they could escape the hazards which occasionally lurked in the narrow mucky streets below. In New York City the Rockefeller Center, designed by Raymond Hood, provided the world's largest privately owned business and entertainment center. It provided a "labyrinth" of underground shopping arcades, sunken plaza theaters, television studios, 25 restaurants, 70 retail stores, the Lincoln Center for the performing arts, and space for 50,000 daytime inhabitants in the "slab-sided" office complexes.

The Rockefeller Center attracted generous urban renewal funds, as did the Los Angeles Bunker Hill Urban Renewal Project, a $500 million effort to refurbish America's largest western city. Bunker Hill included a multi-million dollar Civic Mall featuring gardens, walkways, and cultural attractions, and it boasted a 34.5 million dollar music center which attracted over four million persons to its performances during the first three years. Other cities emulated Los Angeles' idea of bringing the open country atmosphere downtown. In Atlanta the gigantic Regency Hyatt House caught the spirit of the time. The hotel featured a massive skylit courtyard filled with birds, fountains, and greenery reminiscent of the Hanging Gardens of Babylon. Perched at the top was an elaborately decorated cocktail lounge and restaurant that revolved 360 degrees an hour, giving its guests a refreshing view of the countryside stretching to the west. The design, according to architect John C. Portman, was to give patrons "a feeling of complete openness."

Even while Modernism reigned supreme across the landscape of the cities, Post-Modernism began to make its challenge. Philadelphian Robert Venturi, author of a 1966 book titled Complexity and Contradiction in Architecture, articulated a new trend probably more fitting of the pluralism and change in American society. "Architects can no longer afford to be intimidated by the puritanically moral language of orthodox modern architecture," wrote Venturi. "I like elements which are hybrid rather than 'pure,' compromising rather than 'clean,' distorted rather than 'straightforward,' ambiguous... and equivocal rather than direct and clear." Venturi argued for "messy vitality over obvious unity," and for "richness of meaning rather than clarity of meaning." The exaltation of density and plurality by the Post-Modernists challenged the singleness ideal of the Modernists, who continued to build most of the new structures. Nevertheless, intrigue with the city occupied the attention of both groups.

Most Americans considered the city a vital, permanent part of the nation's future. At Disneyland millions of admiring Americans toured General Electric's vibrant "Carousel of Progress," which featured a 21st century model city, equipped with automated highways, smokeless nuclear power plants, and controlled climates. Indeed, America's feelings about the city were not unlike those of the 19th century philosopher Henry James when he first viewed London: "It is not a pleasant place, it is not agreeable, or cheerful, or easy, or exempt from reproach. It is only magnificent."

The fast-paced activity of the city gave the decade the mark of hastening trends and persistent movement, even though the nation itself became more suburban as inner city areas grew more slowly and rural America actually lost population. Rural population decreased from 16 to 10 million while central city population increased from 57 to 65 million and suburban population from 56 to 76 million. Yet the nation became more homogeneous as the wonders of mass media compressed its consciousness. The population continued to shift south and west toward America's glittering new sunbelt cities of Dallas, Houston, and Phoenix.

Improved transportation facilities made the nation more mobile than ever before; nearly 40 million persons changed residence each year. Interstate highways and air travel--highlighted by the fabulous Boeing 747, which could travel at 625 miles per hour and carry 490 passengers--made mobility a normal part of life. Millions of Americans alive in the Sixties could expect to travel over three million miles during their life, compared to a mere 100,000 in 1914.

The more than 40,000 miles of interstate highway virtually laced the nation together. What could not be moved by automobile, moved by truck. Thousands of giant 19-wheel rigs--reefers, dry boxes, and flatbeds--thundered over the nation's highways by day and by night. Their "claustrophobic" cabs were occupied by a new breed of American cowboy; the day of the American trucker had arrived. "The truck is their horse and they are the cowboys," reported one observer of these proud and independent wranglers of the road. "Stetson hats, tooled leather belts and pointy-toed boots trimmed iguana or wildebeest, buttoned denim shirts barely covering bellies bulging out from too many orders of mashed potatoes and chocolate cream pie"--such were the marks of the trucker, constantly on the move like the nation itself.

The rambling, growling sound of huge semi-truck transports and moaning moving vans replaced the distant, forlorn whistle of the slow moving railroad engine, thus marking the new mobility. "The pigeons at Boston's South Station sometimes outnumber the people," wrote one observer as he noted the decline and fall of railroad travel. "Inside the station the bustle subsides, silence steals in, the ticket windows are shuttered one by one and the platforms sprout weeds." The airport terminal replaced the railroad depot as the nerve center of American life, producing a new jet set of hurried travelers, who in restless and footloose fashion proudly mounted the "silver princes of the sky" as these new "locomotive gods" aimed their mighty thrust onward and upward toward the boundless limits of American life.

The quiet hum of the automobile engine probably characterized the increasing mobility of American life more than anything else. Americans enjoyed one automobile for every 2.4 persons, compared to one for every 234 people in Russia. By the Sixties the automobile had become more than a necessity; it had become a status symbol as well as a modern instrument of convenience and pleasure. "It turns its driver into a knight with the mobility of the aristocrat and perhaps some of his other vices," wrote economist and social critic Kenneth E. Boulding. "The pedestrian and the person who rides public transportation are, by comparison, peasants looking up with almost inevitable envy at the knights riding by in their mechanical steeds." The sturdy new turnpikes and expressways not only connected the great cities but made even the most remote areas of the nation more accessible to traveling adventurers, and this greatly increased the feeling of freedom and flexibility. America's increasing propensity to travel could be witnessed in the numbers visiting the national parks; visitors increased from 9,216,000 in 1946 to almost 20,000,000 by 1970.

In an age of relatively cheap energy American auto companies produced cars powered by huge V-8 engines which could easily travel at speeds of 80 miles an hour. Automobiles came equipped with improved suspension-tortion bar mechanisms for quieter and smoother rides; air conditioning for removing dirt, pollen, and humidity from the air; FM and AM multiple speaker stereo-sonic radio equipment and tape decks for musical entertainment; soft-ray tinted glass to protect from sun glare; floor four-speed stick shifting; comfortable steering wheels, power steering, brakes, and windows; bucket seats; shielded headlights; remote control spotlights; padded instrument panels; floor and side panel carpeting; center fold-down arm rests; and cornering lights.

Decorated with flowing body lines, topped by smartly padded vinyl roof covering, postured on a "wide-track" wheel base, and placed on steel-belted tires which eliminated pavement whining and thumping, the automobile--a modern chariot of elegance and flavor--provided many Americans with an important source of identity, individuality, and a sense of accomplishment. "This machine itself appeared as a compensatory device for enlarging an ego which had been shrunken by our very success in mechanization," chided social critic Lewis Mumford. Even the fashion industry took its cue from the automobile. Upon reintroducing the zipper as a fashion piece in 1965, designer Emmanuelle Khan remarked that they "go with the times--the machine, fireball sports cars and speed."

A Buick Electra advertisement captured well the place of the automobile in the American mentality. "Think back over the years," the caption read. "Were all your cars as good as you deserve? Were they eloquent, long, graceful, infinitely luxurious? Did they lift your spirits? Make you soar? Make the merest turn around the block feel like a cruise to Nassau? Did they come equipped with every last thing needed to make driving (or just riding) an unmitigated pleasure?"

Not everything about the automobile culture was worth extolling, of course. "A good transportation system minimizes unnecessary transportation," complained Lewis Mumford, who stated that the American automobile system encouraged a lack of diversity and extracted too high a percentage of resources. Automobiles led to rush-hour congestion, polluted city air, and over 50,000 highway deaths a year, 20,000 from drunken driving. In the soaring Sixties, however, most Americans took little time to concern themselves with the evil side of automobile usage.

The automobile actually strengthened America's confidence in the idea of progress. In the estimation of James M. Roche, Chairman of General Motors, "The history of America has been one of steady progress. The automobile is a perfect example." General Electric advertised that "progress is our most important product," and indeed the reassuring signs of progress pervaded the landscape. Larger machinery, automated equipment, computers, electronics, new chemical processes, and laser technology seemed to lighten the burden of work and increase the comforts of life for millions. Life became as easy as pulling the handle of a vending machine--an industry, incidentally, that grew immensely by catering to the increasing demand for convenience and the instant gratification of human needs and demands.

Cheap electricity brought about household gadgetry which would have left earlier generations in awe. Electric dishwashers, self-cleaning ovens, toothbrushes, and vacuum cleaners all but eliminated the burdens of household chores. Paper dishes, formica table tops, washable synthetic clothing, stronger cleansing agents, aluminum siding and indoor-outdoor carpeting added to America's impulse toward convenience. Pride in one's home and the ownership of it remained prominent in a decade when two out of three families owned their own home and a growing number began purchasing a second home in the country. It led millions to search for even faster and cheaper methods of completing household tasks; they read religiously such newspaper columns as "Hints From Heloise," authored by the peppery and eccentric Heloise Bowles of Texas.

These conveniences left more time for watching the new phenomenon of colored television, by now the nation's major pastime. Over 95 per cent of America's homes owned at least one television set; and some programs, such as comic Johnny Carson's Tonight Show televised from New York and offering a variety of witty and light-hearted hilarity and entertainment, enjoyed upwards of 15 million viewers. Media critic Marshall McLuhan, in his The Medium Is The message, argued that the electronic media might soon replace the written word as the principal means of communication. Yet millions of children remained fervent admirers of Dr. Seuss' zany animal heroes, Horton the Elephant and Yertle the Turtle; and novels continued to sell at all-time levels because such perceptive authors as John Updike, Truman Capote and Jacqueline Suzanne managed to write about amouring themes that tantalized the interest of the reading public.

The comforts of modern life were enhanced by medical technology which provided new healing procedures and pain relievers for almost every illness. Geneticist Dr. Edward L. Tatum confidently predicted at the 1966 Symposium on the Future of Medicine that in a few decades the causes and cures for most diseases would be available to society. Retired Professor James H. Bedford was so optimistic about the future of medicine that he arranged for his body to be preserved after death in a steel capsule at 200 degreess below zero, along with provisions for his revival when cures for cancer were discovered.

Heart transplants and artificial organs strengthened the promise of a longer and more fruitful life. In 1966 Dr. Michael De Bakey implanted an artificial heart in the chest of a 65-year-old Illinois coal miner. Alloplastic wonders such as brain-drain tubes, eyeball girdles, starr heart valves, and silicone-covered pacemakers prolonged life, as did such drugs as fluroiouiacil, thiolepa and choriocaicinoma. Wonder drugs and tonics such as Alka-Seltzer for pep, Sominex for sleep, and aspirin for pain relief promised less pain and more pleasure. Excedrin, purporting to be 50 per cent stronger than aspirin, promised users quick relief, long-lasting relief, a tension reliever to relax, and an anti-depressant to restore spirits. Other tonics such as Lady Clairol, which removed gray from hair, appealed to the urge to preserve youth. "Is it true...that blondes have more fun?" read one caption. Revlon Eterna "27", a facial cream, promised to keep skin looking young and unwrinkled. Actually, the average age of the population was growing older. Widespread use of the Salk vaccine had all but eliminated concern for polio, and the heart-lung resuscitator was developed into a common life saver. The new medical technology increased life expectancy to almost 70 years compared to less than 50 at the beginning of the century.

Not all was well on the health scene, however. Such ills of an advancing technological society as heart disease, cancer, and mental disorder were striking Americans down with increasing rapidity. The death rate from cancer alone increased from 112 per 100,000 population in 1930 to 130 by 1970. Much of the ominous increase could be attributed to the growing number of chemicals in the environment, an estimated 50,000 by 1970, of which 12,000 were considered harmful and 1,500 believed to be linked to cancer. The use of chemical fertilizers increased from 20 million tons in 1960 to 70 million tons in 1970. From 70 to 90 per cent of all cancer was believed to result from environmental conditions.

Cigarette smoking grew into a national health hazard. The use of tobacco had been a controversial practice in western society ever since the 17th century when Sir Walter Raleigh introduced the smoldering weed into England's high society. In 1604 King James penned a pamphlet against smoking, calling it "loathsome to the eye, hateful to the nose, harmful to the brain, and dangerous to the lungs." In the 1880's American James B. Duke introduced the conveniently packaged cigarette; and as millions of Americans in the 20th century adopted the "showy" habit, they generally scoffed at the puritanical critics who dared to suggest that smoking represented a health hazard. Indeed, smoking, like automobiles, became a mark of jet-set activity.

In 1964, however, science came down hard on the side of the critics when the U.S. Surgeon General reported a positive link between cigarette smoking and lung cancer. The male death rate from lung cancer had risen since 1950 from 18 to 52 per 100,000; among women lung cancer deaths tripled during the same period. Congress quickly passed a law limiting cigarette advertising and forcing cigarette makers to place a warning label on each package, but it could not muster the fortitude to eliminate the tobacco industry altogether. This was a matter of personal choice, it was argued. Even the sternest warnings did not faze Americans much ,as the percentage of people smoking only dipped slightly; and by the end of the decade the nation still remained one of puffers, smoking 10 cigarettes per person per day--the highest average in the world.

Death from smoking tended to concern Americans little because the experience of death itself was largely ignored in a society dedicated to the celebration of life. Eight out of ten deaths in America occurred in the isolation of hospitals or nursing homes, the patient surrounded by strangers and medical technicians rather than family and clergyman as in the old days. "The priest has been replaced by the doctor, whose training gives him no way of satisfying the psychological needs of the dying and who hides death from the patient," wrote one critic. "The patient therefore shuffles into death unknowingly; far from being exposed to any ultimate reality, he dies as if death were merely the last drop in the graph on the temperature chart." Funerals were expensive and impersonal. "The art of the American mortician paints death to look like life, sealing it up in water-tight caskets and spiriting it away to graveyards camouflaged as gardens," wrote another critic.

Americans had little time to contemplate death while they worshipped the largesse of new technological systems considered necessary to progress. The gigantic systems boggled the mind and brought confidence in the corporate economy which produced them. The giant Apollo moonship hangar--one million square feet, 525 feet high, covering eight acres--offshore oil-drilling rigs which could operate in 300 feet of water and cut through 30,000 feet of rock, and supermarkets which provided up to 8,000 brightly packaged items, five times as many as in the early fifties--all of these images served as reminders of ever-increasing plateaus of progress.

America's confidence in its own largesse was hardly shaken even when failures in the massive systems resulted in tragedy and death; these failures, perhaps, should have been stronger reminders of human frailty in the face of nature and machine. An earthquake caused millions in damages in Alaska on Easter weekend, 1964. In November, 1965, a massive power failure left 30 million northeasterners without electricity and blackened the New York skyline for the first time in memory. In January, 1966, a sudden internal fire instantaneously snuffed out the life of three Apollo astronauts while they ran through a simulated countdown on the launching pad. In January, 1967, a 23-inch snowstorm brought the bustling Chicago to an abrupt halt as travel and normal communication became impossible. A West Virginia coal mine explosion in 1968 entombed 78 men in a matter of seconds, and a 52-inch rainfall in the San Gabriel mountains in 1969 caused massive mudslides, wrecking hundreds of homes and businesses. In 1967 the famous 2,235 foot Silver Bridge, spanning the Ohio River near Point Pleasant, West Virginia, collapsed under the pressure of high winds and bumper-to-bumper traffic, sending over 100 unsuspecting people to their violent death in the icy waters below. Other disasters such as tornadoes, hurricanes, and airplane crashes killed and maimed thousands of persons but presented relatively small cause for hesitation since Americans believed that society had nearly conquered the capricious hazards of nature. Overconfidence in the "technological fix" represented the outcome of an attitude once attributed to Americans by de Tocqueville, who, upon viewing the nation's seemingly inexhaustible resources, commented that "the great privilege of Americans is to be able to commit reparable mistakes."

Americans were convinced more than ever that nature would be overcome through the healthy application of inventiveness and ingenuity. Without the application of more pure scientific research "our national ambitions will greatly outrun our national competence, " predicted America's pre-eminent space scientist James Van Allen. Others recalled Albert Einstein's belief that "imagination is more important than knowledge." Experimentation with better methods went on undaunted in thousands of public and private laboratories as Americans praised the miracles of scientific discovery.

The confidence in science was reflected in the fantasy of "huge spheres, boxes, cones, cylinders, ovoids, and curving pylon" which highlighted the United States Pavilion at the 1964 New York World's Fair, where Fair President Robert Moses, New York City's masterful Park Commissioner and America's most renowned city builder, bravely proclaimed the theme: "Man's Achievements in an Expanding Universe." America's faith in science and ingenuity was again captured in the United States Pavilion at Expo '67, for which architect Buckminster Fuller designed an exquisite 20-story geodesic dome to "show the craftsmanship, inventiveness and creativity of the American people." The "great glove celebrated our release from the tired old methods of enclosing a given area. It was a clean sweep of stuffy thinking," wrote William K. Zinsser, exemplifying the

American tendency to boast of practical solutions to sticky problems. Dean Gordon Brown of M.I.T.'s College of Engineering was so confident of America's ability to solve its problems that he said: "I doubt if there is such a thing as an urban crisis, but if there were, M.I.T. would lick it in the same way we handled the Second World War."

The apparent success of science, coupled with the traditional insistence upon tolerance, openmindedness, and the free discussion of ideas, provided new opportunities for experimentation with alternative life styles and with new, sometimes feral, ideas. "How else could an individualistic people be expected to evolve an indigenous cultural tradition out of social confusion but by consulting, observing, and censuring each other?" asked social critic Rowland Berthoff. Americans strived for uniqueness and distinctiveness in both character and manner; they longed to "do their own thing" even when that proved embarrassing and absurd, and they generally tolerated the same in others.

Americans hardly winced at the frivolous frolics of Tiny Tim, the tulip patch falsetto minstrel; and the uncanny popularity of Britain's 90-pound Twiggy, scrawny as a "cockney dowsing rod," demonstrated America's flair for the unconventional. An orthopedist concluded of Twiggy that "practically everything is wrong with her--she has a humpback, exaggerated curvature of the spine and a hanging abdomen." It all seemed to demonstrate that "the more things were out, the more they were in," commented one observer. The "brash, Brooklyn, smart alecky" actress-singer Barbra Streisand, "the gal who really belts out a song," and the every woman type--probably America's most emulated movie personality--explained that "I'm so far out I'm in." The passion for individualism was perhaps best expressed in the song "My Way," popularized by the aging songster Frank Sinatra, the Pack Rat, himself an erstwhile example of one who firmly resisted the imposition of Victorian social mores and traditions: "And now the end is near, and so I face the final curtain/ My friend, I'll say it clear/ I'll state my case, of which I'm certain/ I've lived a life that's full/ I traveled each and every highway/ And more, much more than this / I did it my way."

The search for the unconventional made "to tell it like it is" a vogue. Often those who did came under a barrage of criticism, yet Americans showed an amazing capacity for what the Rochester Bishop Fulton J. Sheen would call "suffering from tolerance." American society proved flexible enough to contend with the ideological aberrations of both the atheist Madalyn E. Murray, who campaigned vigorously to eliminate any reference to God in public life, and the ultra-conservative Reverend Carl

McIntyre, who campaigned just as vigorously to place the stamp of Christianity on every facet of human endeavor. Symbolically, at least, Americans went to great lengths in order to preserve the idea of individuality. In 1967 when little Billy Churchill of Satellite Beach, Florida had his television tray pop stand closed by county health officials, the flamboyant Governor Claude Kirk gained wide public attention by leading the drive to reopen the boy's business. "It was symbolic of a nationwide problem of individual initiative stifled by governmental red tape and foolishly administered regulation," surmised Kirk.

For all their individualism, however, Americans continued to be a nation of joiners, a people who enjoyed being at gatherings of many sorts. The urge for togetherness was celebrated in Barbra Streisand's hit song "People." "People, people who need people/ Are the luckiest people in the world/ We're children needing other children/ And yet, letting our grown up pride/ Hide all the need inside/ Acting more like children than children." Americans gathered at county fairs, commemorative parades, family and class reunions, picnics, weddings, funerals, dedication ceremonies, concerts, farewell and welcoming parties, and especially at the increasingly popular cluster called the cocktail party.

Prosperity re-established the old American pastime of eating out. Outdoor grilling sent curls of smoke ascending from the back yards of Suburbia on warm summer evenings as Americans by the millions indulged themselves with freshly cut beefsteak made less costly by the amazing new technology in the meat processing industry. Steak houses flourished like never before. Many became luxurious restaurants where the community elite came to wine and dine. At Manhattan's renowned "21" restaurant, for example, an updated speak-easy, highlighted by richly paneled walls and graced with Old English silver and $750,000 worth of paintings, a mere hamburger lunch could cost as much as $14. The restaurant became "the place" for the famous to be seen. Those who could not afford the more luxurious pleasures of eating beefsteak could satisfy their urge to eat out by frequenting such drive-in restaurants as A & W Root Beer, Dairy Queen, McDonald's, Burger King, Arby's Roast Beef, Kentucky Fried Chicken, Dunkin' Donut, or the Copper Kettle.

Aided by the convenience of modern jet travel, nearly eight million Americans gathered annually at a variety of gorgeous and extravagant vacation resorts located in such faraway places as Hawaii, Acapulco, Casablanca, and Las Vegas, where the International Hotel was graced by the world's largest eternal flame (35 feet high), and where the slot machines clacked merrily as hopeful and frantic gamblers stood six deep next to craps and blackjack tables. Millions celebrated to the hyperbolic drum beaters at the famous hotels at Miami Beach, proclaimed still as "the sun and fun capital of the world." "Indulge yourself--live a little," went the slogan. "Miami Beach was built for big-city people. It's the big city's idea of a tropical setting," asserted one publicity agent. "I'm not designing hotels," commented Morris Lapidus, designer of Miami's fabulous $40 million Fontainebleau, "I'm designing stage settings on which people will play out their two-week vacations." Millions of Americans vacationed in Europe, where they often behaved in a profuse and extravagant manner.

The middle and lower classes were not to be outdone as the traveling camper trailer became a prominent part of many family weekends. Interstate travel allowed campers to go miles away from the city to countryside camp sites. This provided an opportunity for fishing, water sports, and a good deal of friendly laughter and chatter around campfires. Prosperity did not mark every gathering, of course. Once a year American's most colorful hobos, a breed of independent people becoming extinct along with the railroad, met at Britt, Iowa, where admirers could listen to such ragged, time-worn, but stubborn characters as the Hard Rock Kid and Steamtrain Maury chortle about yesteryear and spin exaggerated yarns describing the rambling adventure of the tramping life.

Some gatherings were huge affairs. The Illinois State Fair, for example, attracted over a million people each year during ten hot late summer days. The fair offered over one million dollars in contest prizes, livestock shows involving over 25,000 animals, harness races, home and cooking demonstrations, midway entertainment, and rock concerts. This was considered a good, clean affair. Another massive annual gathering, however, the New Orleans Mardi Gras, left some questions, but no one argued that it was not filled with spectacular fun. "It is a hedonist's paradise," wrote one admirer, "a visual kaleidoscope, a festival of glorious sounds, smells, tastes, and other pleasures that may overload all your circuits." Each year over a million Americans squeezed into the famous areas stretching from Napoleon Avenue to Canal and Bourbon Streets along the French Quarter, to watch 50 parades, attend some 60 balls, participate in extravagant street dancing, herald the famous marching clubs, see the costume contests, and to listen intently for the jazz music sounds rising from the wheezing trumpets of Al Hirt and Pete Fountain.

Every community sponsored an annual celebration, even the smallest. In Waynesburg, Pennsylvania, the community's annual Rain Day, with festivities ranging from square dancing to a town picnic, provided evidence that the nation still relished very common things. "Fink Day," a celebration in the little northern Texas community of Fink which honored a flower by the same name, drew thousands of Texans who came to enjoy a rodeo, a parade, a barbecue, a domino championship, and most importantly, a chance to meet old friends and make new acquaintances in a setting of relaxed, festive fellowship. Some such events were given gargantuan dimensions. Beaver, Oklahoma sponsored the World Champion Cowchip Throwing Contest, the winners receiving bronzed trophies featuring a tiny, gold-plated cowchip.

The festive spirit virtually enveloped the nation during each New Years' Eve celebration--an event characterized as a frivolous mixture of carousing, feasting, ribaldry, and tippling, marked by big bands, dancing, sparkling champagne, pointy party hats and funny noisemakers that blew in long squiggles. The annual revelry provided Americans with a fanciful ritual for reviewing past mistakes and for restoring personal hope in the future as they jubilated to the soothing, quivering saxophones of Guy Lombardo's "Auld Lang Syne."

More than anything, scientific and technological progress bestowed upon Americans an ever-increasing amount of leisure time, almost 50 hours a week. In an urban nation dedicated to celebration and entertainment the search for self-gratification and activity satisfying to the lighter side of the spirit could not be thwarted, puritanical principles aside. Americans immersed themselves in the visual pyrotechnics of such melodramatic movie extravaganzas as _Cleopatra,_ _Dr. Zhivago,_ _Sound of Music,_ _Patton,_ and _2001: A Space Odyssey._ Box office ticket sales grossed nearly a billion dollars in 1966, the best year since 1947. The movie industry was "back in high gear," boasted the quixotic and imperious Darryl Zanuck, who, as president of 20th Century Fox since 1962, had made the company a very profitable enterprise once again.

The new interest in cinema resulted partly from a greater emphasis on sex and violence, which were increased to help movies compete with television. Taking advantage of the relaxed public view of pornography and the greater permissiveness of the production code, movie producers often complemented the sex and violence with serious efforts to achieve realism and meaningful social commentary. In the 1961 production _Splendor in the Grass,_ for example, sex was prevalent in the theme, but so was a responsible critique of puritanical moral codes. As the decade wore on, love-making became a common feature of films such as _Georgy Girl,_ _Alfie,_ _The Prime of Miss Jean Brodie,_ _Goodbye Columbus,_ and _Blow-up,_ but not without treating along with it the guilt, jealousy, complexity, and misunderstanding that could be involved with love-making. Casual sex without permanent commitment became a prevalent theme in such films as _John and Mary,_ which featured Mia Farrow and Dustin Hoffman in a love-making encounter before they even knew each other's name.

In Elizabeth Taylor and Richard Burton's 1966 movie, Who's Afraid of Virginia Woolf? the bickerings and connivances of upper middle class life were revealed with stunning clarity. The film which included "some of the most searing dialogue ever heard in a Hollywood movie...won the movies' right to explore forbidden realms," reported Life. Even the National Catholic Office for Motion Pictures, once known as the National Legion of Decency, gave the film its qualified endorsement. Elizabeth Taylor proved to the be decade's most durable sex goddess. She was paired with Richard Burton, her knightly suitor of grandeur and fame. Burton symbolically established the reign of the mellifluous pair over the swinging international jet-set elite in 1968 when he purchased for Liz the 33.19 carat Krupp diamond, one of the world's most coveted gems, at a price of $305,000. "My little girl is ecstatically happy about getting it," reported Burton in a gesture of humble gallantry.

Another important film, In the Heat of the Night, starring Sidney Poitier and Rod Steiger, dealt with circumstances which caused brotherly love to overcome racial prejudice. In Poitier's Guess Who's Coming to Dinner, the issue of interracial sexual relationships was portrayed with vivid certainty. Warren Beatty's film Bonnie and Clyde, which involved a story of carefree killers in the 1930's who pursued their murderous tirade from Iowa to Texas before themselves being brutally killed in ambush, drew stunning parallels between the violence of the Thirties and the Sixties. In the 1968 film The Graduate, starring Dustin Hoffman, the plot proved to be an excellent commentary on the hypocrisy and loneliness of middle class suburban life. In 1969 the movie Easy Rider, starring Peter Fonda, explored the social conflicts arising from the clash between the hippie-like motorcyclist who sought the freedom of the road and main street America, which wrenched at the prospect of changing values and attitudes.

The cinema, then, represented a socialization process as well as entertainment. "Even as it strives to entertain, the new Cinema is part of the broad cultural movement of an age that is searching for contemporary redefinition of man's place in the universe," wrote Time. In spite of all the talk about social commentary, however, the emphasis on sex themes remained an important reason for the success of the movie industry, and sex goddesses received much attention. Raquel Welch, for example, who was introduced to the nation in 1967 wearing a tattered fur bikini as the star of One Million Years B.C., became a salacious reference point. By the end of the decade movie-goers came to expect at least one good nude scene in every major production. The zest for sensual experience carried over into the theater with productions such as Che, Grease, and Oh! Calcutta! ,a play highlighting an exotic and humorous series of skits exploring sexual intercourse, oral sex, and masturbatory fantasies.

The technique of mixing sex and social commentary was epitomized in Hugh Hefner's publication of Playboy magazine, which came to enjoy sales of almost six million copies a month and monthly advertising receipts of $3.5 million. "We want to make clear from the very start, we aren't a 'family magazine,'" pronounced Playboy in the initial 1953 issue. "If you're somebody's sister, wife, or mother-in-law and picked us up by mistake, please pass us along to the man in your life and get back to your Ladies Home Companion." Hefner promised the magazine would provide "a little diversion from the anxieties of the Atomic Age."

Playboy featured such sensate fantasies as glossy nude photographs of sumptuous and unblemished women whose creamy perfection excited the male imagination. This was designed to release American males from their repressive Victorian attitudes of the past and make them "healthy" in business and sex alike, argued Hefner, whom one critic called the modern "prophet of pop hedonism." Another described him as the "mass producer of plastic-wrapped sex, the purveyor of pop hedonism, the great anti-Puritan who is out to make every square feel that he too can be a swinger." His genius was "that he has linked sex with upward mobility," wrote Time; Playboy represented "the ultimate life of material and sensual pleasure."

The advertising of luxurious clothing, sleek cars, plush stereo sets, and elegant foods and wines informed the budding playboy of the other accessories accompanying success according to Hefner's formula. Playboy gained some respectability from its featured articles and interviews with many of the leading cultural and intellectual authorities of the land. Hefner's empire included Bunny Clubs, such as the nine-million-dollar complex at Lake Geneva, Wisconsin, where tired executives could come to relax and vicariously enjoy some sensual pleasure in a world so busy that, in actuality, it left less time than in the "good old days" for sexual fulfillment. Hefner ruled his empire from the top of Chicago's Palmolive Building, where a huge Bunny beacon reportedly beamed for 500 miles. When criticized, the controversial and gaudy recluse simply answered by saying that "everyone should have the right to go to heaven or hell in his own way."

The link between sex and success in modern times was also a constant theme in the character of James Bond, novelist Ian Fleming's fictional secret agent 007, who zipped from triumph to triumph with serene confidence. Employing the latest technology known to police science, and some tactics not yet known, Bond was presented as a cosmopolitan, clever, fashionable, versatile, brilliant, handsome consorter with powerful people, a man who always maintained a modest posture but came out the cool winner against uneven odds. Many American males enjoyed identifying with his jet-set pace. He drove the finest sports cars, consumed the most expensive alcoholic beverages, smoked especially tailored cigarettes, and seduced--almost without trying and only when time permitted--the prettiest and most eloquent women. In a typical Bond movie females were portrayed like birds, flying in and out of scenes without any forethought or afterthought. Female resistance to him "tends to collapse at the moment he appears," wrote one critic, and he "gives a good account of himself in bed." Somewhat in keeping with the American dedication to the work ethic, of course, sensual gratification never came for Bond until after his task had been well accomplished. The success of Bond prompted NBC television to launch a weekly series called The Man From U.N.C.L.E., starring Robert Vaughn, soon to be known as 006 7/8.

The so-called "sex craze" carried over into the glamours of night life where topless and bottomless Go-Go dancers performed endlessly before enthusiastic clients. By the end of 1965 San Francisco's Broadway section of the North Beach contained over a dozen rock-n-roll cabarets, each featuring the scantily clad girls doing new dances such as the "Swim." In Chicago the famous Living Room was reopened under the name of Whiskey A-Go-Go. In New York City, where Chubbie Checker's Peppermint Lounge had inaugurated the decade with a tossing, turning dance called "The Twist," the Village Vanguard became popular for such entertainment, and even the prestigious hotels Drake and Gotham opened discotheques featuring Go-Go entertainment for the city's dreamy cafe society.

Women's fashions strongly emphasized the sensuous tenor of the age as skirt lengths (miniskirts) crawled higher and higher above the knees, complemented by seamless, textured stockings and knee-length glove-like patent leather boots, probably the "boots" Nancy Sinatra had in mind in her 1965 pop hit, "These Boots Were made For Walkin.'" Even women's formal wear began to flirt "with the lower limits of modesty." Fashion has become "boobs and butts, anything to make pictures sexy," lamented fashion beauty Wilhelmina Behmenburg Cooper, whose classical high-piled hair represented the aristocratic look--a style fast giving way to the more earthy, natural, laid-back look. Yet her 5 foot 11 inch, 38-24-36 frame allowed for the claim that she was "one of the few high fashion models built like a woman."

"Rarely have so many designers been so intent on uncovering so much," wrote Time in 1968, "and as a result, the fashions this summer will be the breeziest and barest in memory." Seventh Avenue designer Chester Weinberg conjectured that "if I bare the back any more I may be jailed." Yet in that same year Yves St. Laurent introduced the braless, see-through blouse. "It's the hottest thing we've had for years," commented Bernard Goodman of Sportwhirl. The bikini swimming suit became standard women's beach wear; it clung "to every curve and dimple like a coat of suntan oil." Swimming suits became scantier and more "seeworthy." In 1968 Rudi Gernriech introduced the topless swimsuit. Although few women ever donned a topless suit, the fashion industry continued to emphasize the baring of the breast, which, in turn, prompted a growing number of women to implant silicone in their breasts in order to achieve a more sensuous, wholesome appearance.

Some suggested that the sensuous fashions represented a new sense of freedom felt among women, inspired partly by the introduction of oral contraceptives, which were used by as many as 10 million women. Sexual restraint became more a matter of conviction than fear. Others argued that the sensuous fashions represented a manifestation of prosperity. British scholar of costume and contemporary fashion James Laver put it: "The disappearance of corsets is always accompanied by two related phenomena--promiscuity and an inflated currency. No corsets, bad money and general moral laxity." One thing was certain. Women's fashions catered more to the fancies of men than the fulfillment of women, something that would change drastically toward the end of the decade with the rebirth of the women's movement.

Another sign of affluence during the high Sixties was the burgeoning population of pets. Pets became a national preoccupation. President Johnson set the example with his mawkish fondling of a white mongrel named Yuki, who followed him around the Oval office and became a droll feature at Presidential press conferences. In 1967 it was estimated that 25.5 million pet cats, 24.5 million dogs, 20 million birds, and 650 million tropical fish existed in the United States. New York City alone boasted more than 600,000 dogs, more than the human population of Delaware. Around 30,000 New Yorkers a year required medical attention for dog bites.

In the decade of the unconventional people did not hesitate to possess unconventional pets. In Chicago a pet shop offered black bears, in Seattle, baby elephants, and in Canyon City, Colorado, mountain lion cubs. Snakes, monkeys, squirrels, hawks and wolves became subject to the pet world. Chicago dealer Bernie Hoffman sold vultures. "A vulture makes a wonderful conversation piece sitting on the chandelier," insisted Hoffman, who also sold tarantulas. They could "really be quite tame," observed Hoffman. "They learn to love their masters. You can teach them to crawl up your arm." Food experts complained that the new high-protein pet mixtures, a $2 billion a year industry, provided overly pampered pets with better nutrition than that enjoyed by many of the nation's poor. The nation boasted over 400 pet cemeteries where grieving masters held elaborate funerals for their deceased. Bonheur's in Baltimore, for example, offered bathing and grooming to give the "sleeping" appearance, satin and velvet-lined caskets, viewing in a "slumber" room, religious services, and candles lighted at the grave site on the anniversary of the pet's birth or death.

Nowhere was affluence more evident that in recreational and sports activities. "The U.S. appetite for sports has never been so insatiable," wrote Time. "The greatest opportunity in the United States today is to invent new ways for people to do nothing," chided one pundit in a quippish commentary on the demise of the work ethic. America's attitudes toward recreation had changed significantly since the nation's inception, when Dr. Benjamin Rush had labeled "enjoying oneself on the Sabbath by swimming, sliding and skating" as sin. In the Sixties the famous psychiatrist Dr. Karl Menninger felt compelled to write a book entitled Whatever Became of Sin?, in which he criticized the selfish notion that nothing was wrong as long as it was not prohibited by law or stigmatized by psychiatry. So the great search for pleasure went on, unabated by any twinge of conscience that might have bothered earlier generations.

Seventy-five percent of the American people over nine years old involved themselves in some form of outdoor recreational activity. By the end of the decade the nation boasted over seven million pleasure boats, many of them tri-haul, inboard-outboard crafts made of fiberglass for the boaters' comfort and convenience. Over 50 million Americans spent over a billion dollars a year on boats and operating costs. An increasing number of Americans also purchased yachts for weekend pleasure cruising. Encouraged by technology we have "learned to stamp out fiberglass yachts like so many costly cookies," commented Life.

The nation included over 11 million regular golfers who, in using the new high compression golf ball and other improved equipment, made a 300-foot tee-off a normal expectation, something that Twenties golf star Bobby Jones could never have accomplished. A less costly form of recreation was bowling. Millions of Americans joined once-a-week bowling leagues and spent approximately $40 million annually for equipment. Game hunting of all kinds increased as an important recreational activity. Deer hunting was probably the most spectacular. On the night before the opening of deer season on the Upper Peninsula sector of Lake Superior, for example, as many as six hundred thousand hunters could be found waiting around campfires for their chance to bring down a "big horse." Tennis flourished during the decade, involving an estimated eight million people, many of whom were willing to pay hundreds of dollars a year to belong to indoor-outdoor racquet clubs.

The popularity of skiing continued to increase as six million skiers spent $1.5 billion a year on equipment, lodging, and transportation. For the first time, American people spent more on skiing than on golf. The introduction of new light-weight metal skis allowed a good skier to travel thirty miles an hour faster than before. The number of skiing areas in the United States doubled to 700 during the decade, and such places as Stowe, in Vermont; Sun Valley in Idaho; and Aspen and Vail in Colorado became renowned panaceas where jet-setting "free stylers" and "hot doggers" came to twist and spin down the slippery slopes.

For all the fanfare about boating, golf, and skiing the more traditional and less expensive, if more time consuming, pastime of fishing still maintained its predominance as an American recreational activity. "The charm of fishing is that it is the pursuit of what is elusive but attainable, a perpetual series of occasions for hope," wrote adventure novelist John Buchan in _The Thirty-Nine Steps._ Perhaps this sensation explained why 50 million happy anglers attempted the somnolent sport each year.

The newest sport to achieve significant popularity during the decade was snowmobiling. The streaking snowmobiles, skooters on skis, amounted to a lawnmower-type engine on skis propelled by rear belt treads and steered with handle bars. A snowmobile could travel at speeds of 50 miles an hour and could reach areas where even skiers feared to tread. By 1968 snowmobile groups held what were called weekend rallies. The number of snowmobile sales jumped from 15 thousand in 1964 to almost 600 thousand by 1970.

The decade was filled with the establishment of new sporting records, a fact which served as evidence of progress to many. It all began in 1961 when New York Yankee slugger Roger Maris slammed out 61 home runs, besting Babe Ruth's record of 60 established in 1927. Back in 1954 U.S. Olympic Coach Brutus Hamilton had compiled a list of "ultimate track records," most of which tumbled in the Sixties. American sports heroes seemed to become tougher and more resilient because of advances in nutrition, training methods, equipment and medicine. The introduction of aluminum and fiberglass vaulting poles in place of the old hickory or ash, for example, helped John Pennel establish a record 17 foot 10 1/4 inch jump in 1969. Curtis Mills ran the 440-yard sprint in 44.7 seconds, and Jim Ryan ran the mile in three minutes and 51.8 seconds.

Nowhere did Americans anticipate their capacity to break records more than at the annual Memorial Day Indianapolis 500 auto racing spectacular. The Indianapolis 500 represented the frontier of engineering technology. Engineering discoveries introduced at the Speedway over the years included the rear-view mirror, four-wheel and disc brakes, hydraulic shock absorbers, ethyl gasoline, low-pressure balloon tires, improved suspension systems, fuel injection, turbocharged engines and improvements in motor oils and high-temperature lubricants. Development of aerodynamic principles and devices reducing drag and resistance helped cars to roll easier and improve mileage.

The real excitement of Indianapolis, however, was reserved for the competition itself. Competition began early in May with the four-lap qualification runs conducted as the process of selecting the 33 fastest cars. The first day of time trials could attract as many as 125,000 spectators. The "race-day" crowd attracted as many as 350,000 people, making it the largest single sports event of the year.

On race day the atmosphere fairly crackled with anxious anticipation. The beginning of the race eventually came down to the crucial "chilling moment" with ritualistic certainty. It featured the playing of Taps, the sentimental sound of "Back Home in Indiana," the release of thousands of brightly colored balloons, and finally, the crisp announcement from speedway owner Anton (Tony) Hulman, "Gentlemen, start your engines!". Trembling and anxiety accompanied the chilling moment at the start of the race because most of the fatal, fiery crashes occurred during the opening moments. "The final 30 minutes of planned pomp and circumstance sends a tingle through you," observed historian Donald Davidson of the United States Auto Club. "There is just an incredible surge of emotion coming from 350,000 or 400,000 people." The start of the "500" reminded the famous journalist Ernie Pyle of "an armada of B-29's taking off for a mission to Tokyo; both driver and pilot after weeks of training find 'now is the hour of fate.'"

As the race quickly gained speed, the cars became multi-colored blurs as they streaked past the grandstands, whipping sometimes just inches from the concrete wall. They would drive low on the track and disappear around the first turn with a raspy whine that would echo for a moment after they sped out of sight. Bad luck and grisly disasters were only part of the exciting scene. The foremost concern involved the establishment of new records. Here aerospace technology and dazzling speeds represented the epitome in the worship of progress. During the Sixties drivers continued to reduce the qualifying and racing times. Rene Thomas first completed a lap over 100 miles per hour in 1939. Parnelli Jones first exceeded

150 in 1963, and afterward speeds ascended steadily upward. Scotsman Jimmy Clark topped 160 in 1965. England's Graham Hill reached 170 in 1968, and Bill Vukovich soared above 180 in 1970. In 1969 speedster Mario Andretti drove his Hawk Ford to victory at an average speed of 156.867 miles per hour. The 1970 contest brought auto racing's first million-dollar purse.

"The cars keep getting better, the competition gets better and racing is better," exhalted Indy's premier qualifier and winner A.J. Foyt. "There's no other place like Indianapolis anywhere in sports. It's one of a kind." The Indianapolis 500 had become an All-American folk festival steeped in colorful tradition and an unequaled celebration honoring the wonders of modern technological advancement and the daring skill of the individuals who piloted the missile-like chargers around the Speedway race track.

America's wide-spread enthusiasm for spectator sports made professional sports a leading business enterprise. Competitive professional sports presented a romantic panorama in which average citizens could vicariously experience the clash of prowess and brawn seemingly unbridled by the mundane surroundings of a machine-oriented society. In many ways professional sports mimicked the reality of life itself. The principles of good sportsmanship, which purportedly involved the exercise of competitive integrity, a spirit of team cooperation, undaunted persistence, coolness under pressure, and excellence in performance became so important to Americans wishing to emulate the greats that the first principles of sportsmanship were drilled into the minds of boys, and some girls, from the early grades through completion of their formal education. Furthermore, sports provided the thrill of upset, the opportunity for the "underdog" to come out the winner against almost insurmountable odds. This phenomenon was played over and over again in sporting events but was probably best demonstrated in 1969 when the scrappy New York Mets, under the canny leadership of manager Gil Hodges, won baseball's World Series.

These elements of the American sporting spirit provided the popular foundation for professional sports and brought wealth into the coffers of the sporting heroes. The fearsome trio of professional golfers, Arnold Palmer, Jack Nicklaus and Gary Player, earned well over one hundred thousand dollars a year. Arnold Palmer's famous late match charges attracted so many enthusiastic fans that they became known as "Arnie's army." Palmer's charm with the spectators, his gracefulness in victory or defeat, and his gentlemanly dedication to abiding by the principles of competiveness won him the designation as the decade's outstanding athlete from the Associated Press. In 1968 the leading golf money winner, Billy Casper, earned over 200 thousand dollars, a figure unimaginable in Bobby Jones' generation of the Twenties.

Boston Red Sox player Ted Williams became the first player in baseball history to consummate a $100,000 annual contract. Wilt "the Stilt" Chamberlain, who often scored more points that the rest of his Philadelphia Seventy-Sixers teammates put together, won a $250,000 contract in 1968 after an uncomfortable holdout that lasted until just eight days before the basketball season began. Jockey star Willie Shoemaker, who guided some the nation's best horses to victory at the annual Kentucky Derby and won 260 races by the end of the decade, boasted lifetime earnings of $40 million. Horse racing drew up to 70 million fans annually, highest of all spectator sports. The Kentucky Derby remained the premier horse racing contest. Thousands flocked to the resplendent Churchill Downs each spring to watch such greats as Decidedly, Northern Dancer, and Majestic Prince break gallantly from the gate, set the pace through the back stretch, dominate the field past the furlong pole, and sweep majestically under the wire to victory which earned a garland of roses in the winner's circle and a huge treasure of money.

Professional football reached its zenith during the decade, providing not only large gate receipts but a variety of brawny heroes as well. Jimmy Brown, for example, the Cleveland Browns' running back whose bulldozing tactics brought him a record seven 1,000-yard rushing seasons, put on an awesome field display. A New York Giant linebacker complained that the "best way to tackle Brown was to grab hold, hang on, and wait for help." The Detriot Lions' colorful tackle Alex Karras disagreed, suggesting that if Lion linemen "were equipped with axes they could have a better chance of stopping him." Most of the hero worship was reserved for quarterbacks such as Green Bay Packer Bart Star, Baltimore Colt Johnny Unitas, and "Broadway" Joe Namath, whose lightning-like passing brought the gallant young New York Jets a Super Bowl victory in 1969. But by the Sixties even husky defensive experts could become notable stars. Chicago Bears' 245-pound linebacker Dick Butkus, for example, who some thought was let out of his cage only on Sunday afternoon, averaged 200 tackles a season and became renowned for his meanness. "He's like a mule," complained an opposing lineman after Butkus had been accused of biting another lineman in a pile after a tackle. A quarterback complained that "if he doesn't tackle you, you can still hear him coming. You know he's going to be there eventually. It's savage!" "He'll be alright," commented teammate Ron Smith, "as soon as he has a couple cups of blood." Even the nation's leaders recognized the new status of defensive players. Senator Robert Kennedy, for example, engaged Los Angeles Rams Roosevelt Greer as his body guard during the 1968 presidential campaign.

The volatile rough-and-tumble action on the playing field increased America's appetite for football. Football attendance had increased by almost 500 percent since World War II, and gate receipts reached $25 million a year. A football franchise carried a value of six million dollars by the end of the decade compared to one million in the late Fifties. In Houston, Texas, citizens eagerly spent $431.6 million to build the huge Astrodome, a monument to the growing American faith in sportsmanship. The new Dallas Cowboy stadium featured 184 "Circle Suites" costing owners $50,000 each. One wealthy oilman spent $24,000 to decorate his suite in Louis XIV decor. Most suites were equipped with several television monitors for instant replays of the more valiant field action. Violence and action made football entertaining, at least to the approximately 25 million loyal fans who watched their heroes crunch and grind away on television every Sunday afternoon.

The first Super Bowl occurred in 1966. It featured the invincible Green Bay Packers led by the iron-willed coach Vince Lombardi, a man who demonstrated a brand of toughness, single-mindedness, competitiveness, and old-fashioned persistence profoundly attractive to Americans in a decade otherwise marked by limited wars and uncertain goals. "Lombardi is a hard-nosed disciplinarian and an advocate of forthright, bone-rattling football," observed *Time.* "Winning is not everything. It is the only thing," snapped Lombardi, who hated to lose. "This isn't a circus, it's a contest. There's a winner, and there's a loser," barked Lombardi to his admiring players. "We are in a time when society seems to have sympathy only for the misfit, the losers. Let us also cheer the doers, the winners!" he insisted.

Lombardi's insistence on the struggle for victory drew an image of potency in an age otherwise softened by automation. Man's greatest fulfillment "is that moment when he has worked his heart out in a good cause and lies exhausted on the field of battle--victorious," asserted Lombardi. "There is something in good men that really yearns for, needs discipline and the harsh reality of head-to-head combat."

Lombardi believed that the primary objective of football should be the "building of character." He once told the American Management Association that "we need to develop in this country a strong spirit of competitive interest. We fail in our obligation unless we preserve what has always been an American zeal--that is, to win and to be first, regardless of what we do." This pure zeal to succeed presented Americans with an attractive alternative to the frustration of bureaucratic life. Speaking of Lombardi's transfer to the Washington Red Skins in 1969, one admirer wrote that our "appetite for idealism and appreciation of romance has been starved on a diet of platitude, bombast and forked-tongue aphorism as dished out by Washington's ruling-class population of politicians, bureaucrats and the captains of vested interests. A few arararararararghs can only be counted as a welcome sound in such an environment."

Lombardi's image of strength and resolve was replayed week after week in football stadiums around the country. Even in high schools and colleges "the coach" symbolized the pillar of resolve and strength. For many coaches football paralleled war as a builder of character and community spirit. "This whole country has been built on one thing--winning," contended Ohio State coach Woody Hayes, whose favorite hero was General George Patton of World War II fame.

Whether or not football surpassed baseball as America's "national game" in the Sixties remained a debatable question. Baseball represented more than gallantry and brute strength. It was more individualistic and represented more intimacy between fans and the players. Football came in fall and winter while baseball represented the warm sunshine of spring and gentle summer breezes rippling the flags in center field, the aroma of freshly prepared popcorn, and the cheerful catcalls among players and from fans. In baseball there was time for lazy commentary between plays.

Probably the preeminent sports hero of the decade turned out to be New York Yankee slugger Mickey Mantle, whose courageous, injury-ridden career singularly gave the American spirit an uplift. The broad-shouldered Mantle annually dueled with Babe Ruth's home run record and excelled in every facet of playing-field action. "When Mickey Mantle got up that day in August, 1963, after being out of the line-up for two months, and pinch-hit that beautiful home run into the left field stands," wrote author John O'Hare buoyantly, "I jumped to my feet, let out a yell that was heard in my kitchen, and then sat down and cried. I was happy for Mantle, happy for the Yankees, and happy for the human race." Mantle's valiant contribution to the American sporting spirit found expression in the words of U.S. Supreme Court Justice Earl Warren, who told a convention of newspaper editors, "I always turn to the sports section first. The sports page records people's accomplishments. The front page usually records nothing but man's failures."

Not all sporting figures presented an image of traditional Americanism, however. Some, like Joe Namath, represented instead the nation's changing values and life styles. Sports, like cinema and popular music, became more embroiled in the arena of politics and social causes. Symbolic of this trend was World Heavy Weight Boxing Champion Cassius Clay, later to be known as Muhammad Ali--the boxer who "floated like a butterfly and stung like a bee."

Not only was Ali probably the greatest boxer of the century, he was also the most eccentric and outspoken sports figure. Out of the ring he presented the public with a pugnacious, self-centered, and egotistical performance that created a genuine love-hate relationship with fans who helped bring the sport of boxing from a struggling $4 million industry to an $11 million industry in 1966. According to Time, Ali generated around himself a mythology growing from "his ridiculous, irreverent verses, his portentous prophecies, his jazzy clothes..."

Star sportscaster Howard Cosell estimated that "Ali was the most important athlete of the 1960's. He was to become a figure transcendental to sports." Ali's antics successfully challenged the established domain of commissioners and operators, continued Cosell, and "revealed how sports invaded the economics, the law, the politics, the sociology of this society." Along the road to success Ali was converted to the Black Muslim faith and on that basis, he had been ordained a Muslim minister. As a minister, he refused to heed the draft in 1967 and received a five-year prison term. As a result, the World Boxing Association stripped him of his title which he promptly won back after the furor over the Vietnam war had subsided.

Affluence also provided Americans with greater opportunity to patronize the finer things of life such as symphony and art, even if they probably understood it less. In Philadelphia's Academy of Music, Eugene Ormandy's Philadelphia Orchestra drew audiences from around the world, and in New York City Leonard Bernstein drew almost as much acclaim. It seemed almost providential that the world's most advanced society should patronize and encourage the advancement of art--whether that be conceptual, process, video, body, or assorted other new art forms. In the prevailing liberal atmosphere, Americans eagerly supported the so-called avant garde artists who, as outsiders, purported to have a more profound insight than society's more traditional insiders.

Patronization of the arts became a status serving device as well as a real aesthetic experience. By obtaining the world's most precious art pieces, Americans could demonstrate the dominance of their civilization. The nation would become the new Rome and New York City, where most of the budding artists hung out--the new Paris. Los Angeles tried hard not to be outdone. In 1967, for example, the Los Angeles County Museum sponsored the " American Sculpture of the Sixties" exhibition highlighted by David von Schlegel's 42 foot jet delta wings which sparkled cool and in geometric fashion against the prodigal background of Hollywood Hills. Much of america's sculpture reflected the nation's infatuation with urbanism and largess. Commenting on the magnificent work of leading sculptor Alexander Calder, *Look* praised his "delicate ornaments of motion with massive monuments of repose...torch-cut out of heavy metal sheeting and bolted like monster machines, they match the sweep and the thrust of our sky scraper."

Such sculpture represented a romance between art forms and the American people, which, in turn, resulted in an interesting union of culture, social status, capital and official power. THe rich scrambled after the world's most precious art pieces. In 1961 Ailsa Mellon Bruce paid $850,000 for Fragonard's *La Liseuse;* in that same year the Manhattan Metropolitan Museum paid $2,3000,000 for Leonardo da Vinci's *Aristotle Contemplating the Bust of Homer,* and the Washington National Gallery of Art paid $5,000,000 for Leonardo da Vinci's *Ginevra Dei Benci.* In 1965 California industrialist Norton Simon purchased Rembrandt's *Titus* for $2,300,000. The epitome was reached in 1970 when New York's Metropolitan Museum purchased Velasquez's *Juan de Pareja* for $5.5 million.

Art became good business and good promotion. David Rockefeller, President of New York's Chase-Manhattan Bank, spent $800,000 for paintings, sculptures and graphics to decorate the offices and reception areas of his bank's headquarters building in New York City. At the end of the decade he invited 290 of the world's famous artists to a "thank you" celebration at the bank's lavishly decorated top-floor restaurant. As it turned out, his collection by then was worth over $1,500,000, and corporate leaders everywhere scrambled to emulate the patronizing antics of this modern "corporate Medici." Some critics charged that the art museum, once a place of secular spiritual elevation, a place of quiet contemplation, a place of serious intellectual exhibition, was transformed now into a market place spectacle where price supplanted meaning. "Everyone with something to invest was blundering about in its turbid flood like a shark, snapping up artworks," wrote *Time.* The artists considered outstanding, chided *Time,* were those "whose work was underwritten by the capital and by the social opinions of a powerful empire."

What art America could not possess it still sought to be associated with. This was demonstrated during the 1964 World's Fair when Chairman Thomas J. Deegan arranged to bring *Pieta* to New York city, the first time in over 400 years that Michelangelo's splendid sculpture had left Rome. The decade's culminating art event happened appropriately in New York City where Metropolitan's Henry Geldzahler organized a dazzling exhibition called "New York Painting and Sculpture: 1940-1970," in order to demonstrate that the "Big Apple" still commanded the best of American culture.

America's yearning to be associated with high culture did not escape the attention of President Johnson. During June of 1965 the President sponsored the First White House Festival of the Arts in the East Lawn Rose Garden, attracting over 400 poets, painters, sculptors, writers, actors, musicians, photographers, and other accomplished artists. "Culture reigns at the White House for thirteen hours," chided the New York Times. The President then initiated the establishment of the National Endowment for the Arts, and the Endowment for the Humanities soon followed. LBJ also pushed legislation through Congress which would allow Uranium King Joseph Hirshborn to endow a museum of modern art next to the Capitol mall. In spite of all the outward fanfare, however, the nation spent only about seven and one-half cents per person per year on art compared to $2.42 in Germany, $2.00 in Sweden, $1.40 in Canada and $1.23 in Britain.

LBJ's patronization of art demonstrated how the subject served curiously as a vehicle for magnifying the importance of public events. A good example of this occurred in Chicago, Carl Sandburg's "City of the Big Shoulders," where Spain's great sculptor Pablo Picasso received much public attention in 1967 when his 50-foot, 162-ton rusting Cor-Ten steel sculpture was unveiled in the new Civic Center Plaza. Thousands of the city's leading citizens gathered, the Chicago Symphony played Beethoven, poet Gwendolyn Brooks read a special poem, and Mayor Richard Daley called the statue a "free expression" of the "vitality of the city," but no one could tell whether it was "a bird, a woman, an Afghan hound, a Barbary ape, a cruel hoax, a Communist plot, or Superman." A policeman declared that he liked "it fine--whatever it is," a statement which well revealed America's incessant but naive fancy for art.

The advent of Pop Art in 1962, Op Art, and then Kinetic and the Assemblers, who attempted to free art from the constraints imposed by traditional materials, made art more acceptable to the casual viewer's sensibilities than the Abstract Impressionism which had enjoyed previous dominance in the art field. Pop made art less difficult; it seemed almost as easy as advertising both in its creation and interpretation. "I didn't understand it totally, but then again, why should I have to understand everything?" commented Pop Art admirer Robert C. Scull of New York City; "I liked the idea that I didn't have to say to an artist--or to myself--what is it?" For Scull and many other Americans Pop Art was transient, expendable, low cost, and mass-produced, its production appealing to the urgings of a convenience-oriented society.

Pop Art featured banal subject matter and mundane images of common everyday life such as soup cans, flags, targets, numbers, automobiles, hamburgers, typewriters, cakes, billboards, neon signs, comic books, Coke bottles, and neckties. It drew the viewer's attention to things otherwise not contemplated in a civilization which seldom experienced the romantic image of nature's undisturbed landscape. "By using such familiar props, the Pop artists are commenting on the new urban landscape of supermarkets and motel rooms, of roadsides and TV commercials," wrote Time. "Pop works contain a tacit indictment of a society that allows life itself to be rolled off an assembly line: standardized, specialized, fragmented, and beautifully packaged." It was an art form that "could be grasped instantly by young and old, highbrow and low, farmer and office worker, millionaire and pauper," wrote Carla Gotlieb in Beyond Modern Art, "It depicted subject matter they all were familiar with."

The leading Pop artist was Andy Warhol, described as a "cross between Peter Pan and W.C. Fields." "The thin, acrid sensibility of Andy Warhol remains naggingly insistent, an idiosyncratic talent that can be derided, but not dismissed," wrote Time. Warhol himself found it a little difficult to describe precisely or even define his work, probably because it embodied the bumbled diversity of the complex society in which he lived. "I just paint things I always thought were beautiful, things you use every day and never think about," he conjectured. Warhol believed his art represented the "impersonal products and brash materialistic objects on which America is built today. It is a projection of everything that can be bought and sold, the practical but impermanent symbols that sustain us."

Not all critics were so sympathetic with Pop Art and the other new art forms of the Sixties, however, calling it "kitsch" and "vulgarity." "Somebody piles glass on the floor and that's art. Somebody digs a hole and that's art," admitted Warhol's associate Paul Morrissey; "and to think of the mindless ninnies who devote attention to this gibberish." For all of its social and financial success, many questioned whether anything significant had been contributed by American artists to the world of culture during the Sixties.

Affluence, liberality, complexity, and the yearning for modernity diminished the cloak of provincialism and made Americans generally less dependent on established ways and institutions in the Sixties. The loyalty of the people shifted away from the more localized institutions of government, the church, schools, and the traditional concept of neighborhood toward the federal government and highly organized national institutions such as corporations and labor unions, all political and economic bastions responsible for the phenomenal economic growth. Even the nation's heroes and villains became national in character rather than more regional and local as they had once been.

The shift in loyalty to the massive organization manifested itself especially in the declining emphasis on the nuclear family. Divorce rates increased dramatically; people married later and had fewer children. Divorce increased from 2.2 per 1,000 population in 1960 to 3.5 in 1970. According to the Gallup poll, the percentage of persons believing that four or more was an ideal number of children decreased to 23 percent, compared to 49 in 1945. The birth rate fell below 2.11, the estimated population replacement level; and the rate of population growth slowed by almost 50 percent during the decade.

The concept of marriage was de-emphasized in the mass media. Heroes and heroines seldom appeared shackled by the bonds of marriage or permanent commitment. The general public seemed to prefer the excitement of spontaneous romance over the image of mundane married life. The public eagerly followed the decade's most dramatic romance, involving Elizabeth Taylor and Richard Burton, which began during the filming of Cleopatra in 1962. Their lustful antics around the night club circuit stirred up a mild furor, and the couple forsook their mates in 1964 for marriage to each other in order to avoid the stamp of scandal.

By the end of the decade, however, the public ceased to frown on such relationships as long as they did not materially interfere with professional and career responsibilities. Illicit affairs no longer presented much of a threat to the careers of conspicuous people; in fact, large portions of the public vicariously enjoyed these affairs. Living together outside of marriage and having children out of wedlock could hardly be said to be a social taboo anymore for those who could afford it. Composer-conductor Andre Previn and actress Mia Farrow became parents without considering marriage, as did actress Vanessa Redgrave and actor Franco Nero. "I don't think marriage would make me a very nice person to live with," observed Redgrave; and her actress sister, Lynn, conjectured that "it's so easy to go wrong, I think you should live for quite a while with the man you love before even thinking of marriage." Upon ending her marriage with Roger Vadim, actress Jane Fonda suggested that "two people living together all their lives is almost unnatural." International playgirl Brigitte Bardot frankly stated, "I live and love by no rules but my own."

Divorce was probably a greater emotional and economic problem for average people. Marital distress prompted some clergy to call for sanctioning trial marriage. It "would be vastly superior to our present system which is marriage, divorce, and re-marriage," argued Dr. Edward Craig Hobbs of Berkeley's Episcopal Divinity School. According to Dr. Robert

Lee, San Francisco Theological Seminary, however, since "intercourse during engagement is becoming standard," the time of betrothal, in effect, "has become a trial marriage." Philosopher Sydney Harris suggested that the increasing divorce rate related to an "overinflated concept of romantic love in modern society" and offered a principle once asserted by Goethe: "Love is an ideal thing, marriage a real thing; a confusion of the real with the ideal never goes unpunished." Whatever the reasons, divorce increased loneliness and anguish in society; and even with the adoption of no-fault divorce, the courts became overburdened with civil suits and their property settlements.

Affluence and the prosperous liberalism of mid-decade granted Americans a time to reflect, refine, and expand upon the opportunities of democratic life. The strenuous debates of the Thirties over the nature of America's modern political economy had subsided with the return of postwar prosperity. For a rare moment in their history Americans enjoyed the leisure of considering the quality of human life in a materially rich society. The democratization process manifested itself most poignantly among those who sat behind the great mahogany bench inside the Corinthian temple that housed the United States Supreme Court. Here, under the persuasive leadership of Chief Justice Earl Warren, the highest court sensed that the time had come to make principles of equality and harmony a reality in law rather than just theory.

Earl Warren, once Governor of California, was a lifelong politician who possessed an inordinate capacity to achieve consensus among his more loquacious colleagues and to give the Court historical direction. An "activist" jurist, Warren "brought to the bench an expansive and unremitting belief in the strength and power of the law." Under his astute leadership, the High Court became more subjective in its decision making and even practiced what some might call judicial legislating; it began to forsake the traditional judicial process which emphasized analytical reasoning, hewing to precedent, and social neutrality. Yet the Warren Court was probably more in harmony with its time than any other, and the profound social impact of its decisions typified a statement once made by the revered former Justice Oliver Wendell Holmes: "We are very quiet there, but it is the quiet of a storm center."

Earl Warren was appointed Chief Justice in 1952 by President Eisenhower, who later sometimes regretted his choice. "It was the most damn-fool appointment I ever made," exclaimed Ike, who had expected Warren to be a moderate conservative. Warren quickly established his judicial liberalism in the <u>Brown</u> vs. <u>Topeka</u> cases, which represented his belief that an infringement on the rights of even a single individual was an infringement on the rights of all as guaranteed in the Bill of Rights. In that sense "he went back to the roots of the national being," wrote Max Lerner. "In the modern American Babylon he was a prophet of the 'civic religion,' which Cushing Strout has located at the point where liberty, law, religion and morality converge."

The Warren Court moved resolutely to strengthen the right of free expression. Throughout most of American history the Court had based its decisions on the English common law doctrine of "bad tendency," which favored governmental stability over potentially disruptive criticism. Not until the Twenties did Justice Oliver Wendell Holmes define the "clear-and-present-danger" doctrine which favored the free expression of critics unless their criticism presented a direct threat to the ability of government to maintain order. During the McCarthy period the tide turned back toward a "bad tendency" view. But by the late Fifties the Court, led by the tireless prodding of Justice William O. Douglas, began dramatically to expand once again the purview of free expression.

"Secrecy in government is fundamentally anti-democratic, perpetuating bureaucratic errors. Open debate and discussion of public issues are vital to our national health," maintained Justice Douglas. Even though "ideas have been the most dangerous forces in the history of mankind," Douglas believed that a free people must bear the risk. "Free speech has occupied an exalted position because of the high service it has given our society," argued Douglas. "Its protection is essential to the very existence of a democracy." Free expression would serve the nation better than repression because "the airing of ideas releases pressures which otherwise might become destructive." Douglas argued that free expression expedited progress. "When ideas compete in the market for acceptance, full and free discussion even of ideas we hate encourages the testing of our prejudices and preconceptions," which, in Douglas' mind, often needed practical rearranging in order to accommodate stable change. "Full and free discussion keeps a society from becoming stagnant and unprepared for the stresses and strains that work to tear all civilization apart."

The famous 1957 Yates vs. United States case probably revealed more than any other decision how Douglas' faithfulness to free expression influenced the Court's determination to protect the rights of individuals from the infringement of highly-organized institutions, especially the government. In Yates the Court limited the powers of government to prosecute unpopular political minorities under the infamous Smith Act passed by a panicky Congress in 1940. Justice Hugo Black, one of the most progressive and colorful jurists of the century and absolute defender of First Amendment guarantees, spoke for the

Court. "Governmental suppression of causes and beliefs seems to me to be the very antithesis of what our Constitution stands for. Unless there is complete freedom for expression of all ideas, whether we like them or not, the government becomes the censor," argued the luminous Black. "The First Amendment provides the only kind of security system that can preserve a free government, one that leaves the way wide open for people to favor, discuss, advocate, or incite causes, however obnoxious and antagonistic such views." For opinions such as these Justice Black, who had usually served in valorous dissent prior to the Warren majority, became known as the jurist who hammered the Bill of Rights through the fabric of American law. His constant proddings enhanced the Court's efforts to make America a more free and open society.

During the Sixties the High Court moved to protect the freedom of expression in many other areas. In Sullivan vs. New York Times, a landmark 1964 case, the court ruled that a public figure could successfully sue a publication for libel only when the writer clearly demonstrated a reckless disregard for whether the material contained in an article might be false. In this case Justice William J. Brennan, Jr., speaking for a unanimous Court, defined a "national commitment to the principle that debate on public issues should be uninhibited, robust, and wide open." The "Times Rule" gave the press more freedom to criticize public officials and cured the ever-growing appetite of those in power to suppress information. The benefit of doubt now lay on the side of the press. "The special nature of liberties is that they can be defended only as long as we still have them," contended CBS commentator Eric Sevareid, "so the very first signs of their erosion must be resisted."

Another area of free expression involved student demonstrations. When students were expelled from a Des Moines, Iowa, high school in 1965 for wearing black arm bands in silent protest to Vietnam, the Court, speaking through Justice Abe Fortas, ruled in the famous Tinker case that such protest was "closely akin to pure speech" and protected under the First Amendment, as long as it did not create disorder.

The "dim and uncertain" line between obscenity and constitutionally protected free expression continued to be a problem for the Court. Three tests of whether material was pornographic had been worked out in a series of decisions: (1) whether the material was "utterly without redeeming social importance;" (2) "whether to the average person, applying contemporary community standards, the dominant theme taken as a whole appeals to prurient interest;" and, (3) whether it "goes substantially beyond customary limits of candor" to the point of "patent offensiveness." No two judges applied these tests in the same way, of course, leading to many controversies. In the case of John Cleland's Fanny Hill, a 200 year old memoir of an exotic, sensual woman, the lower courts remained hopelessly divided. In New York the book was allowed for its "literary value," while in Massachusetts it was sanctimoniously banned. In the midst of controversy, the restraints on obscenity were relaxed, however. The Court let stand a ruling that "no photograph of the female anatomy, no matter how posed, if no sexual activity is being engaged in, or however lacking social value, can be obscene."

While the Court generally held that sex-filled publications could be censored, the members themselves, found it impossible to arrive at a satisfactory definition of obscenity. In Ginzburg vs. United States (1966), the Court upheld Ralph Ginzburg's conviction based on advertising in his magazine Eros which one Justice said, featured "the leer of the sensualist." Justice William Brennan for the Court wrote that "where the purveyor's sole emphasis is on the sexually provocative aspects of his publications, that fact may be decisive."

In the dissenting opinion in the Ginzburg Case, Justice Hugo Black demonstrated how obscenity represented a matter which defied precise definition. The criteria employed by the Court was "so vague and meaningless," wrote Black, "that they practically leave the fate of a person charged with violating censorship statutes to the unbridled discretion, whim and caprice of the judge or jury which tries him." The problem with obscenity was like beauty; it essentially rested in the eyes of the beholder. Given strict definition, even the Bible could be interpreted as unsafe reading material for the immature mind. Confusion resulted from the fact that no two individuals held exactly the same viewpoint regarding offensiveness. Individual viewpoints could be inconsistent from one time to the next. The effects of a publication depended upon unpredictable variables.

Justice Black argued that no "average" individual existed to whom the question of obscenity could be reasonably addressed. Every individual came to the question with a different mix of "personality, habits, inclinations, attitudes, and other individual characteristics." He contended further that it was impossible to define the "community" by whose standards publications were supposed to be judged. "Nothing that has been said," complained Black, "leaves me with any kind of certainty as to whether the 'community standards' referred to are world-wide, nation-wide, section-wide, state-wide, country-wide, precinct-wide, or township-wide." He questioned whether "community standards" could be expected to be the same "in Mississippi as in New York, in Vermont as in California?"

Justice Black also argued that "redeeming social value" could never be determined objectively. This element of interpretation was as uncertain as "the unknown substance of the Milky Way," conjectured Black. "Whether a particular treatment of a particular subject is with or without social value in this evolving, dynamic society of ours is a question upon which no uniform agreement could possibly be reached among politicians, statesmen, professors, philosophers, scientists, religious groups or any other type of group, "warned Black. "Not even the most learned judge, much less a layman, could possibly determine obscenity "as that term is confused by the Court today."

The obvious confusion over the definition of obscenity left the interpretation of pornography unsettled in the Sixties. Most believed that the sexual experience represented a highly important arena, but many feared that erotic realism in some publications had gone too far. A future Court would come along and confuse the matter even further.

Another vital area of free expression involved the right of privacy. The Court became embroiled in the questions concerning the employment of electronic bugging and eavesdropping devices by law enforcement officials. In _Berger_ vs. _New York_ (1967) the Court struck down a New York State statute which permitted trespassory invasion of a constitutionally protected area by general warrant. The statute infringed upon the "zone of privacy" guaranteed by the Fourth Amendment, wrote Justice William O. Douglas, known by now as the Court's "mover and shaker," whose single-minded goal was getting "the government off the backs of the people." According to Justice Tom C. Clark, who wrote the majority opinion, "few threats to liberty exist which are greater than that posed by the use of eavesdropping devices." In the ruling the Court obliged law enforcement officials to make their eavesdropping warrants more specific about information which was to be gathered, to show more probable cause that a crime was in process, and limit the warrants to more specific periods of time. A few weeks later in _Katz_ vs. _United States_ the Court ruled that Fourth Amendment protection extended to people as well as places, thus disposing of the government's argument that "search and seizure" involved only the defendant's residence. Earlier in _Mapp_ vs. _Ohio_ (1961), a case involving the invasion of Dollree Mapp's home by police, a Cleveland court had ordered state courts to exclude evidence obtained in violation of the Fourth Amendment.

The High Court's determination for individual rights carried it into the foggy area of insuring the rights of the accused. In _Gideon_ vs. _Wainwright_ (1963) the Court ruled that defendants must have the right to counsel in all felony trials. As a result Clarence Gideon, an indigent Florida wanderer, later won retrial for attempted burglary and was declared innocent.

In Escobedo vs. Illinois (1964) the Court ruled that under the authority of the Sixth and Fourteenth Amendments counsel must be present at the moment police interrogation begins. This resulted in the dropping of murder charges against Chicagoan Danny Escobedo, who had previously been forced to confess without the benefit of legal assistance. When a suspect finds himself in "police custody, surrounded by antagonistic forces, and subject to the techniques of persuasion" belonging to the modern interrogator, wrote Warren, he "cannot be otherwise than under compulsion," and a "badge of intimidation."

In its most controversial decision, Miranda vs. Arizona (1966), the Court placed strict safeguards around criminal defendants' rights of self-incrimination, ruling that confessions obtained without informing defendants of their precise rights must be excluded. Again the court contended that criminal suspects were at an enormous disadvantage in the normally coercive atmosphere of arrest and interrogation. It placed the burden of informing suspects of their rights squarely on the police. Police activities came under the Court's scrutiny in other areas as well.

The Supreme Court also moved into the sticky area of reapportionment, which until the Sixties had been mainly a province of the states. In the view of the Court this issue related fundamentally to the individual's right to function equally in the democratic process. The Constitution guaranteed equal voting representation, yet the states were grossly malapportioned. The malapportionment favored reactionary "country interests" and greatly reduced the ability of state governments to accommodate the needs of burgeoning urban areas. In Baker vs. Carr (1962) the Court ordered the state of Tennessee, which had not been significantly reapportioned since 1901, to create voting districts based upon an equality of numbers. This was followed by the famous Reynolds vs. Sims (1964) decision.

Chief Justice Earl Warren spoke the mind of the Court: "Undeniably the Constitution of the United States protects the right of all qualified citizens to vote....The right to vote freely for the candidate of one's choice is the essence of a democratic society...." Legislatures should "represent people, not trees or acres," continued Warren. "Legislatures are elected by votes, not farms or cities or economic interests. As long as ours is a representative form of government and our legislatures are those instruments of government elected directly by and directly representative of the people, the right to elect legislatures in a free and unimpaired fashion is a bedrock of our political system." The Court tried to further impose its concern for pure majoritarian democracy in later cases by requiring as closely as possible legislatures to achieve "precise mathematical equality." One-man-one-vote brought vociferous complaints from the traditional parochial interests who had become accustomed to rule by gerrymander, but the decisions clearly represented a victory for those who struggled to perfect the democratic process.

One of the most controversial of the Warren Court decisions was Engel vs. Vitale (1962) which outlawed officially sponsored prayers in the public schools. The case involved the New York Board of Regents which had approved a brief prayer to be recited in the classroom at the beginning of each school day. Speaking for the Court, Justice Black called this "wholly inconsistent with the Establishment Clause" of the Constitution. The decision merely outlawed "officially sponsored" prayers; any student still possessed the right of free religious expression.

The decision received support from the National Council of Churches, which explained that "teaching for religious commitment is the responsibility of the home and the community of faith rather than the public schools." But to most Americans this represented an affront to their religious predilections. "An outrageous edict which has numbed the conscience and shocked the highest sensibilities of the nation," complained Georgia Senator Herman E. Talmadge. The Court has "now officially stated its disbelief in God Almighty," lamented the trenchant Congressman L. Mendel Rivers of South Carolina. Former President Herbert Hoover expressed his deep concern for the "disintegration of a sacred American heritage," and recommended that Congress submit a constitutional amendment establishing "the right of religious devotions in all government agencies, national, state and local."

Some citizens, however, such as the brisk Madalyn Murray O'Hair, "the most hated woman in America," attempted to persuade the Court that it should eliminate all reference to God in public affairs. Murray crusaded to get "under God" out of the Pledge of Allegiance and to eliminate government-paid military chaplains, income tax deductions for church contributions, and tax exemptions for church-owned property, and even to eliminate Christmas carols in the public schools. "If people want to go to church and be crazy fools, that's their business," stormed Murray, "but I don't want them praying in ball parks, legislatures, courts and schools. I don't want to see their religion emblazoned on the public buildings I look at. They can believe in their virgin birth and the rest of their mumbo jumbo, as long as they don't interfere with me, my children, my home, my job, my money or my intellectual views." In later cases the Court upheld such references to God as "In God We Trust" on the American coin and sided with those who argued that Christmas carols had long ago lost any purely religious significance but rather represented part of a cultural inheritance that marked a civilized society.

The decisions concerning religious freedom best exemplified the Warren Court's capacity to accommodate the "felt needs" of the time without destroying the fundamental traditions which undergirded the national consciousness. Warren's story "was the triumph of sheer character over the doubts and divisions of American life," wrote Max Lerner. Indeed, the Court's activistic brilliance of the Sixties proved to be a modern manifestation of English author Dr. Samuel Johnson's 18th century insistence that "the law is the last result of human wisdom acting upon human experience for the benefit of the public."

Affluence and the cosmopolitan, urban-oriented atmosphere of the high Sixties caused religion to lean in the direction of modernism and liberalism along with an accent on social activism and political involvement. Even though 42 percent of Americans still summoned the minister first in time of trouble, church membership barely held steady while church attendance declined drastically, as parishioners became increasingly more enthralled with the glamour and glitter of temporal affairs. More than 80 percent of Americans believed in the Ten Commandments, according to a Gallup poll, but fewer than half could identify five of them. Religious apathy, coupled with the growing complexity of modern social and theological challenges, rubbed harshly on the conscience of church leaders as they sought to reassert the influence of religion in a predominantly secular society. At least they wanted to avoid the designation English clergyman Sydney Smith once ascribed: "What a pity it is that we have no amusement in England but vice and religion."

Presbyterian theologian Dr. Sam Keen described the religious mood of the time as a "wonder eclipse." Most Christians regard religion as "nothing more than an insurance policy against fire in the next world," complained one dejected clergyman. "The problem now is that 96 percent of us claim at least some affiliation with a church," complained Dr. Franklin H. Littell, Professor of church history at the Chicago Theological Seminary, but do not participate--"what we've got to do is evangelize the 'Christians.'" Writing from Birmingham's city jail, Dr. Martin Luther King warned that "if the Church of today does not recapture the sacrificial spirit of the early Church, it will lose its authentic ring, forfeit the loyalty of millions, and be dismissed as an irrelevant social club with no meaning for the 20th century." Churches can no longer afford to "stew in their own juice," proclaimed Earlham's Professor D. Elton Trueblood; they must "penetrate the world." Hence, the new watchword for religious action would involve "comforting the afflicted and afflicting the comfortable."

The wave of religious activism was highlighted by the rise of profound new theological ideas aimed at achieving an urban spiritual reality. In large part the new theology was based on the ideas of Christian realism forwarded earlier in the century by such super-theologians as Reinhold Niebuhr, Paul Tillich, and John Robinson. Contending that the old-time religion depended too much on outmoded tribalistic and rural images, Harvey Cox, in his Secular City (1964), called for a drastic modernization of America's theological precepts. In the new "age of urban secularization," dominated by the "supercity" and "technopolis," argued Cox, theology must forsake its agrarian motifs of the past for motifs relevant to automation, mass communication, superhighways, and high-rise living. "Life is a set of problems, not an unfathomable mystery," asserted Cox pragmatically, and "we shall have to stop talking 'God' for awhile" as Christians move beyond existentialism and demythologized religion in order to bring religion back to relevance. "One of religion's most important features is its intractable irrelevance, its eccentricity, its downright inconvenience," complained Cox. "Religion is an antique settee on the freeway, an almost indecipherable old song disturbing the beep of computers."

Most leaders within the religious establishment accepted Cox only to a degree. His thoughts represented good commentary for spiritual thought, maybe, but he was not to be taken too seriously. Some theologians, however, moved beyond Cox, declaring God dead. They hoped that this dichotomous imagery would shape the American religious consciousness into a more realistic experience of God through the life of Jesus Christ. Convinced that the old religion was pervaded with "self-delusion and more than a little antiquarian romanticism," such spokesmen as Thomas Altizer and William Hamilton called for a theology that would bring "the ancient church from the universe of discourse" into the real world. According to Altizer, the original transcendent Biblical God "died" when he became Jesus, no longer "wholly other," as Karl Barth would have it, but "an eminent part of mankind, a divinity that men could reach for in themselves."

Altizer later admitted that this talk about the death was really the death of neo-Orthodoxy. Nevertheless, the "God Is Dead" idea became the subject of many fiery sermons among the more traditional clergymen and awakened some interest in religion even in the universities where stodgy professors anxiously drew comparisons to Friedrich Nietzsche's 19th century criticism of conventional Christian piety. Actually the movement served to broaden America's religious perspective. It "cleared away some simple-minded notions of what the life of God means," admitted one critic, Dean John Killenberger of Berkeley's Graduate Theological Union.

Conventional theology received a further jolt with the publication of The New Morality (1965), a book written by Joseph Fletcher of the Episcopal Theological School in Cambridge, Massachusetts. The new morality represented the ultimate application of pragmatic philosophy to religion. Fletcher attacked the dogmatism of traditional morality, claiming that its inflexibility usually rendered itself inapplicable in modern circumstances. Fletcher called for "situation ethics," based more on neighborly concern and social responsibility than traditional restraints. In the situational approach, "one enters into every decision-making moment armed with all the wisdom of the culture, but prepared in one's freedom to suspend and violate any rule except that one must as responsibly as possible seek the good of one's neighbor," wrote Fletcher.

Under careful scrutiny Fletcher's new morality appeared more like a modern restatement of the Biblical Golden Rule than heresy, even though it was attacked vociferously by conservative clergymen. Liberal churchmen embraced the new morality seriously, however. Princeton theologian Paul Ramsey argued that St. Paul himself taught that through Christ "we are delivered from the law," and added that a "list of cans and cannots are meaningless" anyway. Yale chaplain William Sloan Coffin hailed Fletcher's substitution of "guideposts" for "hitching posts," and Harvard's Gordon Kaufman suggested that in an age of contraceptives situational ethics had become more applicable anyway than most people would readily admit.

In an era dedicated to action even the new theology could not restore the traditional importance of religion. Yet the concern for fundamental human values seemed irrepressible, and it was left to Charles Schulz, himself a lay preacher and the creator of the popular Peanuts comic strip and cartoon series, to translate value lessons into a language that common people best understood. Millions of Americans followed Schulz's main character, Charlie Brown, through overbearing dilemmas which related exactly to such theological questions as original sin, neighborly concern, and the worship of graven images. The cartoon series was "more important than making cracks about the President," explained Schulz, uneasy at times with the shallow cynicism of the activist critique; "It's getting down to the problems that people have, fears and anxieties." In the comic strip Pogo, Walter Kelly's comment on human nature later punctuated the decade: "We have met the enemy, and he is us."

One mark of the new theology was its search for religious mutuality. This bolstered the ecumenical movement which flourished at mid-decade. The National Council of Churches enthusiastically sponsored ecumenicalism, envisioning a new unity among Christ's believers and the transcending of old differences based on creed, ritual, and policy. The movement seemed natural in an atmosphere which revered administrative and organizational efficiency, stressed social compassion rather than ideological differences, and advocated the reduction of international barriers. The movement was world-wide but received its most significant impetus at the direction of Pope John XXIII when he told the Second Vatican Council in 1962 that "the whole world expects a step forward."

The ecumenical movement was led in the United States by the Reverend Eugene Carson Blake, Stated Clerk of the United Presbyterian Church and soon to be Secretary of the World Council of Churches. From the pulpit of San Francisco's beautiful Grace Episcopal Cathedral, Blake called for a united church "truly catholic, truly reformed, truly evangelical."

Ecumenical cooperation "could carry the Christian message more effectively to city slums, expand missionary efforts overseas, and make the word and the sacrament available to every person in every acre of the land," predicted Blake. "By 1965 the Lutherans, Presbyterians, and the Roman Catholics were thick as thieves, working together on a common theological program," boasted Blake. "If you take the decade of the Sixties, when historians write it, it will be a tremendous, almost miraculous development of the idea of the unity of the one church of Jesus Christ." Under Blake's meticulous direction the prestigious Consultation on Church Union (COCU) was organized, involving mainly Presbyterians, Methodists, Episcopalians, and the United Church of Christ; and, eventually, many smaller protestant denominations plus Roman Catholics and Jews. Episcopal Bishop C. Kilmer Myers of California summarized the prevailing optimism concerning church union when he went so far as to advocate "a reunited church under the Pope as chief pastor and spokesman."

Church unification among large denominations never materialized, but the ecumenical spirit provided for the establishment of a unique series of cooperative ministries dedicated to rendering social and religious relief in the new urban climate. The practical model for these ecclesiastical ministries came from Manhattan's liberal Riverside Church, where the famous Harry Emerson Fosdick had once preached and served. Under the astute leadership of the Reverend Robert James McCracken, the church welcomed all faiths in a common effort to alleviate urban problems in the heart of New York City. It sponsored integrated housing projects, day care services, adult education courses, an experimented with more relevant forms of music in its worship services. "The Christian faith has not been tried and found wanting, it has been found difficult and left untried," asserted McCracken, quoting Lord Chesterton.

Important new ideas for cooperative ministries came from Chicago's Ecumenical Institute, founded in 1957 by a group of persons believing that the conventional parish could no longer serve "the missionary needs of the modern city." In this modern monastery dozens of interns, fellows, and regular clergy pursued common community projects, worshipped, ate, worked, and prayed together. The experience oriented "the minds of clergymen to secular realities," explained Dean Joseph Mathews, and set "the mood, style, and pattern of the post-modern world view," while promoting "life styles and structures necessary for Christianity's years ahead."

In Detroit a coterie of clergymen organized and Industrial Mission to minister among industrial workers during lunch and shift breaks. "We have in America an industrial society dominated by great corporations," explained the ministry's founder, the Reverend Richard S. Emrick, an Episcopal Bishop, "yet the church has no relevance unless the tremendous insights of our spiritual heritage are ... applied to industry."

The new emphasis on cooperative ministries inspired many refreshing forms of creative ministries, designed to close the gap between the pulpit and the laity. Dr. Truman Douglass, champion of creative and experimental ministries from the United Church of Christ, complained that "all of us are obsolete. The new world emerging demands a new style of church and leadership for which we are unprepared. Douglass urged modern clergymen to "meet people where they carry on their most vital tasks." Douglass inspired the Homeland Ministries Board to sponsor a ministry among the tenants of a new high-rise apartment building in Pittsburgh. The ministry occurred in "the laundry room, the sundeck, the lobby--anywhere that residents gather to talk," reported _Time._

Many creative ministries followed. In Chicago, the Reverend Donald N. Kelly established a marketplace ministry amidst the bustling Oakbrook shopping center. We hear "about things that people won't say in a church meeting or to their pastor," commented Kelly, and we talk "to people who have become disenchanted with the church." At the famous California Squaw Valley ski resort, the Reverend Frank Evans organized a weekend ministry around simple hillside worship services and private marriage counseling. In Las Vegas, America's Sin City, the Reverend Richard Mawson doubled as a desk clerk at the infamous Sands Hotel and as a religious consultant in the hotels and casinos along The Strip. Along San Francisco's North Beach the Reverend Donald Stuart ministered to the "night people" in taverns and coffee houses, and inside Manhattan's rambling Erie-Lackawanna commuter train the Reverend Craig Biddle III could be found conducting "worship-on-wheels" for homeward-bound commuters.

One of the decade's most successful experimental ministries involved the "walk-in, drive-in" worship services pioneered by the Reverend Robert Schuller at Garden Grove, California. Sunday morning worshippers could view Schuller and the choir through 25-foot high moveable glass sections while listening through speakers attached to the automobile. On a typical Sunday morning, reported Time , "the church lots are invariably packed with cars carrying rooftop boats, surfboards, golf clubs, and picnic hampers." The cars also brought "sick and disabled, parents with small children, celebrities trying to shun crowds, and many unchurched Christians who just like to meditate by themselves." This "shiny new model for church life," easy-going and informal, further signified how convenience-oriented American society had become.

The new ministries inevitably raised questions about the church's social and political involvement. Christ himself had left uncertain guidelines when he instructed his followers to be "in the world, but not of the world." Liberal churchmen interpreted this dictum as a rationale for social and political activism. "Surely, if chambers of commerce, labor unions, university faculties, and women's clubs properly influence political decisions," contended Eugene Carson Blake, "it is a basic rejection of the importance of God himself if the church is to be inactive or silent." Religion was not "simply a spiritual affair," said Blake, but "interest in the salvation of men, both souls and bodies." Tex Sample, Director of social relations for the Massachusetts Council of Churches, agreed: "The church should be involved wherever there are human values at stake."

More conservative churchmen, such as the decade's most popular preacher, Billy Graham, objected to using the church as an instrument for social and political reform, arguing that "the biblical approach is to change men and men will change society." Yet in the middle Sixties public opinion supported involvement. In 1964 the Christian Century for the first time endorsed a Presidential candidate--LBJ--and wrote strongly-worded editorials castigating Goldwater.

Religious activism manifested itself most dramatically in the civil rights movement. As early as 1960 a United Presbyterian position paper suggested the possibility of creative civil disobedience: "Some laws and customs requiring racial discrimination are, in our judgment, such serious violations of the law of God as to justify peaceable and orderly disobedience or disregard of these laws." In 1963 Eugene Carson Blake led a group of clergymen in a peaceful demonstration against segregation policies at Baltimore's Gwynn Oak Amusement Park. "I don't question that the law is constitutional," Blake said as police arrested him, "but I question whether the law is right."

In Milwaukee, Wisconsin, Father James E. Groppi led a series of massive demonstrations in favor of open housing through the city's Inner Core. Other clergymen became involved with the voter registration campaigns in the South. The National Council of Churches itself strongly supported the massive civil rights march on Washington in 1963. The religious left later became deeply involved in the antiwar movement. One activist, Father Philip F. Berrigan, drew a prison sentence for vandalizing draft boards and conspiring to blow up governmental heating tunnels in Washington, D.C. "It is madness to squander the world's resources on lethal military toys, while social misery and despair rise around a chorus of the damned," asserted Berrigan.

The economic and social plight of black Americans, as accentuated by the civil rights movement, helped reveal the growing divisions of wealth and power in the country. Many clergymen felt guilty about the resulting inequality of opportunity and took action. This prompted the National Council to organize Project Equality in 1965, an ecumenical effort aimed at getting churches to withhold business from companies guilty of racial discrimination in employment. Tax shelters and exemptions had resulted in church denominations owning approximately seven billion dollars of stock in American companies. "The use of church funds in the corporate-responsibility struggle provides vast moral educational possibilities," wrote Frank P. White of the National Council, author of a new booklet entitled, "Corporate Responsibility and Religious Institutions." According to Dr. Howard E. Spragg, Executive Vice President of Homeland Ministries, the church's role in this matter was "to sensitize the conscience of corporations, using our economic power responsibly in terms of raising issues, while avoiding overblown rhetoric and moralistic judgments."

The movement had some impact in 1967 when the United Methodist Board of Missions retracted its ten million dollar investment portfolio from New York City's First National Bank because of a loan it had made to apartheid South Africa. In the Roman Catholic church Bishop Sheen, once renowned for his conservatism, tried to sell a church and give the money to poor blacks. For that his unhappy parishioners helped have him ousted as the Bishop of Rochester.

Religious activism created deep, noticeable divisions within most church denominations later in the decade, yet the Sixties proved to be one of the richest eras of religious history in America. De Tocqueville's famous century-old observation that "not until I went to the churches of America and found the flame for righteousness did I understand the greatness and genius of America" still applied. And Billy Graham was probably more correct than even he himself realized when he conjectured that "you take the church out of America and see what kind of hell you'd have here overnight."

Prosperity, optimism, convenience, and confidence--these were words that helped describe American civilization during the high Sixties. The roaring good times gave Americans a smug sense of superiority; and none expressed much surprise in 1967 when Joseph Stalin's daughter, Allilueva Stalina, defected from the Soviet Union to taste the rich fruits of democracy. Americans gloried in the belief that the entire world envied the astounding material success of democratic capitalism. Americans lived munificently as though the good times were permanent; and LBJ lavished in popularity, certain of his greatness in history.

Yet just below the surface of the glamour lurked explosive historical forces which would bring about President Johnson's political demise and soon leave American society bitterly divided. These forces were unleashed in the course of the civil rights movement, the Vietnam war, and the youth rebellion--a combination of events which would render America prostrate by 1970, the illustrious expectations of a temporal millennium tragically shattered.

CHAPTER VI

THE RISE AND FALL OF THE CIVIL RIGHTS MOVEMENT

By the time Lyndon Johnson entered the presidency, civil rights had become a primary national concern endorsed by liberals and widely covered by the press. America "is a country where institutions profess to be founded on equality, and which yet maintains the slavery of black men," once observed British philosopher John Stuart Mill as he contemplated the guilt Americans felt about their racial dilemmas. The Civil War had eradicated slavery but not discrimination against blacks; and in the new atmosphere of democratic liberalism, Johnson sensed the opportunity to place the full weight of the presidency behind stronger civil rights legislation. "One of the presidents (Lincoln) I admire most signed the Emancipation Proclamation 100 years ago," Johnson told members of the National Urban League, his fists clenched, "but emancipation was a proclamation and was not a fact. It shall be my purpose, and it is my duty, to make it a fact." Johnson told Congress that "should we defeat every enemy, and should we double our wealth and conquer the stars and still be unequal to this issue, then we will have failed as a people and as a nation."

Johnson's personal commitment aside, the pressures on any President for new civil rights legislation would have been strong. Public opinion had swung in favor of legislative action. In 1942, for example, only 30 percent of those sampled believed that black and white children should attend the same schools, compared to 67 percent in 1965. Supported by favorable public opinion, the modern civil rights movement had already established a history of its own and gained widespread support from other institutions. For years the NAACP had persisted before the United States Supreme Court in order to eliminate legally sanctioned segregation. Finally, in 1954, Thurgood Marshall, Special Counsel for the NAACP, persuaded the Court in _Brown_ vs. _Topeka_ to overturn the "separate but equal" doctrine which had been established by _Plessy_ vs. _Ferguson_ in 1896.

Brown vs. _Topeka_ provided the guiding principles for the civil rights movement. The segregation of students by race represented a deprivation of the equal protection of the laws as guaranteed by the 14th Amendment, concluded Chief Justice Earl Warren for the majority, and "in the field of public education the doctrine of 'separate but equal' has no place." The separation of black students "from others of similar age and qualifications solely because of their race generates a feeling of inferiority as to their status in the community that may affect their hearts and minds in a way unlikely ever to be undone," opened Warren, as the Court ordered school districts to implement desegregation plans "with all deliberate speed." In a series of cases during the Sixties the Court strengthened its desegregation posture, even to the point of condoning the busing of students as "a normal and accepted tool of educational policy."

Bolstered by the Coleman Report released by the United States Office of Education in 1966, which showed that lower-income black children performed better in classes with an economic and racial mix than in all-black classrooms, the Court in its 1968 Green decision went so far as to order desegregation plans which promised "realistically to work now." Thus in education as well as in other areas the highest judicial tribunal stood fast for civil rights. Liberals everywhere were elated.

President Johnson understood that the Supreme Court's insistence on civil rights obliged the other branches of government to follow suit. The best model for presidential leadership came in 1957 when Eisenhower had ordered federal troops into Little Rock, Arkansas, to support the integration of Central High School. Eisenhower's initial reluctance was overshadowed during the 1960 presidential campaign when both Nixon and Kennedy campaigned for favorable civil rights planks. Kennedy captured the imagination of blacks, however--and 68% of their vote--when in October he made a special plea for the release of Dr. Martin Luther King from an Atlanta, Georgia, jail where the prominent civil rights leader had been sentenced to four months hard labor for leading a sit-in demonstration at a department store.

President Kennedy initially moved cautiously on civil rights, fearful of political recrimination from the southern Democrats. He appointed a prestigious commission on equal employment opportunity, declared an end to hiring discrimination in federally financed projects, pushed for an end to segregation in interstate transportation, placed a record number of blacks in federal offices, and ceremoniously issued an Executive Order against discrimination in federally-aided housing projects. Kennedy ordered federal troops into Mississippi in support of James Meredith's admittance to the university, but he grimaced at the activities of the Freedom Riders and shied away from recommending the legislation liberals desired.

The real impetus for stronger legislation had to come from the the blacks themselves behind their own indigenous leadership. By the Sixties Dr. Martin Luther King, head of the Southern Christian Leadership Conference, had become America's most prominent black civil rights leader. Born in Atlanta and graduated from Boston University, Dr. King first rose to national fame in 1956 when he led a yearlong boycott against the segregation of public transportation facilities in Montgomery, Alabama.

King's non-violent protest activities at first electrified some Americans and made most of them uncomfortable. Former President Harry Truman called him a "first-class troublemaker," and FBI Director J. Edgar Hoover referred to him as a "liar" and a "communist dupe." By 1964, however, when he received the Nobel Peace Prize, King enjoyed widespread moral support from both blacks and whites. Even then few Americans understood the true philosophy of this modern prophet whose message of brotherhood was rooted fundamentally in traditional American religious and democratic principles. "Injustice anywhere is a threat to justice everywhere."

King appeared as a modern day Moses leading his people from the bondage of second-class citizenship toward the promised land of equal justice and opportunity. Yet King's mission involved the redemption of the entire nation not just blacks. His promised land amounted to a truly integrated community founded on the principles of mutual love and concern rather than the capricious principles of competition and intrigue which he believed had come to dominate American life. According to King, segregation represented a "blatant denial of the unity which we all have in Christ," and the nation could not be at peace with itself until this terrible condition was removed.

King's non-violent tactics flowed from his redemptive mission. By attracting public attention to segregation, thereby forcing it into the political arena, King hoped to challenge the public's conscience to remove this incongruity and establish a more perfect union. "Non-violent direct action seeks to create ... a crisis and establish such creative tension that a community that has constantly refused to negotiate is forced to confront the issue," wrote King in his letter from the Birmingham jail. "It seeks so to dramatize the issue that it can no longer be ignored." King had learned much from Mahatma Gandhi, Indian liberator, and America's 19th century spokesman of non-violent protest, Henry David Thoreau. King believed with Thoreau that "under a government which imprisons any unjustly, the true place for a just man is also a prison." And King understood with Thoreau that "a minority is powerless while it conforms to the majority; but it is irresistible when it clogs by its whole weight. If the alternative is to keep all just men in prison, or give up war and slavery, the State will not hesitate which to choose."

King's democratic idealism was mixed with a pragmatic notion of stimulating redeeming action. On the one hand, he believed in working through established order, never advocating overthrow of the government or special privilege for blacks. Even when nervous authorities became violent, King did not physically retaliate but turned the other cheek. "Let no man pull you so low as to make you hate him," warned King, quoting Booker T. Washington. "Along the way of life, someone must have sense enough and the morality enough to cut off the chain of hate." This powerful image of persistent righteousness greatly influenced his fellow Americans, as revealed in a comment by Cleveland Browns' rambling Jimmy Brown: "He never struck back. So he became my idol." On the other hand, King remained firm in his mission. Even though he did not ask for charity, he demanded long-withheld justice. He persisted unremittingly in his strategy without compromise or exception. "In any non-violent campaign there are four basic steps," he wrote: "collection of the facts to determine whether injustice exists; negotiations; self-purification; and direct action."

While King remained hopeful about the fulfillment of the great American dream, he harbored a few illusions concerning the enormous amount of vociferous resistance his actions would generate. The ultimate racial peace that King sought would surely rattle the very foundations of the comfortable old order and bring about bitter and often unreasoned recrimination not unlike that experienced by unpopular Biblical prophets of old. King became fond of quoting Christ: "I have not come to bring peace, but a sword." King's idealism was tinged with fatalism. "It may get me crucified. I may even die," King once speculated, "but I want it said ... in the struggle that he died to make men free."

Hence the historical paths of the determined prophet King and the reluctant President Kennedy converged once again during the spring of 1963 when the civil rights leader brought his struggle to Birmingham, Alabama, probably the most segregated city in the country. King led a series of marches against discrimination in shops, restaurants, and in public and private employment. Once he was jailed but released on bail. The tension mounted. On May 3, 1963, a thousand demonstrators marched from the Sixteenth Street Baptist Church into the downtown area. Suddenly violence broke out as a horde of helmeted policemen, led by the indomitable police Chief Eugene "Bull" Connor and armed with electric cattle prods, high-pressure fire hoses, and growling police dogs, descended unmercifully upon the hapless black throng, injuring several.

The brutal scene shocked and outraged the nation.

In Birmingham an accord soon followed which desegregated public facilities, expanded employment opportunities for blacks, and established a bi-racial study group. But tension still remained, and it could spread elsewhere. Clearly, the time had come for Kennedy to exercise the moral leadership of the Presidency. "We are confronted primarily with a moral issue," announced Kennedy, "it is as old as the Scriptures and is as clear as the American Constitution."

Kennedy's study of history and politics had convinced him that unabated injustice could lead to serious social disruption and even revolution. "In these moments of tragic disorder," Americans have an obligation "to reject the temptations of prejudice and violence and to reaffirm the values of freedom and law on which our free society depends," Kennedy told a Vanderbilt University audience. In June, after Alabama's pugnacious young Governor George C. Wallace had arrogantly tried to frustrate the admission of blacks to the state university, Kennedy decided to make a nationwide television appeal as he submitted a strengthened civil rights bill to Congress. "We face a moral crisis as a country and as a people," admonished Kennedy. "It cannot be met by repressive police actions. It cannot be left to increase demonstrations in the streets. It cannot be quieted by token moves or talk. It is time to act!"

Southerners balked at Kennedy's new civil rights initiative. Just hours after his television appeal Medgar Evers of the Mississippi NAACP was murdered. A few weeks later four small girls died in an Alabama church bombing. Meanwhile, Senator James O. Eastland, Chairman of the Senate Judiciary Committee, blocked Kennedy's civil rights bill in committee.

In spite of Southern intransigence, public opinion continued to mount for Kennedy's demands for strong civil rights legislation. In August of 1963, one century after the Emancipation Proclamation, over 200,000 Americans marched in Washington, D.C., singing "We Shall Overcome": "Black and White together/Black and White together/ We shall overcome, some day." At the Lincoln Memorial Dr. King delivered, in resonant tones, what might have been the most moving sermon of the century. "Even though we face the difficulties of today and tomorrow, I still have a dream," affirmed King in his magnificent drone. "I have a dream that on the red hills of Georgia the sons of former slaves and the sons of former slave-owners will be able to sit together at the table of brotherhood.... I have a dream that even the state of Mississippi, a state sweltering with the heat of injustice, will be transformed into an oasis of freedom." He closed with a dramatic appeal: "Free at last! Free at last! Thank God Almighty, we are free at last!"

The momentum created by the Washington march and Kennedy's assassination transfixed public opinion so that Johnson could make civil rights a reality. While in the Senate Johnson had been a formidable civil rights foe, but, as President, he became an unswerving supporter. He made his position clear in the 1964 State of the Union Message. "Let this session of Congress be known as the session which did more for civil rights than the last hundred sessions combined," exhorted the President. In an address at Howard University the President used the "foot-race" analogy to rationalize his position. "You do not take a person who, for years, has been hobbled by chains and liberate him, bring him up to the starting line of a race, and then say 'You are free to compete with all the others,' and still justly believe that you have been completely fair," admonished LBJ. The President demanded more than equal treatment; he demanded action which would guarantee equal opportunity, a principle as old as the American dream. In this sense Johnson appealed to a fundamental American notion of equity which emphasized individual merit as the standard of human worth and dignity.

In the U. S. Senate Minnesota's loquacious Hubert Humphrey, who personally had a hand in most of the decade's significant legislation and whose outspoken support for racial equality dated back as far as the 1948 National Democratic Convention, where he had insisted on placing a strong civil rights plank in that year's party platform, led the struggle in the Senate against one of the longest and most acrimonious southern filibusters in history. "The Negro in the South is a happy person. He understands the members of the white race, and they understand him," protested Arkansas Congressman Ezekiel "Look" Gathings. Finally, the liberals resorted to cloture in order to secure the most comprehensive civil rights legislation since Reconstruction.

The Civil Rights Act of 1964 prohibited the use of literacy tests as a voting qualification, made unlawful discrimination in public facilities, authorized the United States Attorney General to file desegregation suits, outlawed discrimination in programs receiving federal funds, made discrimination in employment illegal, and established an Equal Employment Opportunity Commission for enforcement purposes. In 1965 a second act guaranteed voting rights by authorizing the federal government to perform registration procedures and suspending the use of literacy tests. Almost one million new black voters were registered by 1970. In 1968 a third civil rights act sought to guarantee open housing. Thus Johnson accomplished his grandiose civil rights goals. No other president since Lincoln could match his record. "For generations Negro Americans have prayed for a President who would not only see their peculiar disabilities but would do something about them. Lyndon Johnson was such a one," wrote Roy Wilkins of the NAACP. Most Americans believed that civil rights had now been put behind them. Dr. Martin Luther King captured the optimism of the moment when he said, "it has been a sea of great moments for us all."

In the midst of this apparent success, however, a series of ironical, if not inevitable, events turned the civil rights movement into directions which few Americans had anticipated. The ominous events began with Barry Goldwater's capture of the Republican Presidential nomination in 1964. Goldwater had voted against the Civil Rights Act, ruefully citing his states' rights philosophy. His obdurate stand attracted a surprising number of white bigots and other anti-civil rights people. The Congress on Racial Equality (CORE) paraded a coffin outside the Republican convention in order to signify the death of the movement should Goldwater become president.

At the Democratic National Convention a few weeks later civil rights advocates were profoundly disappointed when the most prominent white liberals failed to support the persistent Fanny Lou Hamer and the Mississippi Freedom Party in their effort to unseat the all-white regular delegation. Meanwhile, in California, Proposition No. 14, which would repeal the state's open housing laws, received overwhelming support from voters; and in other parts of the country the middle class and blue collar workers began rallying around the saucy George Wallace.

The facade of racial progress was further stripped away in 1965 when Dr. Martin Luther King brought his movement north to Chicago, where the vile reaction in the blue-collar suburb of Cicero demonstrated that racism was as insidious in the North as the South. King came to Chicago from Selma, Alabama, where he had faced the violent obstinacy of Sheriff Jim Clark, who opposed efforts to register black voters. A 50-mile march from Selma to Montgomery was interrupted by beatings and death. Selma and Cicero proved that mountains of prejudice could not be wiped away with the mere passage of legislation.

Meanwhile, the first of more than fifty inner big city racial explosions occurred in the Watts section of Los Angeles in 1965, when five days of rioting left 34 persons dead, 853 wounded, and 4,000 under arrest. The main business district along 103rd Street was destroyed; the area later became known as "charcoal alley." The bellows of curling black smoke and intermittent exchange of gun fire presented an uncommon and disturbing scene for millions of Americans who had grown complacently accustomed to domestic tranquility. In the next few years riots occurred in other major cities, leaving 107 dead and almost 4,000 injured.

The big city riots were largely spontaneous, the tragic result of horrid living conditions, hot summer weather, unemployment, and police oppression. Whitney Young, Jr., President of the National Urban League, called them the result of "poverty and dope, and the refusal of authorities to crack down on the Mafia, which traffics in narcotics." Many black families had only recently moved north, refugees of southern agricultural mechanization, and were suffering the consequences of being unprepared for northern industrial life, where economic opportunity remained scarce.

The underlying causes of the riots escaped the attention of most whites, however, who preferred to blame communist agitators and irresponsible radicals rather than to grapple with the truth. In Chicago Mayor Richard J. Daley emphatically ordered the police "to shoot to kill any arsonist or anyone with a Molotov cocktail in his hand." The Mayor received applause from poor whites, who, struck by fear, were busily arming themselves against an invasion from black ghettoes, and from the more affluent middle class, which demanded repressive governmental measures. Whites were also beginning to resent not only violence but welfare, court-ordered busing, and open housing legislation. The liberal social architects were left confused and baffled.

The growing white backlash prompted younger, more impatient blacks to advocate a more drastic course of action based on separatism and forceful confrontation. Much of the new black furor took its inspiration from Malcolm X, desperado prophet of the Black Muslim movement. Malcolm X preached racial separation, moral self-improvement, economic self-sufficiency, and pan-Africanism, which meant an ultimate black exodus "back to our own African homeland." Malcolm X showed contempt for American liberalism, calling it a mere placation of blacks. He dubbed Christianity as a White man's religion and taught that blacks "can sometime be 'with' whites, but never 'of' them."

Malcolm believed that "the Negro is better off by himself, so he can develop his character and culture in accord with his own nature." Malcolm X criticized King's non-violent tactics, claiming that "the Negro is justified to take any steps at all to achieve equality.... There can be no revolution without bloodshed," he insisted. "When our people are being bitten by dogs, they are within their rights to kill those dogs," claimed the embittered leader. "No man in our time aroused fear and hatred in the white man as did Malcolm," wrote Melvin S. Handler in the introduction to Malcolm's autobiography, "because in him the white man sensed an implacable foe who could not be had for any price--a man unreservedly committed to the cause of liberating the black man in American society rather than integrating the black man into the society." Malcolm's life was cut short by brutal assassination engineered by a detractor from within the Black Muslim movement in 1964, but by then he had already implanted a fierce black nationalism in the minds of many younger black leaders.

"Black Power" became the symbol of the new black nationalism; "Black is Beautiful" was its slogan. Black Power was not necessarily to be equated with black militancy. Even though it drew much of its rationale and inspiration from persons such as Malcolm X, it represented not so much a radical departure as a maturation of the black-American movement. It represented a tough-minded realistic formula for achieving practical goals. A good many moderate blacks viewed the movement as a wholesome stage in positive advancement toward equality. Responsible black opinion was well represented by Robert S. Browne, Executive Director of the Black Economic Research Center, who said that "we will never again allow ourselves to accede to 'integration' as the sole possible route." "There is nothing in the concept of community control that differs with the belief in an integrated, open society based on pluralism," wrote Urban League Director Whitney Young. "The failure of white institutions to provide equal services for the ghetto means that the black community itself must control its institutions."

Black Power in its best sense emphasized the need for blacks to acquire an indigenous Afro-American consciousness rooted in a pride for black culture and life styles not unlike that of other nationalities which had immigrated to American shores. It called for the repudiation of white majority values, morals, and ethics and for the eradication of the traditional Negro image of "the lazy stupid, crap shooter, chicken stealing idiot," as one proponent put it. Black Power involved both an affirmation and a search for identity. According to one spokesman, it represented "not so much a negation of white power as it is an affirmation of the worth and dignity of the black man without reference to the white ideal."

Black Power represented "an exploration of black culture and the realization that within this culture are those values which a black minority can, without shame, embrace," wrote activist author Addison Gayle, Jr. Gayle described it as "a creative concept aimed at destroying one hundred years of mental enslavement, distorted images and meaningless cliches." He saw it further as "a rebuke to white experts who do not realize that to be black in America is to journey through the fiery labyrinthine corridors of hell."

Black Power called upon blacks to gain control over their own affairs and institutions. At issue was the black individual's "ability to control a part of his life, the ability to control some of the economic forces that now only act on him, the ability to make them act in his own behalf," asserted Julian Bond, Georgia legislator and a founder of the Student Non-Violent Coordinating Committee (SNCC). "Every group in this country owns its own neighborhoods but us," pointed out SNCC's leader Stokely Carmichael. "If we are to proceed toward true liberation, we must cut ourselves off from white people. We must form our own institutions, credit unions, co-ops, political parties, write our own histories," stated a SNCC position paper. By banding together to insure the force of numbers, blacks, much as organized labor a generation earlier, could bargain collectively with whites in order to win their rightful share of American prosperity. "Black Power means black people coming together to form a political force," explained Carmichael. "It's an economic and physical bloc that can exercise its strength in the black community." Put more plainly, Carmichael told a group of whites: "Look, buddy, we're not laying a vote on you unless you lay so many schools, hospitals, playgrounds and jobs on us."

Black Power had many positive results. It resulted in the election of such politicians as Mayors Richard Hatcher of Gary, Indiana, and Carl Stokes of Cleveland, Ohio. It led to rent strikes against absentee landlords who extracted exorbitant rents without maintaining the property, supermarket boycotts against food chains which reserved the highest quality products for suburban stores without differentiating in price, and the beginnings of black capitalism and the organization of citizen police protection associations. It prepared blacks for employment opportunities. The Center for Community Action led by CORE founder James Farmer, for example, stressed remedial education, job training, and retraining. The Center operated upon the proposition that while "picket lines may pay off old scores, vocational training will pay the grocery bill." Such activities envisioned economic and neighborhood control for blacks.

"Operation Breadbasket" in Chicago, under the leadership of Jesse Jackson, sought to bring food to the inner city poor. In Detroit the East Side Voice of Independent Detroit, under the direction of the burly Frank Ditto, who called himself a responsible agitator, initiated several "black pride" projects. "Operation Bootstrap" in Watts found employment for skilled blacks. In Indianapolis black clubs removed trash in massive neighborhood clean-up efforts. "Slums are made by people, not by plaster or bricks," asserted sponsor Mattie Rice Coney proudly. "Civic rebuilding begins with people who care about themselves." On Broadway an all-black cast brought _Hello, Dolly_ to its audience in a most refreshing style. These accomplishments gave blacks a new self-confidence and a new sense of purpose necessary for the assertion of their race and culture.

Some of the symbolism and inciting rhetoric connected with the Black power movement, however necessary to stimulate blacks, tended to disturb whites who had not taken the time to understand the experience behind the rhetoric. Whites were offended, for example, when during the 1968 Olympics two black medal winners saluted the playing of "The Star Spangled Banner" by raising gloved fists. Allusions to violence and disruption by Carmichael and his SNCC associate H. Rap Brown proved especially disconcerting to whites. Carmichael first gained national attention in 1966 when he publicly advised blacks not to participate in Vietnam: Tell LBJ "hell no, I won't go." According to Carmichael, ghetto blacks shared more in common with such suppressed groups as the Viet Cong than with their white American compatriots; both groups existed in a colonial status, victims of white capitalistic imperialism. Dark-skinned brothers and sisters should not become instruments of white imperialism against each other.

While seldom advocating outright violence, Carmichael and his followers came armed and prepared to fight back in defense of their neighborhoods. "We believe in violence," claimed Carmichael. "I am using all the money I can raise to buy arms." H. Rap Brown claimed that "violence is as American as apple pie." "If President Johnson is worried about my rifle, wait until I get my atom bomb," shouted Brown. "If you are gonna loot, brother, loot a gun store. Don't be running around here looting no liquor, cause liquor's just for celebrating," harangued Brown. "We ain't got nothing to celebrate about. You better get yourselves some guns, baby." "If America don't come around," warned Brown, "we are going to burn it down, brother. We are going to burn it down if we don't get our share of it."

From San Quentin Eldridge Cleaver, who described himself as a "full-time revolutionary in the struggle for black liberation in America," in his <u>Soul on Ice</u> justified violence by arguing that the black male had systematically been robbed of his masculinity through the years. Soladad brother George Jackson spread revolution among other black prisoners who could easily point to injustice in the legal system. At the University of California the militant Angela Davis, a brilliant young philosophy instructor, provided a Marxist rationale for black revolution.

Black Muslim world heavyweight boxing champion Muhammad Ali told the National Conference of Black Students that "by nature, blacks and whites are enemies." In New York City James Foreman,

Director of the United Black Appeal, demanded $500 million in "reparations" from the nation's white churches and synagogues. "The Church is the jugular vein of the country, because wrapped up in the church is a vital system which helps perpetuate the kind of exploitation of blacks which goes on," explained Foreman.

When Black Power rejected white leadership, the movement lost the crucial support of the Jewish community. Not only had Jews sympathized with the horrors of persecution, but a strong civil rights consciousness served to protect themselves as well. In the early days of the movement Jews stood as martyrs alongside blacks. For example, the two white men who were summarily murdered in Philadelphia, Mississippi, in 1964 along with black James Chaney were Jewish.

A bitter struggle involving the community schools in the Brownsville section of Brooklyn, New York, in 1967 led to a clash between Jews and blacks for control. The dispute drew national attention when the Jewish head of the American Federation of Teachers, Albert Shanker, got involved in an ugly dispute with local blacks over the issue of black anti-Semitism. The Jews were becoming increasingly uneasy about problems of reverse discrimination. While blacks had almost no representation in high influential places such as university faculties, Jews were proportionately overrepresented. Things began to appear too much as if a gain for blacks would be a loss for Jews, hence there was less than complete agreement on a host of civil rights issues ranging from affirmative action to school desegregation. By 1968 Jews had become deeply disturbed about the violence.

The year 1968 proved to be a bad year for the civil rights movement. The Six Day War of 1967 caused further alienation. Radical blacks began to see Israel as a major perpetrator of colonialism in such places as Southern Africa, where many black brothers were falling before rifles obtained in Israel. For their part, the Jews became pre-occupied with the survival of a Jewish state in the face of growing Arab and Soviet hostility.

A group of radical blacks led by Bobby Seales and Huey Newton had organized the Black Panther Party, which actively began preparations for guerrilla warfare in the urban ghettoes. Newton charged that Cleaver had led blacks down the road to "reactionary suicide." In his book <u>Revolutionary Suicide</u>, Newton called for "a United Nations-supervised plebiscite to be held throughout the black colony in which only black colonial subjects will be allowed to participate, for the purpose of determining the will of black people as to their national destiny."

The assassination of Martin Luther King on April 4, 1968, triggered a wave of violence that left forty persons dead. The tragic death of King severely damaged any dreams of racial unity. Instead racial polarization prevailed, and the color line was laid bare. "When White America killed Dr. King, she declared war on us," snapped Stokely Carmichael. "We have to retaliate for the death of our leaders. The executions of those deaths are going to be in the streets." Blacks must "abandon the nonviolent concept used by Dr. King," urged Lincoln Q. Lynch, Chairman of the United Black Front, "and adopt a position that for every Martin Luther King that falls, ten white racists will go down with him." King left a leadership vacuum that the more radical civil rights elements quickly sought to fill, thus reducing further the tentative support previously enjoyed among whites. At the White House President Johnson could see the reflections of a burning city dancing off the Capitol buildings. The idealism had gone out of the civil rights movement. Thus made vulnerable, the movement was destined to grind slowly to a halt under the stern law-and-order policies of the upcoming Nixon Administration.

Lyndon Johnson could point to only scanty progress toward racial equality. The Supreme Court would remain firm, and the media was eliminating many of its most blatant stereotypes. In the film Grasshopper Jimmy Brown would embrace Jacqueline Bisset, remarking that "it couldn't have been done years ago." But in real life basketball star Lew Alcindor would have to file a lawsuit in order to rent the apartment of his choice.

Most disappointing was the fact that equal economic opportunity still eluded blacks. Family incomes for blacks increased 55 per cent during the Sixties compared to 64 per cent for whites. While blacks comprised 11 per cent of the population, only 5.1 per cent possessed an annual buying power of more than $15,000, the estimated income needed to maintain a comfortable standard of living. Only two per cent of the nation's business enterprises belonged to blacks, and only three of the 3,182 highest corporation executives and board directors were black. In the building trades, described as the "bastion of discrimination" by Roy Wilkins, Executive Director of the NAACP, only four per cent of the construction workers were black. Among plumbers, electricians, and skilled manufacturing, the percentage was even lower. Economist Sylvia Porter concluded that for blacks "giant economic strides" had simply not been made "except in the publicity handouts."

Federal assistance for the employment of blacks proved even more disappointing. A soft drinks manufacturer received $950,000 in federal contributions over two years but employed only 22 of the promised 300 blacks. Twenty-two California firms received $11.6 million from the federal poverty program for creating only 1,010 new jobs. Father Theodore M. Hesburgh, Chairman of the United States Civil Rights Commission, summarized the sorry record. "This commission has had it up to here with ... communities that have to be dragged kicking and screaming into the U.S. Constitution," admonished Hesburgh. "People aren't serious about equality of opportunity and the government isn't serious about equality of opportunity."

In the final analysis Americans proved unwilling to face the dire implications of racial equality. Even the President's Kerner Commission, appointed to study racial affairs, declared that "our nation is moving toward two societies, one black, one white--separate and unequal." First white backlash and then black backlash brought about disenchantment, reaction, and withdrawal similar to that which had diminished the post-Civil War civil rights movement a century earlier. Not even the inimitable political antics of Lyndon Johnson could penetrate the unyielding color line, and now the President himself stood to reap the blame for all the violence and default.

CHAPTER VII

THE VIETNAM WAR

While struggling to maintain racial peace at home, President Johnson resolutely backed the nation into a major military conflict abroad. The war which developed in Vietnam eventually became a fundamental matter of conscience with the nation, one greater than any since the Civil War. British novelist Thomas Hardy once argued that "war makes rattling good history; but Peace is poor reading." Such had never been the case with Vietnam, an agonizing foreign policy problem since the late Forties, when President Truman--in an exchange for Europe's support of containment--agreed to support France's claims to a colonial empire in Southeast Asia.

The United States stumbled into the war largely as a result of a bi-partisanship foreign policy. This political practice had been inaugurated along with containment after World War II when leaders of both parties strived to avoid the kind of domestic political divisiveness associated with America's failure to become part of the League of Nations after World War I. Senator McCarthy's vicious anti-communist campaign in the Fifties made it risky for liberal politicians to question the direction of American foreign policy for fear of being labeled "soft on communism." Such conservatives as former President Hoover or Ohio Senator Taft who questioned containment principles found themselves simply labeled as "isolationist" and not taken seriously by the press or the public. Thus criticism became dwarfed. Few anticipated the dangers of bi-partisanship in foreign policy. In retrospect, more Americans should have heeded the warning of nineteenth century philosopher Nietzsche about open debate in a democratic society: "In all institutions from which the cold wind of criticism is excluded, an innocent corruption begins to grow like a mushroom." Mistakes will be discovered only at great cost. Vietnam represented not so much a conspiratorial wrong as much as it represented an unchallenged and well-intentioned wrong-headedness on the part of American policy makers.

Under Truman and Eisenhower two billion dollars in American foreign assistance failed to solidify the French position in Southeast Asia. The Viet Minh nationalists, under the astute political leadership of Ho Chi Minh (He Who Enlightens) and buoyed by the clever guerilla warfare tactics of General Vo Nguyen Giap, brought the French down to humiliating defeat at Dienbienphu in 1954. The French signed the Geneva Accords which provided for unilateral withdrawal and the unification of Vietnam under a single elected leader.

Instead of joining the Geneva Accords, which would have almost certainly left the communist-connected Ho Chi Minh in control, President Eisenhower sponsored the establishment of a pro-western regime in the southern half of Vietnam under the leadership of Roman Catholic Ngo Dinh Diem. Eisenhower resisted pressures for military involvement and strictly limited American aid to diplomatic and material support. "We want to help you to help your people keep from going Communist, but we will not furnish the men," Eisenhower wrote Diem in 1957. Eisenhower's stubborn refusal to accept the Geneva Accords prompted the Vietnam nationalists to organize the National Liberation Front (NFL), the Viet Cong, which successfully began turning the Vietnamese people against Diem.

By the time Kennedy entered office, the Diem government was in serious political trouble; yet Kennedy placed Vietnam squarely in the context of American's cold war containment policy, equating freedom in Vietnam with that of West Berlin. Vietnam represented the "cornerstone of the Free World in Southeast Asia, the Keystone to the Arch, the finger in the dike," proclaimed Kennedy as he significantly increased the material aid to Diem and introduced about 20,000 special advisors into Vietnam. Kennedy, like Eisenhower, however, understood that victory would remain illusive without indigenous support from the Vietnamese people. "In the final analysis, it is their war," conceded Kennedy. "We can help them, we can give them equipment, we can send our men there as advisors, but they have to win it." Kennedy resisted Pentagon proddings to introduce ground forces, telling Florida Senator George Smathers, "Old Eisenhower had more sense than these people. They didn't get him suckered in." Twice Kennedy consulted with former General Douglas A. MacArthur who unequivocally warned against becoming locked in a land war in Asia. Yet Kennedy did not call the war off, fearing serious domestic political repercussions. Eventually Kennedy realized that the Diem government was too ridden with corruption to establish a credible ruling mandate, and the Administration stood quietly by as a military coup marked the bloody end of Diem in November, 1963, just days before Kennedy himself would fall to an assassin's bullet.

President Johnson, not suspecting that he had inherited a triumphant wrong, became the fourth postwar American President to anguish over the Vietnamese enigma. More hawkish than

Kennedy, Johnson harbored few reservations about the ultimate success of American policy in Vietnam. "This nation will keep its commitments from South Vietnam to West Berlin," he confidently told Congress upon Kennedy's death. "The confusing nature of this conflict cannot mask the fact that it is the new face of an old enemy," insisted Johnson, who obviously believed in the inherent goodness and inevitable soundness of American democratic ways. "Regardless of what you hear and regardless of what some of the bellyachers say, we are much beloved people throughout the world," contended Johnson. Anxious to prove that a Southerner could be just as forceful in defending America's international interests as the northeastern foreign policy elite, concerned about potential Red Chinese expansionary designs, protective of Asian trade routes, feeling the need to demonstrate America's invincibility to guerilla warfare, buoyed by the confidence of generals bearing a brand new array of conventional arms, subtly influenced by the military-industrial establishment's desire for still more governmental contracts, and fearful of becoming the first American President to lose a war, Johnson moved the nation toward further involvement in Vietnam.

Johnson' early approach to Vietnam policy enjoyed widespread support from almost the entire foreign policy establishment. Ambassador to South Vietnam Henry Cabot Lodge Jr. suggested the need for escalation to Johnson only hours after he entered the Presidency in November of 1963. Lodge reported grimly that Viet Cong "incidents" had sharply increased. Such limited war advocates as Chairman of the Joint Chiefs of Staff General Maxwell Taylor, the tenacious Army Chief of Staff Harold Johnson, Defense Secretary Robert McNamara, National Security Chief McGeorge Bundy, the new National Security Advisor Walter Rostow, and Secretary of State Dean Rusk all backed Johnson's war position. They advised the President that an escalation of activities in Vietnam could be held to a "clean war" fought from the skies and further contended that LBJ could apply his majestical political skills at home, carefully orchestrating a "peace action" that would hardly cause a ripple on the surface of domestic affairs. Among the President's closest advisors only Under Secretary of State George Ball demurred. "No matter how many hundred thousand white foreign troops we deploy," warned Ball, "I think humiliation would be more likely than the achievement of our objectives--even after we have paid terrible costs."

Secretary of Defense Robert McNamara supported escalation strongly. He argued that as long as Russia and China continued to involve themselves heavily with so-called "wars of national liberation," the challenge must be met by America in the name of democracy and world order. "If we fail to meet it here and now, we will inevitably have to confront it later under an even more disadvantageous condition," McNamara told the House Arms Services Committee. "This is the clear lesson of history which we can ignore only at our peril." Secretary of State Dean Rusk convinced Johnson that Vietnam represented the "ultimate test" of America's resolve to defend the Free World.

In Vietnam "we represent most of the rest of the people of the world," argued Rusk. The guerrilla activities represented the front line of Chinese communist expansion and deserved fundamental American opposition. We "must stay their hand," insisted Rusk, who became even more urgent in his hawkish advice after Red China managed to detonate its first nuclear bomb in October of 1964. "The United States must be prepared for the day," argued Rusk, "when there will be a billion Chinese on the mainland, armed with nuclear weapons, with no certainty about what their attitude would be towards the rest of Asia." In tones resembling Eisenhower's "falling domino" theory, Rusk contended that "the national security and the whole position of the non-totalitarian states of the world may well depend upon the manner in which the United States deals with the challenge of Communist China."

These attitudes attracted bi-partisan support from the U.S. Senate where the silver-tongued Minority Leader Everett Dirksen proclaimed that "if we let South Vietnam go, another giant step in the march of communism will be taken and the remaining nations of the southeast Asian peninsula will be in ever-deepening danger." New York Governor Nelson Rockefeller insisted that "winning the fight for freedom in Vietnam is essential to the survival of all Asia." Johnson could indeed take comfort from this early wide ranging support for his position on Vietnam. Support came all the easier in 1964 because during the Presidential campaign Johnson promised, in response to Goldwater's suggestion to use low-yield nuclear weapons, that as President he would not send "American boys nine or ten thousand miles away from home to do what Asian boys ought to be doing for themselves."

During the first sixteen months of Johnson's Presidency the situation in Vietnam continued to deteriorate ominously. The government seemed to change hands on almost a regular basis. General Nguyen Khan gave way to an upstart 32-year-old flying ace, General Nguyen Coa Ky, who commanded only tenuous control. Senator Goldwater made Vietnam a major political issue in the 1964 campaign, demanding stronger military action. Goldwater complained that once again Democrats were not "winning" global confrontations with the Communists. It was in this rather confused and disruptive political atmosphere that Johnson made his first crucial moves toward war.

The President endorsed a plan involving surreptitious strikes against North Vietnam by Asian mercenaries. The campaign of sabotage would be conducted under American military direction. The operations included commando raids against transportation facilities, PT boat raids against coastal installations, and a kidnapping campaign against key citizens who could be interrogated for information. The President also ordered American destroyers into the Gulf of Tonkin for patrol purposes and to protect South Vietnamese commando groups raiding North Vietnamese positions along the gulf. In early August of 1964 two U.S. destroyers, the Maddox and the C. Turner Joy, were reportedly attacked by North Vietnamese gunboats while operating along the gulf coastline. President Johnson retaliated with a flurry of air strikes against North Vietnamese military installations.

While the brief flurry of air strikes moved forward with almost surgical precision, the President presented his deceptive Gulf of Tonkin Resolution to the U.S. Senate. The resolution authorized the President "to take all necessary steps," including "the use of armed forces," in his efforts to turn back North Vietnamese aggression. The prestigious Chairman of the Senate Foreign Relations Committee, J. William Fulbright, known back home as the "Arkansas hawgcaller," agreed to sponsor the resolution because he viewed it mostly as a political campaign ploy to blunt Goldwater's charges about Democrats being soft on communism. From a strategic point of view Fulbright believed the resolution provided LBJ with only limited authority similar to that granted Eisenhower in 1958 when the American military intervened to help quell a short-lived rebellion in Lebanon. Only two Senators, Wayne Morse of Oregon and Ernest Gruening of Alaska, voted against the resolution. It gave the President too much authority in an affair that could lead to great mistakes and even greater humiliation, they contended. Their contention soon proved correct. The Gulf of Tonkin Resolution, as Under Secretary of State Nicholas Katzenback soon began to argue, represented the "functional equivalent" of a war declaration.

In the months following the Gulf of Tonkin Resolution the temerity of the embittered Viet Cong began to reveal itself in no uncertain terms. A devastating series of attacks were conducted against American installations in South Vietnam. In early November of 1964 a surprise mortar barrage at Bien Hoa Airfield killed five Americans, wounded 76 more, and destroyed six B-57 bombers. On Christmas Eve a bomb exploded in an American officers' billet at Saigon's luxurious Brink Hotel, killing two and wounding almost 100 more. During a vicious six-day battle early in January of 1965 at Binh Gia the American-backed South Vietnamese forces experienced what was reported as a "disastrous" defeat. In response to the dismal reports President Johnson dispatched a hastily organized fact-finding mission led by special Presidential Advisor McGeorge Bundy. Even as Bundy began his mission the Viet Cong struck again. This time the strike hit with devastating quickness at Pleiku just hours after the lunar New Year celebration had ushered in the Year of the Snake. While guerrillas smacked the compound with a barrage of mortar fire, Viet Cong soldiers slipped unseen from the surrounding tall grass, cut their way through the barbed wire encirclement, and blasted several helicopters and light reconnaissance planes with satchel charges. When the smoke of battle cleared, eight Americans lay dead and more than 100 were wounded.

Pleiku spurred Johnson into action. Assistant Secretary of State for Far Eastern Affairs William P. Bundy, George's brother and Dean Acheson's son-in-law, campaigned hard for increased American military pressure that would convince Hanoi "that the price of maintaining the insurrection in the South would be too great." Meanwhile George Ball, who was a protege of Adlai Stevenson, who died during the summer of 1965, and of W. Averell Harriman and who was known in Administration circles as a "Europe Firster," decided to quietly leave the Administration. With voices of moderation leaving, all caution was about to be thrown to the wind. "The worst thing we could possibly do," stormed the piqued President, "would be to let this go by.... It would open the door to a major misunderstanding." Once again the lengthy procession of chauffeured black Cadillac limousines, bearing to the White House the members of the National Security Council for top priority meetings, signaled that a critical turning point in the war was in store. "The time has come for harder choices," McGeorge Bundy reported back to the President. Bundy advised that the South Vietnamese government's downfall seemed imminent.

President Johnson's next decision echoed like a gargantuan thunder clap through the corridors of the world's diplomatic community. Johnson ordered "Operation Rolling Thunder," a highly concentrated and devastating bombing attack against targets in North Vietnam. Operation Rolling Thunder, featuring the mighty B-52 bombers, would continue with only brief interruptions for almost three years. Much of the bombing was aimed at the so-called Ho Chi Minh Trail, a maze of hidden roads and paths that allowed infiltration from North Vietnam south. The trail soon became known as "the highway of death." Johnson ordered the first combat troops--3,500 Marines--into Da Nang, where expansive war preparations were already under way. By the end of 1965 almost 200,000 American military personnel were in Vietnam. The President authorized the Seventh Fleet to begin patrolling in the territorial waters of both North and South Vietnam. The military build-up was accompanied by special pacification teams which penetrated the Vietnamese countryside trying to isolate the common people from Viet Cong political influence.

During the next two years Johnson would commit over 500,000 American troops and over $100 billion to the war effort while insisting that his policy represented one of "gradual response" fashioned after modern limited war theory. He confidently promised the American people that the nation could have both "guns and butter," arguing that a limited war abroad would not interfere with the accomplishment of his ambitious Great Society goals at home. "This nation is mighty enough--its society is healthy enough--its people are strong enough to pursue our goals in the rest of the world while still building a great society here at home," insisted Johnson.

Johnson contended that military force had become necessary in order to bring the North Vietnamese around to negotiating a settlement which would preserve the political autonomy of South Vietnam. Whenever the North would agree to relent, LBJ promised, peace talks could begin anywhere at any place at any time. The reward for North Vietnamese cooperation would be a one-billion-dollar American social and economic development program for all of Southeast Asia. But North Vietnam, in turn, made negotiations contingent upon a commitment from LBJ for an eventual American withdrawal, something the wary President refused to accept. Johnson refused to become involved in peace talks incorporating demands for American withdrawal even when they had been secretly arranged by United Nations Secretary General U. Thant. "I know the other side is winning; so they do too," grumbled the President privately. "No man wants to trade when he's winning," estimated LBJ as he informed his advisors that he would "apply the maximum deterrent till," as they say in Texas, Ho Chi Minh "sobers up and unloads his pistol."

President Johnson's clearest public statement of Vietnam policy came during his Johns Hopkins University speech on April 7, 1965. "We are there because we have a promise to keep." "We have made a national pledge to help South Vietnam defend its independence," stormed Johnson in his often-resorted-to "believe me please" manner. "To leave Vietnam to its fate would shake the confidence of people around the globe in the value of an American commitment. The result would be increased unrest and instability, and even a wider war," warned Johnson. "We are there because there are great stakes in the balance. Let no one think for a moment that retreat from Vietnam would bring an end to the conflict. The battle would be renewed in one country and then another. The appetite of aggression is never satisfied," contended the President. "The only peaceful settlement," concluded Johnson, would involve "an independent South Vietnam securely guaranteed and able to shape its own relationships to all others--free from outside interference--tied to no alliance--military base for no other country. These are the essentials of any final settlement."

President Johnson exemplified his outward confidence in victory and the rightness of the American cause in the 1966 State of the Union Message when he told Congress that "the enemy is no longer close to victory." According to Johnson "time is no longer on his side. There is no cause to doubt the American commitment." In February Johnson demonstrated his resolve by flying to Hawaii for top-level meetings with South Vietnamese leaders. He was then whisked off to Cam Ranh Bay in Vietnam, where one of the largest military build-ups in history was in process. The confident Johnson could not hide his feelings of bellicosity amid such a glamorous array of power. American boys would soon "come home with the coonskin on the wall," he shouted. In March of 1967 LBJ demonstrated his commitment anew by traveling with his top aides 8,700 miles to Guam for a planning parley with South Vietnamese leaders.

As the war escalated out of control, the inherent contradictions in Johnson's policies began to surface with dismaying frequency. The more pressure exerted by the United States military, the more vehemently the Vietnamese people resisted the "white man's" invasion of their society. American superior firepower proved counterproductive to the war aims when trained against illusive enemies hiding in villages, jungles, and swamps. The power was unleashed as often against friend as against foe. The friendly village of Deduc was mistakenly attacked in October of 1965, killing at least 48 civilians and wounding 55. A month later American planes accidentally bombed Locthoughiel. This only served to strengthen Vietnamese resistance. Clearly, the Vietnamese were not about to accept American democratic capitalism "at the point of a gun."

The Americans grossly misjudged the complicated Vietnamese domestic political situation, ultimately settling for the unpopular and undemocratic Thieu-Ky regime, which itself nearly fell to Buddhist anti-war demonstrations in 1966. The incredible situation was reminiscent of an observation once made by English philosopher John Stuart Mill: "A government which needs foreign support to enforce obedience from its own citizens is one which ought not to exist." Insensitive American advisors relied on individuals such as Thieu, a politician strongly allied with Western traditions, rather than attempt to understand better political leaders of other factions with closer and more indigenous connections with the local culture and society. Americans remained oblivious of Vietnamese society and custom, never taking time to gain some appreciation for the religious and social power structure, the influence of the family system on government, business, and the military elites, and the crucial role of the important Chinese community within Vietnam. Rather than create a genuinely broad-based consensus among supporting political and social institutions, American policy makers became entrapped in their support of narrowly-based, shaky elites who ruled on the basis of stern personal loyalty and intrigue rather than on the basis of enlightened self-interest.

Rather than build a model system of democratic capitalism, American material and financial assistance programs actually debased the Vietnamese currency and caused the economy to fall under the control of commodity manipulators and corruptionists of every stripe. Diversion of funds and material aid bolstered corrupt elements in South Vietnam and served ultimately to strengthen the rapport between Viet Cong tax collectors and quartermasters. Dr. Nguyen Van Hoa, Director General of the United Nations Agricultural Development Bank, frankly told a group of American businessmen that "we have been extremely wasteful in using that aid. We must assume full responsibility for our unintelligent and unreasonable use of it and suffer the consequence." Billionaire industrialist Cyrus Eaton, who contended many years that trading with the Communists was preferable to fighting and perishing with them, was appalled by the waste. "Here we would call it bribery; over there they call it 'efforts in behalf of democracy'," complained Eaton after his return from a tour of the region. "We are just buying people by the thousands to get people to adhere to democracy."

American and French speculators got rich from the waste and graft while the Vietnamese people became more and more destitute. "Instead of catalyzing an undeveloped feudalism into a modern political economy," charged the unreserved economist Eliot Janeway, "we are left with an old loan-shark's racket. The loan sharks we are financing are profiteering not merely at the expense of their own people but at the expense of ours." According to "Silent Sam" Berger, the career diplomat so responsible for the economic boom in South Korea, the Vietnam effort was doomed because the United States had tried "to win the war with money and people instead of brains." Rather than glory, advantage, and friends, then, Johnson's war policies in Vietnam were reaping a poisoned harvest of misery and ruin.

The unexpected high financial cost of the war fanned the fires of inflation and dislocated America's domestic and international social and economic priorities, throwing heaps of doubt on LBJ's pretensions about both guns and butter. American productivity and manufacturing efficiency declined as European and Japanese business interests began easing into world markets traditionally held by Americans. "From transistor radios to whole steel mills, the Japanese have been able to sell the rest of the world just about everything," reported _Time._ The cost of war increased deficit spending and moved America toward a greater trade deficit which, in turn, weakened the stability of the dollar in the international monetary exchanges. This led to devaluations, revaluations, and shifting monetary exchange rules. Bankers began to lose confidence as they rushed to exchange their dollars for American gold, forcing the United States to begin forsaking the once thought invincible gold-dollar link. "No single event would do more good for the nation's economy than ending the war," complained economist Arthur Smith of the First National Bank of Dallas. While allies took economic advantage of America's growing preoccupation with Vietnam, Russia quietly increased its influence in the oil-rich Middle East, an area ostensibly much more important to America's real international economic and strategic interests.

The constant spectre of cruelty--the indiscriminate B-52 aerial "terror" bombing which killed and maimed thousands of civilians, the application of dangerous chemicals which ruined crop land and endangered human life for generations, the burning children running naked and helpless along the highway, the beautiful green hillsides suddenly enveloped in a lethal orange lava of napalm, the South Vietnamese officer blowing the brains out of a Viet Cong suspect--all of these brutal images caused America's international reputation of goodness and generosity to plummet. "America now looks like the most dangerous country in the world," claimed the aging British historian Arnold Toynbee. Ironically, America, the nation which had fought the first successful modern war for colonial independence, now found itself in the same precarious position as its British oppressor of 1776. "I dread our own power and our own ambitions," warned Edmund Burke at the time; "I dread our being too much dreaded." Now, Martin Luther King echoed Burke's fears of 1776. "The United States which initiated so much of the revolutionary spirit of the modern world" had become "an arch counter-revolutionary nation," warned King.

President Johnson had endorsed escalation of the war in Vietnam originally in order to demonstrate the invincibility of American power. Johnson's inability to stabilize the situation demonstrated just the opposite. The United States seemingly possessed neither the power nor the will to fulfill its self-proclaimed role of world policeman. America's failure in Vietnam helped complicate Johnson's foreign policy problems elsewhere. The failure carried with it ominous signs of declining American influence and placed peace around the world in growing jeopardy.

At the United Nations the United States became a growing target of Communist bloc and Third World detractors, who charged that Johnson's policies animated from the selfish and imperialistic instincts of American corporate capitalism. Johnson understood the crucial connection between public opinion and the disposition of power. So as the growing vulnerability of his war policies drew heavier criticism in the United Nations, he, in turn, became increasingly reluctant to rely upon the organization for resolving world conflict.

Before Vietnam became a burdensome international issue, Johnson was able to engineer a successful resolution of the Turkish-Greek conflict over Cyprus in 1964. Cyprus had been granted independence from Britain in 1960 and came under the respected leadership of neutralist Archbishop Makarios, who was unable to quell the internal conflict between Greek and Turkish Cypriots. In March of 1964 the conflict erupted into open fighting along the important Nicosian-Kyrenia road, which separated Turkish guerrilla fighters in the mountains around St. Hilarion from the Greek villagers below. The fighting threatened to draw Greece and Turkey into the conflict and, ultimately, the two superpowers, both of which were very concerned about the balance of power in the eastern Mediterranean. In April the United Nations introduced a 7,000-man peace-keeping force and sent a special representative, Galo Plaza Lasso of Ecuador, to conduct exploratory talks designed to reduce tensions. Lasso eventually persuaded both sides to establish a 200-yard-wide "truce zone" along the Nicosian road, a solution that managed to maintain an uneasy peace for the remainder of the decade.

In April of 1965, however, when Vietnam had become a sensitive international issue, Johnson choose to largely ignore the United Nations when he decided to order the military invasion of the Dominican Republic. The Dominican crisis resulted from a military coup engineered by young rebel military officers sympathetic with former President Juan Bosch, a man known to embrace democratic principles, who himself had been the unfortunate victim of a coup two years earlier. The pro-Bosch regime, lead by Jose Rafael Molina Urena, distributed arms to civilians in a desperate effort to strengthen itself against the expected onslaught from the old military guard under the command of the abrasive General Elias Wessin.

Anguishing over the lessons of Cuba, fearing another embarrassing setback in the Caribbean, and spurred on by the frantic counsel of Ambassador W. Tapley Bennett in the Dominican Republic, Johnson ordered American Marines to intervene in the name of protecting the lives of Americans and other nationals. The intervention proved unfortunate for hemispheric relations because it abruptly reversed the 38-year-old Good Neighbor pledge by the United States not to employ military intervention in Latin America. Nevertheless, the intervention did bring back political stability. Through the Organization of American States the United States negotiated a cease-fire. Both the military junta and the anti-government rebels agreed to an uneasy coalition government under Dr. Hector Garcia Godoy. On

September 4, 1965, the United States extended formal diplomatic recognition to the new government and resumed foreign assistance programs to the reunited country.

The Dominican rebellion resulted mainly from poverty and poor living conditions among the masses, but President Johnson based his intervention on the threat of a Communist takeover. Johnson frankly declared that what had "began as a popular democratic revolution" had been seized by "a band of Communist conspirators." Johnson claimed that he intervened "to prevent another Communist state in this hemisphere." "What is important," declared Johnson, "is that we know, and that they know, and that everybody knows, that we don't propose to sit here in our rocking chair with our hands folded and let the Communists set up any government in the Western Hemisphere." Secretary Rusk added that "the Communists had captured the revolution according to plan, and the danger of a Communist takeover was established beyond any question." Thomas C. Mann, the influential Under Secretary of State for Latin American Affairs, stated that the intervention was "not so much a question of intervention as it was of whether weak and fragile states should be helped to maintain their independence when they are under attack by subversive elements responding to direction from abroad." Thus, the rationale for intervention in the Dominican Republic was no different than in Vietnam, except that one nation was located much closer to American borders.

Johnson's heavy-handed military intervention in the Dominican Republic presaged the President's deepening concern over the diminishing ability of the United States to influence the course of events in Central and South America. The Alliance for Progress had by now failed to produce the kind of political reform and economic expansion once envisioned by Kennedy. Most Latin American leaders had interpreted the new offer of American partnership as a shallow combination of Yankee imperialism and conscience-clearing do-goodism. The Alliance assistance was accepted not so much as charity or aid for development as it was as a reparation payment for offenses past and future. The resources were too often used for immediately pressing needs rather than for long-range goals. "They use the Alliance to fight crisis, not cause," complained Chile's President Eduardo Frei. By the time Johnson embarked upon his much publicized trip to Punta del Este in April of 1967 "to breath new life into the Alliance," he knew very well that most thoughtful observers had given up hope.

As the failure of the Alliance became more apparent during the Johnson years, United States policy makers anxiously shifted their support toward the budding Christian Democratic movements in such countries as Venezuela, Peru, Columbia, and especially Chile. These independent-minded movements represented the only acceptable alternative now to the rigid conservative politics of the right and the more violently radical politics of the left. Leftist guerillas such as Che Guevara were becoming romanticized and popularized in leftist circles in the United States, their anti-colonial cause linked to the one being fought in Vietnam by Ho Chi Minh. Johnson was hopeful that the Christian Democratic model would instead stand as the model for the future, and he anxiously sought for ways to assist.

In Chile the Christian Democrats, under President Eduardo Frei, captured power from the ultra-conservative Allesandri in 1964. Frei promised a variety of reforms under the auspices of the Chilean government and the eventual chileanization of industry. With American encouragement, the government purchased 51 percent of the stocks in the huge United States-owned Anaconda and Kennecott copper firms, and also purchased over half a million hectares worth of land from wealthy aristocrats for later distribution among landless peasants. Unfortunately, Frei's bold moves also failed to bring legitimate reform and progress toward modernization. Frei fell victim to constitutional restraints, a lack of genuine support from the United States, bad weather, and the so-called revolution of rising expectations. The Socialist Dr. Salvador Allende took power in 1969, signaling a more radical course away from the ideals of the Alliance for Progress. By then President Nixon had sent Governor Nelson Rockefeller on a special tour of Latin America to assess the diminished prospects for progress. Rockefeller grimly advised that United States policy must shift toward easier recognition of militaristic, autocratic governmental elites for the sake of maintaining a semblance of stability. Such disappointing advice was rather ironic, coming as it did from a leader since 1938 in the movement to spread the New Deal formula for democratic capitalism South, and it represented a sad commentary on interhemispheric affairs. Perhaps if Johnson had been less arrogant in his approach to Vietnam, more resources could have been available for the development of a durable Alliance for Progress in Latin America.

President Johnson's abortive efforts to stabilize governments south of the equator revealed a certain frenzy that had crept into the American foreign policy. American policy makers were becoming ever more haunted by the notion that the United States could not prosper as the lone island of democracy in a worldwide sea of totalitarianism. Yet Johnson's volatile policies in Vietnam and elsewhere seemed to strengthen the hopeless feeling that democracy was subsiding almost everywhere. In Indonesia Sukarno's "guided democracy" grew into a dictatorial nightmare which fell ingloriously before the harsh rule of a military junta in 1966. In Rhodesia Ian Smith's "democratic revolution," which placed four million blacks under the political control of 250,000 whites, proved to be democratic in name alone. In Algeria Ben Bella employed such repressive tactics that some of his fellow countrymen longed for a return to colonial rule. In Ghana the so-called "Redeemer" President Nkrumah ruled with an autocratic iron hand that denied his subjects many fundamental freedoms.

Even in Greece, the cradle of democracy, representative government faltered before the sword. In late 1966 the popular Prime Minister Papandreou, leader of the Centre Union Party, resigned under pressure from King Constantine after a bitter split over control of the military. In April of 1967 the King himself relinquished control to the military after an outbreak of violent street demonstrations. Once in control, the military suspended freedom of the press and assembly because they reportedly represented a "danger to public security." The junta then proceeded to place so-called political dissenters in "protective custody." In Greece, as it was in so many other countries, American military assistance, which had been intended for the protection of democracy from outside or internal communistic influence, instead armed ambitious military officials who looked for an excuse to snuff out democracy and place themselves in power.

The decline of democracy and multinational solutions to conflict became clearly evident during the Six-Day War in the Middle East during June of 1967. Ever since the creation of the state of Israel in 1948 the Arabs had staunchly refused to recognize its legitimacy. The historic hatred between the Israelis and the Arabs erupted in armed conflict in 1948 and again in 1956, when United Nations interventions resulted in the establishment of a peace keeping force along the Gaza Strip and the Sinai Peninsula in an attempt to keep the combatants apart. By the middle Sixties tensions again started to mount as Syrians on the heights above Galilee, edged on by Egyptian President Gamal Abdel Nasser, stepped up their harrassment of Israeli farmers who persisted in their violation of the old armistice line. In May of 1967 the terrorism reached such proportions that Israeli Prime Minister Levi Eshkol partially mobilized the armed forces.

President Nasser responded by mobilizing the forces of the United Arab Republic. Suspicious of the United Nations peace keeping force and confident of his own ability to defeat the Jews, Nasser bluntly ordered U Thant to withdraw. This was followed by Arab occupation of the strategic Sharm el-sheikh and the unilateral closing of the Gulf of Aqaba, Israel's most vital sea port. On May 24 U Thant rushed the United Nations Security Council into a special session as troops massed on both sides of the disputed frontiers. The Council became deadlocked amidst Russian charges that the United States and Britain were tacitly supporting Israel's aggression. On May 31 the council adjourned, unable to agree and unable to act.

On June 5 the war began with the Israeli armies virtually sweeping the Arabs aside before their quick and proficient thrust. By June 8 Israeli armies, under the astute command of the dynamic General Moshe Dayan, had occupied Arab Jerusalem, the Gaza Strip, Sinai west of the Jordan River, and had reopened the Gulf of Aqaba. The sunken ships in the Suez Canal caused traffic through the vital trade route to come to a complete halt. The Soviet-equipped United Arab armies were retreating on every front. On June 10 both sides accepted a United Nations-sponsored cease-fire. From that point the debates shifted to the General Assembly, where bitter charges and countercharges dominated the atmosphere. On June 14 the General Assembly rejected a Soviet-sponsored resolution condemning Israel and demanding her complete withdrawal from occupied territory. From June 17 to July 21 the General Assembly met in emergency session.

A long-winded parade of Presidents and Prime Ministers came to denounce the war and capture a little public attention. Finally, the General Assembly agreed on only two things. It voted, with the United States abstaining, to call on Israel to rescind its annexation of the Jordanian sector of Jerusalem and unanimously called on both sides to treat war victims fairly and humanely. Otherwise, the United Nations debate deteriorated into a sideshow over frivolities while the important negotiations occurred via the hot line extending between the White House and the Kremlin, signifying that unilateral rather than multilateral actions by nation-states was coming to characterize world politics.

In 1968 the Soviet Union took its own turn at unilateralism when it unscrupulously invaded Czechoslovakia. Johnson Administration protestations fell on deaf ears in the international community, which remembered the Dominican Republic and Vietnam. The United States under Johnson had lost much of the moral authority it was able to exercise during the Eisenhower-Kennedy years. Under the dynamic leadership of Alexander Dubcek, Czechoslovakian Communist Party leader, the small Eastern European nation had begun to liberalize its political, social, and economic structures to the point where Western influence might replace that of the Soviet Union. Deputy Premier Ota Kik talked confidently of issuing "people shares" in the state owned industry. Czech bankers began enthusiastic private talks with Western bankers, freeing for investment uses $20 million in Czech gold which had been captured from the Nazis in 1945. Dubcek went so far as to begin negotiating for "most favored nation" trade treatment in the West.

The Soviet Politburo viewed the situation in Czechoslovakia as an ominous threat to socialist and Russian security in eastern Europe. Dubcek's economic program threatened to edge Czechoslovakia toward the western orbit; and even worse, the reform fever could well spread to the other eastern European members of the Warsaw Bloc. Therefore, Soviet leaders arranged for an invasion of Czechoslovakia by Warsaw Pact countries beginning on August 18, 1968. Dubcek was quickly deposed, and an orthodox Communist government was placed in charge of reversing the embryonic trend toward democratic capitalism and national autonomy.

Soviet Ambassador Jacob Malik made a ceremonious voyage to the United Nations in a vain effort to rationalize the blatant intervention. His rationale sounded much like Johnson's concerning intervention in the Dominican Republic. It had been "requested" by loyal elements within the Czech government and in neighboring states, he said. His country had been bound to "meet its treaty obligations" in order to protect the security of Poland, East Germany, Hungary, and Bulgaria from the subversive outside forces of Western capitalism. Malik promised, of course, that Russian armed forces would "be immediately withdrawn as soon as the threat to security was eliminated." Throughout the episode, the United States severely criticized the Soviet action but carefully avoided intervention. The cruel invasion brought the same kind of bitter recrimination upon the Soviets from international liberal and progressive elements as the United States had received for its actions in the Dominican Republic and Vietnam. The exercise of unilateral power might bring victory or even some respect from other countries, but not honor and acceptance.

Honor was certainly something that eluded President Johnson. Even traditional allies were concerned about his policies concerning Vietnam. The growing political opposition of the Allies to Johnson's Vietnam war efforts left the President in an even more precarious international position. The President loathed the torrent of criticism and was visibly disappointed when, with the exception of South Korea and Australia, none of the Allies lent diplomatic and military support even though they were more or less bound by SEATO treaty commitments. LBJ never fully appreciated, of course, the historical fact that the United States had hardly come rushing to the aid of the French and British after world wars broke out in 1914 and in 1939 and that his country had waited for the French colonial collapse in Vietnam before making its 1954 commitments. The Allies well remembered the self-interested point of view that since the United States had inherited the world order--one that operated in its own favor--the United States should be its principal defender.

The Allies had suspected LBJ's Vietnam policies from the very beginning as wrong-headed and contrary to the flow of historical reality. "In Asia there is an Asian way, a blend that results from the interplay of Asia's historical, geographic, and other forces, and which defies full comprehension when seen through the rational eyes of Western people," Japan's Prime Minister Elsaku Sato warned Johnson in a speech before the National Press Club. "A spirit of tolerance and harmony, in particular, is essential in dealing with the problems of Asia. The establishment of peace and freedom in this area requires enormous effort, wisdom, and time." Such advice was foreign to the understanding of the impatient and impulsive Johnson.

The most devastating criticism of Johnson's war policies came from French President Charles De Gaulle, who cleverly capitalized on LBJ's dilemmas to fulminate his own agenda within the Western Alliance. Enthralled by the notion of a new French grandeur, depressed by the Americanization of French culture, irritated by the American tendency to ignore the French in making serious nuclear decisions regarding Cuba, jealous of the Anglo-American connection, and confident that a united Europe could serve as a positive force in diffusing cold war tensions, De Gaulle resolutely moved now to chart for France an independent diplomatic course. His awesome personal demeanor helped him forge a foreign policy otherwise beyond France's means. "One had the sense that if he moved to a window, the center of gravity might shift, and the whole room might tilt everybody into the garden," observed Henry Kissinger.

De Gaulle's first diplomatic blow had actually been struck before Johnson and Vietnam gave him more manueverability. It came on January 31, 1963, when he dramatically announced his intention to veto Great Britain's entry into the Common Market, a reprisal for Kennedy's plan to make nuclear submarine and warhead information available to the British but not the French. De Gaulle went on to deviate from the United States in tariff and monetary policy, at times threatening to disrupt the sagging American-dollar gold standard. In 1964 he became the first western statesman to formally recognize Red China. In 1966, as Johnson's war problems deepened, De Gaulle endorsed the so-called "Free Quebec" movement in Canada and one year later he toured Mexico City, where he walked among the poor and criticized Yankee imperialism. De Gaulle stubbornly refused to support America's escalation in Vietnam and stood firmly on the side of the Arabs in the Middle East. His final dramatic act before being forced out of office by radical student demonstrations in 1968 was to withdraw French military forces from NATO. Clearly, earlier Kennedy talk of Grand Design for Europe had faded. The sheer intensity of the debate over

Vietnam by now overshadowed all other foreign policy concerns among the beleaguered Allies.

The growing sense of failure among Americans concerning foreign policy abroad helped to fan the flames of war opposition at home. As the muffled drums of war in Vietnam grew louder, the human cost intensified. Hundreds of flag-draped coffins came back weekly, signifying the cost in human blood. Incensed American citizens began to swing into action. The Friends Committee on National Legislation and the Americans for Democratic Action called for an early end to the conflict during the summer of 1965. Martin Luther King submitted a comprehensive four-point peace plan to United Nations Ambassador Arthur J. Goldberg in September of 1965, arguing that domestic priorities now stood in grave jeopardy. In November of 1965 Norman R. Morrison of the Baltimore Stony Run Friends Society burned himself to death at the river entrance to the Pentagon within full view of Defense Secretary McNamara's office.

A whole generation of youth, many under threat of draft and death, became dispirited and demoralized over their prospects and the Vietnam War. "Draft Beer, Not Boys," read one poster as 125,000 New Yorkers marched against the war. Massive demonstrations such as this were followed with ceremonial draft card burnings, campus teach-ins, and organized marches on Washington, D.C.

The draft card burning case of David J. Miller, convicted under a 1965 law prohibiting the knowing destruction or mutilation of draft cards, went all the way to the U.S. Supreme Court, where Chief Justice Earl Warren held that such acts offended patriotism. The Court refused to review a lower court opinion against Miller, reasoning that draft card burning fell outside the category that had been defined as protecting "symbolic speech." Miller became an instant hero among the Vietnam protestors, and slowly but surely public opinion began to turn bitterly against the war effort.

The fearful realization that in the eyes of the world the war might turn America into a dangerous armed camp spurred several of the nation's leading creative thinkers and commentators to begin openly attacking Johnson's Vietnam policies. Pulitzer Prize poet Robert Lowell flatly refused LBJ's invitation to the White House Festival of the Arts during the summer of 1966. Authors John Hersey and Dwight MacDonald appeared under protest. The President had tersely reminded his guests that "your art is not a political weapon," but hastily added: "Yet much of what you do is profoundly political." His worst fears were soon realized, however, especially when a growing number of establishment intellectuals began to break with his war policies.

Retired General James M. Gavin, a noted military analyst, argued that American troops should be consolidated in stategic enclaves. "In Vietnam we have lost sight of our national objectives and let what started as a limited war expand in time, cost, and effort," contended Gavin, who predicted that the massive destruction would so transform Vietnamese society as to "make impossible the objective for which we entered the war." Much to LBJ's chagrin, Gavin was joined in his criticism of Administration policies by the dean of America's political commentators, Walter Lippmann. "It was a mistake to invade the mainland where the masses of Vietnam and of China can march against us," wrote the fluent scholar. "The right thing to do now is to take a stand on territory separated by blue water from the mainland." Another important postwar containment strategist, Hans Morgenthau, a University of Chicago political scientist, protested that "this war is really the result of absent-mindedness. We slipped into war." By now even Defense Secretary McNamara warned LBJ privately that he no longer believed the war winnable.

Historian Ronald Steel's Pax Americana reached the top of the non-fiction bestseller's list in 1967. "America's worth to the world will be measured not by the solutions she seeks to impose on others," argued Steel, "but by the degree to which she achieves her own ideals at home." "What is the use of physicians like myself trying to help parents to bring up children, healthy and happy, to have them killed in such numbers for a cause that is ignoble?" asked the famous pediatrician Dr. Benjamin Spock, who later went to trial in Boston for his war protest activities."

Singer Eartha Kitt carried her protest right into the White House, where her impromptu attack on Vietnam policy at a Women Doers' Luncheon also demonstrated how Vietnam was sapping the vitality of LBJ's domestic reform efforts. In a discussion on street crime Kitt blurted out to Lady Bird: "We sent the best of this country off to be shot and maimed.... They don't want to go to school, because they are going to be snatched off from their mothers to be shot in Vietnam." Much to LBJ's surprise, even Rochester Bishop Fulton J. Sheen, one of America's foremost postwar anti-communists, called upon the President for an immediate troop withdrawal. "May I speak only as a Christian and humbly ask the President to announce 'In the name of God, who bade us love our neighbor with our whole heart and soul and mind, for the sake of reconciliation I shall withdraw our forces immediately from South Vietnam,'" pleaded Sheen graciously.

The growing unpopularity of the war manifested itself in the political arena, where representatives of both the left and right aimed a volley of criticism at LBJ's policies. The war "has settled like a bitter frost over the American political landscape," wrote Newsweek. Conservative Michigan Congressman Gerald R. Ford, House Minority Leader, charged that LBJ had "hand-cuffed" the military; and he called for a more extensive bombing of the North. As a representative of the liberal wing of the GOP California's Congressman Paul A. (Pete) McCloskey complained that the South Vietnamese people lacked the determination to create their own government and that all the force in the world would not provide that basic ingredient. McCloskey suspected that the Viet Cong enjoyed more support from the Vietnamese than the Thieu-Ky regime in Saigon. "It has now become clear that there is some sort of native resilience in the Vietnamese opposed to the Saigon government which has enabled them to withstand heavy casaulties, heavy bombing, and immense hardship, and yet fight on," proffered McCloskey, who had supported the war until he personally visited Vietnam. "We begin to perceive that there must be something more than Russian and Chinese aid which enables these people to stand fast." Prominent Republican Senator Thurston B. Morton of Kentucky complained that LBJ had "squandered his credibility" on Vietnam, and presidential candidate Governor George Romney of Michigan charged that Vietnamese leaders "wouldn't last a couple of weeks without our support."

More serious for LBJ's badly sagging political fortunes was the growing impatience within the ranks of his own Democratic party. "I consider the life of one American boy worth more than this putrid mess," shouted Alaska's Senator Ernest Gruening, who, along with Oregon's Wayne Morse, was on of the only two Senators to oppose the Gulf of Tonkin Resolution in the first place. Some day the war would "be denounced as a crime," warned Gruening as support for this view began building in the Senate. In early March, 1967, New York Senator Robert F. Kennedy in a Senate speech called for a unilateral bombing halt. This came only a few weeks after a 45-minute confrontation at the White House between the aspiring Senator and the beleaguered President, where reportedly LBJ furiously told Kennedy, "I never want to see you again."

The most forceful and legitimate criticism of LBJ came from Senate Foreign Relations Chairman William Fulbright who bluntly labeled the war endless, futile, debilitating, indecent, and contrary to America's best democratic traditions. He charged that the United States was "losing its perspective on what exactly is within the realm of its power and what is beyond it." The stubborn and resourceful Senator, half-rimmed glasses perched on the end of his nose, launched a long, arduous committee hearing destined to slowly but surely expose the contradictions in LBJ's war policies--policies that Senator Fulbright contended would lead to the permanent militarization of American institutions. "The true mark of greatness is not stridency but magnanimity," argued Fulbright as he frankly proposed a unilateral cessation of bombing, guaranteed Viet Cong participation in a new government, and neutralization of all Southeast Asia. Fulbright drew strong support from Senate Majority Leader Mike Mansfield of Montana, who complained bitterly that "the reports of progress are strewn like burned-out tanks all along the road which has led us ever more deeply into Vietnam."

Outside of the Senate disgust with the war spread like an old-fashioned prairie fire. A group of high-minded liberals led by the unabrasive and highly-respected Gilbert Harrison, editor of the prestigious New Republic, established the "Dump LBJ" movement. James Gavin echoed the growing public sentiment. "The war was having disastrous consequences on the national economy," complained Gavin. "As a result, the President's domestic programs are grossly underfunded. I simply will not support Johnson for President in 1968." California clothier Harry Roth spent almost $8,000 in the New York Times on advertisements which publicly urged LBJ not to seek renomination. The bitterness of the war debates rendered the national political atmosphere almost noxious. "We are in danger of losing our sense of confidence in each other," warned Massachusetts Senator Edward Kennedy. A Johnson aide could well say, "We're winning that war out there. The real war is back here."

Indeed, Johnson had sacrificed his credibility on the war effort. A Gallup poll showed that between 1966 and 1967 those believing that ground troops should never have been introduced in Vietnam increased from 24 to 41 per cent. A Louis Harris poll showed that only 23 per cent agreed with LBJ's handling of the war and that only 38 per cent were favorable to his overall conduct of the Presidency. Polls indicated that both Governors Rockefeller and Reagan could swamp a Johnson-Humphrey ticket in 1968, and they also showed that the popularity of New York Senator Robert F. Kennedy had soared ahead of the President's. The tested old political pros still stuck uncomfortably with LBJ, but the rank and file Democratic workers made no secret of their preference for Kennedy. Speaking of LBJ's political fortunes in the largest electoral state of California, Governor Pat Brown sighed gloomily and reported that "right now, we're dead in the water out here."

Meanwhile, Minnesota Senator Eugene McCarthy announced his 1968 Presidential candidacy, making the war his sole issue. His astonishing success in the early precinct caucuses and primaries left the President, in a political sense, "sitting naked on the windmill." LBJ began to feel his political Gotterdammerrung almost at hand. Johnson probably heard what Satan heard in Milton's Paradise Lost: "On all sides, from innumerable tongues a dismal universal hiss, the sound of public scorn." Once shed of his credibility, the President became a pathetic figure, sounding more like a forlorn and tired old hoot owl than a great leader presiding over the high noon of his Presidency.

Nevertheless, as the fateful year of 1968 dawned, LBJ clung relentlessly to his war policies, declaring that "we shall not be defeated," and calling his critics "nervous Nellies, eat and run people." He specifically called Fulbright "a frustrated old woman" who could not appreciate "that people with brown skins value freedom too." According to Vice President Hubert Humphrey, there could be "no doubt of our ultimate success." General Earle Wheeler, Chairman of the Joint Chiefs of Staff, purported that "the enemy's chance for a military victory is gone." Vietnam Commander General William Westmoreland reported that "we are winning, slowly but steadily." "We have begun to hurt the enemy in his home territory," stated Pacific Ocean Commander U.S. Grant Sharp. National Security Affairs Advisory Walt Rostow confidently claimed that as much as 85 per cent of the South Vietnamese people supported the United States as a result of pacification and search and destroy missions.

In the midst of the Administration's optimistic proclamations, the Tet Offensive delivered its deadly psychological blow. Traditionally the lunar New Year represented the most festive of occasions, marked by colorful parades, operas, dances, and feasts of cakes, fruit, and rice wine. The gala holiday atmosphere was abruptly interrupted, however, by a massive Communist offensive against several large cities that reached to the very doorstep of the American Embassy in Saigon. Though the Viet Cong suffered a devastating military defeat with perhaps 10 percent casualties, the attack seemed to demonstrate persuasively that the United States enjoyed only limited support among the people of Vietnam. The offensive extracted a tremendous human cost. In Hue, once the imperial capital and traditionally the center of the country's intellectual and artistic elite, a month of house-to-house fighting left thousands dead and 80 per cent of the once-beautiful city destroyed. Many other cities and villages were destroyed by American aerial bombing. The ultimate contradiction of the war was revealed when a beleaguered American officer inadvertently explained to a television reporter that the smouldering town in the background had been destroyed in order to be saved.

Meanwhile, at Khe Sanh, a major American defeat seemed imminent. Khe Sanh was a pivotal base located in the northeastern part of South Vietnam, close to the Ho Chi Minh trail of infiltration, where American military strategy and prestige hung in the balance. A large American garrison there had come under constant siege and heavy artillery bombardment--reminding many observers of the fateful final days of French involvement at Dienbienphu. The vulnerability of the American position lay open for the whole world to witness. It was not American might nor power but the tenacious spirit of the Vietnamese revolutionaries which seemingly prevailed.

The Tet offensive prompted, at last, a fundamental reassessment of American policy in Vietnam along with its worldwide implications. "We are coming to the end of a policy," lamented former Ambassador to Japan Edwin R. Reischauer. "It is now crystal clear," announced Senator Mansfield, "that we are in the wrong place fighting the wrong kind of war."

It became the responsibility of the new Secretary of Defense, Clark Clifford, crafty advisor to Democratic presidents since Truman and a man of impeccable manners and penetrating insight, to reverse Johnson's policies of escalation. While Clifford reviewed the dire situation, the military asked for yet another 200,000 troops without giving any assurance of early victory. War costs were projected to increase by another $12 billion, prompting the necessity of credit restrictions, tax increases, and wage and price controls. Even with the exercise of these draconian options, experts would not guarantee that aerial bombing would end the war without pulverizing the entire countryside. The clamor for the use of tactical nuclear weapons among military circles was becoming more and more intense.

The Vietnamese army was in sad disarray with a 30 per cent desertion rate. Drugs, prostitution, and demoralization had reduced the effectiveness of American forces. The Thieu-Ky regime, which some suspected was connected with the huge heroin traffic among American soldiers, was neither interested in reform nor serious about peace negotiations. The Chinese-Soviet split had by now reduced the fears of monolithic Communist expansion, and support for American Vietnam policy among other Free World governments had dwindled to a mere trickle.

"The nation which lets its duty get on the opposite side of its interests is lost," England's author George Bernard Shaw once wrote. "Our political leaders are learning that Sophocles was right," concluded CBS commentator Eric Sevareid. "Nothing that is vast enters into the affairs of mortals without a curse, and that vast American power has now produced its curse." Most of all the nation had finally learned through hard experience the gamy consequences of playing God with the destinies of other peoples, an act that represented an unreasonable international attitude of big brotherism and indiscretionary insistence on selfish national purpose. "Selfishness is not living as one wishes--it is asking others to live as one wishes to live," novelist Oscar Wilde once proffered. The observation seemed to apply to what the nation had to learn in Vietnam.

Secretary Clifford had vaguely begun to understand the lessons of Vietnam when he called for a frank "A to Z" appraisal of war policy and patiently coaxed the deeply anguished President into a posture of conscious deescalation and serious negotiation toward a peace settlement. Sensing the strain at last, the harried LBJ recognized that the fire of his popularity had grown too dim to rekindle, so in characteristic fashion he decided to take expeditious action before becoming any more entangled in the inevitable.

Sensing his political demise, President Johnson appeared on national television on March 30, 1968, to announce a bombing halt and America's new willingness to negotiate. In a surprising move, which he hoped would truly demonstrate his sincerity about peace, LBJ announced irrevocably his intention to leave the Presidency--perhaps his most noble public act. "I shall not seek and I will not accept the nomination of my party," the stone-faced LBJ told a stunned nation. "I cannot recall a more momentous event of this kind in our entire history," declared Alf Landon, former GOP presidential candidate.

CHAPTER VIII

THE YOUTH REBELLION

Lyndon Johnson's withdrawal from the Presidency signified the end of the Great Society consensus, with its ambitious package of confident hopes and expectations, and marked the rise of an anti-establishment movement involving one of America's most serious social and political disruptions--a disruption against constituted authority fully as serious as the Populist Revolt of the 1890's. The enormity and unpredictability of the historical forces impacting on American life helped create a restive mood among the people not unlike that which prevailed in the colonies prior to the American Revolution of 1776.

Such periods are times "in which confidence in the justice or reasonableness of existing authority is undermined; where old loyalties fade, obligations are felt as impositions, law seems arbitrary, and respect for superiors is felt as a form of humiliation," wrote the eminent historian R. R. Palmer, "where existing sources of prestige seem undeserved, hitherto accepted forms of wealth and income seem ill-gained, and government is sensed as distant, apart from the governed and not really 'representing' them." According to Palmer, "in such a situation the sense of community is lost, and the bond between social classes turns to jealousy and frustration. People of a kind formerly integrated begin to feel left out."

Such was the case in the Sixties. The rebellion of the 1960's resulted most directly from LBJ's persistent Vietnam policies, but in many ways Vietnam served more as a manifestation of serious contradictions rooted deeply in the structure and operations of America's modern highly-integrated political economy.

The rebellion's initial leadership, like that of 1776, came from youthful zealots who bore the brunt of Vietnam policies; but even without the apparent contradictions of war, youth would have been vigorously questioning the modern structure of American society in the Sixties. Anyway, the "first duty of youth" after all, as the historian Charles Tawney put it, was "to make a tradition, not to perpetuate one." From youth the rebellion quickly spread, gaining sympathy from persons of all ages. Relatively few Americans ever served on the barricades of confrontation--many were deeply disturbed by the spectacle--yet, as Time reported, "the disquiet that suffused the spectacle was certainly shared to a degree by most Americans." The rebellion would leave in its wake the 20th century's second "lost generation," more alienated and more disillusioned than the first, which had been deeply embittered by the disappointments of World War I.

The symbol of youth in dissent and rebellion was natural to the times. America had always idealized the youth spirit, and society itself strived for a youthful accent. "Everyone wants to be youthful and mature," observed columnist Sidney Harris. America thought of itself as a youthful nation, and, indeed, Aristotle's perceptive description of youth characterized the tone of American society in the Sixties. "They have exalted notions, because they have not yet been humbled by life or learned its necessary limitations," wrote Aristotle. "They overdo everything--they love too much, hate too much, and the same with everything else."

In the early Sixties American society patronized youth more than ever and encouraged even greater youthful social and political involvement. "Not since the founding of the Republic has there been a generation of Americans brighter, better educated, more highly motivated than this one," exclaimed Senator Robert F. Kennedy. "We see the hope of tomorrow in the youth of today, better educated, more committed, more passionately driven by conscience than any generation in history," exalted former Vice President Richard M. Nixon. "Today nowhere in the world are there elders who know what the children know," claimed sociologist Margaret Mead, and Caltech's President Lee DuBridge proudly announced that "there is no question that today's teenager is better educated and more seriously motivated than ever before." According to St. John's sociologist William Osborne, "this generation has what other generations have lacked--a holy discontent, courage, and willingness to sacrifice." Young people found themselves placed on a pedestal not unlike that once reserved for the yeoman farmer, the 19th century mythical symbol of morality, honesty, integrity, and resourcefulness. But they began to discover remorsefully that such patronization was exaggerated and unreal. In reality Americans expected youth in docile fashion to accept gratefully a symbolic place on the pedestal placed in the center of the modern American garden of Eden. But ironically the Howdy-Doody generation, born and bred on technophonics and plenty, found the garden objectionable and the pedestal insufferable. Young people were not allowed the flexibility to exercise their creative impulses. They began to discover the difficulty of fulfilling themselves. As H. L. Mencken once put it: "Youth, though it may lack knowledge, is certainly not devoid of intelligence. It sees through shams with sharp and terrible eyes." Actually, the "now generation" found itself treated as "marginal individuals," expected to live by a rather narrowly defined stereotype which in an industrial society compelled them to be consumers and watchers rather than builders and doers.

Youth in the Sixties became the first to experience the devastating boredom that Russian critic Dostoevsky prophesied would accompany industrial prosperity. People will "suddenly realize that they have no life any more, no freedom of spirit, no freedom of will and personality, that somebody has stolen all that from them. People will become depressed and bored," predicted Dostoevsky. At the Detroit Institute of Technology Dr. S. I. Hayakawa, of San Francisco State, addressed the same issue more bluntly. "We keep them out of meaningful participation in adult life. No wonder they are bored and angry," he complained. America provided little opportunity for youth to exercise its creative impulses in a self-fulfilling way. Philosopher Sidney Harris summarized the problem. People "maintain their self-respect chiefly by doing a difficult job and doing it well," wrote Harris, "and the widespread loss of self-respect noted in the modern world is largely owing to the increasing number of jobs that can be done repetitively, perfunctorily, mechanically, uselessly, and cynically."

Youth yearned to escape from the specter of such a gloomy existence. "The majority of adults in this country hate their work," conjectured Charles A. Reich in his The Greening of America. "Whether it is a factory job, or the role of being a housewife, they hate their work as much as young people rebel against the prospect of similar work." Under the shadow of magnificent wealth and celebration which dominated the Great Society years, then, a dismal mood of restiveness and rebellion began to take shape.

The youthful discontent began in a disjointed, incoherent, and undirected fashion. It grew from "invisible dynamics that is turning the whole world into a society that spends most of its time on arms, entertainment and therapy," complained one youthful critic worried about America's apparent confusion of priorities. "The collapse of our pretensions both at home and abroad has struck our young men and women with devastating impact," wrote historian Arthur S. Schlesinger, Jr. "The frustration that is overwhelming to American college youth is that they cannot understand why this nation, with unlimited resources and ability, as they see it, seems to place such little priority on the realization of the American dream," explained Chancellor Roger W. Heynes of the University of California. "We need good schools and houses for people to live in and it could be done and we're going to make this country do it," activist Simon Kunen wrote in his The Strawberry Statement: Notes of A College Revolutionary. "I'm going to stay mad until things change. You change them, or we change them. I don't care. But the choice isn't going to be yours much longer."

Rapid change and the specter of instant nuclear destruction added to the feelings of impermanence and instability. The hope of a long, fruitful life which had characterized the Victorian times could not be shared by this generation faced with deafening talk about bomb shelters and nuclear overkill. The reduced hope for long life generated a spirit of contemporariness: "live and be merry for tomorrow will almost surely never come." The discontent was magnified by a broad and incomprehensible feeling of dissatisfaction with the status quo, the meaninglessness of materialistic values, the crassness of society's purposes, the hypocrisy in high places, the inability to establish one's identity, the failure to be granted legitimate responsibility, and the fear that individuality would be crushed in the frantic pace and complexity of modern life.

Adults may have lauded John Glenn's space feat for its demonstration of individualism; youth shuddered at its organizational implications. "We look at the complexity and hugeness of life and wonder how we'll keep our individuality," complained one youth. Youth felt aimless, stranded and confused. Youth indirectly perceived Henry Adam's late 19th century vision of the virgin and the dynamo. Modern society, which worshipped the machine, lost authenticity, enshrined cold calculating pragmatism, and stifled warm human relations. "Unable to reconcile themselves to the stated values and implicit contradictions of contemporary western society," youth have "become internal emigres," complained _Time._ The alienating aspects of modern industrial life, then, rather than Vietnam, represented the real causes behind the youth rebellion of the Sixties.

The youthful rebels heralded mainly from the middle and upper classes of suburbia. Their protests involved a "root-and-branch" rejection of suburban standards and moral values. Bored with temporal possessions, starved for some attention, and craving to be taken seriously, they struck out first against mass education. Over 90 per cent of America's youth were obliged to attend high school compared to 13 per cent in 1900. LBJ had hoped that Great Society billions for education would produce "the cultivated mind," the "guardian genius of democracy." But the billions were spent mostly to provide elaborate facilities, not to teach students. The situation was grasped by radical sociologist Paul Goodman, who charged that "education had become mere exploitation, the abuse of the abilities and time of life of school youth for others' purposes."

Upon introspection youth began to realize that educational institutions actually mirrored American society itself with its assembly line mentality, its rows upon rows of identical houses, and its subtle quest for conformity, serialization, and regimentation. "The University like the nation seems to be like a great, complex vending machine that has become rusted with age," proclaimed one disgruntled critic; "the only way to make it work right is to kick it hard." Out of this realization grew a "class consciousness," a new camaraderie under stress, and enthusiastic dedication for creating new traditions rather than perpetuating antiquated ideas and systems. "Students have become somebody in being able to act together," boasted a Yale student.

The new esprit de corps converted young people from aimless drifters into emigres seeking liberation from modern industrial constraints, and the revolt against convention quickly spilled out of the classrooms and into the streets. The nation's adults would soon come to appreciate what Lebanese prophet Kahlil Gibran once said of youth: "Your children are not your children. They are the sons and daughters of Life's longing for itself. You may give them your love but not your thoughts. You may house their bodies but not their souls, for their souls dwell in the house of tomorrow."

The youth movement gained official attention in 1964 during the Berkeley Free Speech Movement led by the fiery Mario Savio, the brilliant son of immigrant parents, who had become disenchanted after failing to find a college he thought able to accommodate people's actual educational needs. The immediate cause of the Berkeley uprising involved a decision by University President Clark Kerr, model practicioner of America's liberally-educated elite, to prohibit students from using a small strip of pavement adjoining campus, eventually dubbed the "People's Park." The People's Park had become an accepted place for a variety of student political activity, and Kerr's rather summary decision represented a serious infraction upon the right of free expression. When the university tried to arrest students for trespassing in the area, the issue exploded into a campus-wide rebellion requiring police intervention. When Governor Edmund G. Brown ordered state police to clear demonstrators from occupied buildings, thousands of students filed out of class in support of Savio's Free Speech Movement. Mass arrests, bloodshed, and bombastic rhetoric followed.

The tone of the rebellion was set by one placard which read, "I am a human being. Do not bend, fold, or mutilate." FSM leader Jack Weinberg gave the movement a slogan which demonstrated youth's growing distrust of the nation's bureaucratic and hierarchical liberal establishment. The slogan read: "Don't trust anyone over 30." Another FSM leader explained that the "university came to be the mirror-image of liberal social values, a growth economy, competitive, progressive, expanding, upwardly mobile." Academic life stifled "thoughtful participation in the common affairs" of life and drove youth into "a frenzied existence," he complained. Before 13,000 persons shouting "We want Mario," police came, grabbed Savio by the throat, twisted his arm in a hammer lock, and dragged him away; but not before Savio echoed the battle cry of the rebellion: "Put your bodies upon the gears, upon the wheels, upon the levers, upon all the apparatus and ... make the university stop!"

The tactics of the FSM served as an early model for youthful protest on several other campuses. At the University of Kansas students clogged the hallways outside of the Chancellor's office, protesting segregation in sororities and fraternities. At the University of Washington students demonstrated against mandatory membership in the student association. At the University of Chicago students threatened a "sleep-out" in protest against curfew rules. At St. Johns University students demonstrated against convocation policies which prohibited the campus appearances of such luminaries as Senator Robert F. Kennedy and Malcolm X. The time-honored and heavily ceremonialized graduation exercises became favorite targets of student protesters. Some colleges felt obliged to cancel graduation ceremonies for fear of campus turmoil. "There is no place so safe as a good college during the critical passage from boyhood to manhood," boasted Charles William Eliot upon becoming President of Harvard in the 1860's; few would have agreed in the 1960's.

As the rebellion spread from the campus into the streets, leadership fell to the Students for a Democratic Society (SDS), the most notorious of the radical student political action groups. SDS was organized in 1962 under the leadership of Tom Hayden, editor of the University of Michigan campus newspaper and veteran of the early civil rights marches in the South. Hayden produced the Port Huron Statement, which served as an early rationale for SDS action. "We are people of this generation, bred in at least modest comfort, housed now in universities, looking uncomfortably to the world we inherit," read the Hayden document, in which he called for a truly participatory democracy. Hayden called for patient working through the labor movement and the major political parties to bring about individual self-respect and the feeling of connection. He believed the establishment would change, hence overcoming the alienation so inherent in modern industrial life.

SDS began primarily as a ghetto action group. During the election of 1964 SDS volunteers helped canvass the inner city areas of Cleveland, Ohio, in order to register voters. They also helped SNCC register black voters in Mississippi. In Newark, New Jersey, SDS volunteers established the Newark Community Action Project, which consisted of neighborhood surveys to determine housing needs. On Chicago's North Side SDS established an organization called JOIN (Jobs or Income--Now) which drew public attention to slum housing, police harassment, and inoperable welfare programs. The SDS shifted its attention toward the antiwar movement in 1965 when LBJ escalated American participation in Vietnam. During the first week of May SDS sponsored Vietnam Emphasis Week, including teach-ins, marches, and demonstrations designed to inform the public of what SDS considered as escalating folly. Soon SDS members could be found distributing anti-war leaflets at army recruiting and induction centers and setting up counseling centers around the country designed to help young men avoid the draft. These tactics met with bitter criticism from such establishment type as Senator Dirksen, Attorney General Katzenbach, and even President Johnson, who promised that his policies would not be influenced in the least by the SDS antics. Such recalcitrance in high places caused the SDS to become more radical by 1967, as its leaders began advocating more confrontational tactics. In place of teach-ins came angry charges that men fighting in Vietnam were "suckers," "baby-killers," and "warmongers." The establishment slowly became the enemy to be defeated rather than an instrument to be manipulated in the name of social justice.

As the confrontation between the establishment and the youthful agitators sharpened, youth sullenly began to question basic western assumptions and values. Like the 19th century Romantics, youth railed against a society that appeared overregulated, oversystemized, and overindustrialized. Youth mistrusted rationalism because it destroyed spontaneity and interfered with the uninhibited release of emotions. Youth believed that institutions tended to corrupt human nature. Rational materialism corrupted the innate innocence and virtue that characterized humans in their natural state.

The movement began to seek ways to liberate individuals from the alienating influences of modern institutionalization. "Our ideology focuses on the inability of the individual to make meaningful decisions in society. Individuals are deprived of power over their own lives by a corporate elite which manipulates people economically and politically," complained one youthful critic. "Their crass materialistic values reduce human beings to 'consumers of things.' This depersonalization plus the separation of most people from power produces a sense of apathy and resignation." Arthur Miller captured the intensity of this feeling in his play _Death of a Salesman_ when Biff told his mother, "I just can't take hold, Mom, I can't take hold of some kind of life."

Youth's disenchantment with the system was manifested in its attempt to experiment with alternative ideals and life styles. Youth forsook such time honored models as the lovable bad guy Huck Finn and the successful Horatio Alger for more contemporary heroes such as James Dean and Lenny Bruce. Fifties star James Dean provided early inspiration because of his unbridled defiance of adult authority in the motion pictures Rebel Without a Cause and East of Eden. Dean reflected "their own inner image of themselves," wrote one biographer.

In the half-educated, devastatingly alert Lenny Bruce, fiesty entertainer who died, disillusioned, from a drug overdose in 1966, youth found a quasi-mythical martyr for the cause of free and uninhibited expression. "Most of his career was devoted to demolishing the hypocrises inherent in the notion of good taste," wrote Michael Murray in Commonweal. "Bruce's satire helped begin the process of cauterizing long ignored social wounds," wrote Time, and "his use of previously forbidden words to make jokes about subjects long forbidden in public was in some small way liberating." The belief that Bruce had been somehow driven to suicide by a "repressively puritanical Establishment," eventually became an article of faith among his youthful sympathizers. In his final years Bruce carried on a running battle with the courts over charges of obscenity and narcotics. After his death an attorney reflected upon Bruce's legacy to youth: "We drove him into poverty and bankruptcy and then murdered him.... We all knew what we were doing. We used the law to kill him."

Both Dean and Bruce looked to the emerging rock-n-roll musical phenomenon for their new models and life styles. The rock music phenomenon held within it all of the potential that the leading 19th century Italian patriot revolutionary Giuseppe Mazzini had grasped: "Music is the harmonious voice of creation; an echo of the invisible world; one of the divine concord which the entire universe is destined one day to sound." Meanwhile, Mazzini's American contemporary, Thomas Edison, had invented his historic tin foil phonograph, the speaking telegraph as he called it. Little did he realize that he had planted the seed which would provide the mechanical grist for an explosive emotional revolution of the Sixties. In the bumping and grinding gyrations of rock music youth, which had been "snoring along to the croons of Sinatra, Crosby, and Como," found a long-awaited release from the humdrum of highly-structured modern life. Songs by such new rock stars as Chubby Checker, the Big Bopper, Buddy Holly, and Chuck Berry began crowding the popular charts.

Elvis "the pelvis" Presley, the southern troubadour with "greased-back hair, tight pants, black leather jacket, heavy-lidded eyes and a sneer that played at the corners of his mouth," became a super phenomenon among youth as early as the middle Fifties. Presley's intrusive on-stage demeanor offended polite society. The deep groans, the hard edges, cutting angles, and incessant beat seemed hedonistic to staid, well-mannered adults still heavily influenced by the appropriateness of Victorian life. During Presley's first appearance on the Ed Sullivan show, the television cameras carefully avoided showing his wiggling hips.

What appeared repulsive to adults of Ozzie-and-Harrietland, however, proved keenly appealing to youth. "This loud, unbridled, extravagant, hyperbolic, primitive, catchy, mindless, rebellious, exultant, fatuous, exhilarating music nicely delineated the Generation Gap of the '50's," wrote critic John Christensen. Presley's music touched the many moods of youth from the time of his first big hit song in 1956 entitled "Heartbreak Hotel," described by one critic as "a blood-stirring dirge about love and loneliness." Adult disapproval of Presley's instinctive expressions helped make youth his natural constituency. A youthful generation, which itself felt unrepresented and oppressed, easily identified with "this bad boy from the wrong side of the tracks." Presley provided a refreshing, if unreasoned, alternative outlet for deep-seated and unarticulated feelings and frustrations.

By the early Sixties rock music had become more than just fun and harmless funk. It had become a tribalizing phenomenon drawing youth together in a bond of immediate communion. "Many of the things that young people cared about were reflected and distilled in the lyrics of the songs: the meaning of freedom; the quality of life; the care of the earth; the reality of sex; the political and social problems of war, racism, and poverty; the personal crisis of identity; and the religious meaning of love, peace, and truth," observed one critic. Such songs as "Little Boxes" and ban-the-bomb elegy "What Have They Done to the Rain?", written by Malvina Reynolds and made popular by Joan Baez and Pete Seeger, gained early favor among youth. "Ticky Tacky Little Boxes" intoned the growing frustration. "And the children go to school/ and the children go to camp/ and then to the university/ where they are put in boxes/ and they all come out the same/ and they're all made out of ticky-tacky/ and they all look just the same."

Rock "exerts a fearful centrifugal force," wrote *Time.* In many ways rock music became the equivalent of the "underground newspaper of the air, prophetically criticizing society's moral failures and standing up for the hopes and dreams of American youth." It was to the Sixties what the angry literature of Fitzgerald and Lewis had been to the Twenties. In no other age had popular music contained so many signals about society. "Rock became the centerpiece to a new way of life," wrote an observer. "Next to humanity's need for food to exist and air to survive, it must have music," bandleader Stan Kenton once contended. That contention proved true in the Sixties. The phenomenon reminded some of the ancient poet who boasted that "I don't care who writes the nation's laws as long as I can write its music."

The new prophet and seer envisioned by Dean and Bruce emerged in the shy and unaspiring person of Bob Dylan, a Minnesota troubadour bearing a harmonica around his neck and a guitar on his hip and singing in a raspy voice, "The Times They Are A Changin'." "There's a battle/ outside and it's ragin'/ It'll soon shake your windows/ And rattle your walls." Dylan's mission began at the bedside of the dying Woody Guthrie, whose songs like "This Land is Your Land" in the Thirties had captured the meaning of the catastrophe being visited upon the dispossessed of the Oklahoma Dust Bowl. Dylan's lyrics and beat represented a mixture of Guthrie's folkish and desolate dust bowl ballads and a new humanistic concern "for the lost, the lonely, and the despairing." "Old New York City is a friendly old town/ From Washington Heights to Harlem on down/ There's a mighty many people all millin' around/ They'll kick when you're up and knock you when you're down/ It's hard times in the city/ Livin' down in New York town." His songs empathized with the downtrodden victims of the capitalistic system and showed contempt for class and privilege.

Dylan's terse protestations went well beyond the vague moralisms of the earlier "hootenannies," popularized by the folk music of Joan Baez, Pete Seeger, The Kingston Trio, the Lamp Lighters, Burl Ives, the Weavers, and Peter, Paul, and Mary, the trio that popularized Seeger's "Where Have All the Flowers Gone?" in the early Sixties, when American public opinion was still oblivious to the growing war threat in Asia. Dylan's early sensitivity to the tragedy of the war was demonstrated in 1964 when he published such songs as "Masters of War," "John Brown," "Talking W.W. III Blues," and "With God on Our Side." Dylan's lyrics were more heartfelt than Country Joe McDonald's cynical satire of the 1964 LBJ election called "Superbird." Dylan's quiet lamentations of bigotry, nuclear destruction, war profiteering, racism, and social emptiness crystallized "once vague discontents," thus transforming dissent from an intellectual hobby to a public cause," reported *Time.* "He's all of us," cried one frenzied coed; "he's all the things we always felt but could never eloquently express." Dylan's intense style bolstered the message. "In his haunting nasal howl he spits out his message like a cobra," observed one student.

Dylan soon attracted attention in New York City's Cafe district where songstress Joan Baez and poet Allen Ginsberg would sometimes come by to join him. Dylan became the subject of numerous campus "rap sessions," the "inspiration" for essays, and "the brooding presence uniting thousands of unsatisfied students." Dylan's music filled the spiritual vacuum inside many beleaguered middle class youth otherwise constrained by the superficiality of surburban life. "We're concerned with things like the threat of nuclear war, the civil rights movement and the spreading blight of dishonesty, conformism, and hypocrisy in the United States, especially in Washington," noted one student, "and Bob Dylan is the only American writer dealing with these subjects in a way that makes any sense to us." Dylan was "more than a poet, prophet or guitar player, he was, quite simply, a phenomenon," recounted one observer. His popularity on campus should not have been too surprising since he captured in a few concise lines what youth felt so deeply: "Johnny's in the basement/ Mixing up the medicine/ I'm on the pavement/ Thinking about the government/ The man in the trench coat/ Badge out, laid off/ Says he's got a bad cough/ Wants to get paid off/ ....Lookin' for a new friend/ The man in the coon-skin cap/ In the big pen/ Wants eleven dollar bills/ You only got ten." So sang Dylan in "Subterranean Homesick Blues."

The Dylan mystique resulted largely from his inordinate sensitivity to the changing mood of the times. So as the politics of confrontation became more intense, so did Dylan's music. "Yes, my guard stood hard/ when abstract threats/ too noble to neglect/ Deceived me into thinking/ I had something to protect/ Ah, but I was so much older then/ I'm younger than that now."

In his 1965 "Bringing It All Back Home" Dylan portrayed a vision of a nightmare world of social chaos and psychic dread. In "Subterranean Homesick Blues" Dylan sings of street activists being repressed by the police in a vengeful and insane manner. "You don't need to be a weatherman to know which way the wind blows," crooned Dylan. "Look out, kid, it's something you did/ God knows when but you're doing it again/ Look out, kid, they keep it hid/ Better jump down a manhole, light yourself a candle." In "Highway 61 Revisited" Dylan portrayed a world of disorientation and madness.

"Desolation Row" represented a bleak diatribe against the loneliness and emptiness of urban life. "They're selling postcards of the hanging," the song opened. It then went on to describe a totalitarian state ruled by a death force "At midnight all the agents/ And the superhuman crew/ Come out and round up everyone/ That knows more than they do." The song ended in hopelessness not unlike that felt by many youth. "Yes,

I received your letter yesterday/ About the time the doorknob broke/ When you asked me how I was doing/ Was that some kind of joke?...? Right now I can't read too good/ Don't send me no more letters, no/ Not unless you mail them from Desolation Row." Thus, reflecting the growing anger of youth, Dylan had moved in a few short years from coherent narratives of social protest to bitter diatribes about lost visions and an impossible world.

The rise of Dylan was matched by that of the cosmopolitan British singing group called the Beatles. Beatlemania came to America early in 1964 when the frisky foursome--donned in bizarre Edwardian costumes, lace ruffles, and "great pudding bowls" of hair--appeared on the Ed Sullivan show, pushing the program's television ratings to the highest level in history. The slamming guitars and drums, secondary rhythms and melody, harmonics and the bawling "yeah, yeah, yeah," proved to be especially appealing to the young, who had become fascinated with the new electronic amplifiers, tuners, magnetic cartridges, air suspension speakers, and wide-angle sound effects of the new stereophonic technology. According to a _Life_ magazine observer, the new sensational sounds, soon known as the "Liverpool Sound," amounted to "an attempt to blow the public mind with technological voodoo."

In 1964 the Beatle "Ragmopheads" had placed an unprecedented six number-one pop hits. In 1965 their recording "Yesterday" sold over one million copies in the first ten days after its release. By 1966 Beatle John Lennon observed that his group "had more of a hold on teenagers than Jesus. Christianity will go. It will vanish and shrink," predicted Lennon. "I don't know which will go first--rock or Christianity." Such pretension caused a brief furor in America, but back in England the Beatles performed before Queen Elizabeth. "People in the cheaper seats, please clap," jested Lennon wryly, "the rest of you just rattle your jewelry."

The Beatles were to the music of the decade as the Kennedys were to politics, setting a tone which would be emulated everywhere. In 1965 Amex Corporation introduced the stereo tape cartridge, making tape decks a must in stereo sets, automobiles, and even pleasure boats. Listening to popular music almost became an obsession. One observer admitted that "when the Beatles started out they were a pretty bland bunch playing subdued ... harmless stuff." But as the decade grew more tense, they followed Dylan into the field of social protest. John Lennon expressed an early fondness for Dylan's "striving to tell it like it is." The Beatles' transition to self-conscious lyrical beats filled with "metaphysical subtleties" and "surrealistic epigrams" became evident in their 1967 album _Sgt. Pepper_, which sold an unbelievable 2,500,000 copies in the first three months. This package of "psychic shivers" denoted the growing generation-gap. In that same year the Beatles song "Nowhere Man" described the person without direction or point of view in dislocated times: "Nowhere Man, Living in your nowhere land/ Doing all your nowhere things, for nobody." Like Dylan, the Beatles gave profound expression to a new culture.

Numerous rock groups emulated the beat and lyrics as well as the social consciousness of the Beatles, often adding a few new twists of their own. The loud and nasty sounds of the Rolling Stones, which brought screaming and electrified rock to its maximum, ignited almost as much havoc and hysteria as the Beatles. "Everywhere I hear the sound of marching, charging feet/ Hey, think the time is right for a palace revolution," blasted their lyrics. The rough-hewn sound of the Stones sung in a mock Negro dialect presented youth with the ultimate rebel image. "I don't give a damn about convention," decried lead singer Mick Jagger, whose grinding performances reminded one critic of a "spastic marionette."

The sounds of rebellion against convention filled the air. Simon and Garfunkel intoned the mood of the dispossessed: "And people bowed and prayed/ To the neon god they made/ And the sign flashed out its warning/ In the words that it was forming/ And the sign said: The words of the prophets are written on the subway walls and tenement halls/ And whispered in the sound of silence." "All the cities will burn/ You are the people who will build up the ashes," sang the Motor City Five. Barry McGuire became famous for such war protest songs as "The Eve of Destruction." A group called Chicago Transit Authority included taped sound of actual street violence from the 1968 Democratic Convention in their early music. Chicago Transit Authority, composed of University of Chicago graduate students in music, became known by its trademarks--denim fatigues, dove-crowned peace flags, and bottles of Ripple wine--and by its use of hard political lines. From San Francisco's Haight-Ashbury the Grateful Dead, led by Jerry Garcia, known affectionately as "Captain Trips" or "Uncle Jerry," dominated the rock scene. Later Crosby, Stills, Nash, and Young were its "social conscience," conjectured _Time._

The Doors' Jim Morrison, clad in black vinyl pants, carried rock protest to new heights. "I'm interested in anything about revolt, disorder, chaos, especially activity that has no meaning," snapped Morrison, who got arrested for public indecency during a Florida performance; "it seems to me to be the road to freedom." The Doors acted out their music. In "The Unknown Soldier," an antiwar diatribe, the sounds of battle, gruff commands, fearful shouting, and even death rang from their blazing orchestration. The rock group The Who demonstrated its emotional frustration with the times by smashing the guitars and amplifiers as part of its onstage act. Jimi Hendrix, whose twisting and banging performances represented total release from inhibition, actually set his guitar on fire during his concerts. Sex and violence burned through the beat of his music. "You only remember each town by the broads," boasted Hendrix, whose hippie Latin American bandito outfit--black boots, silver-belted denims, Navajo vest, and pure purple velour gaucho hat--brought profound feelings of rebellion and liberation to his frantic worshippers.

At a typical rock concert audience participation became a central and fascinating part of the foray. There they were "arms linked together, swaying in unison, chanting in time to the psychic current," described Time. "There's a significantly greater communication between the music itself, the people who make it, and the people who listen to it than in Elvis Presley's day," explained Paul Kantner of the Jefferson Airplane. A concert could suddenly turn its attention away from social and moral criticism to sheer hedonistic ritualistic escapism and an appeal to the physical and the carnal. This was exemplified by the "San Franciscan Sound" introduced by Grace Slick of the Jefferson Airplane. By maneuvering the sound systems and lighting, the Jeffersons appealed to all of the senses. Their presentations were "raw, raucous, rough-hewn" with the "spark and spontaneity of a free-for-all jam session," reported Time.

The Jefferson Airplane, along with the Grateful Dead, represented the rise of "acid rock," a combination of rock and drugs which gave youth an opportunity to escape rather than to come to terms with the realities of modern life. The group's "Plastic Fantastic Lover" characterized the wounds technology visited upon humanity. "Her neon mouth with the blinking soft smile/ Is nothing but an electric sign/ You could say she has an individual style/ She's part of the carnival time/ Super-steel lady, chrome-colored clothes/ You wear 'cause you have no other/ I suppose no one knows/ You're my plastic fantastic lover/ The electrical dust is starting to rust/ Her trapezoid thermometer taste/ But all the red tape is mechanical rape/ Of the TV program waste/ Data control and IBM/ Science is mankind's brother/ But all I see is draining me/ On my plastic fantastic lover."

Along with the hard rock diatribe against modern society, the use of drugs, electric Kool-Aid as they were first called, would supposedly help youth better define the reality of human existence. The prolific smell of "pot" at rock concerts indicated that drug usage had become a significant part of the developing youth culture. Drug usage became a fashionable youthful fad, a welcome relief which freed youth from the "bonds that tie you down." Beyond that it was supposed to give youth a feeling of unknown potency, making "your body feel like a conductor for tens of thousands of volts." The lyrics of the song-poets encouraged experimentation with drugs. Peter, Paul, and Mary sang of "Puff, the Magic Dragon," the Doors sang of the "Crystal Ship," Jimi Hendrix sang of the "Purple Haze," and the Beatles sang "I Get High With a Little Help From My Friends" and "Lucy in the Sky With Diamonds." Marijuana became widely used because exponents claimed it was not habitual, dangerous to health, or psychologically repressive. It supposedly expanded one's mind, relaxed the body, and allowed for clear and sensitive perception. Youth experimented with other mind expanding drugs, but none were as significant as a drug called LSD.

Harvard professor Timothy Leary, 1966 founder of the League for Spiritual Discovery, became the generation's foremost advocate of LSD, arguing that an LSD experience was truly creative and liberating. Leary's League headquarters stood amidst the woodlands of New York's Millbrook estate. Newsweek called it "a strange mutation of Thoreau's Walden and a Tantric Buddhist temple." The woods were filled with statues and shrines, and there was a "Bavarian baroque hut "provided for individuals who wished to come and fast or meditate."

Wearing a magenta shirt and fringed-leather jacket, Leary, the guru of psychedelia, argued that LSD was "the sacrament that will put you in touch with the ancient two million-year-old wisdom inside you." This ancient wisdom would become the principle force behind the adornment of a new political city on earth, a new nation. Youth "are courageous enough to experiment on themselves with the psychedelics," asserted Leary, "and are sufficiently free from prejudice to consider the truths with which the visionary experience confronted them." "It will be an LSD country within fifteen years," claimed Leary. LSD could tune you in, turn you on, or drop you out. It produced good trips and bad trips; but for youth seeking freedom and new realities, it was a chance worth taking. A trip intensified perception, caused one to float outside himself, brought about vividness and newness, and flung one into ecstasy. Any object, even a fire hydrant, could "become an object of surpassing beauty." The experience helps you "follow the river inside you to its source and then out again," explained one user. Another LSD experimenter spoke of a majestic quietude, "an indescribable mood of great calm and peace. The problems and strivings, the worries and frustration of everyday life vanished," he wrote; "in their place was a majestic, sunlit, heavenly inner quietude. I seemed to have finally arrived at the contemplation of the eternal truth."

Along with the use of drugs many youth turned their attention to Eastern mysticism. The turning began as early as 1962 when poet Allen Ginsberg made a voyage to India to "connect" with ancient Eastern culture. This turning eastward coincided with the ranking among youth of Indian pacifist Mohandas K. Gandhi as the most prominently admired person in recent history. The quest for a more meaningful social and ethical medium based on Eastern culture was bolstered in 1966 when the Beatles, in a highly-publicized excursion, discovered the Zen-Buddhism of the Far East. The glamorous foursome made a pilgrimage to India for a visit with the Great Sage, the bearded guru, Maharishi Yogi, who offered a method of "transcendental meditation" which promised to achieve spiritual reality and inner tranquility. "When the conscious mind expands to embrace deeper levels of thinking" explained the Indian guru, "the thought wave becomes more powerful and results in added energy and intelligence." Claiming that his method could be "of special spiritual benefit to affluent, tension-ridden Westerners," Maharishi taught that ultimate reality came "through the soul's intuition of itself," not through pure reason as Westerners would have it. Coincidentally, his method was based on once-a-day meditation, stripped of the laborious and soul-searching penance and asceticism associated with traditional Hinduism. This provided the Beatles and their millions of youthful Western followers with an easy "ready-made" pattern of life dedicated to poverty, simplicity and meditation.

The symbol of Zen soon became the standard of the new counterculture. Zen provided values beyond logic and reason; it enshrined intuition and mysticism and glorified the spirit of the individual. Its absence of strict discipline and rigid formulation attracted freedom-searching youth. The amorality of Zen represented neither "a proselytizing creed nor a theology," wrote one admiring commentator, but, "rather, a personal illumination." In the quiet contemplation of Zen, youth could escape the "competitive exactions and conformities of technocracy."

In its efforts to achieve the feelings of Zen, youth turned to such domestic prophets of "angelic raving" as Allen Ginsberg and Alan Watts. Ginsberg, secular prophet of the Old Left, the mutterer, sought to be the voice, the instrument, "of powers beyond his conscious direction." His poetry expressed the "angry distress" of all creative and visionary people who felt stifled by bourgeois ideas and institutions. Ginsberg reached beyond his art in search of alternative modes of consciousness. "At poetry readings and teach-ins, he need not even read his verses: he need only appear in order to make his compelling statement of what young dissent is all about," wrote one contemporary. "The hair, the beard, the costume, the mischievous grin, the total absence of formality, pretense, or defensive posturing" prompted youth to appreciate more their inner existence. The old "vagabond proselytizer" attracted youth in its search for alternative life styles. For youth the

Indian-sign necklaces and Hindu temple bells stood for feeling, emotion, and mastery of truth and reality over the time-honored Western approaches of science, rationality, and skepticism. In an era of expertise, Pentagon worship, and superpragmatism, the Ginsberg method proved both refreshing and dangerous to established order.

The plastic flower culture of San Francisco's Haight-Ashbury became the most significant symbol of youth's attempt to experience the new psychedelic, mystical life style. Haight-Ashbury featured mind-liberating drugs, nudity, casual sex, obscenity, and absurd dress. "Strollers wear jingle bells at their ankles, beads or flowers at their throats, and strum guitars or tootle flutes," reported Time, which characterized the area not so much as a neighborhood as "a state of mindlessness." There shoeless, bearded hippies huddled in doorways, smoked pot, rapped, and fondled with an array of Hippiedom paraphernalia including elephant bells, English kites, love oil, incense, exotic posters of underground heroes, Japanese colored balls, kaleidoscopes, diffraction disks, and pocket-sized comic books. Zap Comix with characters like Mr. Natural and Fritz the Cat, created by Robert Crumb, were favorite underground comic strips. "Love" and "Peace" posters abounded, as did many ceremonious, peaceful demonstrations such as the "Human Be-In" staged in Golden Gate Park during 1967. Over 10,000 hippies participated in singing the praises of folk-rock, worshiping the descent of psychedelic parachutist, and listening to Hindu prayers chanted by various gurus. The Haight-Ashbury mood of transience and rootlessness was captured by balladeer Dion who popularized the song "Are You Going to San Francisco?"

In California's Seal Beach area hippies could be found participating in a "love-in" which featured the use of trash cans for drums and random flutes. In New York's Greenwich Village hippies paraded through Washington Square Park chanting "What is dog spelled backwards?" The hippies reached for the outer limits of cynical expressionism, advocating such anti-establishment causes as an end to the war and pay toilets, the legalization of psychedelic drugs, free food and fiber for the poor, and a heart transplant for LBJ. Exhibitionism became a favorite tactic of attracting attention. In San Francisco fifty young men and women stripped in Golden Gate Park before a crowd of astonished onlookers.

While many experimented with new life styles, the leaders of the youthful rebellion struggled for a philosophical rationale. Norman O. Brown, Marshall McLuhan, Ken Kesey, and Paul Goodwin, among others, became the canonical gurus of the movement. Youth learned from R. D. Laing, who wrote The Politics of Experience and The Divided Self , that the Western intellectual tradition had become dichotomized, chopping reality into undefinable parts and robbing individuals of reality. Laing's thinking was heavily dependent on mysticism. He taught that theory must free itself from the narrow and unimaginative confines of rules and canons of reason and the rational, observable scientific evidence. Laing suggested that in an insane world which condoned such actions as Vietnam, society had lost its sight of what sanity really represented and that those who carried the brand of insanity in a coldly rational world probably knew better the therapies for happiness than the so-called pragmatic experts.

A host of intellectuals, termed by radical writer Bayard Rustin as the "disaffected sons and daughters of the middle class," provided youth with plenty of rationale for rebellion. Novelist Norman Mailer was seen by many as a spokesman for New Left morality. In history William A. Williams, Staughton Lynd, Gabriel Kolko, and James Weinstein insisted, contrary to the consensus historians, that American society could best be understood through the study of class conflict rather than through an emphasis on consensus and continuity. In economics the New Leftist mood was best represented by Robert Theobald and Ben Seligman, while in sociology C. Wright Mills and Paul Goodman became often-quoted authorities. Sociologist Kenneth Winetroute expressed the connection between the New Left and academia: "In our present-day world, it is not enough to be scholarly," he insisted; "one must also be concerned enough to shout. It is not enough to understand the world; one must also seek to change it."

The person who probably represented New Left thinking more than anyone else was the aging Berkeley philosopher Herbert Marcuse, who spent his life modernizing the theories of Old Left hero Karl Marx. In two important essays, One-Dimensional Man (1964) and An Essay on Liberation (1969), Marcuse redefined the nature of oppression in an industrial society and offered new prescriptions for the achievement of happiness.

Through the application of Hegel's "historical dialectic," Marcuse reasoned that people in both the western capitalistic societies and in the communistic systems suffered from alienation resulting from a false consciousness perpetuated by selfish technical-bureaucratic elites, which he dubbed the technocracy. The technocracy rather than the capitalistic class became the culprit. The culprits included all who exercised power in an advanced society no matter what the ideology. Through the implementation of an "advanced industrial culture," the manipulative and devious technocracy superimposed a false individual identity. In modern society individuals were subtly deprived of autonomy, independence, and a true sense of self-fulfillment. Mankind did not experience real happiness, only the delusion of happiness. The average person existed merely as an unidentifiable and vulnerable cog in a vast, impersonal corporate-industrial machine. Man did not control the machine; rather, the machine controlled man. This analysis made good sense to youthful rebels impatient with over-burdening bureaucracy. The Code of Federal Regulation, for example, contained almost 60,000 pages of rules regulating life in America. Up to 5,000 new pages of rules were being added each year. Not even the high priests of technocracy themselves were certain how to interpret or apply many of these rules.

Marcuse believed that technology held in its bosom the possibility of eventual utopia which could some day supersede the current trends toward repression. He called for a revolution which would bring about a truly humanistic system in accordance with man's inalienable natural birthright. The revolution would not be fostered, as Marx would have it, through the working class movement; the modern worker had been "co-opted" by the technocratic system. The revolution would require more than the mere replacement of one elite by another. Rather, society must assert its control over the machine-oriented system. This would require an initial transformation of consciousness. The new consciousness must depend more upon the images and ideas of the romantic tradition and less upon the run-away, cold, calculating, scientific pragmatism of 20th-century liberalism.

Marcuse believed that the revolution would result from confrontation between technocratic elites and the Third World, which felt most acutely modern industrial repression. In the United States youth and minorities--manipulated and exploited elements of society--shared a Third World status. The developing counter-culture consciousness would provide the impetus for the revolt. The universities and inner cities would become the staging areas for the new revolution.

In a decade of growing anti-heroism youth turned to few mentors in the established adult world. Indeed, many looked abroad to embrace such Third World anti-imperialist revolutionaries as Che Guevara, Mao Tse-tung, and Ho Chi Minh, who themselves were victims of American imperialism. Youthful critics of the American system were simply too mistrustful of the compromise necessary to achieve success in contemporary industrial society. One exception to this rule was Ralph Nader, a lanky, sallow-faced graduate of Harvard Law School, who single-handedly challenged the practices of the most powerful captains of America's industrial bureaucratic elite. Zeal, inexhaustible energy, dogged pursuit of fairness, righteous abrasiveness, intolerance for half-truth, and stubborn impatience with corporate skullduggery--all of these characteristics became final elements in Nader's great appeal to youth.

Nader's greatest claim to the allegiance of youth grew from his consistent refusal to "sell out" to the establishment. His unquestioned independence and impeccable integrity could not be penetrated by the subtle forces of self-interest and conformity. Nader's operating style and personal demeanor reminded youth of a sincere, self-sacrificing crusader bent on eradicating the evils of organized society. His life style remained devoid of the customary modern frills. Like an ancient wilderness prophet dedicated to the principles of poverty and simplicity, he wore ragged clothes, refused to own cars and date girls, worked out of a low-rent apartment, and used an old secondhand portable typewriter in combat against the mammon of organized industry. Protest and non-conformity were commonplace to Nader's manner. During his undergraduate days at Princeton he had worn a bathrobe to class in order to protest the conformity in dress styles among his classmates, and on another occasion he disturbed university authorities by protesting the application of DDT weed spray because it killed the songbirds.

Nader's concerted attack on the establishment represented much more than a traditional muckraking campaign in the old Upton Sinclair mold. He was an activist consumer advocate dedicated to correcting as well as revealing problems in the system. He was best described as a relentless nag who persisted until results could be achieved. "You've got to keep the opposition off balance. Once you get them tumbling you can't let up.... That's the only way to get results," he argued. Nader once described his ultimate goal as "nothing less than the qualitative reform of the industrial revolution." Nader's efforts, explained the New York _Times_, stemmed "from the social consciousness of an ultra-individualistic lawyer ... instinctively opposed to any action he views as an arbitrary exercise of power against the individual." Beyond that Nader hoped that youth might learn from his example how vigorous citizen participation could make free enterprise and democratic institutions, principles he believed profoundly in, work for the welfare of all people. Chairman James Roche of General Motors charged that Nader and his followers were out "to start a crusade against corporations." Other corporate sympathizers complained that Nader sought to make business the "whipping boy" for the nation's problems. In reality, however, Nader strived to make the free enterprise system work better by putting competition and incentive back into the market place, a goal with which business could hardly quarrel.

Nader arrived in Washington as an understudy of Daniel Patrick Moynihan, then special assistant in the Labor Department. Astounded by Nader's searching mind, his precise command of substantive facts, and his earnest desire to do good,

Moynihan encouraged his young assistant to publish Unsafe at Any Speed (1965). This amounted to a devastating report on the safety defects in automobiles, especially General Motors' early Corvairs, "one of the nastiest-handling cars ever built." The book became a best-seller but may not have had much impact until it became known that General Motors hired Vincent Gillen, a private detective, to "get something, somewhere on this guy (Nader) to get him out of our hair and shut him up." The investigation included threatening telephone calls and sex traps. This blatant invasion of privacy outraged public opinion and prompted such powerful Senators as Abraham Ribicoff, Warren Magnuson, Gaylord Nelson, and Robert Kennedy to see the passage of the Motor Safety Act of 1966, an act which established a federal agency to set and enforce mandatory vehicle safety standards.

Nader's public relations victory over the auto makers established him in Washington as the defender of consumer interests. He quickly became known as the King of Consumerism, "the nation's ombudsman par excellence." From this unique vantage point he engineered a number of important reforms. His article in the New Republic entitled "We're Back in the Jungle" documented the grisly practices in the meat industry and led to the passage of a stronger meat inspection act in 1967.

Subsequently, Nader brought attention to the laxity in the Food and Drug Administration and launched investigations that resulted in legislation such as the Natural Gas Pipeline Safety Act of 1968, the Radiation Control for Health and Safety Act of 1968, the Coal Mine Health and Safety Act of 1969, and the Comprehensive Safety and Health Act of 1970. Nader's burgeoning popularity prompted President Johnson to predict that consumerism would be one of his "major talking points" in his 1968 re-election campaign. After LBJ had signed the Nader-initiated flammable fabrics act in 1967, he demonstrated his belated concern by lecturing the assembled legislators: "You better get with it," scolded the President, "because women are tired of meat with worms in it, blouses that burn, and pipe lines that blow up under their homes."

"A bureaucracy is like a fish. It rots from the head down," Nader once exclaimed. The essential truth of his contention was revealed when in 1968 he launched an investigation into the practices of the Federal Trade Commission, the agency which had been established in 1914 to regulate corporate practices and protect consumers from abuses in the market place. This agency, more than any other, represented the Progressive ideal of insuring fair play in America's modern corporate economy. The operations of the FTC had always given unsuspecting citizens the impression that Big Government could protect consumers from the more conniving intrusions of powerful private vested interest groups. Nader's report revealed what New Deal critic Herbert Hoover had long ago predicted: regulatory agencies ultimately operated more in favor of the industries supposedly regulated than in the interest of consumers. This allegation represented a fundamental contradiction in America's economic system and served to confirm the hypocrisy which youthful rebels had suspected.

Nader's persistent consumer campaigns greatly diminished the credibility of established institutions and leaders and encouraged criticism from other persons in the establishment, some of whom attracted at least some allegiance from the youthful protesters. Youth was attracted to the wide appeal of New York Senator Robert F. Kennedy, whose untimely death by assassination caused profound distress and a feeling of being cheated by the establishment. President Johnson's liberal Attorney General, Ramsey Clark, drew some praise for his vocal opposition to the brutality of law enforcement officials. Associate Supreme Court William O. Douglas received acclaim for his book entitled <u>Points of Rebellion,</u> in which he wrote that "we must first realize that today's Establishment is the new George III."

The modish-looking New York Mayor John V. Lindsay gained similar acclaim for his night time strolls through that riot-torn city. Dr. Benjamin Spock, upon whose advice many youth had been reared, and Yale Chaplain William Sloane Coffin, Jr. became instant heroes when they were arrested for resisting the draft. Comedians such as the Smothers Brothers, who used television to criticize establishment attitudes, became temporary heroes, as did Dick Gregory, who claimed that "America is the most morally polluted, degenerate, insane country in the world today." Even economist John Kenneth Galbraith, leader in the prestigious establishmentarian organization called Americans for Democratic Action and John Kennedy's Ambassador to India, gained some acclaim for his astute analysis of modern society's contradictions in his book entitled <u>The Industrial State.</u> "In his view, industrial growth often conflicts with esthetic achievement, and pollutes not only the atmosphere, but also the human psyche," wrote <u>Time,</u> "because consumers and employees surrender to the goals of the organization."

Of all the figures who drew allegiance from the youthful rebels, none gained more respect than Minnesota Senator Eugene McCarthy, who decided in 1967 that President Johnson's "cynical" management of the Vietnam War deserved a political challenge from the liberal wing of his own party. McCarthy and many other liberals were concerned that the political system had not offered youth and their supporters a point of participation, hence the rising tide of street demonstration and violence.

Draft resistance had sharply increased as groups of young militants burned draft cards and rifled files, staged lie-ins and sit-ins aimed at blocking troop and weapon movements, and mounted attacks on ROTC headquarters. Young men increasingly evaded the draft by fleeing to Canada.

Late in 1967 LBJ was obliged to employ troops in the nation's capital for the first time since the days of Herbert Hoover's ill-fated veterans march for higher benefits. The protesters carried red and blue Viet Cong flags and posters reading "Dump Johnson" and "Where is Oswald when we need him?" Baby Doctor Benjamin Spock set the tone: "The enemy is Lyndon Johnson; the war is disastrous in every way." "We are now in the business of wholesale and widespread resistance and dislocation of the American society," announced radical youth leader Jerry Rubin.

Even while McCarthy was mounting his campaign, disturbances at New York City's prestigious Columbia University signaled how far the youth rebellion had moved toward radicalism since Berkeley. Throughout the 1967-68 academic year the SDS and the Student Afro-American Society had been agitating against university policies. Mark Rudd of the SDS placed the liberal establishment on notice concerning the nature of the new, violent student mood: "You liberals don't know what the scene's about," Rudd protested. "It's about power and disruption. The more blood the better."

During the spring the university erupted over the administration's plan to construct a gymnasium in an area of Harlem which would deprive many blacks of their homes and significantly alter the esthetic composition of the area. Another issue involved the university's participation in a consortium which performed research for the Department of Defense. Finally, in April radical students occupied campus buildings, destroying property, faculty notes, and records and forcibly resisting arrest by police. Whereas Berkeley had been more concerned with internal administrative matters, Columbia loomed as a revolutionary instrument to force change in society as a whole.

"The real cause was this common feeling of the students, which was more than just the gym," recalled student Peter Kircheimer. The new gym issue merely symbolized "high-handed exploitation of blacks and Puerto Ricans." According to Kircheimer, the rebellion represented "anger against society in general for the war in Vietnam and for the social injustices that were going on, and against the university for its complicity in these things." "Columbia students wanted a new and independent University standing against the mainstream of American society, or they wanted no University at all," wrote one observer; "they are, in Fidel Castro's words, 'guerillas in the field of culture.'" The radicals had in effect rejected "outright a promise for liberal peaceful change."

Senator McCarthy and his followers understood only too well that the feeling of exasperation with the liberal establishment ran deep on the nation's campuses. At Berkeley students still held some hope for the workings of the political system. At Columbia youth in large numbers were ready to forsake the traditional avenues of political communication for underground tactics. This feeling was partly reflected by the fact that some 630 underground radical newspapers enjoyed a circulation of over three million.

The growing propensity of youth to settle its differences outside of the regular political system prompted McCarthy, who had been one of the first to challenge the outrageous activities of Senator Joe McCarthy in the early Fifties, to announce on November 30, 1967, his intention to challenge the incumbent President on the basis of his Vietnam War policies. "The administration seems to have set no limit on the price it is willing to pay for military victory," protested McCarthy, terming the war "indefensible legally, constitutionally, diplomatically, historically, militarily and morally." McCarthy claimed that the war was corrupting the nation's moral and ethical foundations. The war issue "involves a deep moral judgement with reference to national policy and the future of the nation," he asserted. Thus, the Senator with the unpretentious and soft mannered posture, who spoke with a creaky, jerky voice and swore off all pretensions of power, became a hero of youth--a last desperate hope to set the system straight.

"Every great and commanding movement in the annals of the world is the triumph of enthusiasm," Ralph Waldo Emerson once wrote; "nothing great was ever achieved without it." McCarthy gladly embraced youthful enthusiasm for his seemingly impossible effort against the well-placed Johnson. The young "would rather not demonstrate--they'd rather get involved in a political campaign for issues they believe in," pronounced McCarthy. "They are inexperienced; they oversimplify; they may not have a sense of history," admitted the Senator. "They have other shortcomings, but they bring with their commitment intelligence, a deep sense of spirit and hope." From the beginning youthful enthusiasm keyed McCarthy's drive toward the Presidency.

Although McCarthy would remain a mystery to the political world--an "unfathomable blend of intellect, humor, humility, and arrogance," as *Time* reported--in the eyes of youth he soon came to represent the non-politician's non-politician. He would not seek the Presidency, he said, for the sake of power; rather, in a move that could well jeopardize his otherwise secure political future in Minnesota, the slightly-graying, slightly-stooping Senator placed everything on the line on behalf of the war issue--an image not unlike the Biblical David facing the mighty Goliath. The Senator's mild manner, uninspiring nature, wit, and scholarly interests easily captured the imagination of idealistic youth. His professed love for poetry gave him a romantic twinge well suited for an uncertain generation yearning to hear a quiet, soothing voice of good hope. Thousands of youth "shaved, scrubbed, and dressed" to be "clean for Gene," reported political analyst William Manchester.

McCarthy's campaign began simply as a referendum on Vietnam but quickly expanded into a major critique of American institutions, especially the U. S. Presidency, an institution gathering such rapidly expanding powers as to corrupt the sensibilities of any occupant. The Presidency has become an "incarnation of all the hopes and aspirations of the country," complained McCarthy. "I think that is to put too much of a burden on the office." The war, according to McCarthy, represented an outrageous manifestation of wrongful vested power; and the Senator, in whiggish fashion, called upon his countrymen and Congress to take that power back. The excessive power had bred cynicism in high places and left decent people alienated from the political process. "I have sensed a deep uneasiness about the war and about the quality of our leadership," contended McCarthy. "It flows from a profound and growing conviction that something is wrong with the direction of American society." According to the professorial McCarthy, the war transgressed the traditional prudence and decency represented by Democrats Adlai Stevenson and John Kennedy and diverted the nation's energy and high purpose toward terrible destruction. McCarthy called for "a constituency of conscience, of hope and trust in the future."

The political experts did not expect the soft mannered poet-Senator from the nation's hinterlands to make much of a showing against the powerful, haughty incumbent LBJ. The pundits could not imagine that a man who had sponsored little legislation, and who possessed a reputation for avoiding hard analysis and stunning decisions, and who had deprecated executive responsibility would ever occupy the White House. Many suspected that McCarthy would really rather go fishing with his favorite poet, Robert Lowell, than attend the numerous duties of State. Even McCarthy viewed his chances dimly at first.

But McCarthy was destined to become a serious candidate. In the first primary in New Hampshire on March 12, 1968, the erstwhile Senator, who never forsook his cultivated and dignified demeanor, scored 42.2 per cent of the vote compared to Johnson's 49.2 per cent. The astounding outcome was billed as the political upset of the decade. The shock waves of Tet and the extraordinary volunteer assistance from college students provided McCarthy's surprise showing. The experts called it a moral victory. After New Hampshire and then Wisconsin McCarthy became a serious Presidential contender, warding off a spirited challenge from New York Senator Robert Kennedy which ended with Kennedy's bloody assassination in California after having won that key primary.

McCarthy's greatest challenge came from the established politicians, who jealously controlled the Democratic party apparatus and who quickly shifted their support to party stalwart Hubert Humphrey after LBJ's surprising withdrawal from the jumbled race. Humphrey would not challenge McCarthy openly in the primaries, thus thwarting the opportunity for a public debate of the Vietnam issue. Youth fought on anyway, and by the time of the Democratic National Convention, the underdog Senator enjoyed a higher popularity rating among the rank and file voters. Humphrey had to resort to back room bargaining to corral his majority of delegates. The predominance of back room bargaining over open politics caused disillusionment among many youthful activists even before they arrived in Chicago for the convention amidst the late August heat of 1968.

All of the explosive, conflicting forces that had turned American society into a muddle during the decade descended like irrepressible demons upon the windy city of Chicago, where the irascible Mayor Richard Daley, who like a Chinese war lord ruled as the last of the big city bosses, resolved to bare the establishment's teeth. As hippies, yippies, New Leftists, self-proclaimed revolutionaries, and assorted dissidents, numbering upwards of 10,000 strong, moved into Loop area near the convention site, the proud Mayor insisted with fierce and eccentric veracity that "law and order will be maintained." He refused protesters permission to sleep on the soft grass of nearby Lincoln Park, constructed barbed wire barricades around the Amphitheater convention site, placed his 12,000 man police force on 12-hour shifts, and brought in almost 12,000 federal and national guard troops. "Daley virtually invited violence," asserted _Time._

Daley's intransigence actually provided the anticipated opportunity for the more radical elements of the New Left to score political victories in the streets which could have not been possible in the more orderly atmosphere of the Amphitheater. Mobilization chairman David Dellinger, editor of _Liberation,_ understood that careful protest strategy could make the police and party bosses look like "mindless, brutish skull busters beating on helpless youthful martyrs." Dellinger was flanked by chief aide Tom Hayden, author of the Port Huron Statement, Yippie guru Abbie Hoffman, former Berkeley activist Jerry Rubin, and Rennie Davis, the son of former Truman administration economic advisor, who vowed that the radicals would "force the police state to become more and more visible."

Much of the protest activity involved hilarious demonstrations aimed at showing the hypocrisy of the modern political process. One group of hippies promoted the candidacy of a pig, named Lyndon Pigasus Pig, for the Presidency. Others roamed through the Loop area handing out antiwar leaflets and flowers. Some sat quietly along the waters of Lake Michigan listening to Allen Ginsberg recite Yippie poetry. Protesters taunted police with obscenities, calling them pigs, and threw some objects such as bricks and spike-studded golf balls; but real violence did not break out until Wednesday evening, the night Daley refused permission for protesters to parade outside the Amphitheater where Humphrey was to be nominated. The embattled LBJ by then had decided to stay away from the convention altogether.

The demonstrators pressed their case as they moved down Michigan Avenue in front of the famous Conrad Hilton Hotel, headquarters for both Humphrey and McCarthy. That was when the outrageous blood-letting began. Angry demonstrators lowered a U. S. flag in nearby Grant Park, protesting the arrest of some of their leaders. Police hurled tear gas and mace into the crowd. When busloads of armed reinforcements arrived, the police, with billy clubs flailing, began mass arrests. The demonstrators fought back with all their might. Police viciously attacked clergymen, newsmen, photographers, and passerby, as well as unruly demonstrators, turning the city into a fortress of fear. CBS commentator Eric Sevareid called it "Prague West." Eventually, even the McCarthy headquarters got raided. The "cops violated the civil rights of countless innocent citizens and contravened every accepted code of professional police discipline," complained Time; "Thanks to Mayor Daley, not only Chicago but the rest of the U.S. as well was pictured as a police state." "The whole environment of politics had come apart. It became polluted and destroyed and violent," complained Senator Humphrey.

The Chicago conflagration left the nation deeply divided. The division could be seen inside the Amphitheater, where flushed and short-tempered Democrats shouted at one another, some defending while others condemned the actions of the demonstrators. Eastern liberals, such as Abraham Ribicoff, publicly berated the smug Mayor Daley from the convention podium. An angry Daley and his political henchmen from the Illinois delegation shouted back in consternation. George Meany called the demonstrators and their sympathizers a "dirty-necked and dirty-mouthed group of kooks." The tension between Humphrey and Johnson also grew worse. When the beleaguered President heard of fence-mending conversations between Humphrey and some doves, he sent the irascible John Connolly to warn the tearful Vice President that any break over Vietnam would result in a draft-Johnson movement at next day's roll call.

The mayhem confused and shocked the commentators. "Here in Chicago you see America plain with no holds barred, no warts missing from the portrait, with everything there," wrote Max Lerner nervously, "with platform debates, with Lester Maddox and Julian Bond, with hippies and yippies and the New Left, with soldiers and Secret Service and maddening security tightness, with police squads, but with unflinching resolve to show and face what America is really like." Other commentators were not so generous, however. "It is the general proposition of the marchers and protesters that the political convention is beneath their contempt but not their notice; that a convention is not democratic and therefore should be prevented by totalitarian methods," stated CBS's Eric Sevareid in a comparison between Chicago and the Eastern Bloc invasions of Czechoslovakia. "Youths are dying in Prague because they know they are not free; here they will demonstrate because they think they are not free." The gulf existing between those who ruled and those who were ruled, whether in the East or West, had become a major reality of the time.

The circumstances surrounding the McCarthy campaign and the fateful year of 1968 were aptly described by *Time* as a year of "frustration and disruption, of groping and dismay. Many were killed, the timid endured, the vague were exalted, the hesitant lost. Finally, the managers stepped in, good and gray but hardly the stuff to invigorate the imagination." "By 1968 we had a situation where the country really did seem to be coming apart," conjectured historian Erik F. Goldman. The idealism of the youth movement was crushed on the brutal streets of Chicago. After Chicago, youth split into different directions. Some joined the efforts to intensify the violent revolutionary actions. Some members of SDS left to form the Progressive Labor and Revolutionary Youth Movement which, in turn, split, producing a Weatherman faction bent on all-out violent revolution and disruptions, including bombings and such activities as the burning of the Isla Vista office of the Bank of America. "The American school system will be ended in two years," screamed Jerry Rubin. "We are going to bring it down. Quit being students. Become criminals."

Most of the young forsook activism and radicalism, however, and sought escape within themselves, their spirits broken. They turned away from establishment concerns toward the more romantic themes which would provide the foundations for the Age of

Aquarius. Aquarius meant many things, but most importantly it represented total rejection of modern American culture mixed with a search for a simpler, more community-oriented life style. Youth began to search for utopian alternatives resembling those of early 19th century reformers, such as New Harmony, organized in the 1820's, the earliest days of the American Industrial Revolution. The ideals were not that much different; they involved common ownership and use of property and facilities. Aquarius represented a great change in interests from earlier in the decade when the most popular thing on campus was the zany spring vacation trip to Fort Lauderdale or Daytona Beach for what most young men called "beach, broads, and booze."

The Woodstock Music and Art Fair of 1969 characterized the new mood of youth. The phenomenon took place amidst the gently rolling hills around White Lake, New York, a traditional haven for cultural maestros of the avant-garde. Woodstock represented the "most apocalyptic be-in in the history of the rock and psychedelic movement," wrote Time. Abbie Hoffman called it "the birth of the Woodstock nation and the death of the American dinosaur." Allen Ginsberg called it "a major planetary event." Max Lerner called it "an event in a cultural, not a political revolution, but a revolution none the less." And an Aquarian celebration it was. An estimated half million lusty youths peacefully descended upon the site wearing beads, feathers, and bandannas; smoking marijuana; "skinny dipping;" eating macroburgers made of soybeans, rice, and vegetables with slices of cucumbers; and carrying placards which read "Keep America Beautiful--Stay Stoned" and "Head Power."

Woodstock represented more than a rock concert featuring twenty-four different rock groups and such luminaries of protest music as Joan Baez, Arlo Guthrie, Country Joe McDonald, the Rascals, the Guess Who, and Blood Sweat and Tears, singing "Out in the Country." "This festival will show that what this generation is all about is valid," proclaimed promoter Michael Lang. "People will all be going into their own thing. This is not just music, but a conglomeration of everything involved in the new culture." Thousands of the youthful worshippers could neither hear nor see the rock groups but celebrated anyway, feeling a real sense of belonging in this massive expression of humanity.

According to Time Woodstock represented a "tribal gathering, expressing all the ideas of the new generation: communal living away from the cities, getting high, digging arts, clothes and crafts exhibits, and listening to the songs of revolution." The most popular songs were those criticizing Vietnam; and when an army helicopter hovered overhead, hundreds of thousands of those present spontaneously waved the peace sign and cheered for themselves. Even the heavy rain could not dampen the spirit of Aquarius. "Nobody wanted to let go of what we'd had there," wrote an enthusiast. "What we'd had was a fleeting, wonderful moment of what you might call 'community.'"

Another late decade manifestation of Aquarius was the musical Hair, a singular performance which prompted Look to predict that it "might become the most ubiquitous piece of dramaturgy since Uncle Tom's Cabin. " According to columnist Tom Wicker, the musical stood "with Woodstock as symbols of the flower-child experience of the Sixties." "Swing with us, turn on with us," crooned the pop-eyed cast of young rockers and rollers as it moved spontaneously through its free-form, plotless production which included a nude scene and an invitation at the end for the audience to join the onstage festivities. The production represented Joseph Papp's idea of public theater, that of making the audience an integral part of the performance.

Hair tried to "present the hippie phenomenon as the mixed-up but inescapably alive eruption of energy and ... conviction that it is," wrote critic Jack Kroll in Newsweek. "It ignites the key images and issues of the lost-and-found generation--youth vs. age, sex, love, the draft, race, drugs, Vietnam--into a vivid uproar that has more wit, feeling and musicality than anything since 'West Side Story'". Hair provided a final powerful statement of what the rebellion of the Sixties stood for. Its lyrics invited the world to join in the spirit of peace and love. The age of Aquarius would be an era of "... harmony and understanding/ sympathy and trust abounding/ no more falsehoods or derisions/ golden living dreams of visions/ mystical revelation/ and the mind's true liberation." All of the youth's puissant idealism was captured in the lines, "peace will guide the planets/ and love will steer the stars."

Even though youthful protest spilled over into the Seventies, the movement had clearly lost its momentum by the end of the decade. Diminishing economic prospects caused youth to become more concerned once again with securing employment after college. Stricter law enforcement efforts increased the risk of dissent. Drug addiction depreciated the argument that drug usage could lead to liberation. Many turned to the "Jesus" movement in search of relief. The establishment made compromises on such things as the draft lottery and relaxation of university rules which satisfied most of the more moderate youthful protesters. By 1970 the movement had lost its magnetism, inflicted its contributions to historical change, and was ready to be placed in the history books as a significant, if disruptive, episode in the American experience.

CHAPTER IX

SILENT MAJORITY RUMBLINGS

The youthful insurgence rattled the foundations of the establishment and ended the political career of President Johnson, but it also brought down upon itself the unremitting wrath of middle America. A majority of Americans who had spent the decade "behind the sparkling city lights" and sensational headlines, minding their own business, now began to rail against the spectre of dissent and disorder as represented by the New Left. The millions of people who identified with the reaction defiantly associated themselves with what was called the Silent Majority.

Like the Red Scare and McCarthyism before it, the Silent Majority reaction was fueled by unstable economic conditions; rapid change wrought by war, ambitious politicians, and bureaucrats anxious not to take the blame for the decade's failures; conniving business and labor elites; conspiracy-minded conservatives and publicists; traditional anti-intellectualism; and the fear engendered by the violent words and actions of the New Left radicals themselves. By 1968 the reaction had developed into a full-fledged historical movement proclaiming its own beliefs, symbols, and leaders. The appearance of hard hats and VFW caps worn proudly; flag pins on the lapel and patriotic car window decals; mailboxes painted red, white, and blue; flags draped in front of homes; parade floats bearing such themes as "Love--the foundation of Law and Order;" and bumper stickers reading "America: Love It Or Leave It" signaled the nation that the Silent Majority meant to be recognized.

The Silent Majority was comprised mostly of blue collar workers, service employees, farm producers, elderly citizens, and white collar personnel. This number could have included as many as 91 million persons, estimated <u>US News.</u> The Silent Majority tended to live in America's heartland--ordinary main-street folks rather than on the coasts--but many could be found in such opulent suburbs as Queens, New York; Van Nuys, California; and Skokie, Illinois.

One pundit described the Silent Majority as those who were unyoung, unpoor, and unblack, people accustomed to the back of the church, the front of the bus, and the middle of the road. "He's the guy who works hard all day and maybe comes home too tired to move, but he has to moonlight anyway to pay his bills," proclaimed New York City Democratic mayoral candidate Mario Angelo Procaccino in 1969. "He wants to educate his kids. He wants his neighbors to be peaceful and clean. He doesn't have a doorman. His kids go to public schools. He rides the subways and the buses. He never burned his draft card or a flag, and never will. He tries to play the game by the rules, and for that he's getting pushed into a corner," continued Procaccino, who almost unseated liberal Mayor John Lindsay. The Silent Majority represented the "forgotten men" that laissez faire sociologist William Graham Sumner had shown profound concern for in the 1880's, when America's modern political economy was still in its infancy. "The quiet, virtuous, domestic citizen, who pays his debts and his taxes," should not be taken for granted, warned Sumner, or democratic capitalism would be in trouble.

More than anything the Silent Majority amounted to a state of mind, "a construct of values and prejudices and a complex of fears," reported Time. "The values that we held so dear are shot to hell. Everything is being attacked, what you believed in, what you learned in school, in church, from your parents," protested a typical middle American. Rather than establish a clearly-defined ideology, the movement represented a reassertion of traditional American principles--the spirit of entrepreneurship, free and private enterprise, the work ethic, pre-marital chastity, the notion of postponing gratification, sacrifice, frugality, and the goodness and inevitability of growth. Because such family-oriented movies as Funny Girl, 2001: A Space Oddyssey, and Oliver, --all rated for General Audience--were the top money-makers in 1968, the Oakland Tribune suggested "that the 'silent majority' also appears to be a wholesome majority."

Traditional American values aside, the Silent Majority was plagued with a feeling of economic insecurity brought about by the steep rise in the cost of living toward the end of the decade and by the fact that Americans' recent affluence had been based on consumption, not possession. Few Americans owned assets which would permit them to survive beyond their current position of employment; real economic security, then, had never been a factor in the prosperity of the Sixties.

The lavish promise of upward mobility endemic in the jargon of LBJ's Great Society simply did not materialize. While average gross income rose from $75 to $115 per week, additional taxes and inflation brought about by Great Society spending left less than a $10 gain. Between 1965 and 1970 the average cost of a new home increased from $20,000 to $28,000; and home maintenance costs spiraled--house paint and fuel oil by 15 per cent and mortgage payments and taxes by 75 per cent. Medical and educational costs were rising ominously, and Social Security took an ever-increasing portion of the paycheck.

The waning of material abundance and economic opportunity raised, once again, the dreadful spectre of class conflict and social discontent. "The class that calls itself 'middle' is, in fact, up against the wall; it is going nowhere and neither are its kids," wrote Professor John C. Raines of Temple University. Middle America was experiencing "less upward mobility ... less middle class affluence," and suffering increasingly from the effects of "moonlighting, worry and exhaustion," warned Raines. "Being 'middle' in America isn't working--and that is a political earthquake." A representative of Middle America put it another way: "The middle class is sort of losing heart," he complained. "They had their eye on where they were going and suddenly it's all shifting sands."

The economic malaise resulted in a profound feeling of loss of status not unlike that which undermined the confidence of the German middle class after World War I and led to the rise of Hitler's Nazism. The middle class felt its traditional independence being infringed upon. In both the social and political sphere it felt impotent. "Studies of the new suburbia show that neurosis and feelings of helplessness are endemic," wrote political scientist Andrew Hacker; "a sense of isolation and powerlessness is having profound social and psychological effects." Feelings of frustration left "the average American ... more deeply troubled about his country's future than at any time since the Great Depression," reported Newsweek. The frustration provided the impetus for a political explosion more dangerous than anything the New Left could have ever concocted. "You better watch out," warned Eric Hoffer, grass-roots blue collar philosopher. "The common man is standing up and some day he's going to elect a policeman President of the United States."

Middle America might have vented its anger and frustration against the top one per cent of the economic scale, the real establishment which controlled the destinies of the nation in the Sixties. But as it was with the Red Scare and McCarthyism--both movements which grew from the frustrations of wars earlier in the century--the Silent Majority characteristically turned its wrath toward those near the bottom of the economic scale who appeared less representative of the American dream. Middle Americans "blamed the poor and the blacks--those who came to be seen as freeloaders," explained Professor Raines, even though "the vast majority of people on welfare are elderly or disabled." "Ironically, they haven't even the option of hating the system which pinched their personalities, ruined their digestions and deadened their marriages," wrote Hacker; "radicalism isn't possible for them; so they blame the kids, the blacks, and the reds." Anxious to escape retribution itself, the establishment did little to discourage such sentiments. In essence, the atmosphere was ripe for the third Red Scare of the century.

The Silent Majority was primarily interested in purging the New Left student radicals who had proclaimed themselves the vanguard of the revolution. "Back America and her leadership and put the troublemakers in their place," cried one country editor. "As for such hate-mongers, who needs them?" demanded another. "Who the hell would have dreamt that a thing like this was possible?" bellowed philosopher Eric Hoffer; "ignorant, bedraggled, illiterate punks." Hard Hat opinion was further represented by Joseph Siemiller, President of the International Association of Machinists: "Union members are pretty sick of rioters, looters, peaceniks, beatniks, and all the rest of the nuts who are trying to destroy the country."

Middle Americans considered the hippie life style fatuous, vulgar, and idiotic. "A bath, a haircut and a good old-fashioned strap would get most of them back in line," blustered one. "If one of those hippies lays down in front of 'mah' car when 'ah' become President," shouted Governor Wallace, the fastest rising star of the Silent Majority, "it will be the last car he ever lies down in front of." Wallace promised that if elected, he would try war dissenters for treason. Mississippi Senator John Stennis, a dedicated Vietnam hawk who chaired the powerful Armed Services Committee, called for a constitutional amendment eliminating the right of trial for radicals who advocated the overthrow of American institutions. In response to some criticism leveled at J. Edgar Hoover, FBI Chief, for tapping the telephones of radicals, conservative New York Congressman Carleton King snapped: "I think it's high time some people were watched." Iowa Congressman Bill Scherle told his constituents that "when you talk about a college kid being a four-letter man today, you don't know whether he's an athlete or the editor of the campus newspaper." Governors and state legislators took their cue from the national politicians by passing numerous pieces of legislation that placed severe penalties on those participating in campus disruptions. In California alone 100 such bills were introduced in 1969.

California Governor Ronald Reagan excelled at chastizing student radicals. "We have some hippies in California," jested the Governor. "For those who don't know what a hippie is, he's a fellow who has hair like Tarzan, who walks like Jane, and who smells like Cheetah." The Silent Majority lauded Governor Reagan's attempts to deradicalize the University of California, beginning with his engineering of the dismissal of President

Clark Kerr. "You don't negotiate with student groups," proclaimed Reagan bluntly. "You listen to what they have to say. But if they don't abide by the rules, they can pack their bags, get out and seek their education elsewhere." Acting President Dr. Samuel I. Hayakawa of San Francisco State became the symbol of Reagan's hard-line policy. Contending that liberal arts colleges breed "contempt for middle class values and encourage an elitist sentimental identification with the lower class," Hayakawa, known as "Uncle Tojo Tom" to students, deployed police as a preventive measure, suspended the student newspaper, and forced the resignation of four out of five black college administrators who opposed his tactics.

The apparent failure of most college administrators to deal forthrightly with campus disruption disgraced the colleges in the eyes of the Silent Majority and brought out a surge of anti-intellectualism, an attitude always lingering just below the surface of the American mentality. "We have never envisioned the purpose of college as that of providing a base for marauding bands to embark on street rampages, arson, and worked-up confrontations with law enforcement organizations," editorialized the conservative Chicago Tribune. "The Silent Majority has sat quietly far too long while our institutions of higher learning have been used to breed contempt for the traditional and hate for those who are expected to support them," chided another middle-western newspaper; "if our country survives and recovers from this period of noise-making and unreason, it will surely be only because of the grace and wisdom that God might grant us, not because of the academic experts we have nurtured." Retired Army Brigadier General Clyde Watts charged that "more than 100 professors" at Berkeley "are hard-core working members of the Communist Party U.S.A."

Most middle Americans regarded a college education as a privilege, not a necessity. The college should be a place to learn and search, "not the place for gullible young students to be spoonfed a certain ideology by a radical professor," complained a middle American editor, charging that "students have been urged on in their campus dissent by those who are receiving their salaries from the taxpayers." The intellectuals were the intolerant ones, charged Eric Hoffer. "They would be uncommon men, do uncommon deeds, reach uncommon heights, but they are comdemned to be ordinary," he wrote. "So they never achieve the sense of usefulness that a man does who builds something, and they hate the system that requires them to build something in order to earn recognition."

A few intellectuals drew praise from the Silent Majority. New York's conservative William F. Buckley, publisher of the National Review, did receive favorable recognition from the Silent Majority when he conducted a personal campaign in 1968 at

Yale, his alma mater, to correct the "liberal imbalance" on the university's board and faculty. California's flamboyant Superintendent of Education, Dr. Max Rafferty, described by Time as "a spellbinder of alliterative conservatism" also found favor with middle America for his denunciations of "permissive, pragmatic progressivism in education." By the end of the decade American education had moved abruptly away from liberal education toward a new emphasis on trade and technical schools. Happiness was working with one's hands, and a little education could be a very dangerous thing.

Ranking second to student radicalism as a Silent Majority grievance were the manifestations of the civil rights movement. "The niggers are all organized. So are the Mexicans, even the Indians," complained a San Francisco hard hat worker, "but who the hell speaks for me?" The President of the National Confederation of American Ethnic Groups lamented bitterly that "we spend millions and the Negroes get everything and we get nothing."

Civil rights legislation represents "an attempt to destroy the seniority and apprenticeship lists of labor unions," charged George Wallace.

Court-ordered busing upset middle America because it conflicted with America's traditional beliefs about neighborhood schools for white children and threatened to reduce the quality of education received by whites. Open housing legislation engendered new fears of interracial marriage and interfered with the sanctity of private property. "There are certain fundamental rights that cannot be put to vote," protested Ronald Reagan, "and one of them is the right of a homeowner to sell his property to whoever he wants."

In Georgia Lester Maddox, who once brandished a pistol and a pick axe to prevent blacks from entering his restaurant, became Governor in 1966, calling himself the "little man's candidate." A lay Baptist preacher himself, Maddox "hit the campaign trail for God." Referring to civil rights, he claimed it was "them against us." "This civil rights legislation has the idea that everybody is equal," complained Maddox, "and they're not. Only in the sight of God."

Crime ranked third on the Silent Majority's list of grievances. Serious crime had more than doubled during the decade in the cities and almost tripled in suburban areas. The Washington, D. C., Board of Trade became concerned enough to warn Congress that "this city is not a safe place in which to live, work and play." "You just can't paint the picture too bad," exclaimed a Chicago policeman. "The astounding increase in crime could have been attributed to society's excessive stress on material gains," complained Columbia's sociologist

Robert K. Merton. It was due to disappointment in the face of rising expectations, Harvard's Seymour Lipset suggested. Crime resulted from the "development of something like a permanent underclass, not so much exploited as left behind--an economic substratum unable to rise by unskilled labor that is no longer in demand, unable to compete in a highly organized technological society, heavily damaged by being in the cities," wrote New York Times columnist Tom Wicker.

These studied answers to the rising crime rate did not impress the Silent Majority, who preferred to blame it on racism and permissiveness among students and blacks and especially on leniency in the courts. Thus, the courts too entered the grievance list of the Silent Majority, who felt that courts favored criminal rights over police action. "We are creating a climate of fear and horror in this country as long as the courts are going to let criminals loose on technicalities," charged Arkansas Senator John L. McClellan, the cotton country conservative who had inherited the chairmanship of the Permanent Subcommittee on Investigations from Wisconsin Senator Joseph McCarthy. "You can see what's happened," demanded George Wallace, "murder, rape, assault; and the criminals just laughing while the police are crying for help." The courts' "decisions have made it almost impossible for police to arrest a criminal," charged Wallace; "you can't walk the streets of large cities because the criminal would be let out of jail before you even got to the hospital." "We must reject the idea that every time a law is broken, society is guilty rather than the law breaker," argued Ronald Reagan. "It is time to restore the American precept that each individual is accountable for his actions."

The growing disenchantment with the courts was aptly reflected in Congress, where House Minority Leader Gerald R. Ford of Michigan launched an impeachment effort against U. S. Supreme Court Justice William O. Douglas for accepting an annual allowance from the Parwin Foundation, which had received some funds from Las Vegas gambling properties.

The United States Supreme Court came under severe criticism. "The violator of the law--whether he be on a college campus, in the streets, in uprisings that foment strife even while clothed protestingly in non-violence--must be made quickly and decisively to answer," demanded Felix R. McKnight, co-publisher and editor of the Dallas Times-Herald. McKnight charged that the Supreme Court had forfeited its protective arm and dignity, and he called upon "the people and the Congress to demand that the Supreme Court cease by 5-to-4 divided personal vote, making law that clouds enforcement and takes away deterrents to assassination and murder." Rather than coddle criminals, asserted McKnight, America must return to the "full recognition of the rights of the overwhelming majority of American society--the right to peaceful existence under the law."

In McKnight's Dallas, one of the nation's most conservative cities, the City Council exemplified Silent Majority tension over crime and hippies when it passed an ordinance prohibiting "walking about aimlessly, without apparent purpose, lingering, hanging around, lagging behind, idly spending time, delaying, scunering and moving slowly about, where such conduct is not due to physical defect or condition." The law was obviously aimed agaist hippies. Few cities became as stringent as Dallas, but many began to favor the election of public officials strong on law and order. In Los Angeles Sam Yorty became mayor on this issue, as did Chief of Police Phil Rizzo in Philadelphia, the City of Brotherly Love.

Law-and-order and disenchantment with the courts helped build a resentment of big government in general. Middle America never lost its confidence in the "democratic" system, but it came to distrust the so-called policy makers and bureaucrats in charge. Although not opposed to the reasons for Vietnam, many became impatient with what they interpreted as bureaucratic bungling of the war.

In domestic programs the Silent Majority bécame even more harsh. Often bureaucrats were seen as baked-over intellectuals. "The people are going to be fed up with the sissy attitude of Lyndon Johnson and all the intellectual morons and theoreticians he has around him," predicted George Wallace. "Our lives are being taken over by bureaucrat," he complained, "and most of them have beards." In 1968 Wallace campaigned against the "pseudo-intellectual government, where a select elite group have written guidelines ... saying that you do not know how to get up in the morning or go to bed at night unless we write you a guideline." In order to maintain "my perspective," continued radio news star Paul Harvey of Chicago, a favorite of Middle America, I must "stay out of the cloister.... The public is being fed such a steady diet of Manhattan-based myopia that the tail is wagging the dog." Harvey was referring to the entire northeastern establishment, its intelligentsia, press corp, and bureaucrats--the traditional scapegoats of Red Scare fervor.

The Silent Majority, like the New Left, looked to a wide array of heroes, symbols, and assorted expressions to articulate its cause. Wallace and Reagan were heroes in a sense but mostly political spokesmen. The real hero of the Silent Majority was J. Edgar Hoover, the "jut-jawed" Chief of the Federal Bureau of Investigation (FBI) who, through a combination of successful law enforcement and superlative public relations, had established himself over the decades as a granite-faced Chief Policeman. He forged the world's most sophisticated law enforcement agency. "The ideal agent can handle a teacup as well as a tommy gun," he contended.

Hoover's empire grew in the Sixties to 8,500 agents working out of 500 field offices which provided support services for more than 4,000 state, county, and local law enforcement agencies. Hoover's computerized Washington laboratory had on file the fingerprints of an estimated 90 million Americans. When the tempo of violence increased, middle America, as it had during the Red Scare and McCarthyism, again looked to the "Chief Protector" to embellish its sense of security.

Much good could be said about Hoover. In the Thirties he had dared to take on organized crime, and in the Forties he protested the allegedly unconstitutional confinement of Japanese citizens. By the Sixties, however, Hoover had become an anti-communist zealot who too often allowed his respect for law to be exceeded by his zest for patriotism. His antics had embarrassed the Kennedys. He restored his rapport somewhat with Johnson by playing on the President's suspicions about his political enemies and by providing him with secret accounts, for "bedtime reading," of the illicit sexual activities of certain public figures. Hoover conducted a running battle with Johnson's Attorney General Ramsey Clark, calling him a "jellyfish" after Clark had suggested that Hoover's "self-centered concern for his own reputation," hindered effective law enforcement. Hoover also could make Johnson uncomfortable, such as the time he subtly attacked the Supreme Court in his official organ, the *FBI Law Enforcement Bulletin.* The courts must "let the guilty criminal know that when he is arrested, he will be promptly prosecuted and substantially punished for his misdeeds," contended Hoover. Still, neither Johnson nor any other President dared move against this resourceful bureaucrat.

By the Sixties the American Communist Party had fallen into disarray under the lackluster leadership of Gus Hall. Some pundits jested that its membership included more FBI undercover agents than real communist ideologues. The decline of the so-called communist threat caused Hoover to cast his attention to other radical groups left and right. In the early Sixties his men (he flatly refused to hire women and minorities) infiltrated and disrupted the Socialist Workers Party. In 1964 the Ku Klux Klan, the Minutemen, and the American Nazi Party became targets of his sordid operations. FBI agents recruited prostitutes as sex traps in order to compromise leaders of the pro-Castro group called the Fair Play for Cuba Committee. Hoover personally ordered the surveillance, and even secret wire tapping, of Dr. Martin Luther King and other civil rights leaders.

The campus disruptions provided Hoover with a challenge made to order. "It has long been a basic tenet of Communist strategy," contended Hoover, "to control for its own evil purposes the explosive force which youth represents." Hoover assumed personal responsibility for a new counterintelligence program called "Cointelpro-New Left," patterned after his 1956 Cointelpro program to disrupt domestic communist activities. Radical students soon became Hoover's obsession. "I have reminded you time and again that the militancy of the New Left is escalating daily. Unless you recognize this and move in a more positive manner ... this activity can be expected to mount in intensity and to spread to college campuses across the country," wrote Hoover in a memo reprimanding his agents in May of 1968. "This must not be allowed to happen and I am going to hold each Special Agent in charge personally responsible...."

Hoover ordered "a major campaign" against the New Left. "The organization and activists who spout revolution and unlawfully challenge society to obtain their demands must not only be confuted but must be neutralized," commanded Hoover as he ordered Cointelpro agents "to expose, disrupt and otherwise neutralize the activities of the various New Left organizations, the leadership and adherents." Hoover told agents to disrupt "the organized activity of these groups and no opportunity should be missed to capitalize upon organizational and personal conflicts of their leadership."

The special agents dutifully obeyed their Chief's commands. They embarrassed the New Left by distributing concocted leaflets which contained vile language and obnoxious pictures. They infiltrated radical groups, cleverly playing upon the animosities among the leaders in order to disrupt the unity of the movement. They transmitted information to local police concerning the use of drugs. They wrote anonymous letters to newspaper editors, parents, and college officials in order to make the movement look ridiculous. They distributed anti-SDS newsletters on college campuses using fictitious names. One leaflet showed pictures of Princeton College SDS leaders sketched on monkey's bodies, captioned: "Princeton is not 'The Planet of the Apes.'"

One of the most vicious acts promulgated by Hoover's henchmen involved Iowa-born actress Jean Seberg, who had publicly announced her support for the Black Panther movement. Los Angeles FBI agents heard a rumor that Seberg was several months pregnant by a Black Panther leader. "The possible publication of Seberg's plight could cause her embarrassment and serve to cheapen her image with the general public," an agent advised Hoover. "Jean Seberg has been a financial supporter of the B.P.P. [Black Panther Party] and should be neutralized," ordered Hoover. The derogatory leak was promptly made. A few weeks later the Los Angeles Times reported the pregnancy of an unnamed international movie star. "Papa's said to be a rather prominent Black Panther," reported columnist Joyce Haber. The rumor was unfounded and, according to the actress' husband, resulted in her developing a psychotic condition. After discovering how viciously she had been used, columnist Haber called the incident "absolutely shocking and appalling."

Like wolves stealing up on their prey, FBI agents dutifully fomented sullen confrontations between students and police in order to further diminish the image of the New Left. They monitored the activities of prominent persons such as Eugene McCarthy and Ralph Nader, and they urged the Internal Revenue Service to audit the income tax returns of politicians and professors who had expressed sympathy with the radical movement. Hoover ordered Marlin Johnson, special agent in charge of Chicago, to cooperate with the La Cosa Nostra in a counterintelligence attempt designed to neutralize radical black comedian Dick Gregory. "This should not be in the nature of an expose, since he already gets far too much publicity," ordered Hoover; "instead, sophisticated, completely untraceable means of neutralizing Gregory should be developed." Hoover's FBI collected secret files on some 11,000 individuals who expressed opposition to Vietnam. The list included such luminaries as Rock Hudson, Joe Namath, Marlon Brando, and Jane Fonda--all Americans who, in Hoover's view, did not conform with the "100 per cent Americanism" he sought to sustain.

Like so many middle Americans, Hoover found it difficult to separate his religion from his nationalism. Hoover's pious religious expressions endeared him all the more with the Silent Majority. In Billy Graham's Decision magazine, which had referred to him as "the structure of integrity," Hoover said that Jesus was "a living reality" to him and that he hoped "for joy and salvation." "No matter what problems confront me," pontificated Hoover, "I know that I can count on our Redeemer for strength and courage." Hoover often reminded his audiences of the Bible he had received as a boy for attending fifty-two consecutive Sunday School sessions and mentioned that he would have become a Christian minister had he not decided to dedicate his life to the FBI.

Hoover believed that the New Left was both unchristian and un-American. "Rioting, looting, burning, and killing--deliberate crimes--are outrages spawned under the banner of civil disobedience, a dangerous philosophy based on shallow reasoning," wrote Hoover in the FBI Law Enforcement Bulletin. Radicals were persons operating "in contempt of all standards by which American society regulates men's baser impulses--faith in an ethical god, love of country, truth and honor in the dealings of men, respect for the family unit." Thus, Hoover presented a solid all-American image that soothed and gave middle America a hopeful feeling of security.

Hoover had good reason to associate his cause with evangelism since the Silent Majority strongly supported the resurgence of revivalism. Ever since the dramatic Great Awakening of the 18th century, led by Jonathan Edwards, revivalism had lingered just below the surface of American consciousness, erupting into public every generation or so. Not since the Billy Sunday crusades of the Twenties, however, had the nation been so ripe for a new wave of evangelism. Not only was there an apparent deterioration in the nation's morals and customs, fueled by the new liberalism in religion, but the growing social confusion had prompted millions of Americans to search for inner solace, a condition in which feelings superseded thought, complexity fell before simplicity, and science caved in to a sort of sorcery.

The new revivalism of the Sixties incorporated most of the old strains, be they Southern Bible Beltism, Protestant Calvinism, Prairie Purifierism, or middle-class pietism. The new outburst was symbolized by the appearance of a 200 year-old hymn, "Amazing Grace," sung by folk singer Judy Collins at the top of the popular music charts; this was followed a few weeks later by "My Sweet Lord," sung by none other than former Beatle George Harrison.

Billy Graham easily became the new revivalism's most buoyant spokesman. Donning a sharply-fitted business suit or a more liberal golden sports jacket and taking advantage of modern electronic communications techniques, this fiery preacher sent revivalism galloping substantially beyond the old-time caricatures of faith healers, holy rollers, counterfeit preachers, and simple-minded hypocrisy. Graham's preaching, remarked one critic, "was somehow an oddly denatured variety of the harsh vinegars of frontier Calvinism--reconstituted into a kind of mild, mass-consumption commodity, a freeze-dried instant sanctity, a rather sensible and efficient salvation."

Graham's efficiently organized crusades, which stressed personal redemption and fundamental faith, netted over 100,000 converts a year. The Billy Graham Association, headquartered in Minneapolis, operated on an annual budget of $15 million; and his magazine, *Decision,* which had been founded in 1960 to articulate profound Christian truths in simple language, enjoyed a circulation of over 3,500,000. Graham Crusades were usually administered by a committee of prestigious local businessmen who vaguely understood the connection between personal salvation and the perpetuation of democratic capitalism. Billionaire H. L. Hunt, for example, fellow parishioner of Graham in the Dallas

First Baptist Church, spent millions on evangelism, gloomily explaining that "we have perhaps three, four, five years to save the republic." By the end of the decade Graham had conducted successful crusades on almost every continent, and the location of the Billy Graham Pavilion just a few yards inside of the New York World's Fair attested to his growing international fame. Yet Graham remained thoroughly American in his sensibilities and in his approach. He viewed himself as "the prophet to call America back to God." "Never having been sullied himself by defeat or tragedy, eternally optimistic and enthusiastic, Billy Graham _is_ America," wrote one associate.

By the Sixties he had shed his early Southern Baptist awkwardness and patterned his delivery after what could almost be called a Madison Avenue technique. "Graham's sermons are masterpieces of popular rhetoric," wrote one critic, employing "drama, mimicry, slang and tension relieving humor. Graham is a master of invective, pathos, and the purple passage." His vigorous persistence, his utter sincerity and impeccable integrity, his superb style--the slicing index finger, the resonant voice, the oratorical control, and the ever-present open Bible lying in his big left hand--all of these elements marked him as the master preacher. His constant analogies between modern America and ancient Israel both calmed the nerves and reinforced the will of his followers.

Graham carefully refrained from attacking traditional institutions and refused to employ divisive tactics. His message of redemption was wholly positive, highly personalized, consensus-oriented, and tailored mainly to relieve the individual from the ignorance of sin involving personal behavior--nightclubs, drugs, alcohol, acid rock, sexual perversion, and sensuous dress. These sins, according to Graham, represent the bitter fruits of American affluence and permissiveness gone awry.

Graham perceived the declining faith in science and rationality and boldly called for a religious conception of a world where change and progress would be based upon the inner transformation of individuals rather than upon elaborate, impersonal social programs administered by thoughtless bureaucrats. By employing the twin passions of apocalyptic fear and the confident conviction that society could be renewed if individuals only made a personal commitment to Jesus, Graham provided millions of Americans, who had grown skeptical of modern humanistic social activism, with new hope for themselves and for America. Graham's unswerving insistence upon a passionate sense of God's presence in everyday life provided lonely converts not only with inner consolation but with a renewed feeling of Christian brotherhood, which sent thousands upon thousands of once complacent parishioners into zealous religious involvement.

Graham reached the pinnacle of his popularity in 1969-70, the early Nixon years. During the summer of 1969 he was instrumental in getting 4,600 enthusiastic delegates, including an Anglican Archbishop and even Pentecostals, to Minnesota for the first U. S. Congress on Evangelism. The six-day conference rallied support for a coast-to-coast crusade. This day "will affect every religious group in the country in the next decade," predicted Graham confidently.

In 1970 Graham, in traditional revivalistic fashion, clearly revealed himself as a spokesman for middle America's urge to combine religiosity and patriotism when he helped to sponsor Honor America Day in Washington, D. C., on the 4th of July. "The American dream is not finished yet," extolled Graham as he reached the Capitol city. I came here to stress "some of the good things about America," professed Graham. "We hope it will remind us that all is not pessimistic and hopeless.... There has been too much negativism." By taking the "what is good about America" line, Graham endeared himself with the Silent Majority, which itself clung to patriotism almost as an escape. Honor America Day eventually harmed Graham's credibility, however, because it associated him too closely with President Nixon, whose policies eventually polarized the nation.

Billy Graham represented the maturing of American evangelicalism during the Sixties. His Americanism provided a hope for stability in disruptive times. His antics proved too moderate for some members of the Silent Majority, however, as they became enthralled with more zealous crusaders such as Oral Roberts and Billy James Hargis, the two firebrands who turned Tulsa, Oklahoma, from the "oil capital of the world" into the "fundamentalist capital of the world." Having gained his fame as a faith healer, Oral Roberts decided in the Sixties to concentrate mainly on emotional television extravaganzas and the establishment of a dazzling new university characterized by a 200-foot-high Prayer Tower with a "crown of thorns" encircling its observation deck. A perpetual flame at the top of the tower signified the omnipotence of the Holy Ghost. Rotating groups of "prayer partners" ascended the tower constantly and made themselves available to counsel visitors or telephone callers about spiritual problems.

Far more flamboyant than Roberts was "Tulsa's number two windbag," as one observer called him, the pudgy, moon-faced Billy James Hargis, founder of Christian Crusade, "for Christ and against Communism." Hargis' targets were Russian Communism and the northeastern foreign policy establishment, which he charged consorted with the Soviets. "Russia has now become so strong that within four years, the United States will be blackmailed into surrender," warned Hargis. "With guns pointed at our back she [Russia] could easily take over the United States, our factories, our cities and our people ... and you."

Hargis attributed a communistic influence to almost everything liberal. In 1968 he launched a vicious attack against those who advocated sex education in the schools. "Sex has become a recruitment weapon in the hands of the devilish Marxist educators," charged Hargis. "Anything goes. Free love, free sex, perverted sex--as you like it, when you like it--this is the siren song of the liberal Marxist educators." Hargis' diatribes on sex netted 25,000 new contributors, which brought his list of major contributors to over 200,000 by the end of the decade. His "superfundamentalistic" broadcasts found air time on more than 500 radio stations and 140 television stations. He lived in a million dollar country mansion, called Rose Sharon Farm, where 90 telephone outlets connected him to his vast religious domain. "New Yorkers may regard [him] ... as a bigger buffoon than Roberts," wrote Martin Gardner in the New York Review, "but in the Middle West he is a greatly admired celebrity."

Much of his popularity with middle America stemmed from the fact that liberal education had become one of Hargis' primary targets. He founded the American College, designed to be even more fundamentalistic than Bob Jones University, which had spawned the career of Billy Graham. The curriculum was based on the premise that "the principles of the [American] constitution were granted to mankind by the Lord, and that the American system was as intimately based on the Bible as the Ten Commandments." Conversely, "communism had been conceived in the brains of the devil, spawned in hell and received its inspiration and direction from Satan." The communist threat represented Satan's latest attempt to demolish the City of God and scatter the faithful.

Hargis attacked the "new neutralism" in other segments of the evangelical movement, proclaiming that no middle ground existed between good and evil or democracy and communism. According to Hargis the forces of good and evil were arrayed against each other in Vietnam. "I wish we had Moshe Dayan leading us in Vietnam," sputtered the ardent hawk; "we could finish the war in a few days." Such simplistic answers sounded good to the Silent Majority.

The only real competition to Hargis' evangelical radicalism came from the Reverend Carl McIntire, who described himself as a responsible extremist against liberal causes. He organized both the American Council of Christian Churches and the International Council of Churches in opposition to the National and World

Council of Churches. This provided McIntire with a self-made forum for attacking liberal Protestantism and the ecumenical movement. McIntire often resorted to activistic tactics. At the 1969 semi-annual meeting of the World Council in Tulsa McIntire personally picketed an address delivered by Russia's Archbishop Nikodim, contending that his presence signified the problem of "creeping communism." As a dedicated hawk on Vietnam, he organized a march on Washington, Bible in hand, demanding that America "use the sword as God intended." Once his band of picketers encircled a church belonging to gay liberationists, still another cause disturbing to the Silent Majority.

Such evangelicals as McIntire were attractive to the Silent Majority because they gave the impression of bringing "good old-fashioned" American religion back to the people, "the rank-and-file church-goers." The Silent Majority had become disillusioned with what it interpreted as the high-brow religious liberalism of the Blakes and Pikes. "I used to go to church and the preacher would talk about God, Jesus and the Bible," complained a Minneapolis churchman; "now he tells me why I shouldn't buy grapes." "Sometimes in their enthusiasm for the have-nots, the activists treated people in far-off funky pews (the very people whose nickels and dimes supported the revolution) with disdain," wrote one critic. "The pew people got in the last licks. They revolted themselves, partly out of the feeling that they had been tossed aside like last Sunday's church bulletin." The new revivalism, then, represented the Silent Majority's reclamation of American religion and its traditional posture.

The Silent Majority's support of the new revivalism represented America's turning inward, away from the cosmopolitan tone of the high Sixties toward the simpler virtues and morals of the past. It represented a rejection of the nation's earlier urban orientation. The growing desire to escape the city was captured by comic Lee Tully who said: "There is only one way to protect yourself in the city--move to the country."

The rejection of the city manifested itself in the phenomenal rise of country and western music. "Country-politan" radio stations increased from 50 to 700 by the end of the decade. Television's _Hee-Haw,_ the country equivalent of the more urbane _Laugh-In,_ commanded prime network time; and a host of new country rock groups resounded up and down the Top 40 popular music charts. Exclusive night clubs, such as North Hollywood's Palomino Club, began to feature country entertainment. Country performers packed Madison Square Garden and Carnegie Hall. "Country music is blowing into the big cities like a fresh breeze from the boondocks," commented _Life_ magazine. According to the New York _Times_ magazine, the nation had gone "country-crazy."

Music Row in Nashville, Tennessee, the "Athens" of country music, clearly reflected the new phenomenon. By the end of the decade it supported four major recording studios, more than 30 record companies, over 100 musical publishers, almost 1,000 writers, and nearly 1500 performers. On weekends Ryman Auditorium, "the mother church of country music," strained under the ecstatic clapping and cheering of thousands of Grand Ole Opry fans. Country music became so popular that the Nashville city fathers constructed a swanky new arena for the Opry, equipping it with modern swivel chairs and air conditioning. They called it Opryland, U.S.A., and the music which ascended from its chambers became known as the new Nashville Sound.

The new sound originated from the many heartlands of America. It was a modern homogenization of Kentucky bluegrass, Delta cotton field sounds, gospel, New Orleans blues, Ozark spirituals, folk hymns, Appalachian melancholy, and western swing. Its folk character could be traced back to early colonial small town life where English and Scotch-Irish fiddlers constructed their homely laments.

By the late Sixties, however, Americans could no longer dismiss country and western as "ignorance put to music." The new Nashville Sound involved a much more sophisticated complex than the half-fledged carnival sounds which had marked the western spangles and the comically-hatted warbles of the past. In their place stood "heart-in-the-throat" balladeers garbed in tightly-fitted jeans and brassy attire. The country bumpkin entertainers had been replaced by "hip hicks and country slickers." Banjos and fiddles had been replaced by mandolins, steel and electric guitars, and string bass.

Country music moved beyond the old themes of "unfaithful wife plus motherly hooker times Jesus Christ and two broken guitar strings over a quart of diesel oil." It had moved from "you broke my heart so I'm gonna break your jaw" to "let's talk it over." Yet country music remained solidly traditional--"Southern in its origin, conservative in its politics (but with a stubborn streak of gut liberalism), blue-collar in its economics, blatantly patriotic, fundamental about God and nostalgic about Jesus," as described by critic William Hedgepath.

Its basic themes now involved home, jobs, and faith, fundamental concerns of the Silent Majority. "It's songs about the average working man, the guy with two kids and a car payment," explained country artist Tom T. Hall. These themes extolled "humble men entrapped in a world of sweet-sad defeats." This melancholy concern for the "little guy" was best expressed in Roger Miller's hit song "King of the Road:" a man of means by no means but King of the Road. The same theme dominated Johnny Cash's "The Legend of John Henry's Hammer," a diatribe of remorsefulness over endless, thankless labor.

The new Nashville Sound glorified the simpler, more folksy, and uncomplicated life of rural society. Honest, straight-forward, and down-to-earth in approach, it often attacked urban hypocrisy. In Tom T. Hall's "Harper Valley PTA," for example, a short-skirted, unmarried mother socked it to the gossipy community leaders who themselves imbibed in a familiar list of evil urban pleasures. The new country music sang of escaping the corrupted clutter of urban life and of going back to the virtues of the small town. Merle Haggard sang "I Gotta Get to Oklahoma," and Guy Drake's "Welfare Cadillac" satirized the city slicker who purchased an automobile from his welfare check. Welfare chiselers and those who refused an honest day's work had never been popular out in the country.

The new country music allowed middle America to vent its nostalgia. It expressed "nostalgic regrets about lost loves, lost opportunities ... lost homes and places." Nostalgia was prevalent in such hits as Glen Campbell's "By The Time I Get to Phoenix," Joe Smith's "Don't It Make You Want to Go Home," and John Denver's "Leaving on a Jet Plane."

Often these warm, lonesome lamentations sought relief from the moral deadness of the present by harkening back to history and heritage, treated as fountains of truth and goodness. "The yen to escape the corrupt present by returning to the virtuous past--real or imagined--has haunted Americans never more so than today," wrote _Time._ Joe Smith's "Age of Worry" expressed the feeling. "We're living in an age of worry/ Living in a time of stress/ A disappointment all around us/ Very little happiness."

The new country and western music possessed a social and political conscience of its own, providing the Silent Majority with a welcome contrast to the raunchy sounds of the New Left. The music called upon individuals to recommit themselves to traditional ideas and institutions, especially the family. Concern for the sanctity of family could be found in the ballads of B. J. Thomas' "Little Green Apples," "Daddy's Little Man," and "Daddy Don't You Walk So Fast," and in Glen Campbell's"Everyday Housewife." This theme was also expressed in Tammy Wynette's "Stand By Your Man," Jim Ed Brown's "Angel Sunday," Bobby Goldsboro's "Watching Scotty Grow," and Johnny Cash's "Big River," the lament of a fellow who wastes his life chasing a fickle woman. Songs such as "The Green Green Grass of Home," "My Son," "Somebody's Always Leaving," and "Ruby Don't Take Your Love To Town," expressed the serious disruption of family life caused by the Vietnam War.

The new country and western songs, then, provided middle America with a musical antidote to the ideas and life styles of the New Left. No song expressed the reactionary mood of the Silent Majority as well as Merle Haggard's "Okie from Muskogee." "We don't smoke marijuana in Muskogee/ We don't take our trips on LSD/ We don't burn our draft cards down on Main Street/ Cause we like living right and being free." The ballad represented a "clear, cool cowboy soul" and topped the country and western charts, selling over four million copies. The success earned Haggard the Country Music Association's Entertainer of the Year Male Vocalist Award.

Haggard explained the impetus behind the song: "The situation ... seemed to be that the left wing had all the floor, and nobody in the other direction was saying anything," complained Haggard. "I wanted to write a song about someone who was still satisfied to be an American." The song was a tribute to those who "still feel it is the greatest country in the world," explained Haggard. "They're still satisfied with a simpler life than some of the people in larger cities are satisfied with." In another song, "The Fighting Side of Me," Haggard's line "when you're running down our country, man, you're walking on the fighting side of me," provided middle America with a feeling of symbolic retribution against student radicals and their high-brow liberal defenders. "We're not the jet set, we're the old Chevro-let set," boasted one country fan after attending a Haggard concert.

Haggard's popularity was demonstrated by his ability to command $15,000 for a concert performance. The pre-eminent star of country and western music, however, was Johnny Cash, who could attract audiences of over 100,000 at state fairs. Cash presented an image of manliness and disenthralled individualism. He was described as a harsh, piercing "man who looks like an outlaw Indian, smiles a crooked smile and plays an ornate Martin guitar." His deep voice exuded confidence. His earthy, visceral sounds were those people could "get involved with and move to." When a blast from his guitar tore into the evening air, his listeners felt a compassionate, romantic power which overcame their feelings of loneliness and isolation.

Cash used his performances to ideologize and editorialize, though subtly, unlike the Haggard hard sell, and his causes were not all conservative. Referring to his constant garb of black satin-like attire, Cash explained, "I wear black for the poor and beaten down; living in the hopeless, hungry side of town." According to *Look,* his politics represented a gut populism endemic of the "hog-and homing belt of the South." Even though he sang out against war protesters, his greatest concern was for the luckless losers--American Indians, country poor, and prisoners. His stellar performance for prisoners at the San Quentin prison demonstrated that concern. Never referring to himself as any more than "a common man," Cash had become a Christian and loved to sing about Jesus and the old-time religion. He often guested at Billy Graham crusades, where middle Americans could sing praises and worship their heroes.

An array of other hero-like personalities came to represent the moods of middle America. The steely, brazen-faced Rod McKuen, who first gained national attention in 1966 with the quiet, lonesome lyrics of "Stanyon Street," appealed to the spirit of forgottenness and underdoggism of the Silent Majority. McKuen represented the image of a carefree, but thoughtful, blue collar drifter and roamer who managed to maintain his independence in the face of modern congestion and interruption. "If I'm still alone by now it's by design," averred McKuen, the iconoclast; "I only own myself, but all of me is mine."

By 1968 McKuen had become more popular than New Left stars Ginsberg and Dylan. The reason according to McKuen: "They say 'I demand,' I say 'I suggest.'" Indeed, McKuen's many years of rambling around the country as a cowpuncher, cab driver, lumber jack, small-town stunt man, and his dutiful service in the United States Navy during the silent Fifties helped the plain-spoken, low-key younder man to give precise expression to middle America's most strongly felt hopes and fears. "We need change but don't offend the society you live in," admonished McKuen. "You can't build anything by tearing it down." McKuen complained about the destructive elements on the college campuses, conjecturing that "there are no children anymore ... they went in search of psychedelic kumquats." Long hair "covers up our eyes and makes us unable to see the world," and miniskirts and pop art ties were "more than modern man can bear," admonished McKuen, who had sold over 50 million records and recorded 35 albums by the end of the decade.

A Silent Majority hero of quite a different nature was actor John (The Duke) Wayne, whose gristly, awesome physique, booming voice, and rolling walk reminded middle Americans of the West, the frontier, and the personalities who made America great. Wayne represented the traditional West, "where a man stood for something and fought for it," wrote Antonio Chemasi in _Newsday._ "He came to embody his screen image: a durable figure clothed in old ideals, burdened with a sense of duty, full of authority." In his movie roles Wayne was tough, resourceful, forthright, and never compromised with principle. "Wayne epitomized the American hero," wrote one critic; "big, rugged, blunt-talking, hard drinking, irresistible to the ladies, unbeatable with fists or guns, but having a heart of marshmallow." He was harsh and decisive with evil, but treated the "right side" with gentleness and loving kindness. An "unabashed reactionary in politics," Wayne was "tough, down to earth, and he says and acts what he believes," reported Time.

The movie Green Berets, in which Wayne led a remnant of Green Berets against the evil hordes of Asian Communists, proved to be a passionate defense of the Vietnam War. In True Grit, with Glen Campbell, Wayne portrayed an aging frontier marshal, Rooster Cogburn, whose drive for instant justice overcame both natural disaster and human deviance--a timely theme for the Silent Majority grown impatient with courts. "Full of booze and passion for justice," the Duke "sees himself as a law and ardor candidate," wrote Time. "His politics are symbolized by the itchy trigger finger, and his judicial philosophy is summed up in a tidy homily: 'You can't serve papers on a rat.'"

Cartoonist Al Capp, the creator of the popular "Li'l Abner" comic strip, became another sort of Silent Majority hero. Capp's low-key political jabs--"What's good for General Bullmoose is good for the country"--had once delighted those on the college scene. But in the Sixties Capp turned his venom against students. A typical episode he created depicted a "boar mitzvah" for pigs. It was a ceremony where "wildly romantic" boars "gotta be sent to California--to Boarkley! They speshulizes in edicatin' swin thar...."

Still another favorite of the Silent Majority was Dallas businessman H. Ross Perot, the 39-year-old electronics billionaire who charted a Boeing 707 jet named Peace on Earth in 1970 to distribute Christmas presents and messages to American prisoners in North Vietnam. Although his mission ended unsuccessfully because of international political complications reaching as high as the Kremlin, middle Americans deemed this humanitarian action as a welcome contrast to the leftist groups which offered blood and supplies to the enemy.

By 1968 the Silent Majority had found a political avenue of expression in the inflammatory George Wallace, who organized the American Independent Party in 1967 as a part of his full-fledged attempt to capture the Presidency. In tones reminiscent of Huey Long's defiant populism of the Thirties, Wallace predicted that "if the politicians get in the way ... a lot of them are going to get run over by the average man on the street." Wallace selected as his running mate former Air Force Chief of Staff, General Curtis E. LeMay, who promptly offered the simple answer to Vietnam frustration--nuclear weaponry.

At first Wallacism had been dismissed as sheer political "boobocracy;" but as his popularity began to grow, even the experts wondered. After watching 4,500 fanatical supporters crowd into a Hammond, Indiana, gymnasium to shout their approval of Wallace's platitudes, the astute political observer David S.

Broder called the movement "a powerful, impressive and frightening phenomenon." "The notion that major party candidates "can easily wean votes back from Wallace is at least open to serious question," warned Broder. A worried George L. Meany publicly pleaded with his fellow Democrats to expel the political "extremists" from the Democratic party or risk losing the rank and file union members to the "country picnic" politics of Wallace. "It is difficult to be precise about the nature of the nightmare year," wrote Presidential election watcher Theodore S. White. "No phrase, no thought can catch, hold and bind together in one frame all the roaring events." "Anybody who attempts to predict the election of 1968 is nuts," commented the seasoned Alf Landon, Republican standard-bearer of 1936.

CHAPTER X

THE NIXON PRESIDENCY

It was at this tumultuous time that former Vice President Richard M. Nixon, never anybody's hero, once again became a factor in American politics. Nixon had helped write himself out of national politics in 1962 when the popular Pat Brown defeated him in the California gubernatorial race. "You won't have Richard Nixon to kick around anymore," he remorsefully told a press conference as he settled back into "anxious exile" in a prestigious New York City law firm. Nixon would go the way of the Edsel while other politicians became embroiled in the explosive issues of the decade.

Nixon remained aloof during the great Rockefeller-Goldwater split of 1964 but loyally supported Goldwater after his nomination. When the Goldwater elements were dislodged by the party reorganization under the more moderate chairmanship of Ohio's Ray Bliss, Nixon saw the possibility of another Presidential bid. He campaigned fervently for Republican candidates in the successful 1966 mid-term election, began acting as an official spokesman in opposition to LBJ's policies, and organized a group of advisors who met frequently at New York's Waldorf Towers to plot strategy.

As the Presidential election of 1968 drew near, Nixon began to understand what columnist Stewart Alsop so succinctly described: "Something has happened in this country which, as any good Marxist will tell you, can't happen. The proletariat has become bourgeois. In non-Marxist terms, the working class has become middle class." Alsop contended that the center of gravity of America had shifted toward conservatism. "The amazingly long-lasting Democratic coalition created by Franklin D. Roosevelt was based squarely on 'the forgotten man,' 'the little guy,' 'the working stiff'--the proletariat," explained Alsop. "Now that the working class has become middle class, the ex-working stiff tends more and more to share middle-class sentiments, about everything from law and order to beards." Nixon decided to adopt the Silent Majority, "the forgotten Americans, the non-shouters, the non-demonstrators, the quiet voice," and forge from it a new, more conservative post-New Deal-Great Society political majority. The population trends had placed the majority in suburbia, where people wanted a "progressive President, but not too progressive."

Nixon waited instinctively as Michigan Governor George Romney made a futile attempt to capture the nomination. Nixon knew that party regulars would be uncomfortable with Romney's unpredictability and emotionalism. Romney withdrew before the New Hampshire primary, his demise due to an impromptu statement about having been "brainwashed" by the Johnson administration on Vietnam. Now Nixon was free to run in the primaries, where he could shed his loser image. Nixon went on to win a smashing primary victory in New Hampshire and impressive victories in Nebraska, Oregon, Indiana, Wisconsin, and Pennsylvania. New York Governor Nelson Rockefeller strongly pressed his candidacy after Robert Kennedy's assassination in June, but he did so only to forestall the only real challenge to Nixon's candidacy--that of Governor Ronald Reagan of California, the darling of the conservatives since Barry Goldwater's 1964 demise. Reagan had become the "hottest speaker on the GOP circuit," raising millions through $100-a-plate fundraising affairs around the country. In South Carolina, the home of the powerful Senator Strom Thurmond, 3,500 turned out for such an affair.

By convention time Nixon's nomination was almost a foregone conclusion. The tally stood at 692 for Nixon, 272 for Rockefeller, 182 for Reagan, and 182 undecided. Most of the moderates and conservatives had by then moved over to the Nixon column. Liberal Governor Walter Hickel of Alaska and Oregon Senator Mark Hatfield, plus conservative Senator John Tower of Texas and even Barry Goldwater, had all announced their intention to support Nixon. From the Army Walter Reed Hospital the dying Ike Eisenhower, by now dear to the hearts of Americans who had come to appreciate more the quiet Fifties, kindly endorsed the Nixon candidacy. With Strom Thurmond's support Nixon easily won nomination. The only aberration in an otherwise congenial convention was Nixon's choice of Maryland's Governor Spiro T. Agnew as his running mate. Agnew had once been considered as a Rockefeller liberal Republican but lately had become more noted for his bitter criticisms of moderate black leaders in Baltimore for not exercising more control over the riot-prone radicals in that city's civil rights movement.

Divisiveness among Democrats, coupled with Wallace's failure to become a credible candidate in the North, caused early optimism in the Nixon campaign. The new Nixon of 1968 proved confident, self-assured, serene, firm, and statesman-like in contrast to the old pugnacious, "sock-and-slash" Nixon of the early Sixties. He hammered away with conviction but in a controlled manner.

Nixon promised to restore law and order at home and "end the war and win the peace" in the Pacific. He possessed a secret plan which could not be revealed for fear of upsetting Johnson's delicate diplomacy in Paris. Promising to unite and quiet the country, Nixon asserted that "a party that can unite itself [after the Goldwater split] will unite the country." Nixon's convincing posture brought in millions of dollars in campaign contributions from thousands of persons who had waxed rich from the Great Society economic boom but who now yearned for stability and order. Richard Mellon Scaife, wealthy Pittsburgh banking executive, gave almost a million dollars; and W. Clement Stone, Chicago insurance tycoon, contributed over one million. I wanted "to change the course of history for the better," he insisted.

During September Nixon appeared the certain winner. But as Wallace's popularity began to fade, it became apparent that the Presidential race between Nixon and Vice President Humphrey, who unrepentantly preached the gospel of social uplift, would be one of the closest in history. The pudgy, smile-laden Humphrey, a man of "durability, consistency, good humor, experience, and heart" was a high-spirited, unflappable, and chronic campaigner of unlimited energy.

Although overshadowed for a time by Johnson's unpopularity, Humphrey continued to exude an undaunting faith in the goodness of mankind and continued to enjoy widespread esteem as a man who had been right on most of the major political issues of his generation. In the eyes of many Americans he was still seen as the foremost spokesman for the downtrodden and the keeper of the national conscience, one who would place the public good before personal self-interest.

Most significantly, perhaps, was the image of Humphrey, the Happy Warrior, speaking directly from his heart in a manner that raised the hopes of millions. "Humphrey is the man for this particular season partly because he has rapport with the established chiefs of the low-income whites," wrote columnist Joseph Kraft. "He speaks their rhetoric and shares their faith in the basic goodness of American life." Standing firmly upon his grass-roots base of support, Humphrey could best be described as a builder of movements, an initiator of events, a hard taskmaster, and a pace setter. "I'm the fellow who likes to set out the big building blocks," he asserted. "I let other people come along and apply the mortar." According to *Time*, "Humphrey was sheer political drive: unquenchable, unstoppable, irrepressible." Few politicians had ever demonstrated such exuberance and good faith in America, qualities which Richard Nixon could hardly ignore.

Humphrey knew he was far behind but boldly announced, "I don't intend to quit as long as there is one ounce of strength left in my body." As the campaign progressed, Humphrey managed to separate himself from the discredited Lyndon B. Johnson and to unite the traditional New Deal coalition around the old "bread-and-butter" issues. Humphrey confidently practiced the "politics of joy," not making excuses for the past eight years but offering a better future based on "open doors rather than iron curtains" abroad and real equal opportunity at home. Skillfully portraying himself as the "Chief Pathfinder," Humphrey was able to make his own appeal to the Silent Majority. "The time has come to speak out on behalf of America--not a nation that has lost its way, but a restless people striving to find a better way," urged Humphrey. "His nature is to dream big dreams, to spin off grand ideas, to talk persuasively in his own behalf," reported Time.

Eventually, Humphrey announced what essentially amounted to a dovish stand on Vietnam, a move which attracted the endorsement of Senator Eugene McCarthy and most of his supporters. Just days before the election President Johnson announced a halt to the American air war and the naval bombardment of North Vietnam. The last minute moves made Nixon the narrow winner in the election, the final result of which was not known until the next morning. Nixon won only 43.5 per cent of the popular vote and became the first minority President since one of his mentors in foreign policy, Woodrow Wilson. Nixon had won the Presidency by appealing to the Silent Majority, but he entered the White House without a clearly-defined constituency, much less a clear mandate to rule.

Nixon promised the nation "the lift of a driving dream." The weary nation, profoundly shaken by the terrible events of 1968, assumed the posture of "watchful waiting" while Nixon secluded himself under Florida's Key Biscayne sunshine to begin the difficult task of stitching his Administration together.

Richard M. Nixon's presidency would become one of the stormiest in American history. The Administration soon became shrouded in the mystery of the man. For Nixon the right principles were not enough; an effective leader also had to possess "street smarts" and the capacity to "play every trick." Nixon seemed driven by two separate and sometimes conflicting instincts--one, the statesman-like instinct to achieve a broad-visioned consensus and to give the nation positive direction; the other, the gut political instinct to seek recrimination and to manage affairs in a clandestine and imposing fashion. Nixon's Administration was destined to be threshed back and forth between these two instincts of the master.

The political pundits and commentators dubbed the Nixon of the first instinct as the "New Nixon," and the second as the "old Nixon"--the real Nixon, however, always maintained an eerie illusiveness. In practice, of course, there were many Nixons, each appealing to broad cross sections of the American public. Historian Clinton Rossitor best summarized the element of mystery which surrounded the character of Richard M. Nixon. "I knew, or thought I knew Nixon in the 1950's. I thought I knew him in 1962," pondered Rossitor. "But now I'm not so sure I know him. I don't think anyone has a clear idea of what Nixon's going to do on any issue."

Nixon was a quiet, introverted man, not boisterous like Johnson or outgoing like Kennedy. Whereas Johnson could become emotional in public, Nixon was always cool, even glacial. Nixon was ill-at-ease in a crowd and not comfortable even in a small group. In all of his years in the White House he only danced publicly twice. Even around his top aides he refused to work in shirt-sleeves, preferring the formal dark blue business suit with tie securely fastened. Nixon spent much time either alone or with his family.

Nixon demanded privacy almost to the point of escape. Unlike Kennedy and Johnson, he preferred to make decisions alone, whether that be walking along the beach next to his bayfront home at Key Biscayne, Florida, dining aboard the 102-foot Navy yacht Sequoia as it cruised lazily down the Potomac River, or on the Presidential Catoctin mountain-top retreat at Camp David. "I find that here on top of a mountain it is easier for me to get on top of the job," remarked Nixon. Midnight often found the President alone in the family quarters playing the piano.

Professor James MacGregor Burns, one of America's leading students of the presidency, observed that Nixon was "probably the most introspective president of this century. He gives the impression of being aloof, brooding, lonely; he lacks ease with his fellow men." Commenting on the impersonal nature of Nixon's presidency, columnist Joseph Kraft complained that Nixon "held himself aloof from the public." As a result of his reclusiveness, Nixon never found his way into the hearts of his countrymen like Kennedy, nor did he present a solid image of direction and resolve like Johnson.

Nixon rode to the Presidency upon the crest of Silent Majority sentiment. Thus, the most public of all the Nixons during his presidency was that of the square, stolid, average American. This Nixon "liked the competitive spirit of Vince Lombardi, the music of Guy Lombardo, the novels of Allen Drury, the piety of Billy Graham, the wit of Bob Hope, and the sales techniques of J. Walter Thompson," wrote William Manchester.

"Nixon's world is one of strawberry shortcake, baseball games and stereo music; of quiet dinners, suspense movies and hamburgers; of Norman Vincent Peale and Billy Graham," commented columnist Jack Anderson. "The Nixon era will be an Emily Post society ... their parties won't differ from those given by a president of a bank in Des Moines, Iowa." The era would be "ho-hum" compared to the churning panorama of the Kennedy years.

Nixon cleverly played upon this image. He initiated Sunday morning worship services at the White House, the first featuring Billy Graham. Critics such as theologian Reinhold Niebuhr dubbed these occasions as the "King's Chapel," but middle America saw them as proper displays of public piety. Nixon praised George Beverly Shea as a great hymn singer and claimed Graham as a close advisor on political as well as spiritual affairs. He had sought Graham's advice in the selection of Spiro Agnew as Vice President, he said.

Nixon further complemented his middle American image by inviting the Silent Majority's favorite entertainers to perform at the White House. He invited Johnny Cash to a White House reception to sing "Welfare Cadillac." One political pundit saw this as the swan song for such Johnson reform programs as OEO and noted the performance's "anti-Lyndsayland" flavor. Merle Haggard came to highlight one of Nixon's birthday celebrations. "Just keep singing those songs about patriotism and the working man," blurted Nixon. Frank Sinatra, Duke Ellington, and Hee Haw's Roy Clark also graced the White House in the name of the Silent Majority. This flurry of White House entertaining was part of Nixon's determined effort to dispel his image as a "loner." He entertained 30,600 personal guests during 1969, an all-time high; and he overspent his entertainment budget by $100,000. During his first eighteen months in office he used up more television time than his three predecessors put together.

Outside the White House Nixon appealed to the Silent Majority by playing the role of the nation's chief sports fan. Whereas Eisenhower had been a golfer, Kennedy a sailor, and Lyndon B. Johnson a hunter, Nixon settled for such less elitist pastimes as football and baseball. He enjoyed telephoning the winning coach after the big game. Sportsmanship, of course, had come to represent the middle American way as much as motherhood and apple pie.

Another image Nixon tried to foster was that of "the Chief Executive," the cool, calculating, self-controlled, even-handed administrator who clicked off decisions with precision and daring. This image found favor among the nation's business elite who admired efficiency and coordination and who relished the fast-pace excitement represented by Air Force I streaking through the skies bearing the President to his various headquarters. Nixon enjoyed spending time at his lavish estate at San Clemente, California, called the western White House; Key Biscayne, where he went on frequent excursions aboard Coco Lobo III, belonging to his close banking friend Bebe Rebozo; and the Bahamas, where he participated in sports and fishing escapades with his millionaire friend Robert H. Aplanalp on board Sea Lion II. This Nixon especially impressed the new rich, who, like the new president, approached the gadgetry and glinting commotion of the jet age with the same excitement as a child playing with a new toy.

Still another Nixon became apparent as he organized his Administration. This was the Nixon who appealed to the old-guard genteel Republican conservatives who enjoyed champagne and quiet string music in contrast to the Georgetown cocktail party circuit, which had characterized the Kennedy years, and who yearned for the return to the slower pace of the Eisenhower years. Nixon depended heavily upon their advice in the organization of his Administration, especially in foreign policy. With the appointment of William Rogers as Secretary of State; Henry Kissinger, Harvard whiz donated by Nelson Rockefeller, as Advisor for National Security Affairs; and Peter Flanigan, U.S. Trade Representative, formerly Vice President of banking house Dillon, Read, and Co.; Nixon's connections with the traditional foreign policy elite within the Republican party seemed complete.

Nixon dreamed of establishing a governing consensus even though he represented the minority Republican party. Nixon sensed the need to pull the American people together. Whereas Johnson had called for reconciliation, Nixon called for restoration, consolidation, and containment--"to get America back to where it was before the great fire-happening of the '60's," wrote Max Lerner, "to limit and contain the rampaging forces of social change." Consensus building was represented in some of the early appointments. Arthur F. Burns, Columbia University's pipe toting, silver-haired, trouble-shooting economist was the Chairman of the Joint Council of Economic Advisors; Paul McCracken, Chairman of the Counsel of Economic Advisors; and the volatile Ivy Leaguer, Daniel Patrick Moynihan, Domestic Counselor--all of these men, stubborn, strong-minded, and independent-thinking, promised to play crucial roles in balancing various interests and opinions.

The problem which haunted Nixon from the very beginning, however--since, at heart, he was instinctively a political man rather than a serious problem solver--was his tendency to rely on political cronies rather than the more determined public policy types when difficult decisions arose. Like President Harding before him, Nixon came to rely more and more on the so-called "palace guard," composed of H. R. Haldeman, Chief of White House Staff, and John Ehrlichman, Chief Domestic Advisor.

Nixon was also prone to carry the notion of regality to extremes. Soon after entering the White House, he employed trumpeters with banners draped from their elongated trumpets in order to herald the appearance of the President at state banquets. He also provided the White House guard with imperial costumes; but he soon abandoned these practices when the press criticized him for trying to create an imperial presidency and, more importantly, when he discovered White House visitors--imbued with democratic traditions--snickered at the pointed hats of the guards. Overreliance on cronies and a conspicuous concern for regality would result in the eventual destruction and disgrace of his Administration; but in January, 1969, when Nixon entered the Presidency, the future looked quite positive, and the country hoped for a slowing of the pace, a period of consolidated progress.

Nixon caught the mood of his countrymen in his inaugural address as he called for reconciliation, restraint, a quieting of voices, and a lowering of the profile. "We cannot learn from one another until we stop shouting at one another," he proffered; "speak quietly enough so that our words can be heard as well as our voices." Nixon called for "conciliation" and "mutuality." Whereas Johnson had been the great "provider," Nixon would be the great "healer" and "peacemaker." "The greatest honor history can bestow is the title of peacemaker," proclaimed Nixon, who had spent laborious hours of pre-inaugural time carefully choosing his words. "We find ourselves rich in goods, but ragged in spirit; reaching with magnificent precision for the moon, but falling into raucous discord on earth."

The new President spoke of bringing the country and the world together toward a common purpose. "The peace we seek to win is not victory over any other people," pronounced Nixon, "but the peace that comes with healing in its wings; with compassion for those who have suffered; with understanding for those who have opposed us." Nixon promised the nation and the world "a generation of peace."

In true Republican style Nixon refused to label his Administration, asking only that his fellow citizens join him in moving "forward together." "Those who have been left out we will try to bring in," promised Nixon; "those who have been left behind, we will help to catch up." This call for a "common destiny," claimed Time, represented Nixon's move "to center stage with measured tread."

Even though Nixon represented consolidation and called for an emphasis on quality rather than quantity, he endorsed the progressive concept of the assertive presidency. "The days of a passive presidency belong to a simpler past," he said. "The President must take an activist view of his office. He must articulate the nation's values, define its goals and and marshal its will." As one commentator aptly put it: "With Kennedy it was 'let us begin,' with LBJ it was 'let us continue,' and with Nixon 'let us start over.'" Nixon saw himself as a "Disraeli conservative," who believed in "reform that will work, not reform that destroys." Nixon promised the American people priority action in three problem areas: 1) a peace settlement with honor in Vietnam; 2) a restoration of law and order domestically; and, 3) a reduction of taxes and inflation.

Conservatives and liberals alike proved receptive to Nixon's early conciliatory tone. "Mainly it fitted in with the mood of the people--far better than most wishful Democrats would admit," wrote liberal spokesman Max Lerner, who described Nixon as representing "a quieter breathing spell in which America can catch up with the gains registered on its statute books and its conscience." Theodore H. White sounded even more positive. "He understood the changes going on both at home and in the world abroad," wrote White; "he was a man of the present with a gift for seeing ahead to the future." In the Senate, Democratic Majority Leader Mike Mansfield assumed a posture of "cooperation" conceding that "I think the fellow is trying." New York Times columnist Joseph Kraft praised Nixon's positive attitude toward the outward forms of government. Every issue seemed to enjoy the attention of the new Administration. Hence, the Nixon honeymoon with the American people and Congress began pleasantly. The modish and muddled skies of rebellion and contempt temporarily cleared. The sunshine of consensus and positive direction warmed the heart of American society as Nixon embarked upon his Presidency.

Foreign policy warranted Nixon's immediate attention. America faced its most crucial crisis in foreign relations since World War II. The international structure of containment as authored by the United States was coming apart at the seams. A postcontainment policy strained to be born which better reflected the realities of the newly developing balances of power--one requiring a more serious accommodation with Russia, a normalization of relations with China, a new economic and monetary policy relative to America's capitalistic allies, a strategy for dealing with the economic nationalism in the Third World, and an adjusted American posture toward what had become a multipolar world.

Vietnam had proven America's vincibility. The United States could no longer carry the burden of being the world's policeman. "The time has passed when America will make every other nation's conflicts its own, or make every nation's future our responsibility, or presume to tell the people of other nations how to manage their own affairs," proclaimed Nixon. Nixon realized, however, that the United States was still clearly the most powerful nation in the international community. Even though America was set on a course of reduced involvement, its power still represented the primary force of stabilization.

Nixon decried the assertion of the purity of America's motives as a substitute for the responsible exercise of power. He believed in what some called the "mad man theory" of diplomacy--that is, leaving open the possibility of acting rashly so that the enemy would be kept off balance by dreading the possibility of the worst. Nixon demonstrated this belief in 1970 when he commissioned Green Beret colonel Arthur, "The Bull," Simons to lead a helicopter raid on a carefully guarded prisoner of war site near Hanoi. Commander Simons was deeply disappointed when, after a flawless assault, the camp was empty. The American people were mystified at the apparent rashness of the operation, but Nixon had made his point to his adversaries in a dramatic way.

Nixon believed that America must continue to deal with the world from a position of strength, but with a lower profile. Nixon substituted McNamara's early decade proclamations of superiority and second-strike capability with such terms as "parity" and "sufficiency." He spoke of achieving "regional balances" of power, dependent more upon subtle diplomacy than overbearing displays of power. The new posture was best demonstrated in Defense Secretary Laird's quiet acknowledgement that the McNamara 2 1/2 war strategy of earlier decade had been dropped down to a 1 1/2 war strategy.

In many ways Nixon came to the Presidency well-equipped to bring about a new balance of power in world relationships. Throughout the years he had become well-acquainted with most of the world's important leaders. His world travels had acquainted him with various cultures and the forces of change. Intellectually, he understood power and was not afraid to employ it; but he also knew when and how to employ compassion and persuasion. He was respected as a tough-minded negotiator whose mixture of pragmatism and cleverness would motivate him toward accommodation rather than confrontation.

Nixon's past history of anti-communism made him the only American politician with suitable credentials to defuse the Cold War and strike a new world balance. The conservative majority still viewed him as the "Cold Warrior," the "tough bargainer" who would not compromise unduly with the Communists. Thus, Nixon found himself in a position to accomplish what a liberal Democrat could never hope for--reversing America's foreign policy toward both Russia and China.

Nixon's much celebrated secret plan for ending the war in Vietnam involved just that approach. He believed that North Vietnam could not continue its war efforts without the support of Russia and China. If only they could be enticed with American capital investment, food, and new technology, Russia and China could be persuaded to encourage North Vietnam along the road to compromise. From a more selfish point of view, Russia and China represented new markets and investment opoportunities, expanding frontiers for the recession ridden American economy. The China Market--Cathay, as it had been known by the earliest American generations--proved no less tempting to Nixon than it had been to Christopher Columbus or later to Thomas Jefferson, who sent Lewis and Clark to find the Northwest Passage. His obsession was as old as the American dream. Besides, if America did not move to take advantage of the crack in the Chinese marketing door, its Japanese and European allies would.

Nixon designated Dr. Henry Kissinger, the adroit and remarkably clever National Security Advisor, to conceptualize and implement his vision of a new world order. Kissinger had long been regarded as a foremost foreign policy scholar, beginning with his professional examination of the Concert of Europe, or Metternich System, which had brought peace to the western world for almost a century after 1814. Essentially, Kissinger updated Metternich's "Grand Design" for Europe and applied it to the modern world. Kissinger believed with Nixon that the United States must lower its profile and not become overly extended; but beyond those reservations he remained a firm internationalist and advocate of containment. He decried the growing isolationism of the late decade. "Whereas in the 1920's we had withdrawn from the world because we thought we were too good for it, the insidious theme of the late 1960's was that we should withdraw from the world because we were too evil for it," complained Kissinger.

Kissinger's "Grand Design" for the world would, like Metternich's system, be double-edged. The United States would continue to solidify and expand its hegemony and firm up its alliances, such as NATO, but would exert more effort to identify and take advantages of common areas of interest with its adversaries, from Russia and China to the smaller satellite countries. Kissinger called this the search for "linkages." This inevitably would lead to a softening of relations with the communist bloc countries and an insistence upon allies assuming more responsibility for their own defense.

Arms control occupied much of Nixon's and Kissinger's attention. Building upon the groundwork laid since Geneva in 1955, Vienna in 1961, and Glassboro in 1967, Nixon moved swiftly to initiate the Strategic Arms Limitations Talks (SALT) in Helsinki, Finland. He traveled to West Berlin to call for an easing of Cold War tensions, and he let it be known that the Formosan question would not effectively block rapprochement with China. The neutralization of such strategic areas signaled the world that Nixon was serious about his policy of detente.

In spite of the great fanfare, the war in Vietnam continued to fester hopelessly, threatening to upset the delicate moves toward detente. Since so much had been committed to Vietnam, the political fates of Nixon and the nation rested on the outcome. As a new President, Nixon faced some policy options. He could have declared the war a disastrous mistake, blamed it on the Democrats, and instituted massive early withdrawals of American troops. He could have called for an immediate cease-fire and negotiations, forcing the Saigon regime to make important concessions. Nixon chose, however, to pursue established policy of coupling negotiations with withdrawals, while equipping the South Vietnamese army to win the war on its own. Nixon probably had little hope for the ARVN but wanted to maintain the appearance of strength and resolve for domestic and foreign political reasons.

Besides the inducements to Russia and China to put pressures on North Vietnam, Vietnamization, under Nixon, involved replacing American troops in the battlefield with South Vietnamese soldiers. America would continue to equip and train the troops. The public objective was still peace with honor but with Asian blood and American treasure. This represented somewhat of a shift back to Eisenhower's policy of the Fifties. Vietnamization would be completed in three stages: 1) ground combat responsibilities would be transferred from American to South Vietnamese soldiers; 2) logistic and support activities would be transferred to South Vietnam; and, 3) a small U.S. military advisory contingent would remain for technical and emergency support. In time, predicted Secretary of Defense Melvin Laird, South Vietnamese forces would be able to cope with any threat. Vietnamization would also involve postwar economic development and democratization. American air power would be employed in order to protect the South's field position and to encourage the North Vietnamese diplomatic posture at the Paris peace talks, where veteran diplomat Ellsworth Bunker now labored for the American side. During the early months of his Administration, Nixon's popularity was buoyed by the hope that Vietnamization would work.

Several Nixon initiatives in domestic affairs further stimulated the people's confidence in his leadership. Nixon's emphasis on cautious reform and consolidation became apparent in his appointment of Warren Burger as Chief Justice of the Supreme Court. Burger promised to streamline and reform the cumbersome operation of the judicial system and lower its profile.

None of Nixon's domestic reforms were presented in the hyperbolic fashion of President Johnson, but each appealed to important segments of the populace. Many carried the promise of reducing the divisiveness of 1968 and especially addressed the grievances of youth. Nixon attempted to demonstrate his good faith by sponsoring a weekend retreat in May of 1969 with major college and university figures in order to determine strategies for making higher education more responsive to the needs of youth. Borrowing from the ideas of Senator Edward Kennedy, Nixon sponsored draft reform which resulted in the establishment of a draft lottery, an all-volunteer army, and the ouster of the cantankerous General Lewis B. Hershey, Chief of Conscription for almost thirty years. These moves also pleased the liberal establishment because they held out the promise of reducing both the growth of the huge defense budget and the number of people economically dependent upon defense spending.

Nixon also sponsored the most far-ranging income tax reform since the inception of this form of taxation in 1913, closing some glaring loopholes, raising the personal exemption from $600 to $750, and increasing social security benefits. Nixon took the inefficient postal system out of politics, placing it under the management of a private corporation; and he called for much needed reform in the OEO, manpower, and the grants-in-aid systems.

In a policy called the "New Federalism" Nixon inaugurated a bold attempt to decentralize the ingrained federal bureaucracy. "The Federal government is increasingly caught in issues of municipal housekeeping that are most appropriately the business of a city council," explained Nixon, "but simultaneously the great fiscal power of the federal government" could "provide local governments with sufficient resources to enable them to solve their own problems in their own way." Under Nixon's revenue sharing plan the federal government would make block grants to state and local governments with as few strings attached as possible. This was based on the somewhat dubious premise that local leaders knew their needs best and could more efficiently disburse funds.

Nixon attacked urban blight with a new housing program named by HUD Secretary George Romney "Operation Breakthrough." The program provided for government-sponsored prefabricated factory built houses, claiming it would do for homebuilding what Henry Ford's assembly lines had done for the automobile industry. Romney proclaimed this as the "beginning of a promising future for volume-produced housing in this country." Operation Breakthrough represented a typical Nixon reform which could appeal to the Silent Majority, the advocates of administrative reforms, the old guard conservatives, and liberals alike. It promised to reduce bureaucratic red tape, to function in a business-like manner, to move the government out of the housing industry, and to provide low-cost housing for the poor.

Liberals were also somewhat impressed with Nixon's ideas about reforming the nation's burdensome welfare systems. In what eventually became known as the "Family Assistance Plan," Nixon moved toward a guaranteed income rather than the myriad of existing welfare assistance programs. The plan was based on incentives for gainful employment and was designed to keep families together. Nixon coupled his concern for welfare with population and food matters, sponsoring the White House Conference on Food, Nutrition, and Health in May of 1969. In the beginning Daniel Patrick Moynihan served as a one-man brain trust to deal with the entire spectrum of domestic problems; he was known as the "domestic Henry Kissinger."

Nixon's most vigorous reforming impulse came in the area of anti-trust prosecution. The new wave of anti-trust activity was executed by the mild-mannered Chief of the Anti-Trust Division, Richard McLaren, who became known as the "biggest buster since Teddy." During his first five months in office McLaren filed anti-trust suits against mergers proposed by three of America's most powerful conglomerates: Long-Temco-Vought, ITT, and Northwest Industries. He filed suit against U.S. Steel, claiming that its reciprocal purchase agreements with suppliers represented a monopolistic activity which established the precedent for "a radical restructuring" of the American political economy.

McLaren followed this suit with one against First National City Bank of New York, blocking its attempt to acquire an insurance company because it had suqqested the establishment of a holding company. McLaren, who had come to Washington from a lucrative Chicago firm specializing in anti-trust defense, flailed the evils of excessive economic concentration, feeling it caused unwarranted human dislocation and inefficiency in the market place. His zeal even surprised the President, who eventually rewarded McLaren's efforts with a federal Judgeship in the Chicago area.

Nixon's reforms of federal Indian policy represented conservative reform in its best tradition. Deploring the plight of Native American Indians, citing "centuries of injustice," and describing the Indian people as "the most deprived and most isolated minority group in our nation," Nixon called "for a new era in which the Indian future is determined by Indian acts and Indian decisions." Nixon's policy of self-determination would grant reservation tribes more control over the use of federal funds. According to Nixon, this would reduce unproductive federal handouts and excessive paternalism. "We must assure the Indian that he can assume control of his own life without being separated involuntarily from the tribal group," explained Nixon, "and we must make it clear that Indians can become independent of federal control without being cut off from federal concern and federal support."

Nixon's performance over the first eight months of 1969 temporarily restored the confidence and self-assurance of the nation. The successful moon landing in July served to accentuate his popularity. For that rare moment people the world over forgot their earthly differences as they riveted their attention on what Nixon characterized as the "greatest week in the history of the world since creation." In an important sense the moon landing fulfilled John Kennedy's promise and made the decade seem almost worthwhile.

Nixon confidently proclaimed the "spirit of Apollo," designed to bring a new sense of community and common destiny. During the summer of 1969 the spirit of Apollo was echoed in many quarters. The Reverend Ralph Abernathy, who was leading a poor people's march on Washington, remarked that "he was so stunned by the sight and so proud of the astronauts that he forgot there was hunger." Poet Archibald MacLeish wrote that "we see ourselves as riders on the earth together, brothers on that bright loveliness in the eternal cold--brothers who know now they are truly brothers." Even Nixon's old opponents momentarily caught the spirit. Senator Humphrey commented that in the matter of Vietnam, Nixon was doing "what I advocated in the campaign." "On balance he's done well" in foreign policy, continued Humphrey, who even expressed "reasonable satisfaction" with Nixon's civil rights record. Eric Hoffer recanted his earlier bitter opposition to Nixon. "The man is a total surprise," remarked Hoffer. "It's wonderful that a man who is so denigrated turns out to be so good. I glory in it."

The time of good feelings prompted Nixon to make a special trip to Independence, Missouri, in order to present former President Harry Truman with his old White House piano for the Truman Presidential Library. There two of history's most bitter political foes sat down in front of the keyboard to pound out the "Missouri Waltz" together. Then Nixon flew off to California for a period of golf and relaxation while he quietly attended to minor matters of state. "The nation found solace in the reassuring trivia of routine," commented _Time_; "for a rare moment, most of the United States seemed to be soothed and quiet as the summer drew to an end and the nation basked in unwanted and unfamiliar calm."

CHAPTER XI

A FAILURE IN CONSENSUS

The late summer solace proved only a temporary quiet before the political storms which would propel the decade towards its disastrous conclusion. Issues and events converged on the national scene which exposed once again the deep divisions plaguing the nation. Nixon's handling of these issues discredited his Presidency, defeated his efforts to achieve a working consensus, and left the nation in a state of shock and disillusionment.

The Nixon consensus-building effort first faltered over the issue of military spending. Nixon's insistence on the deployment of a Safeguard Anti-Ballistic Missile system (ABM) caused much consternation in Congress, where the program had never been popular. As early as February, 1969, powerful Senators such as Cooper, Fulbright, Javits, Mansfield, Symington, and Kennedy had warned Nixon of its unpopularity.

The Senate opponents argued that the ABM system would intensify the arms race, cost an outrageous $40 to $60 billion, leave most of civilization unprotected in the face of a massive nuclear exchange, and be obsolete before its deployment. The Senate was swayed by the strong lobbying efforts of the Council for a Livable World, led by Thomas Halsten and backed by thousands of contributors. The Council supplied crucial scientific data discrediting the ABM system. Even loyal Republicans began to doubt its necessity, and public opinion swung sharply against it when the first deployments brought bitter protests from neighboring homeowners.

In spite of the growing opposition, Nixon stubbornly favored the program, arguing that it could assure America's retaliatory capability against Russia, provide a "thin" line of defense against a Chinese attack, and arm the Administration with a powerful negotiating tool in America's effort to control the expansion of armaments. Nixon treaded lightly at first, calling for a Pentagon review of the program and then modifying Johnson's version (Sentinel) downward by 50 per cent. He also agreed to locate the missile sites away from heavily populated areas.

At least 44 Senators opposed ABM, 35 favored it, and 21 remained undecided when Nixon decided to push forward. "I am going to fight as hard as I can for it," he vowed. The battle was led by Secretary of Defense Melvin Laird and Pentagon research chief John Foster, who came bearing reams of favorable statistics. "Based on the best information available to me," claimed Laird, "the Soviets could have 2,500 long-range missiles by 1975, compared with 1,054 for the United States." Laird warned that the Soviets had installed hundreds of giant SS-9 intercontinental missiles capable of delivering 25-megaton hydrogen warheads. He predicted that the Soviets would soon achieve first-strike capability.

Laird's hard line on ABM drew a bitter reaction from the Senate, where Fulbright accused the Nixon Administration of employing the "technique of fear" rather than reason in order to foist ABM on the American people. Democratic Senator Albert Gore of Tennessee dubbed the ABM as "a defense in search of a mission." The intensity of the debate grew more bitter as the summer of 1969 wore on. Finally, in August, Senator Stennis persuaded the leadership to put the matter up for a vote. The entire Senate was present for the historic vote which ended in a tie vote of 50-50 with Vice President Agnew casting the deciding vote in favor. Nixon's slim victory brought little satisfaction in the White House; however, it revealed anew the deep divisions existing over military spending priorities. The President's arm-twisting tactics alienated some important liberal Republicans and drew an increasing amount of criticism about military spending programs in general.

In an attempt to placate the critics of military spending, Nixon reduced the spending for some programs. He instructed the Pentagon to significantly reduce the C-5A transport plane, cancelled the Cheyenne helicopter program, postponed indefinitely the Air Force's manned orbiting laboratory, and called for a reduction in personnel. Nixon named a blue ribbon panel to investigate spending excesses in military contracts. Unfortunately, the panel was nominated by representatives of the military-industrial-complex so it never gained much public credibility. Nixon also moved to outlaw germ and chemical warfare when public opinion became adversely aroused over a series of tragic revelations--the continuing use of despicable chemical defoliants in Vietnam, the discovery of the Army's efforts to move lethal nerve gas by rail from the Rocky Mountain arsenal across the country to dump it in the Atlantic Ocean, and the accidental death of 1,000 sheep in Utah due to the Army's experimentation with dangerous chemical and gases. These policies, coupled with the announcement that SALT talks would begin in Helsinki in November, gave the impression that the President was serious about lowering America's military profile.

Still, Nixon assumed a pro-military posture partly because his "cold warrior" predilections still convinced him that America must deal with all other nations from a position of strength and partly because defense contractors had contributed heavily to his 1968 campaign, millions of whose dollars would be welcomed again in 1972. When Congressional doves advocated even further military reduction, Nixon attacked them bitterly and unfairly. In a strongly worded address to the 1969 graduating class at the United States Air Force Academy, Nixon characterized the Congressional critics of military spending as the "new isolationists" and accused them of advocating "unilateral disarmament." Such references soon undermined Nixon's effectiveness in Congress and limited his chances of achieving consensus.

Nixon's position was further weakened by the Administration's failure to bring a quick resolution to the Pueblo incident and by the revelations that the ship may have actually been conducting spying activities in South Korean waters. New stories about surreptitious activities on the part of the once-revered Green Berets, scandals in the military service clubs, leaks about secret executive agreements with foreign countries, and massacres of Vietnamese civilians by American troops gave Congress plenty of ammunition with which to bombard Nixon's pro-military stance.

Senator Fulbright again led the attack against the military. He produced statistics showing how the Pentagon's public relations budget had increased from $2.8 million in 1960 to $28 million by 1969. With such an enormous figure at its disposal, the Pentagon could influence large segments of the media through the manipulation of its advertising. Democratic Senator William Proxmire of Wisconsin hammered away at the huge cost overruns in military contracts. Describing his efforts as "an attempt, for the first time in almost two decades, to get Congress and the country to exercise its critical faculties over defense spending," Proxmire moved methodically against numerous defense contract inefficiencies. Contract costs often increased by billions over their original estimations. The cost overruns involved not only inefficiencies but mismanagement, secretiveness, and deception.

Proxmire was assisted in his efforts by Pentagon management specialist A.E. Fitzgerald, who originally discovered $2 billion in cost overruns on the C-5A jet transport but later found his employment summarily terminated in a Pentagon "cost-saving" move; this termination appeared as an arrogant and inglorious action which further discredited Nixon. "This was not a case of some person down the line deciding he (Fitzgerald) should go," Nixon later explained. "It was a decision that was submitted to me. I made it and I stick by it." In the end Congress appeared more serious about arms reduction than Nixon. It reduced the President's proposed military budget request for 1970 by $5.6 billion.

Nixon's political viability was further damaged by the great court fight which raged over the President's nominations of Clement F. Haynesworth and G. Harold Carswell to the Supreme Court. Nixon nominated Haynesworth of South Carolina on August 18, 1969, proclaiming that the Chief Justice of the 4th Circuit Court conformed well to his criteria.of a "strict constitutional constructionist." Haynesworth's rather conservative opinions regarding civil rights and labor drew immediate opposition from liberals. The NAACP called his civil rights record "one of resistance to the movement of racial equality." George L. Meany accused him of being "antilabor," pointing out that in seven labor-management decisions Haynesworth had always sided with management and had been overruled in every case by the Supreme Court. At first these reservations were successfully dispelled by sponsoring South Carolina Senator Thurmond, who explained that Haynesworth's judicial mind does not reside at either extreme of the spectrum, and Senator Hollings, who claimed that Haynesworth would bring "balance where it is needed."

The fate of the Haynesworth nomination cannot be completely understood without examining the connection between it and the failure of Abe Fortas to achieve the Chief Justiceship earlier in 1969. Fortas had been nominated by President Johnson to replace Earl Warren, who had resigned upon learning of the election of his hated political adversary, Nixon. Fortas was eminently qualified but an LBJ crony of sorts, and the nomination was regarded as untimely with a new President coming into office. Senate conservatives conducted a scrupulous investigation into Fortas' "off-the bench" financial affairs and discovered that prior to his judgeship in 1966 he had received a $20,000 fee from the Wolfson Foundation. In September of 1967 Louis E. Wolfson, who created the foundation, was convicted of selling unregistered securities and of illegal stock manipulation. He received a one-year prison sentence and a $100,000 fine. Upon learning of Wolfson's difficulties, Fortas returned the $20,000; but, according to Senate conservatives, led by Michigan's Robert P. Griffin, the appearance of gross impropriety disqualified Fortas and would discredit the highest court of the land, if Fortas were to be confirmed.

At first Fortas resisted the attacks upon his integrity; but after Nixon's Criminal Division of the Justice Department began a broader investigation of his affairs and Attorney General Mitchell informed Chief Justice Warren that he held even more damaging information concerning Fortas and after the Committee on Professional Ethics of the American Bar Association concluded that Fortas' association with Wolfson had been "clearly contrary" to Canon 25 of "The Canons of Judicial Ethics," Fortas decided to resign his position. Fortas claimed "no wrongdoing on my part" but resigned out of consideration for "the welfare and maximum effectiveness of the court to perform its critical role in our system of government." The resignation allowed Nixon to appoint the more conservative Burger as Chief Justice.

The ignominious Fortas affair remained fresh in the minds of Senate liberals as they began to examine the private financial affairs of Haynesworth. Democratic Senator Birch Bayh of Indiana led the way. Slowly and arduously the Senate Judiciary Committee found itself confronted with potential conflicts of interest which could have swayed Haynesworth's decisions. In 1963 he had decided for Darlingon Manufacturing Co. against the NLRB. At the time he owned one-seventh interest in a company doing much business with Darlingon. In 1967 he purchased 1,000 shares in Brunswick Corporation while judging a case involving Brunswick vs. Long. During the excruciating hearings and the long and bitter Senate debate which followed, no single clear example of impropriety could be cited; but, taken together, several instances demonstrated lack of sensitivity and suggested the appearance of ethical impropriety.

The Haynesworth nomination passed committee by an unconvincing ten to seven margin but soon ran into deep trouble in the Senate debate which followed. Three top Republicans quickly deserted the President on the nomination. Scott, Griffin,and Chase all contended that they could not in good conscience support Haynesworth when they had opposed Fortas. Some Senators began to suggest that Nixon withdraw the nomination. Rather than bend to such pressure, Nixon decided to fight it out, again revealing the "Old Nixon" who was always ready for a good tussle no matter how badly it muddled the political waters. Nixon announced bluntly to GOP Congressional leaders on October 14 that he remained "firmly and unequivocally determined" to see the Haynesworth nomination through.

In the belief that the liberals were merely "nitpicking," Nixon enlisted all of the political resources of the Administration in the battle. White House Aides Harry Dent and Bryce Harlow applied a variety of pressure-and-promise techniques. Telephone calling, letter writing, and telegram campaigns were carefully orchestrated from the level of constituency groups. Some even threatened to cut off campaign contributions. House Minority Leader Gerald Ford threatened to renew the impeachment movement against Justice Douglas. John Mitchell applied sarcasm. "If we'd put up one of the 12 Apostles, it would have been the same," he cried. Republican Senator William B. Saxbe of Ohio spoke for most when he complained that the White House pressures were "as strong as anything we've seen."

Nixon's pressure tactics were almost too well organized and brought adverse reaction from Senators of both parties, always conscious of their prerogatives. Senator Mansfield claimed that the outside pressure boomeranged and served only to stiffen the opposition. On November 21 the Senate, in one of the most electrifying sessions of the decade, rejected Haynesworth's nomination by a 45-55 vote, the first Supreme Court nomination to be rejected since Herbert Hoover's recommendation of Judge Parker in 1930.

This drew an ill-tempered response from the White House. For the first time since taking over the Presidency, Nixon could not restrain his anger and lashed out at his opposition. "I deeply regret this action. I believe a majority of people in the nation regret it," stated Nixon curtly. "Especially I deplore the nature of the attacks that have been made upon this distinguished man," continued Nixon; "his integrity is unimpeachable, his ability unquestioned." Nixon served notice on Congress that upon its return he would nominate another person, using the same criteria applied to Haynesworth. "I would be consistent with my commitments to the American people before my election a year ago," asserted Nixon.

When Congress returned in 1970, it found itself confronted with the nomination of Judge G. Harold Carswell of Tallahassee, Florida, a member of the Fifth Circuit Court of Appeals. Like Haynesworth, Carswell was a Southerner, a Republican, and a strict constitutional constructionist. Upon investigation, the Senate Judiciary Committee discovered that Carswell's record on civil rights matters was even more reactionary than that of Haynesworth. His early Dixiecrat political career was stained with blatant racist proclamations. During the Fifties he had helped convert a local public golf course into a private club in order to avoid integration. He served on the board of directors of a housing authority for a fraternity at Florida State University which excluded blacks from membership.

Even more disconcerting, however, was Carswell's lack of qualifications. "The public record of Judge Carswell's career and accomplishments clearly does not place him within even an ample list of the nation's more distinguished jurists," warned Derek Bok, Dean of Harvard's law school. Carswell "presents more slender credentials than any nominee for the Supreme Court put forth in this century," protested Law Dean Louis Pollak of Yale. Carswell's judicial record was found to be badly scarred by higher court reversals and judicial error. The nomination appeared as an affront to the integrity of the Senate. Arrogant lobbying by Administration officials further alienated Senate moderates and liberals; and on April 8, 1970, the Carswell nomination met defeat by a vote of 45-51.

Not since the days of Grover Cleveland had a President been rebuffed twice in a row, and never was a President so resentful. Feeling that the White House had received shoddy treatment, Nixon blasted away at the Senate. "I have reluctantly concluded, with the Senate presently constituted, I cannot successfully nominate to the Supreme Court any judge from the South who believes as I do in the strict construction of the Constitution," complained Nixon. He accused the Senate of subjecting Carswell to "malicious character assassination" and "regional discrimination," and he promised solemnly that the millions of disappointed middle Americans would some day have one of their men sitting on the high court.

Liberals and moderates could not be certain whether Nixon's vindictive manner represented a promise or a threat. Some believed that the shrewd Nixon had known all along that Carswell would not pass the Senate but that the nomination was merely meant to placate Senator Thurmond and the South for the sake of developing political strategy, dubbed the "Southern strategy." Actually, Nixon was so engrossed in the management of foreign affairs that he did not give the court matter enough attention, allowing underlings to make too many fateful decisions which later the President himself felt obligated to defend. Whatever Nixon's motives, the bitter battles over the hurt nominations greatly encumbered his chances of forging a new governing consensus. "The President made the mistake of fighting back himself, rather than leaving it to underlings, and now the Senate is free to continue future battles at that elevated level," wrote columnist Marianne Means.

The great Court debate intensified the controversy surrounding the Nixon Administration's law-and-order policies. The practices of John Mitchell's Justice Department caused grave concern and even consternation in many quarters. Mitchell had been a Wall Street expert on municipal bonds with little experience in Justice Department matters before joining his friend and colleague, Nixon. Speaking of Mitchell, "the flash from Apawamis," Nixon once told his personal staff that "I've found the man. I've found the heavyweight." As columnist Marianne Means put it: "Every administration has its scapegoat, its lightning rod, its evil genius." Mitchell's inconsistency on Fortas and Haynesworth, his shrewd advocacy of the Southern strategy, and his tough law-and-order proclamations made him just that. Even his cool, calculating demeanor reminded many critics of repression. "When you first meet Mitchell," reported TBR in the New Republic, "he seems cold on the surface; but after you get to know him you realize that that is only the tip of the iceberg." TBR went on to speculate that "nothing in his life had brought him in contact or sympathy with the poor, the black or the young. What he seems to lack is human understanding and maybe, compassion."

Equipped with his constantly glowing pipe protruding from under his Romanistic nose, Mitchell's policies seemed to reflect the concern of TBR. In his first year Mitchell advocated "preventive detention" in some cases, proposed the idea that judges withhold bail from persons with criminal records, asked for additional authority to conduct wire taps and plant electronic bugs, urged the adoption of a "no-knock" law, presented guidelines to ease school desegregation, and drafted a bill to weaken the Voting Rights law.

These policies drew sharp criticism. Preventive detention would be "worthless as a weapon against crime," exhorted North Carolina's Democratic Senator Sam Ervin of the Judiciary Committee. "You cannot convince me that this can only be done at the price of our constitutional liberties," complained Senator Harold Hughes of Iowa; "we are living in an era in which bombastic hyperbole and repressive policies are being passed off as public responsibility and concern." "It seems as if the department sees the values of the Bill of Rights as no more than obstacles to be overcome," charged the University of California's Sanford Kadish; "there seems to be a single-minded effort to cut the crime rate, with little sense of the constraints of the Constitution."

By pursing the hard line on law-and-order, Mitchell's image became associated with some of the most spectacular criminal justice matters of the time. The tumultuous trial of the Chicago Seven represented a good example of how Mitchell and ultimately Nixon himself became associated with repression which led to more divisiveness. The trial of Abbie Hoffman, Jerry Rubin, David Dellinger, Tom Hayden, Rennie Davis, John Froines, and Lee Weiner--the most active of the radical New Left--was based on violation of a special provision of the 1968 Civil Rights Act which made it a federal crime to cross over state lines with conspiratorial intentions to cause riotous activities. South Carolina's Senator Strom Thurmond had proposed the amendment, which passed the Senate 85 to 5. Some liberals voted for the provision in order to save the housing bill, others in discreet acquiescence to the subtle establishment movement against the New Left. Mitchell sought the indictments for reasons of political expediency as well as justice. The issue dealt with a disturbance at the Democratic National Convention in Chicago under Mayor Daley's control. In a political face-saving maneuver, Mitchell appointed Democratic U.S. Attorney Thomas Foran as prosecutor in the case.

The spurious law required proof of "intent" in the minds of the defendants before commission of any criminal acts, a difficult proposition to prove. Matters were exacerbated by the obstinacy of Federal Judge Hoffman, the judge responsible for the trial. The crusty old judge could not fathom the youth movement, nor could he be impartial in the case. "If I had been trying the case without a jury, I would have found the defendants guilty right off," he remarked. By persistently demanding strict and unyielding rules of decorum in a highly-publicized and unusual trial, Hoffman alienated Americans both within and outside of the legal system. By showing open resentment toward the defendants, he made martyrs out of them and further alienated their youthful supporters and sympathizers. At the end of the trial he shocked the nation by handing down a series of lengthy contempt-of-court sentences. Upon sentencing David Dellinger solemnly retorted that "you can jail a revolutionary, but you can't jail the revolution."

In his instructions to the jury Hoffman defined conspiracy in its broadest terms. "If you find that a conspiracy existed and that during it one of the alleged overt acts was committed by a member of that conspiracy, that is sufficient to find all members of the conspiracy guilty," instructed Hoffman. "When persons enter the unlawful agreement, they become agents for one another." In sentencing, Hoffman added one more irritation by ordering each defendant to pay a portion of the cost of prosecution, which could have been as high as $50,000 per defendant. He went on to refuse bond to the five convicted defendants, calling them "dangerous men."

Whereas Judge Hoffman alienated the more liberal segments of the American public with his "erratic and irascible" handling of the case, the exceptional antics of the defendants themselves, including the recital of protest song lyrics, Buddhist chanting, exotic dress, and the use of four-letter words, alienated the Silent Majority. Life magazine described the disruptive scene. The defendants "giggle and confer endlessly in court and pass notes back and forth like naughty school children, while between them defendant Lee Weiner calmly reads The Wisdom of Lao-tze." The defendant's main attorney, William Kunstler, the self-styled "people's lawyer," added to the confusion. Kunstler himself received a four-year and thirteen day sentence for contempt-of-court.

By the time the trial ended, the whole episode resembled a "theater of the absurd" rather than a respectable pursuit of justice; and the Nixon Administration came under heavy criticism for its involvement. "The real conspiracy in Chicago is not the one with which the government has charged the eight defendants but its own action in securing their indictment," protested Nation. "The decision of Attorney General John Mitchell to seek indictments might be regarded as the 'overt' act. The intent of the government's 'conspiracy' was to discourage opposition to the war in Vietnam."

The Administration lost considerable political stature among moderates as well as liberals. Vice President Agnew identified closely with the prosecution, calling the defendants "anarchists and social misfits." At a St. Paul fund-raising dinner he commented that "fortunately for America the system proved equal to the challenge." New York City's liberal Republican Mayor John Lindsay disagreed. "When a trial becomes fundamentally an examination of political acts and beliefs, then guilt or innocence becomes irrelevant." Hence, divisiveness in place of consensus resulting from the Administration's tough and uncompromising policy on law-and-order.

Mitchell's tough stance on law-and-order bolstered the resolve of law enforcement officials everywhere in their dealings with the political radicals. But many civil libertarians feared that the energetic and forceful manner in which local police departments now operated denied basic human rights, and in some cases they even worried that law enforcement was taking on the trappings of a police state. During this time police and Black Panthers became involved in a number of violent confrontations. The most conspicuous example of this sordid street warfare occurred in Chicago. While police were conducting a supposed routine check on a Black Panther apartment, shots were fired, leaving Illinois Panther-leader Fred Hampton and a follower dead. The police claimed that the Panthers shot first while the Panthers charged that the raid was part of an intentional policy to destroy their leaders. A Federal Grand Jury concluded that the raid had not been "professionally planned or properly executed." The episode reflected badly on the integrity of Mitchell and the Nixon Administration, which had consciously attempted to woo the law-and-order vote.

In the midst of the great Court fight and the law-and-order debate, the dark clouds of economic trouble continued to gather on the horizon, thus placing the nation on notice that its people faced the greatest economic crisis in a generation. "Seldom has the transition from buoyant optimism to spreading doubt come so abruptly," reported *Time.* All of the leading economic indicators began registering an ominous decline. Unemployment, the most political of the indicators, increased sharply from 3.3 per cent at the end of 1968 to 6.2 per cent by the end of 1970, when the average worker's take-home pay had dipped below that of 1965. Unemployment lines grew distressingly long, and jobless people began to cluster aimlessly on street corners and in taverns to fret about their ill fortune. Meanwhile, corporate profits dropped almost 25 per cent from their peak third quarter of 1968; profit margins declined from well over 5 per cent to well under 4 per cent. Annual corporate profits, which had ranged between 48 and 51 billion dollars during the boom years of the Great Society prosperity, plummeted to $39.2 billion in 1970.

Industrial output declined along with profits, and capital outlays for expansion fell ominously. Orders for durable goods and plant equipment declined as inventories began to bulge and business reduced replacement orders in anticipation of a major economic slump. By 1970 manufacturers operated at only 76 per cent of capacity, the lowest since 1961. In the automobile industry production dropped by 15 per cent. "The market for cars has fallen on its ass," complained an auto industry executive. Railroad profits plummeted out of sight and the nation's leading railroad, the Penn Central, which provided passenger and freight service for large sections of the Northeast, declared bankruptcy.

Aerospace sales in 1969 fell by 4.1 per cent while profits declined by almost 30 per cent and employment dropped by 120,000 persons. Employment in the once-heralded space program fell to less than half of the 420,000 positions needed in 1965, sending highly skilled engineers and scientists scrambling for employment. Airline profits, which had been $412 million in 1967, fell to a deficit of $123 million in 1969, forcing schedule reductions. It has been the "worst year ever" for airlines, reported the Wall Street Journal.

The highly-publicized glamour industries of the Sixties began to fold. In Los Angeles Lytton Industries, once valued at $700 million, succumbed to creditors as the California housing boom collapsed. Long-Temco-Vought, one of the most daring and spectacular conglomerates of the high Sixties, had to sell major holdings just to provide for its interest and debt payments.

Seldom in history had Americans experienced an economic crunch that involved inflation and business decline simultaneously. "We face a problem unknown to earlier generations--namely, a high rate of inflation at a time of substantial unemployment," grumbled Presidential Counsellor Arthur F. Burns as he contemplated reports that the leading economic indicators were falling at an annual rate of 1.8 per cent while wholesale prices were rising 8.4 per cent and the consumer price index was rising by 7.2 per cent. "This is a recession plus a continuing brutal inflation," complained business economist Sylvia Porter, the "worst of all possible worlds."

Some economists called the uncertain phenomenon slump-flation, others stagflation; but none could prescribe a remedy. "We are living in an economic world where we know that the old-time economics religion of cutting budgets, raising interest rates, and tightening money flow simply will not do in dealing with inflation," wrote Max Lerner, "but we have not yet found a latter-day economic religion or even an economic philosophy." Lerner concluded gloomily that America was "caught between an economic world that is dying and one that is straining to be born."

Economists found it difficult to agree on a diagnosis for stagflation. Many blamed Johnson's "guns and butter" economic policies, which had resulted in a $25.2-billion-dollar federal budget deficit in 1968, a prosperous year. Deficit spending had created more domestic demand than supply, generating in turn an almost irreversible cost-push inflation. Other economists blamed the monopolistic practices of powerfully organized conglomerates and labor unions which preferred to curtail production and trim payroll for the sake of maintaining high prices. Artificially high prices at the expense of consumers and unorganized labor seemed an easier course than relying on free market forces.

Still other economists, such as Milton Friedman of the "Chicago School," blamed inflation on governmental monetary policy. Friedman argued that the Keynesians had emphasized changes in taxes and federal spending and paid too little attention to expanding and contracting money supplies in accordance with population demands and industrial growth patterns. Friedman charged that the Federal Reserve Board had supplied too much money in the expansionary years of 1965 and 1966 and then "slammed on the brakes too hard" in 1967.

The Governor of the Federal Reserve Board, William McChesney Martin, reluctantly agreed that Friedman's arguments carried some credence but also admitted that the Board might have been "overly hasty" in lowering the discount rate in 1968. A few economists suspected that interest on debt, both public and private, which exceeded the value of all raw materials produced in the United States, might be slowly debasing the American economic structure. They argued that only a massive economic readjustment (depression) or the reindustrialization of America would restore the vitality of the economy.

Whatever the domestic causes of stagflation, America's changing status in the international market place had no small bearing on the economic crisis. Excessive wasteful spending, especially for arms, had resulted in production inefficiencies which made it more difficult for American corporations to compete with the Europeans and the Japanese. In 1969 alone sales of Japanese automobiles in the United States increased by 50 per cent and sales of Japanese trucks by almost 100 per cent, while American manufacturers barely registered a gain. The Japanese Toyota and Datsun, along with the German Volkswagen, became familiar sights on the highways of America. America had sunk from first place to tenth as a world shipbuilder. American yards produced only 50 ships annually compared to 200 produced by the Japanese.

During the decade America's trade surplus disappeared. In 1961 the United States exported $20.2 billion compared to imports of $14.8 billion. By the end of the decade the situation had been reversed: exports amounted to $44.4 billion, imports were $45.1 billion. Textile imports alone increased from $866 million in 1960 to $2.1 billion in 1969. The deficit was caused in part by the increasing imbalance of international payments. The United States invested, loaned, and granted $40 billion more than it earned in trade and investments overseas. By 1970 foreign institutions held $50 billion American dollars compared to $30 billion in 1961. The United States Treasury held only $35 billion in gold. This imbalance held the threat of displacing the dollar as the international currency of exchange and weakened the gold standard. The possibility of bringing back stability through the use of the Special Drawing Rights of the International Monetary Fund existed. Without the huge U.S. agricultural and arms shipments abroad, the situation would have been far worse.

When Nixon entered office, he seemed to appreciate the seriousness of America's economic crisis. At his first Presidential press conference he unequivocally said that the economy "required urgent attention," and called for "some fine tuning of our fiscal and monetary affairs to control inflation." He warned that "unless we do control inflation, we will be confronted eventually with massive unemployment." His strong language was not reflected in his early economic policy, however; his preoccupation with foreign affairs dwarfed his ability to give attention to domestic economic matters.

Political considerations too often took precedence over tough economic policy making. Labor Secretary George Schultz refused to intervene in the collective bargaining process. Nixon pushed for more defense spending in spite of Budget Director Robert Mayo's stern warnings that such programs would be inflationary. Nixon accepted deficit spending in order to escape being tagged with the Herbert Hoover badge. He encouraged a tight money policy at the Federal Reserve, hoping that it would cool inflation. Nixon chose the goal of "controlling inflation without increasing unemployment in any substantial way." Economic Advisor James McCracken typified Nixon's cautious approach when he reported that the objective "was never to lock the brakes so severely that the economy would be thrown in the ditch."

Nixon chose a moderate approach toward economic restoration in the face of immoderate circumstances. He followed Johnson's 1968 precedent of imposing a ceiling on government spending. He coaxed Congress into extending Johnson's 10 per cent income tax surcharge. He got Congress to repeal Kennedy's investment tax credit on machinery purchases and to cancel scheduled reductions in telephone and automobile excise taxes. On the international level he raised tariffs on such products as automobiles and textiles and hoped that his efforts toward rapprochement with Russia and China would open new markets for American goods.

Nixon's moderate efforts soon proved inadequate in the face of gathering economic storm clouds. Nowhere was the crisis more obvious than on Wall Street, which still served as an important economic barometer. Investors increasingly began to lose confidence in stocks as a hedge against rising prices. They worried more over the continuing drop in the value of the dollar on foreign money markets, and they perceived that the Administration could not cope with the complexities of managing the American economy.

Between December of 1968 and May of 1970 an icy hush fell over Wall Street's plush boardrooms as the stock market fell from 944.65 to 641.36, an overall decline of 36 per cent. During this dire period motion picture stock declined by 74.3 per cent, aerospace by 69.5 per cent, airlines by 60 percent, radio and television by 58.6 per cent, railroads by 54.4 per cent, and home furnishings by 50.7 per cent. DuPont fell to a 15-year low, and United States Steel declined to its lowest level since 1954. Pension funds, foundation investments, and mutual funds lost billions. Some called the market slump the "Great Humbler."

Investors, who a few years earlier had revelled in luxurious suites boasting of the "permanent boom," now scurried for cover as their mood turned to one of despair and then anger. The number of brokerage firms doing business on the New York Stock Exchange decreased from 646 to 518. Established firms laid off employees by the thousands. The price of purchasing a seat on the Exchange dropped from $435,000 to $70,000 as Wall Street became known as a "disaster area." The Sandwich Genie on New Street closed as early as 5:00 p.m., quite a change from 1968 when it carried out sandwiches to ambitious young brokers as late as midnight.

Rumors of pending corporation bankruptcies pervaded the atmosphere fully as much as in 1929. This is the worst "crisis of confidence" I have ever seen, reported one disillusioned broker. Richard Scruggs, prominent Goodby Co. analyst, reported that "certainly pessimism is in every corner of Wall Street." The pessimism quickly spread throughout the entire country. Americans' confidence in the future of the economy fell to 86 based on 100 in 1966. The National Industrial Conference Board, a forum of eleven leading economists, predicted a significant economic slowdown for the early Seventies.

A worried Richard Nixon attempted to inspire confidence and sounded the old Hoover prediction that "prosperity was just around the corner." At an April, 1970, press conference Nixon told reporters that "frankly, if I had any money, I'd be buying stocks right now." The next day the Dow Jones Industrial averages promptly dropped another 10 points. On May 26 the market plunged 20.81 points, the worst drop since the day President Kennedy was assassinated. In June the Federal Reserve abruptly forsook its tight money policy, fearing complete financial panic. During the weekend of June 20 leading Administration officials spent their time calling bankers, telling them that on Monday the "discount window would be kept open" and that the ceiling on larger certificates of deposit could be suspended. The *New Republic* characterized the policy change as "the technical equivalent of a slug of whiskey to a heart patient." The crisis was temporarily blunted, but even leading Administration officials could not be optimistic. Secretary of Treasury David Kennedy admitted that "the problem is much more difficult than I realized. We can't let this escalate into runaway inflation, and we're very close to that now." Ultimately, the crisis brought bad omens for Nixon politically. "Mr. Nixon has repealed the 1960's," complained a Wall Street broker bitterly.

Nixon now realized that such drastic measures as wage and price controls would have to be imposed in order to abate the economic crisis. The fortunes of Republican candidates in the approaching mid-term elections looked bleak. Only by accomplishing some great feat in Vietnam could Nixon reverse his sagging political fortunes. Vietnam still commanded the greatest amount of attention in the press as well as in the minds of most Americans. Increasingly, however, Nixon found himself trapped between a stubborn foe abroad and a rising impatience at home.

Vietnam now loomed as the longest and most divisive war in American history. In simple terms it represented a misguided American intervention in a far-away place, but the international stakes were still high. Nixon had to find a way to wind down the war without greatly impairing American hegemony and discrediting commitments made to other allies. Domestically, the stakes were also high. For both personal and political reasons, Nixon, like Johnson, did not want to be branded as the first President to lose a war. An obvious loss could awaken ugly feelings of patriotism and cause millions of middle Americans to shift their political allegiance to George Wallace, thus spelling doom for the GOP. The threat from the right was far greater than that from the left. So there would be no mistake about it, Nixon made his position perfectly clear: "America has never been defeated in the proud 190-year history of this country, and we shall not be defeated in Viet Nam."

In the implementation of his Vietnam policy Nixon suffered several delusions: (1) that Russia and China could easily manipulate the posture of North Vietnam; (2) that the North Vietnamese would settle for a compromise short of Vietnamese reunification; (3) that the South Vietnamese people and military possessed the determination necessary to resist the North; and (4) that anti-Vietnamese forces in America could be successfully placated. Thus, his policies were destined to fail from their inception.

During the first eight months of the Nixon Presidency, Americans had assumed a rather oblique posture of watchful waiting. This posture was interrupted only occasionally by representatives of the New Left or former Johnson officials who mistrusted Nixon's course of de-escalation. For example, when the Administration charged that a North Vietnam spring offensive was evidence of "bad faith," W. Averell Harriman and Clark Clifford countered that the Administration itself had acted in "bad faith" by failing to respond to a year-end "lull" initiated by the Communist forces.

By September, 1969, as students began returning to campuses, Nixon's Vietnamization policy could hardly boast of any success. The students could say along with the ancient prophet Jeremiah: "They have healed the wound of my people lightly, saying, 'peace, peace,' when there is no peace." Serious negotiations in Paris remained illusive, the fighting continued at pre-Nixon levels, and only token withdrawals had been made. After returning from a four-day tour of Vietnam, Defense Secretary Melvin Laird suggested the possibility of a long, drawn-out war without any early major troop withdrawals. Field reports indicated that the Viet Cong infrastructure remained intact, that the agriculturally rich Mekong Delta continued its tilt toward Communist influence, that pacification progressed only at a slow pace, that the ARVN remained heavily dependent on United States ground forces, that province chiefs and military commanders continued to be replaced at an alarming rate, and that the so-called "home front militia" suffered desperately from apathy and misdirection.

The continuing cost in life and resource swelled the American conscience. Five million acres had now been destroyed by the American practice of spraying herbicides to uncover enemy troop movements, a repulsive statistic to the newly ecology-minded public. Some of the most bloody battles of the war at such remote places as Hamburger Hill, the A Shaw Valley, A.P. Bia Mountain, and Hill 37 caused heavy American casualties. The growing despair with war was reflected in the large amount of adverse publicity surrounding the infamous My Lai incident, in which a platoon of Charlie Company, under the leadership of Lt. William Calley, Jr., allegedly massacred 400 unarmed women and children. The gruesome episode brought back memories of San Creek and Wounded Knee and made the war loom as an unconscionable exercise in futility. The unfortunate Calley was marked for trial; but there loomed a nagging feeling that in a fundamental way the hapless Lieutenant was only the scapegoat and that ultimately the blame, shame, and guilt should be born by the military leadership, the politicians, and the citizens who failed to extricate the country from war. Clearly, time was running out on the war and Nixon's Vietnam policy.

The clearest sounds of a renewed anti-Vietnam sentiment came thundering from the halls of Congress, where anxious Senators began to debate Congressional action to end the war. On September 25 Republican Senator Charles E. Goodell of New York proposed a bill establishing a statutory deadline for a complete troop pullout by December 1, 1970. A Gallup poll showed that 59 per cent of the public supported such a measure. The next day twenty-four liberal Democratic Senators met behind closed doors and decided, in the words of Senator Fred Harris of Oklahoma, "to take the gloves off on Vietnam." Massachusetts Senator Edward Kennedy charged that "we have made only token troop withdrawals on the battlefield, an exercise in politics and improvisation." Senator Edmund S. Muskie declared that "time is running out."

Once again such stalwart Senate doves as Fulbright and Church were locked in hopeless debate with equally fervent hawks such as Goldwater and Stennis, taking important time away from Nixon's other legislative priorities. The doves recommended a firm timetable for withdrawal over an 18-month period, arguing that for Hanoi to interfere would jeopardize its own interest of eliminating all foreign influence. The hawks argued that such a policy would "tie the President's hands," and "undercut his bargaining position with the enemy." Doves bitterly criticized Nixon's unflinching support of the tyrannical Thieu-Ky government. Meanwhile, students began planning massive marches on Washington to demand an end to the war.

Nixon responded to Vietnam criticism in a partisan and divisive manner. He wrapped himself in the flag of patriotism, something Johnson had for the most part resisted. In response to the September 26 liberal Senate parley, Nixon called for unity so as not to weaken the President's hand. The war "will end much sooner if we can have a united front," argued Nixon; "if we have that united front, the enemy will then begin to talk." Nixon had Senate Minority Leader, Hugh Scott of Pennsylvania, who had replaced the effervescent Dirksen, call for a 60-day moratorium on criticism to give the Administration "some elbow room" in negotiations. While calling on Americans to turn on their automobile headlights as a show of support for the President, Scott complained that "somebody should demonstrate against Hanoi. I recommend it." Meanwhile, House Minority Leader Ford called upon Americans not to "bug out" or "buckle under" to criticism at home or recalcitrance abroad, while others encouraged the flying of flags at half-staff in support of Nixon.

For all of his bluster, however, Nixon could not turn back the tide of anti-Vietnam sentiment. Several end-the-war moratorium marches were scheduled around the country on October 15 under the leadership of Harvard divinity student Sam Brown. In Washington thousands of solemn demonstrators followed Coretta King in a candlelight parade from the White House to the United States Treasury building, where candles were planted on the tall black fence spears. On the steps of the Capitol building fellow demonstrators began a litany of dissent which involved the reading of names of service men killed in Vietnam. On the West Coast protesters crowded onto the Golden Gate Bridge and displayed banners calling for immediate troop withdrawal. Others handed out antiwar leaflets on the famous trolley cars that dominated the San Francisco scene.

In Chicago students, housewives, and a sprinkling of businessmen marched through the Loop chanting antiwar songs. Close to 100,000 somber New Englanders gathered on the Boston Commons to endorse South Dakota Senator George McGovern's call for an early end to the war. In Bryant Park 100,000 New Yorkers gathered to hear antiwar diatribes from Mayor Lindsay, Pastor Coffin, and Senators Javits and McCarthy. "Come home America from your sinful journey across the sea. Come home America and redeem your soul," intoned the otherwise staid Ralph Abernathy, new leader of the Southern Christian Leadership Conference, before an audience of 10,000 at the University of Southern California. In Vietnam American soldiers wore black arm bands in symbolic protest against a war they neither believed in nor wanted to fight.

On November 15 over 250,000 Americans converged on the Capitol to join the 40-hour "march against death" singing the peace chant, "All we are saying is give peace a chance." They paraded silently past the White House bearing candles and the names of slain soldiers, which were placed in a line of coffins in front of the Capitol. The atmosphere was one of desperation. "It takes little wisdom to realize that if it was unwise and inept to have gotten into this war in the first place," pleaded Coretta King, "to stubbornly persist in staying in it becomes stupid and evil."

Nixon's reaction at this point was partly positive. He went before both branches of Congress to give the impression that earlier withdrawals might be possible. A more ominous side of Nixon's reaction to the demonstrations, however, was revealed in a blatant statement made by Vice President Agnew at a GOP fund-raising dinner. "If the moratorium had any use whatever, it served as an emotional purgative for those who feel the need to cleanse themselves of their lack of ability to offer constructive solutions to the problem," blurted Agnew, who by now had become the President's political "hatchet man."

By Christmas the protest had quieted, and during early 1970 Nixon managed to rekindle briefly public confidence in his Vietnamization policy. Secretary Laird confidently told Congress in February that enemy activity had declined significantly and that American forces would be reduced by 115,500 troops by April. In March Donald G. MacDonald, Director of the Agency for International Development, told Congress that "the leadership of South Vietnam has begun and is pursuing a process of enlightened social change." Edward J. Nickel, Director of the United States Public Affairs Office in Saigon, insisted before Congress that the South Vietnamese government had "manifested an increasing understanding of the importance of developing better lines of communication with the people." In April Nixon announced plans for the withdrawal of an additional 150,000 troops.

The positive outward assessment of the war belied the real situation, however, in this "Year of the Dog," 1970. As long as Prince Sihanouk, Cambodian Chief of State, insisted upon a strict policy of neutrality, Administration officials could not assure the protection of the remaining American troops because of the large amount of infiltration coming through Cambodian territory. Suddenly, in March, a reactionary clique of generals led by General Lon Nol, thought by many to have the support of the American CIA, overthrew the Sihanouk government. Nol immediately fielded his inadequate army in an effort to dislodge the Communists. In a few short weeks the Pathet Lao and North Vietnamese had defeated Lon Nol, gaining an upper hand in the critical area east of the Mekong River and occupying the vital seaport city of Kep. This new advantage allowed the Communists to solidify their positions in new sanctuaries, exposing South Vietnam's entire western flank. Worried Administration officials feared that the old Eisenhower "falling domino" theory might be coming true. "All right, a year from now I will be sitting here with most of our troops out of Vietnam, and what do I do then?", a perplexed Nixon asked the National Security Council. Actually, both Nixon and Kissinger had determined by now that North Vietnam was intent on total victory and would only be brought to serious negotiation after severe punishment.

Prince Sihanouk's announcement from South China that an "Indochinese People's Army" had been formed to regain control of Cambodia's capital city of Phnom-Penh spurred President Nixon into action. He decided to commit American and South Vietnamese troops to an incursion against the so-called "privileged sanctuaries" along the twisting 6,600 mile border just inside of Cambodia. "Let's go blow the hell out of them," Nixon told the Joint Chiefs of Staff. On paper this represented a violation of the 1954 Geneva Accords, but Nixon argued that these border base areas were not actually under Cambodian control anyway. During the predawn hours of May Day, First U.S. Air Cavalrymen pushed into Cambodia's Kimpong Cham Province, the so-called "Fishhook" area, in search of large caches of military and food supplies and with the intention of disrupting the Communist central command headquarters thought to be hidden in concrete bunkers. South Vietnamese troops accompanied by American advisors and United States air protection moved into the "Parrot's Beak" area, a staging ground located only 35 miles from Saigon. The bombing was significantly increased along the De-Militarized zone (DMZ) between the two Vietnams, and three United States aircraft carriers were brought back into action along the North Vietnamese coastal regions.

The action represented the most controversial decision of Nixon's early years, and the President knew it would reap consternation both at home and abroad. Nixon attempted to ameliorate the impact of his decision in a carefully drafted television message to the nation on May 2. He told the American people that the purpose of the incursion was to protect the lives of American boys. "We will not allow American men by the thousands to be killed by an enemy from privileged sanctuaries," asserted Nixon. The incursion would give the Vietnamization program a chance to work, foster freedom in Southeast Asia, and demonstrate a new American commitment. "I would rather be a one-term President and do what I believe is right than be a two-term President at the cost of seeing America become a second-rate power," proclaimed Nixon.

The domestic furor over the Cambodian invasion turned out to be much worse than Nixon and his advisors had anticipated. Nixon's own divisive demeanor helped incite the furor. In his television message he referred to this "age of anarchy both abroad and at home," an obvious stab at the peace demonstrators. He overstated his case: "If when the chips are down the world's most powerful nation--the United States of America--acts like a pitiful, helpless giant," proclaimed Nixon, "the forces of totalitarianism and anarchy will threaten free nations and free institutions throughout the world." Many Americans felt that this kind of language should have gone out with Johnson. Nixon's belated consultation with Congress, which was mostly through the hawkish Armed Services rather than the more standard Foreign Relations Committee, caused many Americans to suspect that they were being "hoodwinked" into a new and more dangerous escalation of the Southeast Asia war.

A shocked Congress reacted quickly to Nixon's policy. On the day after Nixon's television address, previously supportive Senate Majority Leader Mike Mansfield sadly predicted that "we're sinking deeper into the morass." According to Mansfield, "the feeling of gloom in the Senate is so thick that you could cut it with a knife." To demonstrate its disillusionment the Senate scheduled a vote on repealing the 1965 Tonkin Gulf Resolution. Another resolution was drafted condemning the Cambodian action. Mansfield began drafting legislation which would deny the President use of military appropriations for future Cambodian-like ventures. Liberals openly spoke of legislation which could specifically limit the President's war-making powers.

Around the country the antiwar movement was reborn in a matter of hours. Even such staunch Nixon supporters as Senator Hugh Scott received telegrams running 20 to 1 against the President's action. A Harris poll found nearly 60 per cent of the nation opposed the Cambodian action, and a Detroit Free Press survey discovered 75 per cent against it. Cambodia proved to be the breaking point for millions of Americans who had previously trusted Nixon but now demanded an end to the war at almost any price.

The strongest reaction to the news of Cambodia came from the nation's campuses. Thousands of angry students went on strike, ROTC facilities were fire-bombed, and some major universities had to close down for the rest of the semester. At the University of Wisconsin the Army Math Research Center was bombed, killing a graduate student researcher. Even the most conservative schools, such as the University of Nebraska and Nixon's alma mater, Whittier College in California, experienced serious disturbances. Students poured back into Washington, D.C. to renew their protest against the war. The sons and daughters of leading Administration officials joined in the protest, and federal employees themselves participated in some of the antiwar activities. Secretary of the Interior Walter Hickel wrote a publicly distributed letter which strongly reprimanded Nixon for his insensitivity.

Initially Nixon appeared unnerved by the widespread spontaneous and negative reaction to Cambodia, and he sought a path toward conciliation and understanding. Nixon quickly invited several prestigious college presidents to the White House for a parley and afterwards confidently announced the appointment of Alexander Heard, of Vanderbilt, as special advisor for Student Affairs. The next morning before dawn the beleaguered President motored to the Lincoln Memorial to visit some of the 100,000 antiwar protesters. "I know you want to get the war over. Sure you came here to demonstrate and shout your slogans on the ellipse," said Nixon, "that's all right. Just keep it peaceful. Have a good time in Washington, and don't go away bitter." Later Nixon contended that the students' goal of ending the war was his goal also--only their timing and strategy differed. Unfortunately, the gulf between Nixon and the students had grown too deep.

President Nixon may have had a chance to close this gulf had it not been for a major tragedy at Kent State University, Ohio. Normally a conservative campus, Kent State students reacted much in the fashion of their peers around the country. But a series of heavy-handed responses by governmental officials exasperated the situation. In fact, the beginning of the disturbances may have related more to normal college rowdyism accompanying a routine "beer bust" than antiwar fervor. The mayor of Kent ordered a curfew, and police ejected thousands of students from the bars around campus, where many had been watching a basketball game between the Knickerbockers and Lakers on television. Resentful students began breaking windows, setting small fires, and generally disrupted the area around campus.

University officials wanted to close school, but Ohio's Governor Rhodes, who himself was embroiled in a bitter race for the United States Senate, demanded instead the employment of National Guard troops. Many of the tired guardsmen came from other parts of the state where they had been patrolling a tense Teamsters strike. With loaded M-1 rifles, sleepless nights, and no training in riot control, the guardsmen were hardly prepared to deal astutely with the burgeoning crisis. Angry students began gathering on the university commons amd calling passionately for the evacuation of these intruders. "Pigs off campus," they shouted.

One unit of nervous young guardsmen found itself surrounded by noisy, rock-throwing, shouting students and, filled with fear, shot impulsively into the crowd. "My God! My God! They're killing us!", cried a frantic student. When the guns had quieted seconds later, four students lay dead on the commons and ten more were wounded. Most of the victims had merely been onlookers. This brutal turn of events left both sides nonplussed. No one had expected the confrontation to escalate to such a horrible level.

On that same tragic day violence broke out at Jackson State University in Mississippi over racial stress and Vietnam. Before it ended, police and highway patrolmen fired 200 rounds into a crowd in the front of the women's dormitory, killing two and wounding twelve others. The shootings horrified the nation; crosses went up by the thousands on college campuses, and prayer vigils were organized in many communities to commemorate the latest martyrs. The Kent State "bullets wounded the nation," report _Time._ Ultimate blame for the tragedy was laid directly at the portals of the White House, where a remorseful President Nixon now realized that the possibility of consensus on Vietnam had moved beyond his political reach.

Some Democrats predicted that Nixon's Cambodian invasion would lose the GOP fifty House seats in the fall elections. Nixon himself had been deeply concerned about such political repercussions. But gradually Nixon and his political intimates, especially Attorney General John Mitchell, hatched a new strategy quite contrary to the initial consensus line. The Administration concluded that, in spite of its own good intentions, the northeastern establishment elite--composed mainly of Democrats, liberal Republicans, the intelligentsia, the New York-based television media, the ingrained bureaucracy, professional reformers, and student radicals--would do anything to thwart the Nixon Presidency.

Nixon convinced himself that a new governing consensus was impossible in the face of liberal intransigence. The signs seemed to pervade the landscape. Students protested his Vietnam policies. Liberal economists bemoaned his economic policies. The Georgetown elite snubbed his social affairs. Democrats in Congress refused to support his anticrime proposals. The media criticized his secretiveness. Reformers refused to take his talk about welfare reform seriously. Ralph Abernathy sounded the ingratitude of the liberal establishment. "I really don't think Mr. Nixon is sensitive to the problems of black people," complained Abernathy. "Blacks regard him as a President who is concerned only with the welfare of the rich and the affluent."

The old Nixon, the one who defined political leadership more in terms of embattlement between good and evil than as consensus building, began rising to the surface. "You get knocked down day after day and you keep coming back, and you learn that you can't win all the time," Nixon told students at Whittier College, "but if you keep coming back, you might win at last." Nixon's old self-conscious and insecure nature began showing through. Contrary to Johnson, who regarded himself as one of life's big winners, Nixon viewed himself as one of life's underdogs. Nixon determined to besiege his enemies in the gutters and back alleys of partisan politics. "President Nixon, after a period characterized by compromise, is now apparently ready to show his might," commented the Atlantic <u>News-Telegraph.</u> "Resistance on ... matters of major importance ... have apparently stiffened the presidential backbone."

Nixon determined to steamroller the opposition, and he possessed some sound political reasons for believing it might work. Traditionally Democratic elements of organized labor and the South strongly supported him on Vietnam. During the Kent State foray hundreds of hard-hatted construction workers and Longshoremen had paraded down Wall Street shouting "U.S.A. all the way" and bearing placards reading "We Support Nixon and Agnew" and "God Bless the Establishment." Before the rousing demonstration ended, the "Hard Hats" had severely beaten almost 100 antiwar protesters whom they called "commie bastards" and "yellow bellies." The well-publicized episode carried the endorsement of George Meany and the popular Pete Brennan, head of greater New York's Building and Construction Trades Council, later to become Nixon's Secretary of Labor. "We're supporting the President and the country not because he's for labor, because he isn't, but because he's our President, and we're hoping that he's right," thundered Brennan. These were the words of middle America, an ideological majority that political strategist Kevin Phillips has described in his widely-respected 1969 book, <u>The Emerging Republican Majority.</u> Nixon could not resist the temptation of molding this new conservative majority by brute political force.

Nixon also found encouragement in Senator Edward Kennedy's temporary political eclipse, brought about by a mysterious automobile accident at Chappaquiddick, Massachusetts, in August, 1969. The accident left a young woman drowned in the back seat of Kennedy's automobile after the couple had departed from a cook-out together. Kennedy failed to report the tragedy for several hours and even then could not produce a convincing explanation. The episode all but eliminated Kennedy from presidential consideration in 1972 and greatly hampered his ability to lead his party into the mid-term Congressional elections of 1970. To make matters worse for the Democrats, Humphrey had not yet overcome the Johnson taint; and no other party official enjoyed pre-eminence. The time to deal the Democrats a death-blow had never seemed more opportune.

It was at this point that Nixon decided to unleash fully the implacable Spiro Agnew. Until late in 1969 the Vice President had not been useful for anything more than the occasional mouthing of conservative platitudes. But, slowly, he was finding a place in American politics by rhetorically taking on the so-called radic-libs. At Ohio State University he had complained about the "sniveling, hand-wringing power structure" which "deserved the violent rebellion it encourages." At New Orleans he complained about communist-leaning radicals influencing government. He gained widespread attention in November when, in Des Moines, Iowa, he blasted the major television network commentators for expressing "in one way or another, their hostility to the President and America."

After the Cambodian incursion the Vice President launched a barrage against student protesters. "Let us not be naive enough to believe there are no seeds of revolution in the rebellion that radical young people describe as 'the movement,'" charged Agnew. "Let us be candid enough to face the fact that the spawning ground and sanctuary of the movement is the American university." Agnew warned that the "criminal left" belonged in a "penitentiary," not the "dormitory." The criminal left was "not a problem to be solved by the department of philosophy or the department of English," but "a problem for the Department of Justice." Agnew described the students as "children of the affluent, permissive, upper-middle-class who learned their Dr. Spock and threw discipline out the window." Agnew offered "one modest suggestion" for the "effete liberal snobs" of academia. "The next time a mob of students waving their non-negotiable demands starts pitching bricks and rocks at the Student Union, just imagine they are brown shirts or white sheets and act accordingly."

In true "Red Scare" fashion Agnew sought to isolate the radicals politically. It was time for "positive polarization," argued Agnew. "We can afford to separate them from our society with no more regret than we should feel over discarding rotten apples from a barrel," growled the Vice President. "When our basic institutions are assailed, we quake not for our property but for our very lives and for our future--for the simple assurance that tomorrow will come without any more necessary holocaust than the struggle for existence normally entails."

Conservative Democrats such as South Carolina's L. Mendel Rivers, Chairman of the House Armed Services Committee, assisted in the isolation process. "There are more of us patriotic Americans than those pro-Hanoicrats," stormed Rivers. "Keep up the fight. Spy-ro Agnew is helping us. You back up Spy-ro, and he will continue to pour it on." In many places the politicians supported their rhetoric with symbolism. In Iowa Lt. Governor Roger Jepsen distributed American flag window decals after his speaking appearances. In New Britain, Connecticut, Mayor Paul J. Manafort provided 20,000 plastic lapel buttons for his constituents.

The Silent Majority, most of which resented the college-educated elite anyway, responded by aiming its wrath against the "Long Hairs" while "Hard Hats" and "Fat Cats" went merrily on their way. Agnew became a momentary hero, outbidding all other contenders on the lavish $100-dollar-a-plate Republican inner circuit. Agnew became the driving force in Nixon's attempt to purge his enemies during the 1970 mid-term campaign. Democratic Senators Ralph Yarborough, Texas; Albert Gore, Tennessee; and Joseph Tydings, Maryland, and Republic Senator Charles Goodell, New York--all outspoken doves--became the major targets of the Agnew onslaught. As the campaign progressed, however, and Agnew began to suffer from political overkill--especially when he unsuccessfully tried to associate the term "radic-lib" with establishment politicians--President Nixon discovered that the election would hinge more on traditional pocketbook issues and astute organizational practices than on overblown rhetoric.

Rather than retreat, Nixon allowed himself to become embroiled in the sordid political spectacle. On October 29 the President delivered a speech at the San Jose Municipal Auditorium, where a large crowd of antiwar demonstrators milled around in the growing darkness. As Nixon left the auditorium, he impulsively jumped on the hood of his limousine and taunted the demonstrators with a "V" sign. The infuriated demonstrators belted the Nixon party with eggs and rocks as it edged nervously from the parking area.

During the remaining five days of the campaign, Nixon tried to capitalize on the theme of dissenters attacking their President. At Salt Lake City, Utah, Nixon referred to the "ugly demonstrators ... who carry a 'peace' sign in one hand and who throw a bomb or a brick with the other hand," branding them the "superhypocrites of our time." At a Phoenix, Arizona, airport rally a few days later he charged the "the terrorists, the far left, would like nothing better than to make the President of the United States a prisoner in the White House. Well, let me just set them straight," shouted Nixon. "As long as I am President, no band of violent thugs is going to keep me from going out and speaking with the American people... ." Nixon felt so confident in his forceful attacks on the left that he ordered his Phoenix speech broadcasted over all three major networks on election eve. Nixon had violated a cardinal rule of the Presidency once summarized by Eisenhower Aide Sherman Adams:

"A President should above all understand his own prejudices."

In contrast to Nixon's frenzied declamatory politics, the Democrats produced a cool, calculating address by Maine's Senator Edmund Muskie, who from the quiet and distinguished atmosphere of his study called upon Americans to forsake their divisiveness and seek the traditionally democratic road of reason and rationality in public affairs. The election eve contrast between Nixon's politics of furor and Muskie's appeal to the higher instincts helped deal a final blow to Republican chances for victory in 1970. The Republicans lost nine seats in the House, eleven governorships, and gained only two seats in the Senate. The campaign also produced a nationally-respected Democrat, Edmund Muskie, Humphrey's 1968 running mate, who could now lead the challenge of unseating Nixon in 1972. In Congress the controlling Democrats began sharpening their hatchets for the bitter struggle which now seemed inevitable.

Nixon himself had destroyed any hope of consensus and any hope for establishing a ruling mandate. "There is about Nixon's presidency the feeling of theater. When the performance is over and the lights go out, there is an eerie nothingness--no heart, no feeling of movement or national momentum," wrote Hugh Sidey, _Time's_ Washington Bureau Chief. "The presidency as a positive force is a concept which has escaped Nixon. His administration has an aura of negativism." Meanwhile, the President himself became more inaccessible and isolated. "He surrounded himself with men who, except for Henry Kissinger, were faceless beings unknown for anything except loyalty to Nixon," complained Joseph Kraft. As a result the nation was left deeply divided and disillusioned. Hate seemed on the prowl; the fissures ran deep. Things were "on a downhill slide," commented columnist Marianne Means sadly. Somehow the decade seemed lost.

CHAPTER XII

AN AGE OF CONFUSION

The Biblical passage "thou shalt grope at noonday, as the blind gropeth in darkness" aptly characterized America at the end of the decade. Never had the nation faced such a crisis of spirit. The nation's once cherished institutions appeared to be coming apart at the seams, caught up in racial conflict, economic chaos, an unending war, rising crime, growing drug addiction, campus disorder, and Nixon's failure to restore a feeling of unity. America displayed a desperate and unsettling spectre before the world--the richest, the most powerful, and technologically the most successful nation on earth lay prostrate, tangled in a web of internal divisiveness, frustration, and moral disillusionment. H. G. Wells' 1933 version of a 1984 era of deserted roads, fortified banks, and barricaded homes seemed almost at hand.

During the Sixties America had committed record amounts of intellect, energy, and money for reform and the improvement of the human condition; yet the problems seemed to grow further out of hand. Traditional problems suddenly loomed as insoluble; the magnitude of new problems such as pollution, population, and the environment left sober persons with a nagging feeling of doubt and lack of recourse. Life itself suddenly seemed out of scale. Now, even the most cherished assumptions which had propelled American society in the 20th century lay open to question.

The once comfortable debates over traditional issues had lost their proportion. "The only debates we hold are about the comparative lethal punch which the various forms of destruction pack--nuclear radiation, global pollution, overcrowding, energy exhaustion, terrorism, totalitarianism, the overheating of the earth, the overcooling of the seas, the invasion by insect swarms, the collision of the planets," wrote Max Lerner in a fitting piece of prose entitled the Gloomier-than-thou-Competition. "The difference lies in the change of scale and the sense of powerlessness. In the old days, the radicals and liberals could look forward to the collapse of capitalism on he theory that the workers would inherit," continued Lerner, "but if our world shivered into particles of polluted, overheated, irradiated dust, there will be no one and nothing to inherit."

The nation that Lerner uneasily contemplated had drifted far afield during the decade. The great events of yesteryear which had tempered the nation's thinking in 1960 had been substantially shaken by the onrush of dramatic recent events. Over 60 per cent of those alive in 1970 could not remember the end of World War II in 1945. Only 25 per cent could recall the Great Depression, and only 20 per cent the Great Stock Market Crash of 1929. By 1970 Vietnam, civil rights, and youthful unrest had pushed the nation's perception of itself into new and sometimes ominous directions.

Two profoundly disturbing events occurred in 1969 which suggested that America's problems had grown out of proportion. Both emerged from the excesses of the Sixties" the first, the Manson murders, from social excesses; the second, the Santa Barbara oil spill, from the excesses of economic expansionism. The complex implications of these two deeply disturbing events caused many to appreciate still more fully the contention of the great thinker Henry Adams who, at the end of the 19th century, predicted pessimistically that technological progress would eventually destroy social institutions. "Man has mounted science and is now run away with," complained Adams.

The Manson murders were among the most gruesome and unreasoned in American history. Charles Manson himself was a self-styled cultist prophet who bore a bitter grudge against organized society. Motivated by an incessant hatred for the establishment, Manson used his hypnotic prowess to drive his motley band of mostly female followers into complete submission to his will. "We belonged to Charlie, not to ourselves," testified one of his loyal followers. A man of many faces and moods, Manson's followers knew him sometimes as Jesus Christ and God, at other times as Soul, and sometimes as the Devil.

In the Spring of 1967 Manson was released, against his will, from prison, where he had been committed for running a prostitution ring. He moved to Haight-Ashbury and soon established a group, consisting mostly of displaced middle-class girls, which he called the Family or the Nest. Manson had never experienced real nuclear family life, having been rejected by his father and deserted by his mother. He maintained control over the group by forcing sexual submissiveness. The Family moved to Spahn, a deserted movie location, where Manson strummed his guitar and waited for what he perceived would be a black-white revolution referred to as "Helter Skelter." When that did not occur, Manson decided to act himself, as John Brown had before the Civil War.

On the evening of August 9, 1969, the Manson Family entered the mansion of actress Sharon Tate, a glowing symbol of establishment beauty and grace, who was eight-and-a-half months pregnant. Manson ordered the brutal slaughter of Tate and three of her friends. Their frantic cries for mercy went unheeded as the Mansonites cruelly hacked them to death. On August 10 Manson randomly selected the home of Leon and Rosemary La Bianca. "That man has wronged me. Society has wronged me," shouted Manson. "We'll kill whatever pigs are in that house. Go in there and get them." The brutal murder followed. The murderous groupie became a symbol of "crazed excess," complained Newsweek.

To attribute the Manson murders to crazed excess alone amounted to oversimplification. By focusing attention on what motivated Manson, Americans could see a form of angry alienation representing a horrible failure in the socialization process itself. "I haven't decided yet what I am or who I am," testified Manson, "I never went to school, so I never growed up in the respect to learn to read and write too good." Manson's anger was complete. "I did seven years for a $37.50 check. I did 12 years because I didn't have any parents," related Manson.

"When you were out riding your bicycle, I was sitting in a cell looking out the window and looking at pictures in magazines and wishing I could go to high school and go to proms.... I have ate out of your garbage cans ... wore your second hand clothes ... now you want to kill me.... Ha! I'm already dead, have been dead all my life. I've lived in your tomb that you built." Manson's failure was also America's failure, and nervous citizens began to wonder how many more potential Mansons lurked in a society that President Johnson had promised would be great.

The second horrendous event of 1969 involved the "blow out" of a Union Pacific oil well at Santa Barbara, a recreational area located along the beautiful golden beach-studded coast of southern California. After heated debate within the Johnson Administration, Interior Secretary Steward Udall had finally leased the precarious channel for drilling. On January 28, as an enormous drill was being removed from a high-pressure deposit on the channel's floor, the well ruptured, releasing 10,000 barrels of crude petroleum over eleven days. About 800 square miles of sea and coastline became drenched in sticky sludge. Some 4,000 out of 12,000 birds in the region perished. Seals and migrating gray whales fled for their lives. The sea worms and intertidal fauna came under threat of extinction. "There was much evidence of sickness. Some of the sea lions could scarcely be distinguished from their lethargic cousins, the elephant seals," wrote author David Snell in Life. "Here and there we came upon oil-drenched pups that cried weakly and thrashed about like scalded rats, their eyelids gummed shut, umbilicals stained and caked."

Recreational activity came to an abrupt halt as the noxious odor of petroleum toxins hung in the air and dirty black grease smeared the beaches. The disaster could rival "that of the San Francisco fire and earthquake," warned Congressman Charles M. Teague of California. "This city is known throughout the world as an attractive city," sputtered Mayor Gerald Firestone angrily. "Look at it now. People are mad. You bet they're mad." Bewildered citizens began carrying signs calling for the government to "ban the Blob." President Nixon promised "far more stringent and effective regulation." But there could be little hope of discontinuing the risky search for oil in the face of an ever-growing world demand for energy. Four billion barrels of precious oil lay pocketed under the earthquake-prone gulf floor, crisscrossed as it was with "faults, fractures, and fissures." Even though the eventual damage of the blow out did not equal early fears, the awesome magnitude of the problem, whose prevention and cure were both unknown, demonstrated again that America's problems might be getting out of control.

America found itself drifting helplessly into a historical interlude, a perplexing passage between eras, when old symbols and ideals no longer sufficed and new directions were not apparent. The nation itself seemed caught in the abyss sung about by Simon and Garfunkel in the popular hit "Bridge Over Troubled Waters." Americans found themselves a deeply troubled people, adrift without adequate anchors of faith, moving swiftly away from familiar shores of tradition, and less certain of their underpinning values. Americans could now appreciate former President Eisenhower's contention that "we live in a storm of semantic disorder in which old labels no longer faithfully describe."

Thus, the American people felt as though they stood nervously on the edge of an unsettled time that was out of joint and filled with impossible paradoxes. "The country has entered a period of revolutionary change of which no one can foresee the course or the end or the consequences," warned the aging Walter Lippmann. "One felt a value bleakness, with the sense that the old values had fallen either into disuse or contempt, and that the new ones seemed too shrill or violent to command allegiance beyond a small clannish group," complained Max Lerner. "Moral abdication or valuelessness seems to have become a sign of the times," complained the Reverend Theodore M. Hesburgh, President of Notre Dame and Chairman of the U.S. Civil Rights Commission. "One might well describe the illness of modern society and its schooling as anomie, a rootlessness." Not only had Americans become confused over what to believe, they were losing their capacity to believe strongly about anything at all.

The bygone world of 1960--the brave new world of progress and predictability--now seemed to loom as the world of foreboding and dehumanizing change that Adams had warned about. The depressing atmosphere encouraged pessimism and superstition rather than hope and reason. "The world is changing too quick," complained a middle American from rural Illinois. "We don't have the things we used to in the old days. People don't get to know one another like they used to." "The pace and intensity of change in today's society are unprecedented, making tremendous demands on the individual's ability to adjust," complained social commentator Myron Brenton.

Rapid change seemed to be undermining the American character. The timesaving gadgetry which marked the decade had failed to bring about more time for relaxation and contemplation; instead, Americans tended to be frantically bent upon squeezing more and more activity into less and less time and space. This tendency represented a unique brand of American restlessness; to some it was necessary for progress, but many saw it as a phenomenon leading to the breakdown of the American psyche. One person who noticed this deterioration was Mrs. Emet Sclarenco, for twenty-nine years the telephone voice of Greyhound busing lines. Mrs. Sclarenco retired at the end of the decade after handling more than one million calls and noted that "people are more tense today than they used to be." Americans had taken pride in their faddishness and willingness to adapt quickly to changing styles and circumstances; however, by the end of the decade, change for change's sake had become suspect. "The trouble with having a culture boom in America is that the country may bore itself to death," complained social critic William K. Zinsser.

The rising spectre of uncontrollable change made the disquieting interlude at the end of the decade one of profound soul-searching and fundamental reassessment of ideas and institutions, as Americans struggled to conceive of how a semblance of consensus could be re-established. Pessimism and desperation replaced the optimism which characterized most of the earlier Sixties. A nagging self-doubt, a loss of confidence in America's purpose and promise pervaded the national atmosphere as John Kennedy's dream of a better society began to fade. "John F. Kennedy's New Frontier is fading into history," wrote Parade sadly, "out of time and out of spirit." The lights had gone out on Camelot, the banners were furled, the parade was over.

The generation which so enthusiastically embraced power with Kennedy now faced social and political bankruptcy. It was numbed by the swiftness and intensity of perplexing events and stunned by the thought that the long sought-after treasure of a peaceful and prosperous America had been snatched from its grasp. Suddenly, America no longer represented the last, best hope for the world. "I no longer feel I can change the world," admitted evangelist Billy Graham sadly. New York Times columnist Arthur Krock expressed a visceral fear that "the tenure of the United States as the first power in the world may be one of the briefest in history." His colleague C. L. Sulzberger remarked that "the period of dominance that marked the generation after World War II is rapidly eroding; there was never an American century." Noted political scientist Andrew Hacker published a widely-quoted book entitled The End of the American Era. Gore Vidal, popular, satiric, left-leaning political commentator, wrote cryptically of America's imminent decline in a 1969 book he chose to call Reflections Upon a Sinking Ship. Britain's leading commentators shared the disappointment. "This is not going to be the American century," wrote Sir Denis Brogan.

The generation that had been full of praise for Kennedy, hopeful under Johnson, and disillusioned under Nixon began to lose heart. "We had entered the decade sure of who we were and where we were going," wrote author David Halberstam; "we ended the decade rebelling against what we had become and what we had achieved." "We wanted to believe and we did," wrote Gerald Clarke in the New Republic ; "many of us no longer find it possible--or necessary." Clarke's generation had lost its hope and momentum. "In place of trust, there was disbelief and doubt in the system and its leaders," wrote David Wise in The Politics of Lying. Charles de Gaulle had once contended that France fell to the Nazis in 1940 because of a certain "inability to believe in anything at all." According to columnist Stewart Alsop, America had become "clearly infected with the same disease. It's a kind of political cancer!" "We have a long way to go to lift this country," admitted John D. Rockefeller, III from his snug 56th floor office in Rockefeller Center. In 1969 childhood heroine Judy Garland died, disillusioned, from a drug overdose, symbolizing the lost hopes of her generation. The Wizard of Oz had proved to be a cruel hoax after all, and the "city on the hill" lying just beyond the yellow brick road had become an unreachable mirage.

The disillusionment of the Kennedy generation found symbolic expression in the mashed motorcycle which stood in the corner of Georgetown's Volta Place Gallery. Its maker, Karl Hess, formerly an advisor and speech writer for Senator Barry Goldwater, had believed strongly and drank deeply from the stream of American life during the Sixties. But, like many people of every political stripe, his participation had been diminished by the burden of momentous events. Angered and frustrated, Hess dropped out, forsaking positive participation for self-aggrandizement and an individualistic search for self-fulfillment. The mashed motorcycle could well represent the passing of the New Deal-Great Society consensus for those who had advocated it, as well as for those who had resisted it.

Just as the assumption of inherent virtue in Roman citizenship, or the British belief in a benevolent obligation to carry the "white man's burden," wrote C. L. Sulzberger, "Americans' 'Manichean assumptions' about their country's goodness and virtuosity have now begun rapidly to disappear from the mass consciousness". A Gallup poll in 1969 showed that the average American was more deeply troubled about the country's future than any time since the Great Depression. Another poll showed that 46 per cent of the American people had come to believe that the country had changed for the worse over the decade and that 58 per cent believed it would change for the worse in the next decade. In California, traditionally the focal point of America's pioneer optimism, a poll showed that more than one-third of the residents wanted to leave the state in the near future.

The ideal of sturdy, self-respecting American individualism, which had long served as the prime explanation for the greatness and success, now appeared to be waning--replaced with a selfish, introverted individualism based more on what a person could obtain from the community rather than contribute. The public manners and morals of the people demonstrated an obvious deterioration. Americans preferred "to demand rather than discuss, shout instead of reason together, display mutual recrimination rather than mutual respect, use four-letter words for persuasion rather than depend on the orderly exchange of ideas, confront rather than confer," wrote one disenchanted commentator. "More and more hostility and venom are the hallmarks of any conversation on the affairs of the nation," complained former HEW Secretary John Gardner. "Today all seem caught in mutual recriminations--Negro and white, rich and poor, conservative and liberal, hawk and dove, labor and management, North and South, young and old."

Social habit had taken a decisive turn for the worse. Lenny Bruce had been taken too far. Public inhibitions were being relinquished as the once impermissible and intolerable became commonplace. The determination to affront, the appetite for crudeness, the failure to condemn sleaziness--all of these indicated that Americans had become overly preoccupied with individual greed and self-absorption rather than with positive social decor. They had shed the bonds of social propriety and decency associated with the older Victorian ways. "We have become an ill-mannered society in which rational dialogue is all but submerged in a sea of assertiveness," complained John S. Knight of the Detroit Free Press. "Everyone wants to declaim, few are willing to hear the other person's point of view."

Knight's concern reflected a growing fear that the great American pursuit of happiness had resulted in a frantic, often unsuccessful scramble to fulfill desires and in the brutalization of culture. The classical philosopher Montaigne, in Essays, warned of the folly connected with chasing "transcendental humors." "Instead of transforming themselves into angels, they turn themselves into beasts," wrote Montaigne; "instead of lifting they degrade themselves." These sobering thoughts applied well to what seemed to have become of American society.

The selfish individualism of the late Sixties seemed to be destroying the social bonds which once unified the nation. Columnist Kevin Phillips described the phenomenon as the Balkanization of America. Social bonds which had been strengthening since World War II as a result of the "melting pot" psychology were being torn asunder by the re-emergence of ethnicity. "The proliferation of ... religious cults; the new political geography of localism and neighborhoods; the substitution of causes for political parties;... the fragmentation of government; the twilight of authority:--all of these social patterns," according to Phillips, "indicated an ominous narrowing of loyalties which could bring about the dissolution of the community consciousness that had undergirded" the New Frontier-Great Society years. Edmund Burke once wrote that "all governments--indeed, every human benefit and enjoyment, every virtue and every prudent act--is founded on compromise and barter. For the the time being Americans apparently had forsaken all relish of this founding principle.

As a result, institutions became trapped between what John Gardner characterized as uncritical loves and unloving critics. "On the one side, those who loved their institutions tended to smother them in an embrace of death, loving their rigidities more than their promise, shielding them from life-giving criticism," wrote Gardner. "On the other side, there arose a breed of critics without love, skilled in demolition, but untutored in the arts by which human institutions are nurtured and strengthened and made to flourish. Between the two the institutions perished," lamented Gardner, who organized a new people-oriented group called Common Cause.

Institutions appeared to be collapsing under the contradictory pressures of modern life. Nowhere was this more apparent than in the cities, which during the High Sixties had been represented as the foremost arena of modern civilization. The nation's largest city, New York--America's port of entry and the nation's window on the world, the city that once had served as the nation's financial and social nerve center, boasting the finest parks, best stores, most luxurious hotels, and the highest buildings--now last prostrate in the face of public employee strikes, overtaxation, and general administrative apathy. Over 150,000 junkies roamed the streets, the incidence of robbery was double that of other urban centers, and over 1.15 million people drew public assistance. Companies were moving their corporate headquarters out of the city, and even Broadway began opening theaters early to permit customers a safer journey home. Only fools still dared to go for night-time strolls in Central Part, once an inviting feature of life in the "Big Apple."

Crime of all sorts, from serious offenses to petty white collar abuses, industrial sabotage, and shoplifting, continued to increase dramatically in spite of Nixon's strong law-and-order posture. Violence increased as well. After a long and a bitter debate Congress passed the Federal Gun Control Act of 1968. But the ingrained American frontier fetish about the right to bear arms, coupled with the influence of the American Rifleman's Association, made the act almost worthless for preventing crime. As a result, the per capita gun ownership rate actually increased from five to thirty times that of other democracies; and the statistics and crime revealed what a tremendous difference that made: the murder rate in America in 1969 was 360 times that of Norway. During the decade the number of police officers killed in the line of duty more than doubled in the United States. From 1966 through 1972, 621 officers were killed, seven out of ten by handguns, sometimes referred to as "Saturday Night Specials."

According to an old English adage "the test of civilization is the willingness of a people to obey the unenforceable." Americans saw their country failing to meet this test. Columnist James Kilpatrick sadly conjectured that the nation had become "ungovernable." Kilpatrick's solemn mood was reflective of the dissolution among America's leading commentators. "The Industrial-Scientific revolution has jammed us together, polluted much of our countryside, obliged us to work within greater economic units and increased the tensions of daily living," complained CBS commentator Eric Sevareid. "There must be faith and this for the present, is what we do not have--neither faith in our common purposes, nor in our old religious and philosophic institutions, nor in our present policies, nor in the men who are making or administering them," wrote columnist James Reston of the New York Times.

The fear of social breakdown did not escape the attention of columnist Tom Wicker. "Defrauded consumers, homeowners with uncollected garbage, commuters who cannot get to work, persons awaiting trial in impossibly crowded courts, students in institutions that do not teach, pedestrians breathing air noxious with pollution, utility users unable to get adequate service from protected monopolies, victims of the thousands of crimes that annually go unsolved, motorists in massive traffic jams," charged Wicker, "all are victims either of irrelevant law, lack of law, unworkable law, unenforced law, corruption, official disinterest or official disability." According to Wicker, "for all these millions of people, there is no law."

The situation reminded Americans of a statement once made by Edmund Burke, one of the fathers of democratic society: People "are qualified for civil liberty in exact proportion to their own appetites. Men of intemperate minds cannot be free. Their passions forge their fetters." Even the otherwise optimistic Eric Hoffer showed signs of dissolutionment. "I should sit in my corner and not say anything," bemoaned Hoffer, but, "I'm not convinced anymore that I know the score .... I've got no solutions." Economist Arthur Burns complained that "people have lost faith in the processes of government itself".

As a result of the social and political turbulence that accompanied the last days of the decade, Americans grew increasingly inward, fearful of participation, withholding of a helpful hand, and believing in an unhealthy mercantile sense that the government or some other organization, rather than the individual, would somehow resolve all communal problems and bear the major burden of social order. Americans more and more preferred to remain anonymous, free to forsake society's responsibilities in favor of their private habitats and pleasures. One meaning attached to the popularity of women's pant suits, which replaced the more free-wheeling mini skirts of mid-decade, was that it demonstrated America's new predilection for hiding out and covering up. In New York and Los Angeles about one-third of the people had unlisted telephone numbers. Suburbanites began living nervously behind window grilles and electronic surveillance equipment and slept with loaded hand guns nearby.

A spirit of melancholy began to pervade the national mood. The feeling was one of dreams having succumbed to the hopeless onrush of negative historical forces which had destroyed the best part of life's promise. These feelings were echoed by the nation's songsters. In his ode to burned out causes and lonesome people, "Goodtime Charlie Has Got the Blues," Danny O'Keefe sang of "everybody leaving town." The mid-decade Beatle song "Yesterday" reflected well the melancholy of late decade: "Yesterday all my troubles seemed so far away/ Now it looks as though they're here to stay/ Oh I believe in yesterday/ Suddenly I'm not half the man I used to be/ There's a shadow hanging over me/ Yesterday love was such an easy game to play/ Now I need a place to hide away/ Oh I believe in yesterday." Stevie Wonder caught the spirit in a song entitled " Yesterme, Yesteryou, Yesterday." "What happened to the world we knew?/ Where did it go, the yester glow?/ When we could feel the wheel of life turn our way.'

Another song that captured the melancholy feelings was "Those Were the Days," sung by Mary Hopkins. "Once upon a time there was a tavern/ Where we used to raise a glass or two/ Remember how we laughed away the hours/ And dreamed of all the great things we would do/ Those Were the Days my friend/ We thought they'd never end/ We'd sing and dance forever and a day/ We'd live the life we choose/ We'd fight and never lose/ For we were young and sure to have our way/ Those Were the Days/ Oh yes, Those Were the Days." From San Francisco's Temple of Rock, the Fillmore Auditorium across the land to Manhattan's prestigious Gate nightclub, the sad sounds of B. B. King and his band reflected the nation's rekindled interest in blue mood music. "Someday, baby when the blindman calls my name/ You won't be able to hurt on me no more woman/ 'Cause my heart won't feel no more pain."

The sullen sounds of the songsters did not escape the attention of President Nixon as he peered out despondently from under the long shadows which had gathered around the White House. The sparkle and glitter that had characterized the triumphant entry of John F. Kennedy were by now merely lost echoes in history. A gloomy cloud of despair hung heavily over the capital city. Even the fresh coat of paint that had greeted Kennedy had lost its luster.

A humourless Nixon stood solemnly watching the Washington sunset as he thought about the decade just passed and began to conjecture about the pseudo-classical architecture of the governmental buildings. "Sometimes when I see those columns I think of seeing them in Greece and in Rome and I think of what happened to Greece and Rome and you see only what is left of great civilizations of the past. As they became wealthy," commented the President gravely, "they lost their will to live, to improve, they became subject to the decadence that destroys the civilization. The United States is reaching that period."

America seemed about to suffer the consequences of hubris. As with the mythical Greek god Icarus, whose wanton insolence and excessive pride caused him to fly high, too close to the sun, thus melting his wax wings. America seemed about to be thrown into a pattern of descent--at last atonement must be made for the displaced arrogance and false passion that often lingers on the backside of success. Perhaps, as in Greek mythology, the gods were about to punish Americans for having fulfilled their wishes too completely.

NOTES

I. AN AGE OF CONFRONTATION

Page

8 "The 'us' and the 'ours' ... and the vigorous." *The New Republic,* (January 16, 1971), p. 13.

12 A good discussion of the Kennedy-McNamara nuclear strategy can be found in the following works: Hilsman, Roger, *To Move A Nation: The Politics of Foreign Policy in the Administration of John F. Kennedy* (Garden City, N.Y.: Doubleday, 1976); Kaufman, William W., *The McNamara Strategy* (New York: Harper and Row, 1971); Murdock, Clark A., *Defense Policy Formation: A Comparative Analysis of the McNamara Era* (Albany, N.Y.: State University of New York Press, 1974); and, Trewhite, Henry L., *McNamara* (New York: Harper and Row, 1971). One of Robert S. McNamara's most forthright public statements on defense policy can be found in *Look,* September 3, 1968, pp. 13-16.

"The faster we...never have to." *Time* (November, 10, 1968), p.55.

13 "At cocktail parties...to shelters." *Time* (November 3, 1961), p.22.

16 "The gap between...their grenades." *Newsweek* (August 28, 1961), p. 30.

17 Two early works which recognize the American dilemmas concerning Fidel Castro are: Draper, Theodore, *Castro's Revolution: Myths & Realities* (New York: Praeger, 1962); and, Dubois, Jules, *Fidel Castro: Rebel--Liberator or Dictator* (Indianapolis: Bobbs-Merrill, 1959). Two perceptive works on the Bay of Pigs fiasco are: Johnson, Haynes B., *The Bay of Pigs: The Leaders Story of Brigade 2506* (New York: Norton, 1964); and, Wyden, Peter, *Bay of Pigs: The Untold Story* (New York: Simon & Schuster, 1979).

18 Recommended works on the Cuban Missile Crisis are: Abel, Elie, *The Missile Crisis* (Philadelphia: Bantam Books, 1968); Dinerstein, Herbert S., *The Making of A Missile Crisis, October, 1962* (Baltimore, Mary.: John Hopkins Press, 1976); and, Halperin, Maurice, *The Rise & Decline of Fidel Castro* (Berkeley: University of California Press, 1972). Also See: Kennedy, Robert, *Thirteen Days* (New York: W.W. Norton, 1969).

24 Some insider views on the Test Ban Treaty can be found in Sorensen, Theodore C., Kennedy (New York: Bantam Books, 1965), pp. 739-748 and Schlesinger, Arthur M., A Thousand Days: John F. Kennedy In the White House (Boston: Houghton Mifflin, 1965), pp. 895-913.

26 Kraft, Joseph, The Grand Design (New York: Harper & Row, 1962). A more balanced analysis can be found in Cottrell, Alvin J., & Dougherty, James E., The Politics of the Atlantic Alliance (New York: Praeger, 1964). On matters concerning GATT, see: Calleo, David P., Europe's Future (New York: W.W. Norton, 1967) and Steel, Ronald, The End of Alliance (New York: Delta Books, 1966).

29 Kennedy's AID Program has been critically evaluated by: Baldwin, David A., Foreign Aid & American Foreign Policy: A Documentary Analysis (New York: Praeger, 1966); Coffin, Frank M., Witness for AID (Boston: Houghton Mufflin, 1964); and Mason, Edward S., Foreign Aid & Foreign Policy (New York: Harper & Row, 1964).

31 One of the most thoughtful analyses of the Peace Corps was written by Kimble, George H.P.,"Challenges to the Peace Corps," The New York Times Magazine, Section VI (May 14, 1961), pp. 9, 98-100. Also see, Corey, Robert G., The Peace Corps (New York: Praeger, 1970), pp. 101-122, and Lent, Henry B., The Peace Corps-Ambassadors of Goodwill (Philadelphia: Westminster Press, 1966), pp. 1-88.

32 The initially high expectations of the Alliance are reflected in Alexander, Robert J., "New Dimension: The U.S. & Latin America," Current History, XLII (February, 1962), pp. 68-75 and "The First Year of the Alliance for Progress," State Department Bulletin (December 10, 1962), pp. 897-901. A more sobering review can be found in Draper, Thomas, "The Alliance for Progress: Failures & Opportunites," Yale Review, LV (December, 1965), pp. 182-190, and May, Ernest R.,"The Alliance for Progress In Historical Perspective," Foreign Affairs, XLI (July, 1963), pp. 757-774. A good book on the subject is Perloff, Harvey S., Alliance for Progress: A Social Invention in the Making (Baltimore, Mary.: John Hopkins Press, 1969). For the growing concern in Congress see, U.S. Senate Foreign Relations Committee, Survey of the Alliance for Progress (Washington, D.C.: United States Government Printing Office, 1969).

35 "The Whole United...close to collapse." Time , April 2, 1965, p. 13. Also see, Burns, Arthur Lee and Nina Heathcote, Peace-Keeping by U.N. Forces: From

Suez to the Congo (New York: Random House, 1963), pp. 178-211, and LeFever, Ernest W., Uncertain Mandate: Politics of the U.N. Congo Operation (Baltimore, Mary.: John Hopkins Press, 1967).

II. NEW FRONTIERS: OLD SLOGANS

Page

38 Leo Huberman & Paul Sweezy, editors of the Monthly Review wrote articles in the February 16, 1965 & February 17, 1965, editions which branded the Kennedy-Johnson economic policy as socialism for capitalists. This alternative view is well worth reading. Harris, Seymour E., Economics in the Kennedy Years (New York: Harper & Row, 1964); Pace, Donald, John F. Kennedy & the New Frontier (New York: Hill & Wang, 1966); and Rowen, Hobart, The Free Enterprisers: Kennedy, Johnson, & the Business Establishment (New York: Pittman, 1964).

40 "We had no...the world scene."
Joseph, Peter, Good Times (New York: William Morrow, 1974), p. 277. The popular reaction to Kennedy's space initiative was summarized in a Time Essay: "America's pioneering spirit is well suited to the journey that must never end. This is why we will be on the moon within this decade." Time (November 10, 1961), p. 83. America's optimistic attitude can be seen in American Assembly, Outer Space: Prospects for Man & Society (Englewood Cliffs, N.J.: Prentice-Hall, 1962). The most insightful work on the developments in space is Ley, Willy, Rockets, Missiles, & Men in Space (New York: Viking Press, 1968).

42 "back in the...needed boost."
Time (March 2, 1962), p. 9.

"lifted the self-doubt...of modern life."
Newsweek (March 5, 1962), p. 7.
An interesting commentary on the connection between the moon project and other aspects of American life can be found in Logsdon, John M., The Decision to Go to the Moon: Project Appallo and the National Interest (Cambridge, Mass.: The MIT Press, 1970).

44 Two of the best treatments of the Steel Crisis are McConnell, Grant, Steel and the Presidency (New York: W.W. Norton, 1963) and McManus, George J., The Inside Story of Steel Wages & Prices 1959-1967 (Philadelphia, PA: Chilton Books, 1967). Probably the best insight into presidential posturing can be found in Sidey, Hugh, John F. Kennedy,

President (New York: Atheneum, 1964).

46 "It's almost certain...was challenged."
Iron Age (September 22, 1962), p. 13.

"now belong to...White House."
Business Week (June 14, 1966), p. 23.

"I don't buy...other way around."
Business Week (May 14, 1966), p. 10.

47 "Dammit, I may have my faults, but being wrong ain't one of them," boasted Hoffa.
Time (March 17, 1967), p. 20. The Kennedy-Hoffa friction can be reviewed in: James, Ralph C., Hoffa & the Teamsters: Case Study of Union Power (Princeton, N.J.: Van Nostrand, 1965); Schlesinger, Arthur M. Jr., A Thousand Days: John F. Kennedy in the White House (Boston: Houghton Mifflin, 1965); and, Sheridan, Walter, The Fall & Rise of Jimmy Hoffa (New York: Saturday Review Press, 1972).

48 "He represented...of ourselves."
Dr. George R. Krupp, psychiatrist, in Redbook (March, 1964), p. 281.

49 "The country...trail blazer."
Newsweek (December 2, 1963), p. 9.

"The President...New Frontier."
Look (November 17, 1964), p. 33.

"For the first...inside jokes."
Look (January 2, 1962), p. 12.

"Not since...young men."
Newsweek (December 2, 1963), p. 8.

50 "Never before has...and artists."
Newsweek (June 12, 1961), p. 25.

"Shifted from the...unlikely happenings."
Look (January 2, 1962), p. 12.

"When other children...St. Vincent Millay."
Life (June 16, 1967), p. 74.

"I am an ivory...tower President."
Life (June 16, 1967), p. 74.

"Hang up the...Grand Old Loveable."
McCall's (August, 1966), p. 155.

52 "loved Mamie...the last gala."
Look (March 22, 1966), p. 50.

"Her head was...crowds loved it."
Newsweek (April 3, 1961), p. 18.

"He, because he...a movie star."
From an article entitled "The New Sentimentality," by Robert Benton & David Newmen in Esquire's History of the Sixties.

"Vigorous, exciting...New England."
Time (December 11, 1964), p. 121.

53 "Death, in full...pattern of history."
Life (May 29, 1964), p. 62.
Long time Washington commentator, Drew Pearson, complained that Kennedy lacked "techniques" and "persuasiveness." See Nation (July 7, 1969), p. 37. For an early critical approach to Kennedy, see Carleton, William G., "Kennedy in History: An Early Appraisal," The Antioch Review, XXIV (Fall, 1964), pp. 3-17. Also see, Paper, Lewis J., The Promise & the Performance: The Leadership of John F. Kennedy (New York: Crown Publishers, 1975) and Tugwell, Rexford, Off Course: From Truman to Nixon (New York: Praeger, 1971). A more sympathetic treatment can be found in: Lasky, Victor, JFK: The Man & The Myth (New York: Macmillan, 1963); Manchester, William L., The Glory & the Dream: A Narrative History of the United States, 1932-1972 (Boston: Little Brown, 1974); Lincoln, Evelyn, Kennedy & Johnson (New York: Holt, Rinehart & Winston, 1965); O'Donnell, Kenneth P. & David F. Powers, Johnny, We Hardly Knew Ye: Memories of John Fitzgerald Kennedy (Boston: Little Brown, 1972); and, O'Neill, William, L., Coming Apart: An Informal History of America in the 1960's (Chicago: Quadrangle Books, 1971).

III. THE JOHNSON PRESIDENCY

Page

55 "At the moment...Federal Government."
Newsweek (August 2, 1965), p. 22.
"Lyndon Johnson was never able before 1964 to become President on his own," wrote Theodore H. White, "no Democratic convention would nominate him. The Kennedys opened power to him." See Life (July 2, 1965), p. 71. A good work on Johnson's astonishing political background is White, William S., The Professional: Lyndon B. Johnson (Greenwich, CT: Fawcett, 1964). LBJ's own self-serving

account is in Johnson, Lyndon B., The Vantage Point: Perspectives of the Presidency 1963-1969 (New York: Rinehart & Winston, 1971).

56 "The most boisterous...two decades." Time (September, 5, 1969), p. 14. Early accounts of the Johnson years are: Amrine, Michael, This Awesome Challenge: The Hundred Days of Lyndon Johnson (New York: Putman, 1964); Evans, Rowland & Novak, Robert, Lyndon B. Johnson: The Exercise of Power (New York: New American Library, 1966); Wicker, Tom, JFK & LBJ: The Influence of Personality Upon Politics (New York: Morrow, 1968); and, Bishop, James A., From Dawn to Dusk with LBJ: A day in the life of President Johnson (New York: Random House, 1967).

56 "He yearned to...tomorrow's scholars." Time (January 1, 1965), p. 23. Some of the best insights into the complex Johnson personality can be found in: Goldman, Eric T., The Tragedy of Lyndon Johnson (New York: Knopf, 1969); Kearns, Doris, Lyndon Johnson & The American Dream (New York: Harper & Row, 1976); Lynch, Dudley, The President From Texas: Lyndon Baines Johnson (New York: YY Crowell, 1975); and, Miller, Merle, Lyndon: An Oral Biography (New York: Ballantine Books, 1980).

57 "The President...checks and balances." Newsweek (August 2, 1965), p. 22.

58 Bell's book was an irony since within two years ideology came back into the forefront of American politics. See Bell, Daniel, The End of Ideology (New York: Collier Books, 1961).

59 Philip Geyelin presented several useful insights into LBJ's personality. See Geyelin, Philip, Lyndon B. Johnson & the World (New York: Praeger, 1966). A unique insight into LBJ is in Krock, Arthur, Memoirs: Sixty Years on the Firing Line (New York: Funk & Wagnalls, 1968), pp. 381-403.

62 Max Lerner was one of the earliest critics of the Johnson style. "Before you can get a society, great or small, you need more than a consensus," stated Lerner thoughtfully. "You need a nexus: something to tie the parts into a whole, something to cement the individual wills, something to stir the nation's pulse, not continually feel it." See, Time (January 15, 1965), p. 17. Also see, Deakin, James, Lyndon Johnson's Credibility Gap (Washington, D.C.: Public Affairs Press, 1968).

63 "It was Johnson...in the snow."
New York *Review* (December 16, 1972), p. 11.

"The nation needed...to end trust."
Time (January 1, 1965), p. 24.

"The President...what you've done."
Newsweek (August 2, 1965), p. 22.

Significant insights concerning LBJ's character are provided by: Divine, Robert A., Ed., *Exploring the Johnson Years* (Austin, TX: University of Texas Press, 1981); Gettleman, Marvin E., & Mermelstein, David, Ed., *The Great Society Reader* (New York: Random House, 1967); Schlesinger, Arthur M. Jr., *The Imperial Presidency* (Boston: Houghton, Mifflin, 1973); and, Valenti, Jack, *A Very Human President* (New York: Norton, 1975).

64 For a good discussion on the origin of the term "Great Society," see, New York *Times,* (December 19, 1964), p. 28.

66 Goldwater's most pronounced statement of belief can be found in Goldwater, Barry M.; *The Conscience of A Conservative* (New York:Macfadden, 1960). Sympathetic treatments of Goldwater's ideas are in Donovan, Frank R., *The Americanism of Barry Goldwater* (New York: Macfadden-Bartell, 1964) and Hess, Karl, *In A Cause That Will Triumph: The Goldwater Campaign & The Future of Conservatism* (Garden City, N.Y.: Doubleday, 1967). Goldwater never recanted his 1964 beliefs. See Goldwater, Barry M., *With No Apologies: The Personal & Political Memoirs of United States Senator Barry M. Goldwater* (New York: Morrow, 1979).

68 An example of Rockefeller posturing can be found in Desmond, James, *Nelson Rockefeller: A Political Biography* (New York: Macmillan, 1964).

69 Goldwater's political shortcomings were documented early in: Kessel, John H., *The Goldwater Coalition: Republican strategies in 1964* (Indianapolis, Ind.: Bobbs-Merril, 1968); Shadegg, Stephen C., *What Happened to Goldwater? The Inside Story of the 1964 Republican Campaign* (New York: Holt, Rhinehart & Winston, 1965); and, White, Theodore H. *The Making of the President, 1964* (New York: Atheneum, 1965). Another good analysis is in Novak, Robert D., *The Agony of the G.O.P. 1964* (New York: Macmillan, 1965), pp. 118-464. Also see, McEvoy, James, III, *Radicals or Conservatives: The Contemporary American Right.* (Chicago: Rand McNally, 1971).

IV. THE GREAT SOCIETY

Page

74 A discussion of early medicare expectations is exemplified in Feingold, Eugene, Medicare: Policy & Politics (San Francisco, Calif.: Chandler, 1966). The less optimistic reality is portrayed in Stevens, Robert B., Welfare Medicine in America: A Case Study of Medicaid (New York: Free Press, 1974).

77 "Workout for...material needs." New Yorker (January 1, 1966), p. 35.

"has spawned...into worse pigsties." Saturday Evening Post (August 28, 1965), p. 12.

"basic error in...slum-dwellers." Commentary (April, 1965), p. 29.

78 Robert Weaver came into office well qualified. See Weaver, Robert C., Dilemmas of Urban America (Cambridge, Mass.: Harvard University Press, 1965). Think Tankers representing M.I.T. became heavily involved in promoting urban renewal. See: Frieden, Bernard J., The Future of Old Neighborhoods: Rebuilding for a Changing Population (Cambridge, Mass.: M.I.T. Press, 1964); Anderson, Martin, The Federal Bulldozer: A Critical Analysis of Urban Renewal, 1949-1962 (Cambridge, Mass.: M.I.T. Press, 1964); and, Wilson, James Q., Ed., Urban Renewal: The Record of Controversy (Cambridge, Mass.: M.I.T. Press, 1966). The early growth of HUD was documented in Willman, John B., The Department of Housing & Urban Development (New York: Praeger, 1967). An earlier work by Jane Jacobs influenced many who voted in favor of renewal. See Jacobs, Jane, Death & Life of Great American Cities (New York: Vintage Books, 1961)

80 Two early works on poverty which embodied LBJ's philosophy were Conference on Poverty in America, Poverty in America: Proceedings of a National Conference (Berkeley, Calif.: Chandler, 1966) and Keyserling, Leon H., Progress or Poverty: The United States at the Crossroads (Washington, D.C.: Conference on Economic Progress, 1964). Some of the best discussions of urban renewal & poverty were published in several issues of the Nations Cities published by the National League of Cities. Also see Clark, Kenneth B., & Jeannette Hopkins, A Relevant War Against Poverty (New

York: Harper & Row, 1968).

82 "comes as close...deep effect."
Time (August 18, 1967), p. 19.
Analysis of the eventual lack of success in the anti-poverty programs can be found in Plotnick, Robert D., Progress Against Poverty: A Review of the 1964-1974 Decade (New York: Academic Press, 1975), and Rose, Stephen M., The Betrayal of the Poor: The Transformation of Community Action (Cambridge, Mass.: Schenkman, 1972).

83 A good analysis of LBJ's attempts to promote new frontiers through the Appalachian program is in Walls, David S., Appalachia in the Sixties: Decade of Reawakening (Lexington, VA: University of Kentucky Press, 1972).

84 "be the foremost...20th Century."
Time (November 17, 1967), p. 66.

85 "Performance became...of the hour."
Time (November 17, 1967), p. 23.

87 "the only words...'ebullient.'"
Time (April 23, 1965), p. 43.
The great bull market was well characterized in Brooks, John N., The Go-Go Years (New York: Weybright & Talley, 1973).

The Okun approach can be seen in Okun, Arthur M., Ed., The Battle Against Unemployment (New York: Norton, 1965).

"I shall not...inflationary action."
Newsweek (January 3, 1964), p. 58.

88 "Reuther hit a...only for singles."
Time (September 15, 1964), p. 17.
LBJ and Reuther on Chrysler settlement. U.S. News & World Reports (November 16, 1964), p. 102. For a summary of organized labor's growing political influence see Catchpole, Terry, How to Cope with COPE: The Political Operations of Organized Labor (New Rochelle, N.Y.: Arlington House, 1968). An evaluation of Reuther's masterful ways can be found in Cormier, Frank & William J. Eaton, Ruether (Englewood Cliffs, N.J.: Prentice-Hall, 1970).

89 "Across Iowa's corn...measured intervals."
Time (August 18, 1967), p. 78.

90 "little guys at...conglomerates."
New Republic (September 11, 1964), p. 17.

91 "Shut the granery door, nail it shut. If the market wants the grain, it can bring a crowbar -- a fair price to farmers," insisted Oren Lee Staley. See New York Times (September 5, 1963), p. 38. The dilemmas of collective bargaining are treated in Walters, Charles, Holding Action (New York: Haleyon, 1969) and Walters, Charles, Angry Testament (Kansas City, KS: Haleyon, 1969). One can find the impetus behind the Farm Bureau in McConnel, Grant, The Decline of Agrarian Democracy (Berkeley, Calif.: University of California Press, 1953). An update on Farm Bureau philosophy is in Berger, Samuel R. Dollar Harvest: The Story of the Farm Bureau (Lexington, Mass.: Heath Lexington Books, 1971).

92 "Let me introduce myself, I'm Orville Freeman, the man at the end of the pitchfork," Freeman was fond of saying. Time (July 14, 1967), p. 14.

93 "Instead of letting...held down output."
Fortune (June, 1964), p. 30.
The Kennedy-Johnson food policy was rationalized by such Neo-New Deal intellectuals as Keyserling, Leon H., Agriculture & the Public Interest: Toward a New Farm Program Based Upon Abundance (Washington, D.C.: Conference on Economic Progress, 1965) and Paarlberg, Donald, American Farm Policy: A Case Study of Centralized Decision-Making (New York: J. Wiley, 1964). The contradictions in the policies were documented in Johnson, David G., Farm Commodity Programs: An Opportunity for Change (Washington, D.C.: American Enterprise Institute for Public Policy, 1973). A more balanced summary can be found in Cochrane, Willard W. & Mary E. Ryan, Amercan Farm Policy, 1948-1973 (Minneapolis: University of Minnesota Press, 1976).

Both Freeman and McGovern demonstrated their faith in Food for Peace in such writings as Freeman, Orville L., World Without Hunger (New York: F.A. Pager, 1968) and McGovern, George S., War Against Want: America's Food for Peace Program (New York: Walker, 1964). The political problems with the program are analyzed in Toma, Peter A., The Politics of Food for Peace: Executive-Legislative Interaction (Tucson: University of Arizona Press, 1967). The contradictions in the program are treated in Wallerstein, Mitchell B., Food for War--Food for Peace: United States Food Aid in Global Context (Cambridge, Mass.: M.I.T. Press, 1980).

94 The impact of food stamp policy is analyzed in Segal, Judith, Food for the Hungry: The Reluctant Society

(Baltimore: John Hopkins Press, 1970).

96 "My classic example...Conference Board." Time (July 5, 1968), p. 38.

"Even the economists...fantastic rate." Time (January 24, 1969), p. 27.

"The American...in those terms." Time (July 10, 1967), p. 41.

V. AMERICAN CIVILIZATION AT HIGH TIDE

Page

101 Words from the song "Downtown" sung by Petula Clark, composed by Tony Hatch, and published by Leeds Music Corporation in 1964.

104 "It is difficult...is only magnificent." Time (November 14, 1969), p. 47. Venturi, Robert, Complexity and Contradiction in Architecture (New York: Museum of Modern Art, 1966) and Jordon R. Furneaux, A Concise History of Western Architecture (London: Thames & Hudson Limited, 1969). For a good discussion on mobility see Toffler, Alvin, Future Shock, (New York: Rändom House, 1970), pp. 70-81.

107 McLuhan, Marshall, Understanding Media: The Extensions of Man (New York: New American Library, 1964); Duffy, Dennis, Marshall McLuhan (Toronto, Montreal: McCelland & Stewart, 1969); and, Finkelstein, Sidney W., Sense & Nonsense of McLuhan (New York: International Publishers, 1968).

109 "The priest has...camouflaged as gardens." New York Review (June 13, 1974), p. 66. According to Jessica Mitford, funerals represented the third largest expenditure after a home and car. "Restoring and beautifying corpses and putting them on display is a gruesome and barbarous performance," wrote Mitford, "it has no basis either in American tradition or in the religious teaching of any church." Mitford, Jessica, The American Way of Death (New York: Fawcett, 1972), p. 11. Also see Bowman, LeRoy E., The American Funeral: A Study in Guilt, Extravagance and Sublimity (New York: Greenwood, 1973).

110 Bergaust, Erik, Murder on Pad 34 (New York: Putnam, 1968).

111 "I doubt if...World War."
Time (April 23, 1973), p. 83.

"practically everything...hanging abdomen."
Time (July 7, 1967), p. 34.

"The more...were in."
Manchester, p. 1037.

"I'm so far out, I'm in."
Time (April 10, 1964), p. 57.

Words from the song, "My Way" sung by Frank Sinatra, composed by Paul Anka, and published by Reprise in 1967.

On Madalyn E. Murray, see Howard, Jane, "The Most Hated Woman in America," Life (June 19, 1964), pp. 91-94.

112 On Governor Kirk, see the World Book, Year Book, (1968), p. 450. Words from the song, "People" sung by Barbara Streisand, composed by Bob Merrill and Viale Styne, and published by Columbia in 1969.

114 Among those attempting to analyze the impact of the new cinema were: Crist, Judith, The Private Eye: The Cowboy and the Very Naked Girl: Movies from Cleo to Clyde (Chicago: Holt, Rinehart, & Winston, 1968); Rhode, Eric, Tower of Babel: Speculations on the Cinema (Philadelphia: Clinton Books, 1966); and, Schillaci, Anthony, Movies & Morals (Notre Dame, Ind.: Fides, 1968).

115 "Some of the...forbidden realms."
Life (July 16, 1967), p. 18.

"Even as it...in the universe."
Time (March 17, 1967), p. 65.

"My little girl...getting it."
Time (October 31, 1969), p. 36.

116 "That he has...upward mobility."
Time (March 3, 1967), p. 48.
On James Bond, see Amis, Kingsley, The James Bond Dossier (New York: New American Library, 1965).

117 "Rarely have so...so much."
Time (April 19, 1968), p. 51.
British social critic Malcolm Bradbury wrote that "American women are rude...and are, from the European point of view, men." New York Times Magazine (March 29, 1964), p. 48. According to Dr. George Gallup, the

typical woman was "35 years old, happily married for 14 years to only one husband and has two children and wants one more. She is a full-time housewife and mother; she is not employed outside the home...the chief purpose of her life is to be either a good wife or a good mother." Saturday Evening Post (December 22, 1962), p. 12.

118 "The disappearance...moral laxity."
Time (June 16, 1975), p. 37.
On pets, see World Book, Year Book, (1968), p. 454.

119 A good commentary on leisure time was written by Joad, C.E.M., "The Future of Man," Harpers (September, 1978), p. 493. Also see Talamine, John T., and Charles H. Page, Eds., Sport and Society: An Anthology (Boston: Little, Brown, 1973), pp. 102-112.

124 "We are in...the winners."
Life (October 24, 1969), p. 48.

"is that moment...head-to-head combat."
U.S. News & World Reports (February 20, 1967), p. 14.

"building of character."
Look (October 24, 1961), p. 17.

125 "appetite...such an environment."
Sports Illustrated (March 3, 1969), p. 22.

"I jumped to...the human race."
Holiday (May, 1965), p. 66.

One of the best biographies on Lombardi is Dowling, Tom, Coach: A Season with Lombardi (New York: Norton, 1970).

126 "his ridiculous...his jazzy clothes."
Time (March 10, 1967), p. 44.

127 "delicate ornaments...our skyscraper."
Look (January 9, 1968), p. 30.

"Everyone with...snapping up artworks."
Time (March 3, 1967), p. 68.
Also see Kramer, Hilton, The Age of the Avant-Garde: An Art Chronicle of 1956-1972 (New York: Farrar, Straus and Giroux, 1974).

"whose work was...a powerful empire."
Time (December 18, 1972), p. 37.

128 "culture reigns...for thirteen hours."
New York Times (June 25, 1965), p. 1.

Spending on art per person from the Des Moines Register (February 28, 1970), p. 7.

"a bird, a...whatever it is."
Time (August 25, 1967), p. 55.
129 "By using such...TV commercials."
Time (May 11, 1962), p. 52.

"cross between...W.C. Fields."
Newsweek (December 7, 1964), p. 100.

"The thin, acrid...not dismissed."
Time (October 17, 1969), p. 48.

"I just paint...that sustain us."
Time (May 11, 1962), p. 56.

"Somebody piles...to this gibberish."
Art in America (January-February, 1962), p. 42.
A good account of Warhol can be found in Coplans, John, Andy Warhol (Greenwich, Conn.: New York Graphic Society, 1970).

130 "I don't think...thinking of marriage."
Time (April 7, 1967), p. 34.

"I live and...but my own."
Life (December 9, 1969), p. 67.
"I prefer to be married to a soft and vulnerable woman rather than to an American Joan of Arc." complained Fonda's ex-husband, Roger Vadim. Parade (May 31, 1971), p. 17.

Also see Blake, Nelson M., The Road to Reno (New York: Macmillan, 1964).

131 "brought to the...of the law"
Time (May 21, 1973), p. 17.

"Would be vastly...goes unpunished."
Time (April 14, 1967), p. 110.

132 The views of Black & Douglas can be found in Westin, Alan F., Ed. The Supreme Court: Views from Inside (New York: W.W. Norton, 1961). A concise early review of the Warren Court is Liston, Robert A., Tides of Justice (New York: Dell, 1966). For a broader view, see Bichel, Alexander M., Politics and the Warren Court (Cambridge,

Mass.: Harvard University Press, 1968); Kurland, Philip B., Politics, the Constitution and the Warren Court (Chicago: University of Chicago Press, 1970); and Mitau, Gunter T. Decade of Decision: The Supreme Court & the Constitutional Revolution, 1954-1964 (New York: Scribner, 1967).

137 Engel v. Vitale was one of history's least understood opinions. See Clayton, James E., The Making of Justice (New York: E.P. Dutton, 1964), pp. 15-23. Also see Muir, William K., Prayer in the Public Schools: Law and Attitude Change (Chicago: University of Chicago Press, 1967). Warren's own acute sensitivity to the issues is apparent in Warren, Earl, The Memoirs of Earl Warren (Garden City, N.J.: Doubleday, 1977).

"If people want...my intellectual views."
Saturday Evening Post (July 11, 1964), p. 83.

138 "eclipse of wonder"
Keen, Samuel, Apology for Wonder (New York: Harper & Row, 1970).
Trueblood, Elton, The Future of the Christian (New York: Harper & Row, 1971).

139 "age of urban...beep of computers."
National Review (August 23, 1966), pp. 847-850.
See Cox, Harvey, The Secular City (New York: Macmillan, 1964)

"Life is a set of problems, not an unfathomable mystery," asserted Cox. Time (April 2, 1965), p. 78.
Also see Altizer, J.J. and William Hamilton, Radical Theology and the Death of God (Indianapolis, Ind.: Bobbs-Merrill, 1966) and Robinson, John A.T., Honest to God (London: Westminster, 1963)

"self-delusion and...for in themselves."
Time (May 2, 1969), p. 44.

"cleared away some...of God means."
Time (May 2, 1969), p. 44.

Also see Macquarrie, John A., Thinking About God (New York: Harper & Row, 1975).

140 Fletcher, Joseph, Situation Ethics: The New Morality (London: SCM Press, 1965)

"We are delivered...fears and anxieties."
Time (January 1, 1965), p. 44-45.

"one enters into...one's neighbor."
Time (March 5, 1965), p. 63.
Also see Short, Robert L., The Gospel According to Peanuts (New York: Knox, 1965).

141 "could carry the...miraculous Christ"
World Book, Year Book, (1968), p. 469.

"a reunited...pastor and spokesman."
Time (June 16, 1967), p. 56.

142 "the laundry room...gather to talk."
Time (November 6, 1964), p. 65.

"meet people...most vital tasks."
Time (November 6, 1964), p. 65.

143 "the church lots...by themselves."
Time (November 3, 1967), p. 83.

"Surely, if chambers...values at stake."
Time (April 21, 1967), p. 69.
Christian Century criticized Goldwater for "stridency and military recklessness," "obsessive nationalism," and "promoting racist exploitation." Time (October 9, 1964), p. 63.

"I don't question...law is right."
World Book, Year Book, (1964), p. 460.

144 "The use of...educational possibilities."
U.S. News & World Reports (September 20, 1972), p. 43.

"to sensitize the...moralistic judgements."
U.S. News & World Reports (September 20, 1971), p. 43.

VI. THE RISE AND FALL OF THE CIVIL RIGHTS MOVEMENT

Page

148 The initial optimism concerning civil rights can be seen in the following publications: Berger, Monroe, Equality by Statue: The Revolution in Civil Rights (Garden City, N.Y.: Doubleday, 1967); Casper, Jonathan D., Lawyers Before the Warren Court: Civil Liberties and Civil Rights, 1956-66 (Urbana: University of Illinois Press, 1972); and, Congressional Quarterly Service, Revolution in Civil Rights (Washington, D.C.: Governmental Printing Office, 1965). On Kennedy, see

Harvey, James C., Civil Right During the Kennedy Administration (Baton Rouge: University of Mississippi Press, 1971). On the Freedom Fighters see Wilson, Ruth, Our Blood and Tears: Black Freedom Fighters (New York: Putman, 1972). A sympathetic view of Kennedy and Civil Rights is in Golden, Harry, Mr. Kennedy and the Negroes (New York: World Publishing, 1964).

149 "first class troublemaker"
Time (April 23, 1965), p. 46.
Two good examples of black intellectual thinking are Baldwin, James, Fire Next Time (New York: Dial Press, 1963) and Wright, Richard, White Man Listen (Garden City, N.Y.: Anchor Books, 1964). Support and impetus from the black community is covered in Sitkhoff, Harvard, The Struggle for Black Equality, 1954-80 (New York: Hill & Wang, 1981).

150 "He never struck...my idol"
Chicago Tribune, Sunday Magazine (March 30, 1969), p. 56.

"It may get me...make men free."
Newsweek (April 15, 1968), p. 11.
King's approach can be reviewed in three works: Stride Toward Freedom: The Montgomery Story (New York: Harper & Row, 1958); Why We Can't Wait (New York: New American Library, 1964); and The Trumpet of Conscience (New York: Harper & Row, 1967). Two works on King's importance soon after his death were Lokos, Lionel, House Divided: The Life and Legacy of Martin Luther King (New Rochelle, N.Y.: Arlington House, 1969) and Miller, William R., Martin Luther King, Jr.: His Life, Martyrdom, and Meaning for the World (New York: Weybright & Talley, 1968). Also see Bishop, James A., The Days of Martin Luther King, Jr., (New York: Putnam, 1971).

153 "it has been...for us all."
Time (December 25, 1964), p. 23.
Humphrey's optimism is revealed in Humphrey, Hubert H., Beyond Civil Rights: A New Day of Equality (New York: Random House, 1968). King referred to himself as a "drum major for justice." Chicago Tribune Sunday Magazine (March 30, 1969), p. 41.

154 "poverty & dope...in narcotics."
Ebony (August, 1970), p. 28.
A good analysis of urban black problems is in Geschwender, James A., The Black Revolt: The Civil Rights Movement, Ghetto Uprisings and Separatism (Englewood Cliffs, N.J.: Prentice-Hall, 1971).

"to shoot to kill...in his hand."
Chicago Daily News (July 5, 1969), p. 1.
King's own growing misgivings are revealed in King, Martin Luther, Where Do We Go From Here: Chaos or Community (New York: Harper & Row, 1967).

"No man in...into the society."
Little, Malcolm, The Autobiography of Malcom X on Afro-American History (New York: Grove Press, 1964), p. ix. Also see Lincoln, Eric, The Black Muslims in America (Boston: Beacon Press, 1973) and Lomax, Louis E., When the Word Was Given: A Report on Elijah Muhammad, Malcolm X, and the Black Muslim World (New York: New American Library, 1964).

155 "an exploration of...corridors of hell."
U.S. News & World Reports (August 23, 1971), p. 27. The roots of Black Power could be attributed back at least as far as 1848 when Negro Abolitionist Frederick Douglass declared: "It is evident that we can be improved and elevated only just so fast and far as we shall improve and elevate ourselves." Time (December 1, 1967), p. 20. Also see Scott, Robert L., and Wayne Brockriede, Eds., The Rhetoric of Black Power (New York: Seabury Press, 1969), pp. 3-28; Dymally, Marvyn M., Ed., The Black Politician: His Struggle for Power (Belmont, CA: Durbury Press, 1971); and, Zinn, Howard, SNCC: The New Abolitionists (Boston: Beacon Press, 1965).

157 "full-time revolutionary...in America."
Cleaver, Eldridge, Soul on Ice (New York: McGraw-Hill, 1968). Also see Jackson, George, Blood in My Eye (New York: Random House, 1972).

158 "the church is...which goes on."
Church Herald (May 30, 1969), p. 20.
An early assessment of Black Panthers is Marine, Gene, The Black Panthers (New York: New American Library, 1969). Newton's views are in Newton, Huey P., To Die for the People: The Writings of Huey P. Newton (New York: Random House, 1972). Also see Foner, Philip S., The Black Panthers Speak (Philadelphia: Lippinott, 1970) and Heath, G. Louis, The Black Panther Leadership Speak (Metuchen, N.J.: Scarecrow Press, 1976).

159 For the Nixon-Mitchell crackdown see Commission of Inquiry into the Black Panthers and the Policy, Search & Destroy: A Report (New York: Metropolitan Applied Research Center, 1973) and Freed, Donald, Agony in New Haven: The Trial of Bobby Seale, Ericka Huggins, and the Black Panther Party (New York: Simon & Schuster, 1973).

160 "this commission...equality of opportunity." U.S. Commission on Civil Rights, The Unfinished Business Twenty Years Later: A Report (Washington, D.C.: The Commission, 1977), p. 1.

VII. THE VIETNAM WAR

Page

162 One of the best early accounts of LBJ's war decisions is Kahin, George M. & John W. Lewis, The United States in Vietnam (New York: Dial Press, 1967). Early critical accounts include: Draper, Theodore, Abuse of Power (New York: Viking Press, 1967); Little, David, American Foreign Policy and Moral Rhetoric: The Example of Vietnam (New York: Council on Religious and International Affairs, 1969); and Scott, Peter I., The War Conspiracy: The Secret Road to the Second Indochina War (Indianapolis, Ind.: Bobbs-Merril, 1972). Works with more perspective include: Berman, Larry, Planning a Tragedy: The Americanization of the War in Vietnam (New York: W.W. Norton, 1982); Graff, Henry F., The Tuesday Cabinet: Deliberations and Decisons on Peace and War Under Lyndon B. Johnson (Englewood Clifs, N.J.: Prentice-Hall, 1970); and Podhoretz, Norman, Why We Were in Vietnam (New York: Simon & Schuster, 1982).

163 Vietnam could represent an American attempt to stimulate an industrial revolution in Vietnam. See Rostow, Walt W., The Stages of Economic Growth (New York: Cambridge University Press, 1960). An account of McNamara's approach is in Palmer, Gregory, The McNamara Strategy and the Vietnam War: Program Budgeting in the Pentagon, 1960-1968 (Westport, Conn.: Greenwood Press, 1978). On Ball's early opposition and McNamara's growing doubts, see Weisband, Edward & Thomas M. Franck, Resignation in Protest (New York: Grossman/Viking, 1975).

165 On the Tonkin Gulf Resolution, see Austin, Anthony, The President's War: The Story of the Tonkin Gulf Resolution and How the Nation Was Trapped in Vietnam (Philadelphia: Lippincott, 1971) and Galloway, John, Fulbright and McNamara: An Investigation of the Gulf of Tonkin Resolution (Syracuse, N.Y.: Inter-University Case Program, 1970).

169 "we have been...suffer the consequence." Des Moines Register (August 31, 1969), Sec. G, p. 3.

"From transistor radios...about everything."
Time (March 2, 1970), p. 31.
Also see LeFeber, Walter, "Our Illusory Affair with Japan," *Nation* (March 11, 1968).

170 "No single event...ending the war."
Time (May 3, 1968), p. 69.
On the subject of draft resistance, see Ferber, Michael and Staughton Lynd, *The Resistance* (Boston: Beacon, 1971).

171 Johnson's attitudes on the Dominican Republic can be found in Geyelin, Philip, *Lyndon B. Johnson and the World* (New York: Praeger, 1966), pp. 240-248. Also see Slater, Jerome, *Intervention and Negotiation: The United States and the Dominican Republic* (New York: Harper & Row, 1971).

172 On the problems with the Alliance, see Hanson, Simon G., "The Status of the Alliance After Six Years," *Inter-American Economic Affairs, XXII* (Winter, 1968), pp. 3-40. A critical view can be found in Kolko, Gabriel, *The Roots of American Foreign Policy* (Boston: Beacon Press, 1969), pp. 48-88. Other important perspectives include Lowenthal, Abraham F., "Alliance Rhetoric Versus Latin American Reality," *Foreign Affairs, XLVIII* (April, 1970), pp. 494-508 and Montalva, Eduardo Frei, "The Alliance that Lost the Way," *Foreign Affairs, LIV* (April, 1967), pp. 437-448.

173 On Eduardo Frei, see Gross, Leonard, *The Last Best Hope: Eduardo Frei and Chilean Democracy* (New York: Random House, 1967) and Halperin, Ernest, *Nationalism and Communism in Chile* (Cambridge, Mass.: M.I.T. Press, 1965). The dismal results of the Alliance are documented in U.S. Senate Foreign Relations Committee, *Survey of the Alliance for Progress* (Washington, D.C.: U.S. Government Printing Office, 1969).

179 "It was a...the mainland."
Washington *Post* (October 22, 1967), p. 16.
A review of early opposition is in Powers, Thomas, *The War at Home: Vietnam and the American People, 1964-1968* (New York: Grossman, 1973). Another thoughtful piece by Walter Lippman is in "A Sage Ponders the Modern Revolution," Chicago *Sun Times* (May 19, 1968), p. 54.

"America's worth...ideals at home."
Time (August 11, 1967), p. 38.
Also see Steel, Ronald, *Pax Americana* (New York: Viking, 1967)

"May I speak...from South Vietnam."
Time (August 11, 1967), p. 39.

180 "has settled like...political landscape."
Newsweek (November 27, 1967), p. 25.
On Gruening, see Gruening, Ernest H., Vietnam Folly (Washington, D.C.: National Press, 1968). Kennedy's views are contained in Kennedy, Robert, "To Seek a Newer World," Look (November 28, 1967), p. 34.

181 Fulbright's views are best demonstrated in Fulbright, J. William, The Arrogance of Power (New York: Random House, 1967). Also see Johnson, Haynes B., Fulbright: The Dissenter (Garden City, N.Y.: Doubleday, 1968). A highly influential book was Fall, Bernard A., Vietnam Witness (New York: Harper & Row, 1967). Also see Hoopes, Townsend, The Limits of Intervention (New York: D. McKay, 1969) Tucker, Robert W., Nation or Empire? The Debate Over American Foreign Policy (Baltimore: John Hopkins Press, 1968).

182 "We have begun...home territory."
Time (August 25, 1967), p. 27.

183 According to Richard Barnet, Co-Director of the Institute for Policy Studies, LBJ seriously considered the use of nuclear weapons during this time. See Parade (December 27, 1970), p. 2.

184 "I cannot recall...entire history."
Time (April 12, 1968), p. 12.
Columnist Joseph Kraft called LBJ's withdrawal the "supreme achievement of a career rich in significant accomplishments." See Time (April 12, 1968), p. 49. Also see Christian, George, The President Steps Down: A Personal Memoir of the Transfer of Power (New York: Macmillan, 1977) and Schandler, Herbert Y., The Unmaking of a Persident: Lyndon Johnson and Vietnam (Princeton, N.J.: Princeton University Press, 1977).

VIII. THE YOUTH REBELLION

Page

185 "in which confidence...feel left out." Palmer, R.R., The Age of Democratic Revolution (Cambridgo, Mass.: Princeton University Press, 1959), p. 21.

186 "the disquiet that...by most Americans."
Time (October 27, 1967), p. 16.

"today nowhere in...children know."
Time (March 19, 1965), p. 62.

"there is no...ever before."
Time (March 19, 1965), p. 62.

"this generation...to sacrifice."
Time (January 29, 1965), p. 47.

187 "The majority of...of similar work."
Reich, Charles, A., The Greening of America (New York: Bantam, 1971), p. 196. Another insightful critique of youthful consciousness is Roszak, Theodore, The Making of a Counter Culture (Garden City, N.J.: Doubleday, 1969). Also see Slater, Philip, The Pursuit of Loneliness: American Culture at the Breaking Point (Boston: Beacon, 1970), pp. 10-21.

188 "We look at...our individuality."
Look (January 12, 1965), p. 45.
Also see Katz, Joseph and Nevitt Sanford, "Courses of the Student Revolution," Saturday Review (December 18, 1965), pp. 50-64.

"Unable to reconcile...internal emigres."
Time (July 7, 1967), p. 26.

"education had...for others' purposes."
Dissent (February, 1965), p. 10.

See also Goodman, Paul, Growing Up Absurd (New York: Vintage Books, 1956).

189 "The University...to act together."
Time (March 19, 1965), p. 31.

190 "university came to...university stop."
Time (December 18, 1964), p. 68.
Works documenting the university crisis are: Foster, Julian and Durward Long, Eds., Student Activism in America (New York: William Morrow, 1970); Rose, Thomas, Ed., Violence in America (New York: Vintage, 1969), pp. 195-334: and, Wallerstein, Immanuel and Paul Starr, Eds., The University Crisis Reader (New York: Vintage, 1971), Vols. I and II.

191 "Their crass...apathy and resignation."
Nation (May 22, 1967)

One of the best analyses of why youth turned radical is Keniston, Kenneth, Young Radicals: Notes on Committed Youth (New York: Harcourt, Brace, 1968). Also see Lemon, Richard, The Troubled American (New York: Simon & Schuster, 1969), pp. 161-209.

192 "Most of his...to kill him."
Time (November 25, 1974), p. 58.

"their own...of themselves."
Time (December 24, 1965), p. 36.
Also see Belz, Carl, The Story of Rock (New York: Oxford University Press, 1972); Cohn, Nik, Rock From the Beginning (New York: Simon & Schuster, 1969); and Gilbert, Charlie, The Sound of the City: The Rise of Rock-and-Roll (New York: E.P. Duton, 1971).

193 Words from the song, "Little Boxes," sung by Pete Seeger, composed by Lee Huzelwood, and published by Criterion Music Corporation in 1965.

"this lord...of the 50's."
Cultural Information Service (November, 1974).

"Many of the...peace and truth."
Chronicle of Higher Education (February 19, 1974), p. 2.
Also see O'Hare, J.D.,"Talking Through Their Heads," New Republic (May 20, 1972), p. 28.

194 Words from the song, "The Times They Are A-Changin", sung by Bob Dylan, composed by Bob Dylan, and published by Warner Brothers, Inc. in 1963.
Also see Davidson, Sara, "Rock Style: Defying the American Dream," Harpers (July, 1969), pp. 53-62. And on Dylan, the artist, see Gray, Michael, Song and Dance Man: The Art of Bob Dylan (New York: E.P. Dutton, 1972).

195 "We're concerned...sense to us."
Time (January 21, 1974), p. 32.

"more than a...a phenomenon."
Des Moines Register (May 20, 1974).

Words from "Subterranean Homesick Blues" sung by Bob Dylan, composed by Bob Dylan, and published by Warner Brothers in 1965.

Words from "Highway Revisted" sung by Bob Dylan, composed by Bob Dylan, and published by Warner Brothers in 1965.

Words from "Desolation Row" sung by Byb Dylan, composed by Bob Dylan, and published by Warner Brothers in 1965. Also see McGregor, Craig, Ed., Bob Dylan: A Retrospective (New York: Morrow, 1972); Willis, Ellen, "Records: Rock, Etc.," New Yorker (February, 1969), pp. 55-63; and, Eisen, Jonathan, The Age of Rock (New York: Random House, 1969).

196 "An attempt to...technological voodoo." Life (May 3, 1968), p. 28.

"had more of...rattle your jewelry." Time (August 12, 1966), p. 37.

On the Beatles and revolution, see Wood, Michael, "Four Beatles, Five Stones," Commonwealth (December 27, 1968), pp. 40-41. Also see Murphy, Karen, and Ronald Gross, "All You Need Is Love. Love Is All You Need," New York Times Magazine (April 13, 1969), pp. 36.

197 Words from "Nowhere Man" sung by the Beatles, composed by John Lennon and Paul McCartney, and published by Northern Songs, Ltd., in 1965. Also see Davis, Edward E., Ed., The Beatles Book (New York: Cowles, 1969); Mellers, Wilfrid, The Twilight of the Gods: The Music of the Beatles (New York: Schirmer, 1975); and Schaffner, Nicholas, The Beatles Forever (New York: McGraw, Hill, 1978).

Words from the song "Street Fighting Man" sung by the Rolling Stones, composed by Mick Jagger and Keith Richards, and published by ABKCO Music, Inc., in 1968.

"I don't give...spastic marionette." Time (April 28, 1967), p. 54. Also see Sander, Ellen, "The Stones Keep Rolling Along," Saturday Review (November 29, 1969), p. 47.

"Later Crosby...social conscience." Time (January 6, 1973), p. 29.

"I'm interested in...road to freedom." Time (November 24, 1967), p. 106. Also see Greenfield, Robert, A Journey Through America With the Rolling Stones (New York: Dutton, 1974)

198 "arms linked...psychic current." Time (January 24, 1974), p. 24.

"raw, raucous...jam session." Time (June 23, 1967), p. 38.

Words from the song "Plastic Fantastic Lover" sung by Jefferson Airplane, composed by Paul Kanterner, and published by RCA in 1968.

"bonds that...tie you down."
Time (February 24, 1967), p. 51.

199 "Your body...thousands of volts."
Time (April 28, 1967), p. 73.

"Are courageous...fifteen years."
Rozak, Making of a Counter Culture , pp. 167-168.

"become an object...the eternal truth."
Time (December 18, 1964), p. 63.

200 "When the conscious...of itself."
Time (October 20, 1967), p. 86.

"The hair, the beard...defensive posturing."
Time (April 5, 1968), p. 61.

201 "Strollers wear...tooth flutes."
Time (October 10, 1967), p. 31.

"Wilting Flowers"
Time (May 10, 1968), p. 31.

"The Hippies"
Time (July 7, 1967), p. 18.

"Fresh Look at America"
U.S. News & World Reports (November 30, 1970), p. 46.

202 The philosophy of the New Left is in Lothstein, Arthur, Ed., All We Are Saying: The Philosophy of the New Left (New York: Capicorn, 1970).
On New Left origins see Lynd, Staughton, Intellectual Origins of American Radicalism (New York: Pantheon, 1968). A good discussion on New Left Activism is in Berman, Ronald, America in the Sixties: An Intellectual History (New York: Harper Colophon Books, 1968), pp. 110-171.

203 On Herbert Marcuse, see Breines, Paul, Critical Interruptions: New Left Perspectives on Herbert Marcuse (New York: Herder & Herder, 1970) and Marks, Robert W., The Meaning of Marcuse (New York: Ballintine, 1970). Views from the New Left are in Quinn, Edward and Paul J. Dolan, The Sense of the Sixties (New York: Free Press,1968), pp. 1-58.

204 "You've got to...get results."
Newsweek (January 22, 1968), p. 44.

"Nothing less...industrial revolution."
Newsweek (February 20, 1967), p. 31.

"from the social...against the individual."
New York Times (October 29, 1967), p. 28.
On Nader and G.M., see Whiteside, Thomas, The Investigation of Ralph Nader: General Motors vs. One Determined Man (New York: Arbor House, 1972).

205 Leading works on Nader include: Buckhorn, Robert F., Nader: The People's Lawyer (Englewood Cliffs, N.J.: Prentice-Hall, 1972); Gorey, Hays, Nader and the Power of Everyman (New York: Grosset & Dunlap, 1975); and, McCarry, Charles, Citizen Nader (New York: Saturday Review Press, 1972).

"A bureaucracy...the head down."
Parade (April 21, 1974), p. 11.

"You better get...under their homes."
Time (December 15, 1967), p. 28.

206 "We must first...new George III."
Douglas, William O., Points of Rebellion (New York: Random House, 1970).

"In his view...of the organization."
Time (October 27, 1967), p. 58.
Also see Galbraith, John Kenneth, The New Industrial State (New York: Houghton Mifflin, 1967).

207 "We are now...American society."
Joseph, Peter, Good Times (New York: William Morrow, 1974), p. 315. The growing intensity of the youth rebellion is in Foster, Julian and Durward Long, Eds., Protest: Student Activisim in America (New York: William Morrow, 1970), pp. 365-458 and Lipset, Seymour M., Rebellion in the Unversity (Boston: Little Brown, 1971), pp. 197-264.

"You liberals...blood the better."
Look (February 6, 1968), p. 18.

208 "unfathomable blend...and arrogance."
Time (December 22, 1967), p. 19. McCarthy's views are in McCarthy, Eugene J., The Year of the People (Garden City, N.J.: Doubleday, 1969).

"they are, in...peaceful change."
Look (February 6, 1968), p. 27.

209 "shaved, scrubbed...clean for Gene."
Manchester, William, The Glory and the Dream (Boston: Little, Brown, 1973), p. 1144. The student connection is examined in Hyman, Sidney, Youth in Poltics: Expectations and Realities (New York: Basic Books, 1972).

210 "Daley...invited violence."
Time (September 6, 1968, p. 23. A good description of events in Chicago is in Stavis, Ben, We Were the Campaign: New Hampshire to Chicago for McCarthy (Boston: Beacon Press, 1969), pp. 171-194. The impact of Robert Kennedy's death is in Witcover, Jules, 85 Days: The Last Campaign of Robert Kennedy (New York: Putnam, 1969).

211 "cops violated...a police state."
Time (September 6 1968), p. 24.

212 "frustration and...the imagination."
Time (August 1, 1969), p. 68.
"The American school...Become criminals."
Akron Beacon Journal (March 9, 1970), p. 11. Also see The Report of the President's Commission on Campus Unrest (New York: Discus Books, 1971).

213 "most apocalyptic...psychedelic movement."
Time (August 25, 1969), p. 38.

"tribal gathering...songs of revolution."
Time (August 25, 1969), p. 39.

"this festival will...the new culture."
Newsweek (August 25, 1969), p. 88.
Willis, Ellen, "Musical Events," New Yorker (September 6, 1969), pp. 121-124.

214 "might become the...Uncle Tom's Cabin."
Look (August 12, 1969), p. 46.

"It ignites the...'West Side Story.'"
Newsweek (November 13, 1969), p. 124.

"with Woodstock...of the Sixties."
Okun, Milton, Ed., Great Songs of the Sixties (Chicago: Quadrangle, 1970), p. 5.

Words from the song "Aquarius" sung by the Fifth Dimension, composed by James Rado, Jerome Ragni and Galt McDermot, and published by United Artists in 1966.

Commentary on Hair in Genet, "Letter from Paris," New Yorker (June 14, 1969), pp. 98-102.

IX. SILENT MAJORITY RUMBLINGS

Page

215 On the number in Silent Majority, see U.S. News & World Reports (December 14, 1970), p. 20.

216 "a construct of...complex fears."
Time (January 5, 1970), p. 76.
A good discussion of the origins of the Silent Majority is in Scammon, Richard M. and Ben J. Wattenberg, The Real Majority (New York: Coward-McCann, 1970).

217 "The class that...political earthquake."
Des Moines Register (December 1, 1974), p. 8.

"The middle class...shifting sands."
Newsweek (October 6, 1969), p. 31.

"Studies of the new...are endemic."
Hacker, Andrew, The End of the American Ear (New York: Anthenum, 1970).

"the average American...the United States."
Newsweek (October 6, 1969), p. 30.
"Everything has gone to pieces," complained a Michigan housewife. "People are used by the organization which employs them, ending up closer to clerks than to captains of industry," according to Andrew Hacker in "Cutting Classes," New York Review (March 4, 1976), p. 17.

218 "Back America...in their place."
Rock Rapids Reporter (August 20, 1970), p. 5.

"as for such...who needs them?"
Sioux Valley News (July 16, 1970), p. 7.

"Who the hell...illiterate punks."
Time (January 5, 1970), p. 87.

"A bath, a haircut...back in line."
Newsweek (October 6, 1969), p 26.

"If one of those...in front of."
Time (May 5, 1967), p. 62.

"For those who...smells like cheetah."
Time (October 13, 1967), p. 48.
"Private property and the free enterprise system are under attack by the liberal-Socialist-Communist crowd," asserted Wallace in "Hear Me Out-- This is Where I Stand," New York Times Magazine (April 24, 1966), p. 22.

219 "You don't negotiate...education elsewhere."
Time (March 17, 1967), p. 63.

"contempt for middle...lower classes."
Sioux City Journal (February 23, 1970), p. 9.

"We have never...enforcement organizations."
Chicago Tribune (July 16, 1969), p. 27.

"The Silent Majority...have nutured."
Lennox Independent (July 20, 1970), p. 9.

"more than 100...Party U.S.A."
Time (August 29, 1969), p. 46.

"not the place...from the taxpayers."
Storm Lake Pilot Tribune (August 28, 1970) p. 7.
"they would be...to earn recognition."
Koerner, James, Hoffer's America (LaSalle, Ill.: Library Press, 1973), p. 73. Also see Tomkins, Calvin, Eric Hoffer: An American Odyssey (New York: Dutton, 1968).

200 "The niggers are...we get nothing."
Newsweek (October 6, 1969), p. 29.

"There are certain...whoever he wants."
Time (March 17, 1967), p. 81.

"You just can't...to bad."
Time (June 30, 1975), p. 63.

221 "development of something...in the cities."
Wicker, Tom, A Time to Die (New York: Quadrangle, 1975).

"You can see...crying for help."
National Review (April 18, 1967), p. 44.

"We must reject...for his actions."
New York Times (April 29, 1967), p. 17.
On critics of the Court, see Lyile, Clifford M., The Warren Court and Its Critics (Tucson: University of

Arizona Press, 1968).

"The violator of...under the law."
Tulsa Daily World (May 11, 1968), p. 5.

222 "The people are...around him."
National Review (April 18, 1967), p. 19.

"Our lives are...have beards."
Newsweek (May 8, 1967), p. 77.
"pseudo-intellectual...you a guideline."
Scammon and Wattenberg, The Real Majority , p. 62. Also see Warren, Donald D., The Radical Center: Middle Americans and the Politics of Alienation (Notre Dame, Ind.: University of Notre Dame Press, 1976).

223 "The ideal agent...tommy gun."
Time (March 26, 1973), p. 18.
Works on Hoover include Messick, Hank, John Edgar Hoover: An Inquiry Into the Life and Times of John Edgar Hoover, and His Relationship to the Continuing Partnership of Crime, Business and Politics (New York: McKay, 1972); Lewis, Eugene, Public Entrepreneurship (Bloomington: Indiana University Press, 1980); and, Sullivan, William C., The Bureau: My Thirty Years in Hoover's FBI (New York: W.W. Norton, 1979).

Later Attorney General William B. Saxbe admitted Hoover had "gone too far." See Time (December 2, 1974), p. 28.

224 "It has long...personally responsible."
Chronicle of Higher Education (March 15, 1976), p. 13.

"The organization...of their leadership."
New York Review (March 18, 1976), p. 42.
Cointelpro is treated in Blackstock, Nelson, Cointelpro: The FBI's Secret War on Political Freedom (New York: Vintage Books, 1975).

"Princeton is...of the Apes."
Time (December 5, 1977), p. 62.

"The possible publication...Black Panthers."
Des Moines Register (March 11, 1978), p. 7.

225 "the structure of...strength and courage."
Decision (July, 1971), p. 3.

227 "we have perhaps...save the republic."
New York Review (February 21, 1974), p. 27.

"Never having been... _is_ America."
Christian Crusade (October, 1963), p. 13.

"Graham's sermons...relieving humor."
Time (August 29, 1969), p. 43.
Graham's views are in Pollock, John, _Billy Graham: The Authorized Biography_ (New York: McGraw-Hill, 1966).

229 "Anything goes...Marxist educators."
Des Moines _Register_ (March 9, 1976), p. 22.

"New Yorkers may...admired celebrity."
New York Review (February 21, 1974), p. 29.

"the principles of...from Satan."
Christian Crusade (October, 1963), p. 6.

"I wish we...in a few days."
Time (August 29, 1969), p. 49.
Interesting commentary on Hargis is in Redekop, John H., _The American Right: A Case Study of Billy James Hargis and Christian Crusade_ (Grand Rapids: Abington, 1968).

230 "creeping communism...God intended."
Time (November 14, 1969), p. 81.

"Country music is...from the boondocks."
Life (May 3, 1968), p. 48.
A good discussion can be found in Malone, Bill C., _Country Music U.S.A.: A Fifty-Year History_ (Austin: University of Texas, 1970).

"unfaithful wife...of diesel oil."
Time (January 31, 1969), p. 72.

231 "you broke my...talk it over."
New Republic (January 18, 1974), p. 17.

"Southern in its...nostalgic about Jesus."
Flightime (February 1, 1976), p. 2.

"Its songs about...sweet-sad defeats."
Look (July 13, 1971), p. 25.

232 "Nostalgic regrets...homes and places."
Nation (February 23, 1970), p. 68.

"The yen to...so than today."
Time (January 12, 1970), p. 56.

233 Words from the song "Okie from Muskogee" sung by Merle Haggard, composed by Roy E. Burris, and published by Blue Book Music in 1969.

"the situation seemed...are satisfied with." Life (May 3, 1968), p. 32.

Words from the song "Fighting Side of Me" sung by Merle Haggard, composed by Merle Haggard and Roy E. Burris, and published by Blue Book Music in 1970.

"We're not the...old Chevrolet set." Des Moines Register (October 21, 1973), p. 7.

"I wear black...side of town." Look (July 13, 1971), p. 48.

234 "Where a man...full of authority." Newsday (July, 1969), p. 28.

"Wayne epitomized the...heart of marshmallow." Time (May 16, 1975), p. 43.

"We need change...tearing it down." Time (May 16, 1969), p. 98.

235 "unabashed reactionary...what he believes." Time (August 8, 1969), p. 53.

236 "a powerful...serious question." Chicago Sun Times (August 23, 1968), p. 22. A good discussion of Wallace's views is in Frady, Marshall, Wallace (New York: World Publishing, 1968).

"It is difficult...roaring events." White, Theodore S., Making of a President, 1968 (New York: Atheneum, 1969), p. 2.

"anybody who attempts...1968 is nuts." Time (March 3, 1967), p. 72.

X. THE NIXON PRESIDENCY

Page

237 "Something has happened...not too progressive." Newsweek (January 27, 1969), p. 96. The Republican come back is reviewed in Thimmesch, Nick, The Condition of Republicanism (New York: W.W. Norton, 1968) and Witcover, Jules, The Resurrection of Richard

Nixon (New York: Putnam, 1970). On the 1968 elections, see Baker, Russell, Our Next President: The Incredible Story of What Happened in the 1968 Elections (New York: Atheneum, 1968) and Chester, Lewis, An American Melodrama: The Presidential Campaign of 1968 (New York: Viking Press, 1969).

239 "to change the...for the better."
Des Moines Register (October 26, 1974), p. 9.
"Forgotten American" support for Nixon is in Sexton, Patricia C., Blue Collars and Hard Hats: The Working Class and the Future of American Politics (New York: Random House, 1971) and Wirt, Frederick M., On The City's Rim: Politics and Policy in Suburbia (Lexington, Mass.: Heath, 1972). Also see White, Theodore H., The Making of the President, 1968 (New York: Atheneum, 1969). On the Nixon campaign, see McGinness, Joe, The Selling of the President (New York: Trident Press, 1969).

"I'm the fellow...apply the mortar."
Des Moines Register (December 1, 1977), p. 1.

"Humphrey was...irrepressible."
Time (January 23, 1978), p. 18.
Humphrey was the first to think of himself as a great man. See Humphrey, Hubert H., The Education of a Public Man: My Life in Politics (Garden City, N.Y.: Doubleday, 1976).

240 "His nature is...his own behalf."
Time (May 3, 1968), p. 41.
Works which analyze the politics of Humphrey are: Berman, Edgar, Hubert Humphrey: The Triumph and Tragedy of the Humphrey I Knew (New York: Putnam, 1979); Polsby, Nelson W., The Citizen's Choice: Humphrey and Nixon (Washington, D.C.: Public Affairs Press, 1968); and Sherrill, Robert and Harry W. Ernst, The Drugstore Liberal (New York: Grossman, 1968).

241 "I know or thought...on any issue."
New Republic (April 17, 1971), p. 23.
An interesting insight into Nixon's personality is in Mazlish, Bruce, In Search of Nixon: A Psychohistorical Inquiry (New York: Basic Books, 1972).

"probably the most...his fellow men."
Des Moines Register (August 12, 1974), p. 13.
Works analyzing Nixon are: DeToledano, Ralph, One Man Alone: Richard Nixon (New York: Funk & Wagnalls, 1969); Henderson, Charles P., The Nixon Theology (New York: Harper & Row, 1972); Roth, Philip, Our Gang (New York:

Random House, 1971); and, Spalding, Henry D., The Nixon Nobody Knows (Middle Village, N.Y.: David, 1972).

"liked the competitive...J. Walter Thompson." Manchester, The Glory and the Dream, p. 1127.

242 "Nixon's World...in Des Moines, Iowa." Parade (February 20, 1970), p. 7. The Nixon personality is critically analyzed in Mankiewicz, Frank, Perfectly Clear: Nixon From Whittier to Watergate (New York: Quadrangle, 1973). Good commentary on the political atmosphere of the time is in Dutton, Frederick G., Changing Sources of Power: American Politics in the 1970's (New York: McGraw-Hill, 1971).

244 "those who have...with measured tread." Time (January 24, 1969), p. 65. One of the best contemporary treatments of the Nixon Administration is Evans, Rowland and Robert D. Novak, Nixon in the White House: the Frustration of Power (New York: Random House, 1971).

245 "Mainly it fitted...and its conscience." Time (January 31, 1969), p. 20.

"He understood the...to the future." White, Theodore H., Breach of Faith: The Fall of Richard Nixon (New York: Atheneum, 1975).

246 "The time has...their own affairs." U.S. News & World Reports (November 26, 1973), p. 18. Analyses of Nixon's early foreign policy is in Szulc, Tad, The Illusion of Peace: Foreign Policy in the Nixon Years (New York: Viking Press, 1974) and Van Der Linden, Frank, Nixon's Quest for Peace (Washington, D.C.: R.B. Luce, 1972).

251 "he was so...there was hunger." Time (July 25, 1969), p. 37.

"We see ourselves...truly brothers." Time (January 3, 1969), p. 46.

"what I advocated...satisfaction." Time (March 28, 1969), p. 62.

"the nation found...unfamiliar calm." Time (August 29, 1969), p. 14.

XI. A FAILURE IN CONSENSUS

Page

254 "Based on the...United States."
Time (March 28, 1969), p. 28.
"Reading the latest figures on how the U.S. government spent its money last year," chided the editors of *New Republic,* "we felt a twinge of nostalgia for the drowsy days of Calvin Coolidge, who believed that the business of America is business." *New Republic* (April 3, 1971), p. 11.

258 "the public record...this century."
Newsweek (March 2, 1970), p. 36.
On the Supreme Court battles, see Abraham, Henry J., *Justices and Presidents: A Political History of Appointments to the Supreme Court* (New York: Oxford University Press, 1974); Shogan, Robert, *A Question of Judgement: The Fortas Case and the Struggle for the Supreme Court* (Indianapolis: Bobbs-Merill, 1972); and, Simon, James F., *In His Own Image: The Supreme Court in Richard Nixon's America* (New York: D. McKay, 1973).

259 "The President made...elevated level."
Sioux City *Journal* (April 23, 1970), p. 7.
On the southern strategy, see Murphy, Peg and Hal Gulliver, *The Southern Strategy* (New York: Scribner, 1971).

"I've found...the heavyweight."
Parade (May 31, 1970), p. 9.
On Nixon and civil rights, see Panetla, Leon E., and Peter Gall, *Bring U.S. Together: The Nixon Team and Civil Rights Retreat* (Philadelphia: Lippincott, 1971).

"When you first...of the iceberg."
New Republic (April 3, 1971), p. 13.

260 "You cannot convince...and concern."
Sioux City *Journal* (June 4, 1970), p. 12.

"It seems as if...the Constitution."
Time (July 25, 1969), p. 51.
A strong rationale for civil disobedience at the time is in Coffin, William Sloane and Morris I. Leibman, *Civil Disobedience: Aid or Hinderance to Justice* (Washington, D.c.: American Enterprise Institute, 1972) and Cohen, Carl, *Civil Disobedience: Conscience, Tactics, and the Law* (New York: Columbia University Press, 1971).

261 "If you find...for one another."
Time (October 14, 1969), p. 30.
One of the best accounts of the trial is in Epstein, Jason, The Great Conspiracy Trial (New York: Vintage Books, 1971).

"giggle and confer...of Lao-Tzu."
Life (October 10, 1969), p. 23.

"The real conspiracy...War in Vietnam."
Nation (October 13, 1969), p. 18.

262 "When a trial...becomes irrelevant."
Time (March 2, 1970), p. 27.

"Seldom has the...come so abruptly."
Time (February 16, 1970), p. 36.

263 "The market for...on its ass."
Time (February 9, 1970), p. 18.
For statistics, see U.S. News & World Reports (May 22, 1972).

"This is a...possible worlds."
Sioux City Journal (April 1, 1970), p. 6.
On Nixon's economic policy, see Miller, Roger L., The New Economics of Richard Nixon: Freezes, Floats, and Fiscal Policy (New York: Harpers Magazine Press, 1972).

267 "The technical...heart patient."
New Republic (April 17, 1971), p. 5.

"Mr. Nixon has...the 1960's."
Time (February 9, 1970), p. 22.

268 On the rising tide of debate over Vietnam, see Cooper, Chester L., The Lost Crusade: America in Vietnam (New York: Dodd, Mead, 1970) and Harriman, W. Averell, America and Russia in a Changing World: A Half Century of Personal Observation (Garden City, N.Y.: Doubleday, 1971). On the growing impatience from the Left, see Brown, Sam and Len Ackland, Why Are We Still in Vietnam? (New York: Random House, 1970).

272 "All right, a...I do then?"
Time (May 11, 1970), p. 27.
On Nixon's Vietnam policy, see Caldwell, Malcolm, Cambodia in the Southeast Asian War (New York: Monthly Review Press, 1973); Galucci, Robert L., Neither Peace Nor Honor: The Politics of American Military Policy in

Viet-Nam (Baltimore: John Hopkins University Press, 1975); and Porter, Gareth, A Peace Denied: The United Staes, Vietnam, and the Paris Agreement (Bloomington: Indiana University Press, 1975). A critical review of Kissinger's role is in Shawcross, William, Sideshow: Kissinger, Nixon and the Destructon of Cambodia (New York: Simon & Schuster, 1972).

274 "I know you...go away bitter."
Time (May 18, 1970), p. 17.

275 "I really don't...and the affluent."
Time (May 25, 1970), p. 23.

276 "You get knocked...win at last."
Time (May 11, 1970), p. 16.

"President Nixon...presidential backbone."
Atlantic News-Telegraph (July 10, 1970), p. 5.

"We're supporting...that he's right."
Nation (November 7, 1969), p. 33.

277 "The next time...act accordingly."
Time (May 11, 1970), p. 21.
On Nixon and the use of Agnew, see Keogh, James, President and the Press (New York: Funk & Wagnalls, 1972) and Wills, Garry, Nixon Agnostes: The Crisis of the Self-Made Man (Boston: Houghton Mifflin, 1970).

"We can afford...normally entails."
Nation (November 7, 1969), p. 12.

"There are more...to pour it on."
Newsweek (November 24, 1969), p. 31.

279 "There is about...aura of negativism."
Time (May 18, 1970), p. 19.
Some penetrating perspectives on Nixon are in Osborne, John, The Second Year of the Nixon Watch (New York: Liveright, 1971).

"He surrounded himself...loyalty to Nixon."
Des Moines Register (August 21, 1974), p. 9.

XII. AN AGE OF CONFUSION

Page

283 "crazed excess"
Newsweek (August 21, 1969), p. 16.

"there was much...stained and caked."
Life (October 10, 1969), p. 24.

284 "the country has...clannish group."
Los Angeles Times (June 17, 1970), p. 4.

"Moral abdication...a rootless."
U.S. News & World Report (November 26, 1973), p. 56.

"Look at it...they're mad."
Time (October 1, 1969), p. 45.

285 "the world is...they used to."
Des Moines Register (December 25, 1973), p. 17.

"The trouble with...itself to death."
The American Male, p. 4.

"people are more...used to be."
Sioux City Journal (March 12, 1971), p. 5.
"You're competent today, and our're obsolete tomorrow...We're living in a fast world. We've advanced 30 years' worth in five years," wrote Romie Seals in Look (January 12, 1965), p. 51.

"John F. Kennedy's...parade was over."
Parade (February 21, 1971), p. 5.

286 "I no longer...change the world."
Time (June 27, 1969), p. 48.

"The tenure of...an American century."
New York Times (June 6, 1971), p. 13.
"the power of a mass movement confronting the power of the machine. The discard heap that the machine created may arise to devour its progenitor," wrote Hacker in The End of the American Era (New York: Atheneum, 1971),l p. 24. Also see Melman, Seymour, Our Depleted Society (New York: Holt, Rinehart and Winston, 1965).

"We had entered...we had achieved."
Halberstam, David, The Best and the Brightest (New York: Random House, 1972).

"We want to...or necessary."
New Republic (January 16, 1971), p. 13.

"In place of...and its leaders."
Wise, David The Politics of Lying (New York: Random House, 1973). Also see Wolff, Robert P., The Poverty of Liberalism (Boston: Beacon Press, 1968).

"This is not...American century."
U.S. News & World Report (August 3, 1970), p. 9.

"We have a...lift this country."
Sioux City Journal (May 23, 1973), p. 11.

287 "The mashed motorcycle"
Time (December 1, 1967), p. 35.
The California poll in Joseph, Good Times , p. 354.

"More and more...young and old."
Chicago Sun Times (June 16, 1968), p. 17.

"We have become...point of view."
Detroit Free Press (March 17, 1970), p. 9.

288 "The proliferation of...undegirded."
Phillips, Kevin, "Balkanization of America," Harpers (May,1972), pp. 37-38.

"On the one...institutions perished."
Chicago Sun Times (June 16, 1968), p. 20.

289 "The Industrial...of daily living."
Look (July 9, 1968), p. 22.

"There must be...administering them."
Time (January 24, 1969), p. 17.

"Defrauded consumers...of official disability."
Sioux City Journal (August 30, 1970), p. 4.

290 "I should sit...got no solutions."
Time (March 2, 1970), p. 32.

"people have...government itself."
Chicago Sun Times (June 1, 1969), p. 18.

Words from the song "Goodtime Charley Has Got the Blues" sung by Danny O'Keefe, composed by Danny O'Keefe, and published by Warner Brothers in 1968.

Words from the song "Yesterday" sung by the Beatles, composed by John Lennon and Paul McCartney, and published by Northern Songs, Ltd. in 1965.

291 Words from the song "Those Were The Days" sung by Mary Hopkins, composed by Gene Raskin, and published by Essex Music in 1968.

Words from the song "Yester me, Yester you, Yesterday" sung by Stevie Wonder, composed by Ron Miller and Bryan Wells, and published by Jobete Music in 1966.

"Someday, baby...no more pain." Time (January 10, 1969), p. 46.

INDEX